Analecta Gregoriana
Cura Pontificiae Universitatis Gregorianae edita
Vol. 277. Series Facultatis Theologiae: sectio B, n. 96

LIAM BERGIN

O PROPHETICUM LAVACRUM

Baptism as Symbolic Act of Eschatological Salvation

Premio Bellarmino 1998

EDITRICE PONTIFICIA UNIVERSITÀ GREGORIANA
ROMA 1999

IMPRIMI POTEST

Romae, die 6 iulii 1999

R.P. FRANCO IMODA, S.J.

Rector Universitatis

IMPRIMATUR

Dal Vicariato di Roma, 8 luglio 1999

✠ CESARE NOSIGLIA

Arcivescovo tit. di Vittoriana

Vicegerente di Roma

ISBN 88-7652-827-X

EDITRICE PONTIFICIA UNIVERSITÀ GREGORIANA

Piazza della Pilotta, 35 - 00187 Roma, Italia

"YOU HAVE BEEN ENLIGHTENED BY CHRIST.
WALK ALWAYS AS CHILDREN OF THE LIGHT
AND KEEP THE FLAME OF FAITH ALIVE IN YOUR HEARTS.
WHEN THE LORD COMES, MAY YOU GO OUT TO MEET HIM
WITH ALL THE SAINTS IN THE HEAVENLY KINGDOM."

(*RITE OF CHRISTIAN BAPTISM*)

WITH GRATITUDE TO:

CÁIT AND AUSTIN
TOMÁS
STELLA
AUSTIN
KARL
MARINA

ACKNOWLEDGEMENTS

This text was original submitted as a Doctoral Thesis in the Faculty of Theology at the Pontifical Gregorian University. I am grateful to those members of the Faculty who deemed this work worthy of the Bellarmine Award 1998 and so enabled its publication in the *Analecta Gregoriana* series.

I express my thanks to Bishop Laurence Forristal and to the people and priests of the Diocese of Ossory for affording me the opportunity of undertaking doctoral studies in Rome. I am indebted to Fr. Philip Rosato, SJ for his counsel and direction from my undergraduate days at the Gregorian University. Not only does he provide astute academic guidance, but he also show a deep concern for the overall well-being of his students. I was particularly honoured to have Fr. Gerald O'Collins, SJ as the second reader of this thesis. I thank him for his valuable comments on my work.

I would also like to acknowledge the interest and support of Professor Heinz Schürmann, the late Professor Samuel Amsler and Dr. Fearghus Ó Fearghail. Notable mention should also be made both of Fr. Michael Drumm who provided endless encouragement by reading the full text, and of Fr. Patrick Quinn, TOR, my erstwhile study colleague of many years. Invaluable technical assistance was provided by Fr. Michael Higgins, TOR and by Nicole Domenici.

I express my heartfelt gratitude to Mgr. John Fleming, the Rector of the Pontifical Irish College, to Frs. Con Boyle, Kevin Doran, Gerard Condon and Paul Prior, my past and present colleagues on the College Staff. I am grateful to the seminarians and post-graduates of the Irish College, particularly to those who assisted with proof-reading. I salute Sisters Canice, Conleth and Helen, the last members of the Congregation of St. John of God who ministered in the Irish College from 1922-1998.

I acknowledge the companionship and support of my friends from home, Kilkenny, Maynooth, Rome and beyond. I thank my parents and my brothers and sisters who, more than any, have helped to keep the flame of baptismal faith alive in my heart. This work is dedicated with gratitude to them.

TABLE OF CONTENTS

PART II: THE WATER OF BAPTISM

ABBREVIATIONS[1]

AAS	*Acta Apostolicae Sedis*, Città del Vaticano
ALW	*Archiv für Liturgiewissenschaft*, Regensburg
AmEcclRev	*The American Ecclesiastical Review*, Washington
America	*America*, New York
AmiCl	*L'Ami du Clergé*, Langres
AnBib	Analecta Biblica, Roma
AncB	Anchor Bible Series, Garden City
AncBRL	Anchor Bible Reference Library, Garden City
Ang	*Angelicum*, Roma
AnGr	Analecta Gregoriana, Roma
Aug	*Augustinianum*, Roma
BEThL	Bibliotheca Ephemeridum theologicarum Lovaniensium, Leuven
Bib	*Biblica*, Roma
BiBh	*Bible Bhashyam*, Vadavathoor, Kottayam, India
BiLe	*Bibel und Leben*, Düsseldorf
BiLi	*Bibel und Liturgie*, Klosterneuburg; Düsseldorf
BiTod	*The Bible Today*, Collegeville
BJRL	*Bulletin of the John Rylands Library*, Manchester
BL	J, DANIÉLOU, *The Bible and the Liturgy*, Ann Arbor 1956
BR	*Biblical Research*, Chicago
BZ	*Biblische Zeitschrift*, Padderborn
CBQ	*The Catholic Biblical Quarterly*, Washington
CCC	*Catechism of the Catholic Church*, Dublin 1994
Christ	E. SCHILLEBEECKX, *Christ. The Experience of Jesus as Lord*, New York 1981
Church	E. SCHILLEBEECKX, *Church. The Human Story of God*, New York 1993
CleR	*The Clergy Review*, London

[1] In as far as possible, the abbreviations follow the system proposed by S.M. Schwertner, *International Glossary of Abbreviations for Theology and Related Subjects* (New York/Berlin: de Gruyter, 1992).

ComLi	*Communautés et liturgies*, Ottignies
Comm	*Commonweal*, New York
Conc	*Concilium*, Religion in the seventies/eighties, Edinburgh
Cont	*Continuum*, Chicago
CProt	*Les Cahiers protestants*, Lausanne
CS	K. RAHNER, *The Church and the Sacraments*, New York 1963
CSEG	E. SCHILLEBEECKX, *Christ the Sacrament of the Encounter with God*, London 1963
CTom	*Ciencia tomista*, Salamanca
Div	*Divinitas*, Città del Vaticano
DFT	*Dictionary of Fundamental Theology*, ed. R. Latourelle - R. Fisichella, Middlegreen 1994
DoLi	*Doctrine and Life*, Dublin
DR	*The Downside Review*, Bath
DS	H. DENZINGER – A. SCHÖNMETZER, ed., *Enchiridion symbolorum definitionum et declarationum de rebus fidei et morum*, Freiburg 1976
DSJ	H. SCHÜRMANN, "Die Symbolhandlungen Jesu als eschatologische Erfüllungszeichen. Eine Rückfrage nach dem historischen Jesus," *BiLe* 11 (1970) 29-41; 73-78
DublR	*Dublin Review*, Dublin
DViv	*Dieu vivant*, Paris
ECQ	*Eastern Churches Quarterly*, Ramsgate
EcR	*The Ecclesiastical Review*, Washington
ÉeT(O)	*Église et théologie*, Ottawa
EeV	*Esprit et vie*, Langres
EL	*Ephemerides liturgicae*, Città del Vaticano
Encounter	*Encounter*, Indianapolis
EO	*Ecclesia Orans*, Roma
Esprit	*Esprit*, Paris
ET	English translation
EThL	*Ephemerides Theologicae Lovanienses*, Leuven
ETR	*Études théologiques et Religieuses*, Montpellier
Études	*Études*, Paris
EX	*Ecclesiastica Xaveriana*, Bogotá
ExT	*The Expository Times*, Edinburgh
FCF	K. RAHNER, *Foundations of Christian Faith: An Introduction to the Idea of Christianity*, London 1978
FLANNERY	A. FLANNERY, ed., *Vatican Council II, The Conciliar and Post Conciliar Documents*, Dublin 1975
FV	*Foi et vie*, Paris

Gr	*Gregorianum*, Roma
HeyJ	*The Heythrop Journal*, London
Horizons	*Horizons*, Villanova
Hum(B)	*Humanitas*, Brescia
Interp	*Interpretation*, Richmond
IThQ	*The Irish Theological Quarterly*, Maynooth
JBL	*Journal of Biblical Literature*, Philadelphia
JBR	*Journal of Bible and Religion*, Boston
JES	*Journal of Ecumenical Studies*, Philadelphia
Jesus	E. SCHILLEBEECKX, *Jesus. An Experiment in Christology*, New York 1979
Jesus' Words	H. SCHÜRMANN, "Jesus' Words in the Light of His Actions at the Last Supper," *Concilium* 4/10 (1968) 61-67
JL	*Jahrbuch für Liturgiewissenschaft*, Münster
JQR	*The Jewish Quarterly Review*, Philadelphia
JR	*The Journal of Religion*, Chicago
JSOT	*Journal for the Study of the Old Testament*, Sheffield
JThS	*The Journal of Theological Studies*, Oxford
Jud	*Judaica*, Zürich
JuT	H. SCHÜRMANN, *Jesu ureigener Tod. Exegetische Besinnungen und Ausblick*, Freiburg 1975
JWC	E. SCHILLEBEECKX, *Jesus Christ in our Western Culture*, London 1986
KDE	A. VONIER, *A Key to the Doctrine of the Eucharist*, Westminster 1948
La Communication	S. AMSLER, "Les prophètes et la communication par les actes," in *Werden und Wirken des Alten Testaments*, ed. R. ALBERTZ, Göttingen, 194-201
Lateranum	*Lateranum*, Roma
Les actes	S. AMSLER, *Les actes des prophètes*, Genève 1985
LiZs	*Liturgische Zeitschrift*, Regensburg
LJ	*Liturgisches Jahrbuch*, Münster
Lukas	H. SCHÜRMANN, *Das Lukasevangelium, Erster Teil, Kommentar zu Kap. 1:1-9:50,* Freiburg 1982
LV(L)	*Lumière et Vie*, Lyon
LW	*Luther's Works,* ed. H.T. LEHMANN, Philadelphia
MD	*La Maison-Dieu*, Paris
MThZ	*Münchener Theologische Zeitschrift*, München
Mystery	O. CASEL, *The Mystery of Christian Worship*, London 1962
NCE	*New Catholic Encyclopaedia*, Washington 1967

ND	J. NEUNER – J. DUPUIS, ed., *The Christian Faith in the Doctrinal Documents of the Catholic Church*, London 1983
NDCTh	*New Dictionary of Christian Theology*, London 1983
NJBC II	*The New Jerome Biblical Commentary*, II, J.A. Fitzmyer – R.E. Brown, ed., London 1990
Not	*Notitiae*, Città del Vaticano
NRTh	*Nouvelle Revue théologique*, Louvain
NThR	*New Theology Review*, Wilmington
OBO	Orbis biblicus et orientalis, Freiburg
OF	*Orate Fratres*, Collegeville
ParLi	*Paroisse et Liturgie*, Saint-André-les-Bruges
PCTSA	*Proceedings of the Annual convention of the Catholic Theological Society of America*, New York
PerTeol	*Perspectiva Teológica*, Saõ Leopoldo
Phase	*Phase*, Barcelona
PIB	Pontificio Istituto Biblico, Roma
Présences	*Présences*, Paris
Prophetic Drama	W.D. STACEY, *Prophetic Drama in the Old Testament*, London 1990
Protest	*Protestantesimo*, Roma
PUG	Pontificia Università Gregoriana, Roma
PUST	Pontificia Università di S. Tommaso, Roma
QF	*Les Quattre Fleuves*, Paris
QLP	*Questions liturgiques et paroissiales*, Louvain
QuLi	*Questions liturgiques*, Louvain
RB	*Revue Biblique*, Paris
RBR	*Ricerche Bibliche e Religiose*, Milano
RdQ	*Revue de Qumrân*, Paris
RdT	*Rassegna di teologia*, Roma
RestQ	*Restoration Quarterly*, Austin
RevSR	*Revue des sciences Religieuses*, Strasbourg
RHR	*Revue de l'histoire des Religions*, Evry
RivLi	*Rivista liturgica*, Torino
RMab	*Revue Mabillon*, Abbaye Saint Martin, Ligugé
RPLi	*Rivista di pastorale liturgica*, Brescia
RScPhTh	*Revue des sciences philosophiques et théologiques*, Paris
RSR	*Recherches de science Religieuse*, Paris
RThom	*Revue thomiste*, Toulouse
RThPh	*Revue de théologie et de philosophie*, Lausanne
RTL	*Revue théologique de Louvain*, Louvain
RUO	*Revue de l'Université d'Ottawa*, Ottawa

RVS	*Rivista di vita spirituale*, Roma
SacDo	*Sacra doctrina*, Bologna
Sales	*Salesianum,* Roma
SapDom	*Sapienza*, Napoli
SBT	*Studies in Biblical Theology*, London
ScC	*La Scuola cattolica*, Milano
ScEc	*Sciences ecclésiastiques*, Bruges
Seminarium	*Seminarium*, Città del Vaticano
Sent	ST THOMAS AQUINAS, *Scriptum super Sententiis*
Septentrion	*Septentrion*, Rekkem
SF	J. DANIÉLOU, *Sacramentum Futuri*, Paris 1950
SJTh	*Scottish Journal of Theology*, Edinburgh
SM(E)	*Sacramentum Mundi*, London
ST	ST THOMAS AQUINAS, *Summa Theologica*
StLi	*Studia liturgica*, Rotterdam
StPat	*Studia Patavina*, Padova
StZ	*Stimmen der Zeit*, Freiburg
Tablet	*The Tablet*, London
TDNT	*Theological Dictionary of the New Testament*, Grand Rapids
TDOT	*Theological Dictionary of the Old Testament*, Grand Rapids
TGL	*Tijdschrift voor geestelijk leven*, Schilde
ThDig	*Theology Digest*, Saint Louis
Theol	*Theology*, London
ThLZ	*Theologische Literaturzeitung*, Leipzig
Thom	*The Thomist*, Washington
Thought	*Thought*, New York
ThQ	*Theologische Quartalschrift*, Tübingen
ThRv	*Theologische Revue*, Münster
ThZ	*Theologische Zeitschrift*, Basel
TI	K. RAHNER, *Theological Investigations*, 23 Volumes, London 1961-1992
TPh	*Tijdschrift voor philosophie*, Leuven
TS	*Theological Studies*, Baltimore
TTh	*Tijdschrift voor Theologie*, Nijmegen
TU	Texte und Untersuchungen, Berlin
VC	*Verbum caro*, Neuchâtel
VS	*La Vie spirituelle*, Paris
VT	*Vetus Testamentum*, Leiden
Worship	*Worship*, Collegeville

ZAW	*Zeitschrift für die alttestamentliche Wissenschaft*, Berlin – New York
ZNW	*Zeitschrift für die neutestamentliche Wissenschaft*, Berlin – New York

INTRODUCTION

In the nineteenth chapter of the *Book of Jeremiah,* the prophet is addressed by Yahweh. Jeremiah is ordered to buy an earthenware jar, to take with him some elders of the people and a number of senior priests, and to go to a point outside the city gate. There, he is directed to deliver an oracle of destruction and to break the flask in the sight of the spectators. Jeremiah does what the Lord commands. The account describes the execution of the act and ends with the prophet's words of explanation. This narrative represents a typical example of the many "prophetic acts" which are recorded in the Hebrew Scriptures. The basic claim of this study is that an analysis of these striking actions provides a framework for retrieving the eschatological dimension of sacraments in general, and of baptism in particular.

Exegetical, liturgical and systematic studies insist that any understanding of the person and ministry of Jesus Christ and of the nature and mission of his Church, together with its constitutive rites and institutions, is possible only when the Jewish historical, cultural and religious background from which they emerge is taken into account. Sacramental theology has already benefited from the insights gained from Old Testament concepts such as *zikkārôn*, or memorial.[1] For the Hebrew, *zikkārôn* is not only a recalling of the past salvific action of God, but is also an efficacious re-presentation of the event in the life of the worshipping community (the past influences the present).[2] In continuity with the rites of the old dispensation, the sacraments of the new law not only recall, but also re-enact, by means of the liturgical rites of the Church, the salvation won, once and for all, by Jesus Christ. In this notion, then, the

---

[1] See J.A. Jungmann, "Das Gedächtnis des Herrn in der Eucharistie," 387-399; I. Oñatibia, "Recuperación del concepto de *memorial* por la teología eucarística contemporánea," *Phase* 12 (1972) 335-345.

[2] See B.S. Childs, *Memory and Tradition in Israel*; P.A.H. De Boer, *Gedenken und Gedächtnis in der Welt des Alten Testaments*; R. Martin-Achard, "Souvenir et mémorial selon l'Ancien Testament," *RThPh* 15 (1965) 302-310; J.A. Soggin, "Memoria, ricordo ed anamnesi in Oriente e nell'Antico Testamento," *Protestant* 21 (1966) 83-86.

traditional commemorative and demonstrative aspects of the sacraments coincide in a concept that is biblically based and ecumenically appropriate.

The Jewish concept of *'ôt*, or prophetic act, not only announces a future divine initiative but, at the same time, prognostically activates it in the present (the future influences the present). Here, in the dramatic interplay of word and action, the force of God's imminent intervention in the history of Israel is proleptically unleashed by the prophet. While studies exist on the contribution of this semitic category to sacramental theology in general,[3] and to the Eucharist in particular,[4] no specific study has been undertaken with respect to the sacrament of baptism as *signum prognosticum* of salvation.

This dissertation is a response to the invitation issued by the Second Vatican Council to make the study of sacred Scripture the soul of Christian theology.[5] Concretely, it investigates the diverse contributions towards an enhanced understanding of the eschatological dimension of the sacrament of baptism. These have been made by prominent biblical scholars who have reflected on the Old Testament concept of prophetic act (*'ôt*), and by renowned dogmaticians who have engaged in biblical exegesis. To this end, a dialogue is facilitated between the writings of two biblical and two systematic theologians, namely Samuel Amsler's *Les actes des prophètes* (1985), Heinz Schürmann's *Jesu ureigener Tod* (1975) and *Das Lukasevangelium* (1982), Karl Rahner's *Kirche und Sakramente* (1963), *Grundkurs des Glaubens: Einführung in den Begriff des Christentums* (1976) and writings from *Schriften zur Theologie* (1954-84), and Edward Schillebeeckx's *Jezus, het verhaal van een levende* (1974), *Gerechtigheid en liefde: Genade en bevrijding* (1977) and *Mensen als verhaal van God* (1989). Other works by these authors are also studied to the extent that they throw light on the theme.

This thesis unfolds in three parts, each employing a different methodology. The first ("Eclipse and Retrieval"), in two chapters, follows a historical-theological method as it presents an overview of the eclipsing and of the subsequent retrieval of the eschatological dimension of baptism during the twentieth century. The second part ("The Water of Baptism"), in four chapters, adopts an analytic-

---

[3] P. Brito Guimarães, *Os sacramentos como atos eclesiais e proféticos. Um contributo ao conceito dogmático de sacramento à luz da exegese contemporânea.*

[4] J.L. Espinel, *La cena del Señor, acción profética.*

[5] *Dei verbum,* 24.

expository methodology which considers the relevant writings of each of the four authors in turn. The insights gleaned from the biblical authors are employed in the analysis of the baptismal theology of the systematic theologians. The third section ("Symbol and Anticipation"), in two chapters, is both evaluative and prognostic in scope. It lists, in synchronic and diachronic fashion, the stimulus which the study of the variegated research of others offers to the theme under consideration. It also identifies cogent theological questions which emerge from this treatment of baptism, and sketches a possible intellectual framework on which a new approach to the eschatological dimension of this sacrament can be solidly developed.

Chapter 1 is founded on the conviction that, until recently, Catholic sacramental theology had focused on the commemorative and demonstrative dimensions of the sacramental sign much to the detriment of the prognostic aspect. This narrowing of perspective has had serious implications for the understanding of sacraments in general, and of baptism in particular. This chapter investigates how the eschatological aspect of baptism as *signum prognosticum* is presented in the writings of St. Thomas. Then it examines the extent to which this theme is eclipsed by his commentators during the early part of this century. The investigation notes that, instead of presenting the commemorative, demonstrative and prognostic as three equal dimensions of the one sacramental sign, many commentators relegate the *signum prognosticum* to a tertiary importance compared to that attributed to either the *signum rememorativum* or the *signum demonstrativum*. Three factors — internal, polemical and semiotic — are identified as possible causes for this theological shift.

Chapter 2 presents the re-emergence of the eschatological dimension of baptism in the patristic, liturgical and biblical studies of the early twentieth century. As a representative of patristic research, Dom Ansgar Vonier insists that the very essence of a sacrament is to be a sign. While he notes that every sacrament is a sign of the past, the present and of the future, and that each aspect of the sign is a cause of the sanctification which it signifies, Vonier is unable to ground the prognostic dimension of the sacramental grace in the sign itself. The influence of the Liturgical Movement on Catholic sacramental theology is examined through the writings of Dom Odo Casel. The three dimensions of sacramental sign are evident in Casel's controversial *Kultmysterium*. Indeed, the analysis of his writings suggests that his notion of "anticipation in image" comes close to the understanding of the proleptic power of a prophetic action. The contribution of biblical research is viewed through the baptismal typology of Cardinal Jean Daniélou. The spiritual exegesis of Daniélou calls for a consideration of sacraments as signs in the light of the liturgy of Israel. In the case of baptism the traditional preference for the typology of the Red Sea over that of the Jordan betrays the predominance of the demonstrative dimension of the sacramental sign over its prognostic counterpart. Chapter 2 concludes with an introduction to the four authors whose writings form the central part of this thesis.

The second section of this dissertation exposes the writings of each of the four authors in turn. Chapter 3 explores the twofold source from which baptism flows. First of all, it investigates the notion of *prophetic act* as presented in the works of Samuel Amsler, the Old Testament exegete and biblical theologian. His writings are analysed under three headings: the act itself, the reaction it provoked, and the ultimate end of the act. According to Amsler, the mission of the prophets of Israel is to establish signs of the imminent intervention of God among the chosen people. This the prophets normally do in proclaiming oracles or recounting visions. Occasionally, however, the Hebrew scriptures record that they dramatize their message by performing scandalous actions. The prophetic act not only heralded, but also proleptically anticipated the future intervention of God, grafting it into the present experience of the community. Secondly, the source of the Church's initiatory rite is investigated by applying the results of each of the foregoing sections to the *prophetic act* of John the Baptist. In the River Jordan, John performs the prophetic act *par excellence*, and brings home the urgency of the imminent intervention of God to Jews and Gentiles alike. The future which the washing proclaims erupts into the present as the "Greater One" paradoxically undergoes the rite of his own anticipation, while the promised gift of the Spirit finds fulfilment in the descent of the dove on Jesus of Nazareth.

Chapter 4 examines the emergence of the Christian rite of initiation from the prophetic action of Jesus in the Jordan. First of all, what Heinz Schürmann views as the difference between the Old Testament symbolic actions and the New Testament "eschatological signs of fulfilment" is presented. Then, his analysis of these new covenant signs, enacted before and during the Last Supper, is outlined. Finally, with the help of Schürmann's own exegesis of the Lucan narrative, the insights gained from this review are retrospectively applied to the baptism of Jesus. The analysis shows that, by stepping into the Jordan waters, Jesus is the protagonist of a new symbolic act in which he reveals himself as the pro-existent Son and as the eschatological bearer of the Spirit.

Chapter 5 exposes the understanding of the eschatological dimension of baptism which emerges from the convergence of the writings of Karl Rahner on this sacrament with the preceding treatment of prophetic action. In a first movement, the role of the prophet in the fundamental theology of the transcendental thomist is examined. According to Rahner, Jesus' proclamation of the kingdom can be traced to his identity with the person of eschatological prophet. In a second section, the relationship between the socio-historical manifestation of victorious grace, which is called Church, and Jesus Christ, the fundamental sacrament of salvation, is treated. In the subsequent analysis of Rahner's presentation of the individual sacraments the correspondence with prophetic acts is underlined. In a third step, the baptismal theology of Rahner is exposed, and the motif of baptism as symbolic event of eschatological salvation is employed so as to illumine further the prognostic dimension of this lustral rite. The analysis concludes that, through water and the invocation of the triune God, the form of eschatological life, which non-baptized justified persons receive in the *visio beatifica*, is proleptically bestowed on believers.

In Chapter 6 the baptismal theology of Edward Schillebeeckx comes under scrutiny. The underlying thesis of this chapter is that baptism, viewed as symbolic act of eschatological salvation, provides a key insight into Schillebeeckx's work on this sacrament. Moreover, understood in this vein, baptism is also an architectonic concept which unites the earlier and later moments of his thought. The chapter unfolds in three steps. In a first section, the broad strokes of the sacramental theory of Schillebeeckx, as represented by his writings before 1966, are outlined. Then selected texts are analyzed which throw light on his understanding of baptism as the rite which celebrates a salvific encounter with the triune God. In particular, the eschatological dimension of the sacramental sign is highlighted together with the mutuality of the epicletic and anamnetic moments in the liturgical event. The later work of Schillebeeckx is marked by his methodological turn from the credal Christ of dogmatic statements to the historical Jesus of first-century Israel. The second section of this chapter focuses on the presentation of the prophetic actions of Jesus in the first two volumes of the christological trilogy of Schillebeeckx. The baptism in the Jordan represents the first symbolic action of the eschatological prophet. According to Schillebeeckx, it provides the foundation for the subsequent unfolding of his radical praxis of the kingdom and it finds its climax in the drama of the Cross. In the person and activity of the Nazarene, humanity is confronted with the proleptic anticipation of the new world of the *Deus Humanissimus*. Finally, a third section analyses the place of the sacrament of baptism in the later praxis-oriented thought of Schillebeeckx. According to these writings, baptism is understood as a prophetic act of ecclesial commitment to a praxis anticipating the new creation. By undergoing the ecclesial rite of washing, Christians embark on a life-long mission of being-for-others. Filled with the Spirit of justice, and confirmed as sons and daughters of the heavenly Father, they utter a prophetic protest to the suffering and oppression which enslave humanity and, by word and action, proleptically anticipate the *eschaton* which lies in the future with God.

The dissertation concludes with an evaluative and prognostic section. Chapter 7 re-evaluates the understanding of baptism as *signum prognosticum* in the light of the dialogue between biblical and systematic theology which was elaborated in the central part of this research project. The aim of the first section of this penultimate chapter is to present a methodological evaluation of the response that this thesis makes to the magisterial exhortation that the study of Scripture should be the soul of theology. Then, in a second section, it appraises, in a diachronic movement, the contribution of each of the four authors to the foregoing investigation, and seeks to identify areas which could benefit from further development and research.

Chapter 8 offers a synchronic overview of the enhanced understanding of baptism which emerges from this study, that is, as the sacramental participation in the life and mission of Jesus Christ, the Alpha and the Omega. The points which are proposed in this final chapter refer to the sacramental sign as a prophetic action, the immediate influence of the lustral rite as an incorporation into the Church, and the final effect that the liturgical washing has on its recipients.

The work concludes with "A Prayer Over Baptismal Water" in which, together with its commemorative and demonstrative aspects, the prognostic dimension of the lustral rite is given due emphasis. Baptism can thus be viewed as the initial symbolic act of the eschatological salvation of Christians. In its celebration of baptism, the Christian community which anticipates its hope in the future, awakens its faith in the past and forges a present where love finds a home between memory and promise.

PART I

ECLIPSE AND RETRIEVAL

CHAPTER 1

Eclipsing the Future

The overshadowing of baptism as *signum prognosticum* in the theology of the early twentieth-century commentators on St. Thomas

In his treatise on baptism and confirmation published in 1923,[1] Alexis Maria Lépicier provides a characteristic instance of the dogmatic treatment of baptism during the early twentieth century. Baptism, he writes, may be defined as "a sacrament of the New Law, instituted by Christ the Lord, for the spiritual regeneration of man, performed by the washing of the body in water, under a prescribed form of words."[2] The *ordo tractatus* follows in six articles treating, in turn, the sacrament, the minister, the recipient, the effects, circumcision as its precursor and, finally, the necessity of preparation for its celebration. This is none other than the order established by St. Thomas Aquinas in his *Summa Theologica*[3] almost seven hundred years previously.[4] While Lépicier's exposition adopts a particularly strenuous adherence to the

---

[1] A.-M. Lépicier, *Tractatus de baptismo et de confirmatione* (1923). Lépicier (1863-1936) was at this stage professor of dogmatic theology at the Propaganda Fidei in Rome. His tract on baptism and confirmation was one volume of his massive twenty-five volume *Institutiones theologicae dogmaticae ad textum S. Thomae concinnatae*. Prominent in the neo-scholastic revival, he was appointed cardinal prefect of the Congregation of Religious in 1928, a post from which he later had to resign. See J.M. Ryska, "Lépicier, Alexis" in *NCE* VII (1967) 666.

[2] A.-M. Lépicier, *Tractatus de baptismo et confirmatione,* 15: "Baptismus definire potest: Sacramentum novae Legis a Christo Domino institutum, ad spiritualem hominis regenerationem, per ablutionem corporis in aqua peractam, sub praescripta forma verborum."

[3] *ST*. III, Q. 66, Prol.

[4] Scholars generally agree that Thomas began working on the *Summa Theologica* at Naples in 1265 or 1266 and that he stopped writing on the Feast of St Nicholas 1273. It was unfinished at his death in 1274. See R.M. Coffey, "St. Thomas Aquinas," in *The Summa of St. Thomas Aquinas,* III, 3063-3071; T. Gilby, *Christian Theology*, xxii.

structure employed by St. Thomas, it is not untypical of Catholic baptismal theology of the early twentieth century.[5] To a large extent, these 'manuals' of theology were conceived as a "commentary on the third part of St. Thomas."[6]

From the outset of his treatise on sacraments in general, Thomas states that each rite of the New Testament is a sign with a threefold function: "It is at once commemorative of that which has gone before, namely the passion of Christ, and demonstrative of that which is brought about in us through the passion of Christ, namely grace, and prognostic, i.e. a foretelling of glory."[7] This study is founded on the conviction that, until recently, Catholic sacramental theology has focused on the commemorative and demonstrative aspects of the sacramental sign much to the detriment of the prognostic aspect. This narrowing of perspective has had serious implications for the understanding of sacraments in general, and of baptism in particular.

The purpose of this first chapter is twofold. First it investigates how the eschatological dimension of baptism as *signum prognosticum* is presented in the writings of St. Thomas. Then it proceeds to examine the extent to which this theme is eclipsed in the commentaries of the early twentieth century.

In composing the liturgical texts for the Office and the Mass on the occasion of the institution of the feast of *Corpus Christi* in 1264,[8] St. Thomas offered a rich *précis* of his eucharistic theology in the "*O sacrum convivium*":

---

[5] Among the authors consulted in this regard are the following: L. Billot, *De ecclesiae sacramentis*; C. Pesch, *De sacramentis* Pars I; A.-M. Lépicier, *Tractatus de sacramentis in communi*; A. D'Alès, *Baptême et confirmation*; C. Lattey, ed., *Six Sacraments*; R. Plus, *Baptême et confirmation*; P. Pourrat, *Theology of the Sacraments*; F. Connell, *De sacramentis ecclesiae tractatus dogmatici*, I; A. Piolanti, *De sacramentis*; E. Doronzo, *De sacramentis in genere*; Id., *De baptismo et confirmatione*; H. Lennerz, *De sacramentis novae legis in genere*; Id., *De sacramento baptismi*.

[6] Note, for example, the subtitle of Billot's work: L. Billot, *De ecclesiae sacramentis: Commentarius in tertiam partem S. Thomae*.

[7] *ST*. III, Q. 60, a. 3: "Unde sacramentum est et signum rememorativum ejus quod præcessit, scilicet passionis Christi; et demonstrativum ejus quod in nobis effecitur per Christum passionem, scilicet gratiae; et prognosticum, id est prænuntiativum, futuræ gloriæ" .

[8] Some doubt that St. Thomas is in fact the author of these texts. See P.-M. Gy, "L'office du *Corpus Christi*," *RScPhTh* 64 (1980) 491-507.

O sacrum convivium,
in quo Christus sumitur,
memoria passionis eius recolitur,
mens impletur gratia,
et futurae gloriae nobis pignus datur.

This *Magnificat* antiphon not only highlights the three aspects under which every sacrament may be considered, but also brings the triple dimension of the sacramental sign into focus. The outward sacramental sign or the *sacramentum tantum* is the bread and wine (*sacrum convivium*). The intrinsic state, or the *sacramentum et res,* immediately produced by the outward sign is the presence of the body and blood of Christ under the appearance of bread and wine (*in quo Christus sumitur*). The specific grace produced by the sacrament or the *res tantum* is the unity of the members of the Church with Christ[9] and, in this verse, it is presented under a triple aspect. As a remembrance of the passion of Christ (*memoria passionis eius*), the eucharist is a *signum rememorativum*; it is a *signum demonstrativum* insofar as it represents the grace given (*mens impletur gratia*); and it is a *signum prognosticum* insofar as it is a pledge of future glory (*futurae gloriae nobis pignus datur*).

In baptism the *sacramentum tantum* is washing with water, the *res et sacramentum* is the character which configures the recipient to the priesthood of Christ, and the *res tantum* is interior justification or sanctification.[10] Considered under the triple dimension of the sacramental sign, baptism is a *signum rememorativum* of the passion of Christ,[11] a *signum demonstrativum* of the grace of regeneration, cleansing and rebirth,[12] and a *signum prognosticum* of the future glory opened to those who receive the sacrament in faith.[13] Paralleling the scheme of the "*O sacrum convivium,*" St. Thomas' baptismal theology could consequently be summarized as follows:

---

[9] See B. Leeming, *Principles of Sacramental Theology*, 255.
[10] *ST*. III, Q. 66, a. 1.
[11] *ST*. III, Q. 66, a. 9.
[12] *ST*. III, Q. 66, a. 1.
[13] *ST*. III, Q. 69, a. 8.

O sacrum lavacrum
in quo Christi sacerdotio congruitur,
memoria passionis eius recolitur,
mens impletur gratia,
et futurae gloriae nobis porta reseratur.

The present study of baptism as *signum prognosticum* in the writings of St. Thomas will follow the structure of this verse. By investigating in turn the eschatological dimension of the sacramental sign (*O sacrum lavacrum*), the sacramental character (*in quo Christi sacerdotio congruitur*) and the ultimate reality conferred by the sacrament (*memoria passionis eius recolitur, mens impletur gratia, et futurae gloriae nobis porta reseratur*) it will also be possible to evaluate the extent to which this theme is eclipsed in the commentaries of the early twentieth century.

1. "O Sacrum lavacrum..."

In the *Summa Theologica*, which is considered the first treatise on sacraments in general,[14] the Angelic Doctor gradually unfolds and sharpens his understanding of the rites of the Church. Beginning from the broad augustinian notion of a sacrament as a sign of a holy thing, "*signum rei sacrae*," Thomas rejects other approaches common at the time.[15] However, not every sign of a holy thing is a sacrament: "a sacrament is a sign of a holy thing insofar as it makes human beings holy."[16] Not only are the rites of the new law covered by this definition, but so too are certain rites and ceremonies of the old law.[17] This is reinforced by Thomas' deliberate avoidance of any reference to causality at this stage.[18] The focus in the *Summa* is no longer on sacrament as remedy for

---

[14] See T.S. Centi, "Introduzione" in *La Somma Teologica. I sacramenti in genere*, 7-19.

[15] *ST*. III, Q. 60, a. 1. See H.-F. Dondaine, "La définition des sacrements dans la 'Somme Théologique'," *RScPhTh* 31 (1947) 213-228.

[16] *ST*. III, Q. 60, a. 2: "Signum rei sacrae inquantum est sanctificans homines."

[17] *ST*. III, Q. 61, a. 3.

[18] Compare Thomas' definition (note 15) with that of St. Isodore: "Sacramentum est in quo sub tegumento visibilium rerum divina virtus secretius operatur salutem," or that of Hugh of St. Victor: "Sacramentum est corporale vel materiale elementum oculis extrinsecus suppositum, ex similitudine repræsentans, ex institutione significans et ex sanctificatione invisibilem gratiam conferens." See H.-F. Dondaine, "La définition des sacrements dans la *Somme Théologique*," 219.

sin, but as means of offering cultic service of God and of sanctifying human beings.[19]

1.1 *The Triple Dimension of the Sacramental Sign in the "Summa Theologica"*

Sacraments, according to Thomas, consist both of sensible realities, determined by God to be employed[20] as signs for the worship of the divinity and the sanctification of humanity, and of determinate words which specify the signification of the realities used.[21] The sacramental sign associated with baptism is the act of washing with water[22]; the words determining the signification in the Latin Church are "I baptize you in the name of the Father, and of the Son, and of the Holy Spirit."[23] The sacrament can be reduced neither to the baptismal water as if it possessed a permanent power or presence of the Holy Spirit,[24] nor to the act of washing itself,[25] but is constituted by the unity of matter and form whereby "the word is added to the element and this becomes a sacrament."[26]

That baptism was instituted by Christ is not doubted. The manner and moment of institution, however, are less clear. A sacrament is instituted when it receives the power of producing its effect, and baptism receives this power when Jesus is baptized in the Jordan.[27] Although Thomas places the moment of institution at Jesus' own baptism by John the Baptist, it is interesting to note how he views subsequent Church doctrine and practice as interwoven in the overall fabric of Jesus' words and deeds.[28] While

---

[19] *ST*. III, Q. 60. a. 5: "...in usu sacramentorum duo possunt considerari, scilicet cultus divinus et sanctificatio hominis."

[20] *ST*. III, Q. 60, a. 5: "Et ideo in sacramentis novae legis ... oportet uti rebus ex divina institutione determinatis."

[21] *ST*. III. Q. 60, a. 6: "Et ideo ad perfectionem significationis sacramentalis necesse fuit ut significatio rerum sensibilium per aliqua verba determinaretur."

[22] *ST*. III, Q. 66, a. 7: "... aqua assumitur in sacramento baptismi ad usum ablutionis corporalis."

[23] *ST*. III, Q. 66, a. 5.

[24] This is the opinion of Hugh of St. Victor which was rejected by Thomas. See *ST*. III, Q. 66, a. 1, ad. 2.

[25] Luther's criticism of "Thomas and the Dominicans" that they "forgot the Word (God's institution) and say that God has joined to the water a spiritual power, which, through the water, washes away sins" is therefore unjustified. See D.R. Janz, *Luther on Thomas Aquinas*, 66-68.

[26] St. Augustine. Quoted in *ST*. III, Q. 60, a. 6, sed contra.

[27] *ST* III, Q. 66, a. 2.

[28] IV *Sent*. D. 3, a. 5, ad. 2: "Multiplex fuit baptismi institutio. Fuit enim primo institutus quantum ad materiam in baptismo Christi; tum enim vim regenerativam aquis contulit; et aliquo modo fuit forma figurata per praesentiam

the matter of baptism is established at the episode in the Jordan, the form is alluded to in the presence of the Father, Son and Holy Spirit, and the final end is prefigured as the heavens are opened.[29] The future necessity of baptism is inferred in the conversation with Nicodemus.[30] The practice of baptism in the ecclesial community is legitimated and begun with the disciples' mission to baptize.[31] And, since the sacraments receive their efficacy from the passion of Christ, the obligation of receiving baptism is proclaimed by the risen Lord.[32]

The inextricable link between the event of the Cross and the celebration of baptism is clearly presented in the theology of Aquinas. Baptism is a configuration to Christ's passion, whereby one dies to the old life of sin and is reborn to the new life of faith.[33] In this context Thomas repeatedly cites Rom 6:3-5,

> Do you not know that all of us who have been baptized into Christ Jesus were baptized into his death? We were baptized therefore with him by baptism into death, so that as Christ was raised from death by the glory of the Father, we too might walk in the newness of life. For if we have been united with him in a death like his, we shall certainly be united with him in a resurrection like his.

St. Thomas interprets this passage in neither a figurative nor a metaphorical sense, but "with a literalness that is bold and unprecedented."[34] It is precisely this relationship to the passion which distinguishes the sacraments of the old and new law, and which guarantees the efficacy of the rites of the latter. The sacraments of the old law were prefiguring signs ("*figuralia sacramenta*") and conferred grace insofar as they were signs of faith in the coming passion of Christ. In the sacraments of the new law "grace is conferred by the power of the sacrament itself which it has insofar as it is an instrument of the already realized passion

---

trium personarum in signo visibili [...] et similiter fructus baptismi ibi prefiguratus fuit, quia coeli aperti sunt super eum."

[29] Matt 3:17; Mark 1:18; Luke 3:22.

[30] IV *Sent*. D. 3, a. 5, ad. 2: "Sed necessitas ejus fuit declarata Joan. III,5, ubi dicit 'Nisi quis renatus fuerit, etc'."

[31] IV *Sent*. D. 3, a. 5, ad. 2: "Sed usus ejus fuit inchoatus quando misit discipulos ad praedicandum et baptizandum, ut patet Mat. X."

[32] IV *Sent*. D. 3, a. 5, ad. 2: "Sed efficaciam habuit ex passione Christi, quantum ad ultimum effectum, qui est apertio januae. Sed divulgatio ejus quantum ad omnos nationes praecepta fuit Mat. ult., 19, ubi dixit: 'Euntes, docete omnes gentes, etc.'"; *ST*. III, Q. 66. a. 2.

[33] *ST*. III, Q. 66, a. 2 & 3 & 9.

[34] D. Bourke, *The Sacraments*, xii.

of Christ."[35] In fact, "the sacraments of the Church flow from the side of Christ as he hung from the Cross."[36]

Water, according to Thomas, is a sign of generation and life; its properties are cleansing, coolness and lucidity.[37] The waters of baptism signify regeneration and the new life of Christ which put an end to sin, temper the heat of concupiscence and strengthen faith.[38] These effects are communicated to the recipients by virtue of their being conformed to the passion of Christ. Christians are incorporated into the passion and death of Christ just as if they had actually suffered and died.[39] Then, having been buried with Christ, the baptized rise to live the newness of grace with him.[40] This fullness of grace derives from Christ the crucified and risen Head of the Church and is communicated to all its members.[41] Precisely because the baptized are incorporated into the passion of Christ (past) and raised to glory with him (future), they receive the grace of regeneration (present).

In this context it is important to note Aquinas' insistence that water is a sign not only of the present effects of baptism (as listed above), but is also of "the mysteries of Christ by which we are justified."[42] This aspect finds its fullest signification in baptism by immersion, whereby the old self is buried "as in a type of tomb" from which the new self emerges born anew "to enter the kingdom of God."[43]

While sacraments effect grace "*ex opere operato,*"[44] Thomas is careful not to attribute a magical quality or consequence to them. Clearly, God the Father is the principal efficient cause of grace; the humanity of Christ is the united instrumental cause; and the sacrament is the separated instrumental cause. This leads Thomas to conclude that "the saving power must be derived by the sacraments from Christ's Godhead through his humanity."[45] In this way he reinforces the necessary connection between the grace which is effected by the sacrament and the crucified and glorified

---

35 *ST*. III, Q. 70, a. 4.
36 *ST*. III, Q. 62, a. 5, sed contra.
37 *ST*. III, Q. 66, a. 3.
38 *ST*. III, Q. 66, a. 3.
39 *ST*. III, Q. 69, a. 2.
40 *ST*. III, Q. 69, a. 1.
41 *ST*. III, Q. 69, a. 4.
42 *ST*. III, Q. 66, a. 3.
43 John 3: 3-5. See *ST*. III, Q. 66, a. 3.
44 *ST*. III, Q. 62, a. 1.
45 *ST*. III, Q. 62, a. 5.

humanity of Christ. In baptism the sinner becomes "a participator not merely in the fruits of the passion but in the death, resurrection and 'newness of life' of Christ himself."[46] This is none other than the unity of the cause, form and end of human sanctification as signified by the sacramental sign:

> The term sacrament is properly applied to that which is designed to signify our sanctification. In this three factors may be taken into consideration: namely the actual cause of our sanctification, which is the passion of Christ, the form of our sanctification, which consists in grace and virtues, and the ultimate end which our sanctification is destined to achieve, which is eternal life. Now as signs the sacraments stand for all of these.[47]

It may be helpful to summarize what has been said above as follows. While baptismal washing is a sign of the grace and virtues received in the sacrament (the form or *signum demonstrativum*), it also a sign of Christ's passion (the cause or *signum rememorativum*) and his rising to eternal life (the end or *signum prognosticum*).[48] Further, this incorporation into the passion of Christ and this regeneration unto the kingdom of God actually constitute the grace and virtue communicated to believers in this sacrament.

1.2 *The Fragmentation of the Triple Dimension of Sacramental Sign in the Commentators*

The three dimensions of the sacramental sign are presented by the Angelic Doctor in the *Summa Theologica* without differentiation in terms of precedence or importance. Yet, in the twentieth-century commentators one notices a considerable shift. These writers intended their work neither as mere slavish repetition nor as an up-dated exposition of St. Thomas. Certainly the method has changed. The question and answer format of the Angelic Doctor has given way to a "pedagogical order of explanation" which involves "thesis, *status quaestionis* (that is, an exposé of

---

[46] D. Bourke, *The Sacraments*, xxii-xxiii.

[47] *ST.* III, Q. 60, a. 3: "Sacramentum proprie dicitur quod ordinatur ad significandam nostram sanctificationem. In qua tria possunt considerari: videlicet ipsa causa sanctificationis nostrae, quae est passio Christi; et forma nostrae sanctificationis, quae consistit in gratia et virtutibus; et ultimus finis nostrae sanctificationis, qui est vita aeterna. Et haec omnia per sacramenta significantur."

[48] As we have seen, this is particularly true when the sacrament is celebrated as immersion.

opinions), positive proofs from authority, proofs from theological reason, solution of the difficulties, corollaries, and in particular corollaries for life and piety."[49] Their treatment generally involves a direct quotation of the relevant thomistic text followed by a brief explanation, sometimes using the "*O sacrum convivium*" as an illustration.[50] However, as the next section demonstrates, instead of presenting the commemorative, demonstrative and prognostic as three equal dimensions of the one sacramental sign, many commentators relegate the *signum prognosticum* to a position of tertiary importance compared to that attributed to either the *signum rememorativum* or the *signum demonstrativum*. How can this be explained? Three factors — internal, polemical and semeiotic — appear to be responsible for this shift. Each will now be examined in turn.

1.2.1 Internal Factor

The definition of sacrament which Thomas posits in the *Summa* includes the sacraments of the old and the new law. Past, present and future aspects are presented on a par with no hierarchy of signification. Having established what sacraments are, Aquinas then proceeds to investigate the need for them.[51] It is here that he outlines the difference between the sacraments of the old law and those of the new. The *discrimen primum* lies in their reference to the passion of Christ from which they derive their efficacy. While the sacraments of the old law "foretell realities that lay in the future," the sacraments of the new law "stand for realities which have taken place in Christ in the past."[52] Circumcision conferred grace "insofar as it was a sign of faith in the coming passion of Christ."[53] In baptism, however, "grace is conferred by the power of the sacrament itself which it has insofar as it is an instrument of the already realized passion of Christ."[54] Consequently, in the *Summa* itself it is evident that all sacraments are at once a reminder of the past, an indication of that which is effected in the present and a foretelling of the future. Yet, because they are related to the passion of Christ, the door is opened to consider the sacraments of

---

[49] Y. Congar, *A History of Theology*, 179.

[50] See L. Billot, *De ecclesiae sacramentis*, 23-24; A.-M. Lépicier, *Tractatus de sacramentis in communi*, 25.

[51] *ST*. III, Q. 61.

[52] *ST*. III, Q. 61, a. 4.

[53] *ST*. III, Q. 70, a. 4.

[54] *ST*. III, Q. 70, a. 4.

the old law as merely prognostic. Highlighting the superiority of the sacraments of the new law over those of the old inevitably leads to a diminution of the prognostic dimension of the sacraments of the new law and a corresponding over-emphasis on the commemorative and demonstrative.[55]

St. Thomas does not draw these conclusions in his treatment of the sacraments in the *Summa*. However, he appears to do so in his *Scriptum Super Sententiis*:

> The sacraments of the New Law signify three things: 1) The first sanctifying cause (e.g., baptism as signifying the death of Christ), and under this aspect they are *memorial* signs. 2) In the same way they signify the effect of sanctification which they bring about. This sanctification is of primary importance for them, and thus they are *demonstrative* signs. No problem arises if someone does not receive holiness, a fact that cannot be attributed to a defect on the part of the sacrament, which by its nature exists to confer grace. 3) Thus, they signify the finality of sanctification, that is, eternal glory, and under this aspect they are *prognostic* signs.[56]

In this earlier work the point of departure is the notion of sacrament as remedy for sin.[57] The word *sacramentum* derives from a verbal root which implies an active sanctification.[58] In order to respect the structure of the human person who comes to knowledge through the senses, it is appropriate that this sanctification be accomplished through signs. Thus the two fundamental concepts of active sanctification and visible sign come together. This prompts Aquinas to recognize and to distinguish between three different understandings of *sacramentum*: a sacrament which sanctifies and which is not a sign (the passion of Christ); a sacrament which

---

[55] L. Billot, *De ecclesiae sacramentis,* 25: "Sed respectu horum trium, sacramenta vetera erant totaliter prognostica, tametsi ut dictum est, sua virtute conferrent de praesenti quamdam praefigurationem interioris gratiae. Sacramenta vero nostra sunt rememorativa respectu primi, demonstrativa simul et efficacia respectu secundi, prognostica demum respectu tertii."

[56] IV *Sent.* D. 1, Q. 1, a. 1, ad. 4: "Sacramenta Novae Legis tria significant: scilicet causam primam sanctificantem, sicut baptismus mortem Christi, et quantum ad hoc sunt signa *rememorativa*. Item significant effectum sanctificationis quam faciunt, et haec significatio est eis principalis, et sic sunt signa *demonstrativa*, nec obstat, si aliquis sanctitatem non recepit, quia non est ex defectu sacramenti, quod quantum in se est, natum est gratiam conferre. Item significant finem sanctificationis, scilicet aeternam gloriam, et quantum ad hoc sunt signa *prognostica*. - Sacramenta vero veteris legis erant *totaliter signa prognostica*."

[57] IV *Sent.* D. 2, Q. 1, a. 1, ad. 1: "...omnia sacramenta in remedium alcuius spiritualis defectus instituta sunt."

[58] IV *Sent.* D. 1, Q. 1, a. 1, q. 1.

Christ); a sacrament which sanctifies and which is a sign (the sacraments of the new law); and a sacrament which does not sanctify but is a sign (the sacraments of the old law). The difference, therefore, between the sacraments of the old law and those of the new is that, while both signify, only the latter sanctify. Considered as sign (*qua signum*) each of the sacraments of the old law and those of the new is commemorative, demonstrative and prognostic. But, considered as cause of sanctification (*qua causa*) the Christian sacrament is principally viewed as being able to confer *hic et nunc* the merits of Christ's passion which it signifies. Hence, the demonstrative and commemorative dimensions are stressed over the prognostic, which is chiefly associated with the inability of the Hebrew sacraments to confer grace *ex opere operato*. In his mature work, when he begins from the notion of sacrament as sign, St. Thomas does not find it necessary to make this distinction.

1.2.2 Polemical Factor

The relatively irenic and free atmosphere of thirteenth century scholasticism was reinterpreted in the early twentieth century, marked by the agitated and contentious climate of a neo-scholastic theology grappling with the internal threat of modernism.[59] In fact the anti-modernist intent of many of the commentators is so dominant that their work most often begins with a statement of the errors which they seek to address.[60] Disputed topics such as the number of sacraments, the nature of instrumental causality, the effect of the sacraments *ex opere operato*, the sacramental character and the regenerative effect of baptism take on an importance beyond that originally attributed to them in the thomistic scheme.[61] Since other issues such as the sacramental nature of baptism,[62] the rite of circumcision as a figure of baptism and the preparation

---

[59] See L. Salerno, "Tomismo, pluralismo culturale e Concilio Vaticano II," *SapDom* 18 (1965) 45-86.

[60] See, for example, H. Lennertz, *De sacramentis novae legis in genere*, which begins with citations from the works of Luther, Melanchthon, Zwingli and Calvin as well as the response given by the Council of Trent.

[61] See E. Ruffini, "I grandi temi della teologia contemporanea dei sacramenti," *RivLi* 54 (1967) 39-52.

[62] L. Billot, *De ecclesiae sacramentis,* 207: "De existentia baptismi in ratione sacramenti non est specialiter disputandum; tanta enim evidentia in traditione christiana continetur, ut superflua sit omnis demonstratio."

which should precede baptism[63] were generally accepted, they receive cursory treatment, with only a direct quotation from Thomas affirming the fact. The result is that solidly Catholic positions, such as belief in sacraments as signs of faith are left aside, while other truths contested by Protestants and by Catholics in dialogue with modernity stand at the centre of attention.[64] A brief consideration of the baptismal and sacramental doctrine of M. Luther and the response given to it by the Council of Trent sheds light on the tense and guarded tone of early twentieth-century scholasticism.

At the heart of Luther's protest is the conviction that solely faith in Jesus Christ justifies sinners before God. This is the lens through which his entire fiducial theology must be viewed. When sinners respond in faith to God's word of promise, they die to the world of sin and rise to the new life of grace.[65] Since this, according to Luther, is what is signified in baptism, without faith the ceremony is of no avail, but when baptism is celebrated in faith grace is imparted.[66] This leads Luther to assert that "it cannot be true that there resides in the sacrament a power capable of giving justification, or that they are 'signs' of efficacious grace. All such things are said to the detriment of faith, and in ignorance of the divine promise."[67] This consistent stress on faith also induces Luther to assert that, if the sacraments have their effect through faith in God's word, then there is no difference between the sacraments of the old law and those of the new law.[68]

Having addressed Luther's doctrine of justification by faith alone in the sixth session of the Council of Trent,[69] the bishops then turned their attention to the teaching of the reformers on sacraments in general[70] and on baptism and confirmation.[71] This they did in a series of canons which anathematize statements they considered to be heretical, without developing a more detailed

---

[63] While A. D'Alès, *Baptême et confirmation*, follows Thomas' *ordo tractatus* closely on the first four questions concerning the nature and existence of the sacrament of baptism, the minister, the recipient, and the effects of the sacrament, the remaining two questions on circumcision and on the preparation that accompanies baptism are not treated explicitly.

[64] A.-M. Roguet, "I sacramenti nel loro valore di segni," *SacDo* 45 (1967) 79-92.

[65] M. Luther, "The Babylonian Captivity of the Church," *LW* XXXVI, 66.

[66] M. Luther, "Ten Sermons on the Catechism," *LW* LI, 185.

[67] M. Luther, "The Babylonian Captivity of the Church," *LW* XXXVI, 66.

[68] M. Luther, "The Babylonian Captivity of the Church," *LW* XXXVI, 65.

[69] DS 1520-1583.

[70] DS 1600-1613.

[71] DS 1614-1630.

doctrine on the subjects in question. Their theological approach to sacraments follows the individualistic scheme based on the notion "remedy for sin," but ignores the liturgical scheme based on the concept "acts of worship" which is so emphasized by Thomas.[72] Although Trent reaffirmed that the seven sacraments of the new law differ from those of the old law,[73] and that grace is conferred *ex opere operato,*[74] the theological emphasis was firmly placed on the performance of the rite — matter, form, minister — and on the salvific effect of a licit and valid celebration of the sacrament. While condemning the truncated opinion that "sacraments are instituted only for the sake of nourishing faith,"[75] the council fathers did not deem it necessary to elaborate on the proper relationship between faith and sacrament. Indeed, the word "only" in the condemned phrase seems to have been forgotten in subsequent discussion, and Aquinas' assertion that "sacraments are signs which protest faith through which humanity is justified"[76] was not quoted regularly lest it appear to have an heterodox overtone. In fact the anti-reformatorial intent of many of the subsequent Catholic commentators on the teaching of Trent is so dominant that they fail to note its excessively objective rather than the liturgical understanding of sacrament.

Luther also reacted against the traditional teaching of the sacrament of penance as the on-going renewal of Christian justification. Once baptized, a Christian can lose grace not by sin but only through unbelief.[77] Although the sacrament of baptism is received just once, believers are continually baptized anew by faith as they journey through this life. This process of fiducial rebaptism has an eschatological quality, since it perdures "until we attain to the completion of the sign at the last day."[78] Hence, one can say

---

[72] DS 1600.

[73] DS 1602.

[74] DS 1608.

[75] DS 1605: "Si quis dixerit, haec sacramenta propter solam fidem nutriendam instituta fuisse: anathema sit."

[76] *ST.* III, Q. 61, a. 4.

[77] M. Luther, "The Babylonian Captivity of the Church," *LW* XXXVI, 60.

[78] M. Luther, "The Babylonian Captivity of the Church," *LW* XXXVI, 69: "Thus, you have been once baptized in the sacrament, but you need to be continually baptized by faith, continually to die and continually to live. Baptism swallowed up your whole body and gave it forth again; in the same way that which baptism signifies should swallow up your whole life, body and soul, and give it forth again at the last day, clad in the robe of glory and immortality. We are therefore never without the sign of baptism nor without the thing it signifies. Indeed, we need continually to be baptized more and more, until we fulfil the sign perfectly at the last day."

that for Luther baptism is of necessity a *signum prognosticum*, a pledge or foretaste of the fulness of life that awaits those who have faith in the Lord Jesus.

In the "Decree on Justification" the bishops at Trent stressed that "those who through sin have forfeited the grace of justification they had received, can be justified again [...] through the sacrament of penance."[79] While it is hypothetically possible that one might not lose the grace of first justification conferred in baptism, the weakness of the human condition suggests otherwise. Given this truth, baptism was viewed throughout the Counter Reformation not so much as the sign of future glory, but as the door to the other sacraments in which grace is recovered by those who have lost it, or increased for those who have persevered in faith and in good works.

1.2.3 Semiotic Factor

A third reason for granting priority to the demonstrative dimension of sacramental signification is to be found in the relationship between matter and form. This argument is ably presented by A.-M. Roguet in his notes on the French translation of the *Summa Theologica*.[80] "Of the three significations," he argues, "two are extrinsic: the cause and the ultimate effect or end. Only the form is intrinsic."[81] Sacraments are composed of matter and form. While the matter may naturally possess a variety of meanings, the precise sacramental signification is specified by the form. The baptismal formula ("I baptize you ...") transforms a visible bodily washing into a spiritual cleansing of the soul which "signifies the grace of purification, of regeneration, of entry into divine life."[82] The sacraments produce the grace they signify, and they signify that which they produce. In that the sacraments do not produce the passion of Christ or future glory, their commemorative

---

[79] DS 1542.

[80] A.-M. Roguet, *Les sacrements*. This argument is also presented in J. Pohle – A. Preuss, *The Sacraments*, I, 15: "Note however that, the sacramental signs are always primarily *signa demonstrativa* and only secondarily *signa rememorativa* and *prognostica*. This is owing to the fact that the sacraments by their very nature must produce that which they signify, i.e., sanctifying grace here and now present in the soul, because it is sanctifying grace that they actually effect, whereas they merely signify the Passion of Christ and the glory of Heaven, the former as an indispensable requisite, the latter as a promise and a guaranty."

[81] A.-M. Roguet, *Les sacrements*, 311: "... de nos trois significations, deux sont extrinsèques: la cause et l'effet ultime ou la fin. Seule la forme est intrinsèque."

[82] A.-M. Roguet, *Les sacrements*, 309.

and prognostic aspects are of secondary importance. Since they only produce grace, then, concludes Roguet, they signify this alone.[83]

This preference for the demonstrative signification of the sacraments seems to contradict the opinion of St. Thomas as expressed in his response to an objection. Since "baptism receives its power from the passion of Christ" and "the sanctification of baptism comes through the form" then, the objection concludes, "it seems that the passion of Christ should be mentioned in the form."[84] Thomas' response shows that in, mentioning the Trinity in the sacramental form, the passion of Christ is not excluded, because in this case the principal cause encompasses and implies the instrumental cause.[85] That the passion of Christ is not explicitly mentioned in the form of baptism does not mean that Calvary is not signified by it.

In his article "La triple dimension du signe sacramental" J.M.R. Tillard[86] employs the results of liturgical studies in order to respond to A.-M. Roguet by stating that the sacramental sign must be inserted within the broader context of salvation history. While the matter is projected onto a faith level by the form, the realities employed are not devoid of previous religious significance. The matter of Christian baptism is not simply water in its natural symbolism as a source of life and a means of purification, but is already laden with a complexity of allusion which it has gleaned from the history of salvation.[87] Tillard views Roguet's reduction as symptomatic of a canonically inspired minimalism which focuses on the essential formula and the precise material without which the sacrament would not exist.[88] Nor should the baptismal washing be

---

[83] A.-M. Roguet, *Les sacrements,* 312: "...si les sacrements produisent en nous une certaine grâce, ils ne produisent pas en nous la Passion du Christ, ni la gloire future, puisque, par définition, l'une est passée, l'autre est à venir. S'ils les rendent présentes en nous, c'est la Passion dans son effet qui est la grâce, la gloire dans son germe qui est la grâce encore. Puisque "les sacrements produisent ce qu'ils signifient," on peut dire qu'ils signifient ce qu'ils produisent. Ne produisant que la grâce, ils ne signifient donc qu'elle seule."

[84] *ST.* III, Q. 66, a. 5, obj. 5: "Baptismus virtutem habet a passione Christi. Sed per formam baptismus sanctificatur. Ergo videtur quod in forma baptismi debeat fieri mentio de passione Christi."

[85] *ST.* III, Q. 66, a. 5, ad. 5: "Passio Christi, etsi sit principalis causa respectu ministri, est tamen causa instrumentalis respectu sanctae Trinitatis. Et ideo potius commemoratur Trinitas quam passio Christi."

[86] J.M.R. Tillard, "La triple dimension du signe sacramentel," *NRTh* 83 (1961) 225-254.

[87] J.M.R. Tillard, "La triple dimension du signe sacramentel," 249.

[88] J.M.R. Tillard, "La triple dimension du signe sacramentel," 252-253.

considered in isolation from the other rites of the sacramental celebration. These secondary elements of the rite are the proper context within which the signification of the essential aspects must be understood. "The sacramental rite is not an amalgam of signs; it is a single sign deployed over a period of time, in various stages, in which each has the purpose of setting in relief various aspects of the whole."[89] Within this expanded framework the commemorative, and especially the prognostic, aspects of the sacramental sign are rehabilitated, and an inflation of the demonstrative is rendered untenable.

2. "... in quo Christi sacerdotio congruitur ..."

A valuable insight into the eschatological dimension of sacraments in general, and of baptism in particular, is provided by an examination of their place in the extensive plan of the *Summa Theologica*. This is the purpose of the initial part of this section. In order to participate in the other sacraments, Christians must be deputed or marked by a spiritual sign or character through baptism. The second part of this section is devoted to a study of the eschatological dimension of sacramental character.

2.1 *Situating Baptism*

It has already been noted that Thomas' approach to the sacraments evolves from that used in the *Scriptum* to that used in the *Summa*.[90] In the later work Aquinas insists that sacraments are not only signs of human sanctification but also means of divine worship.[91] The place granted to the sacraments within the overall scheme of the *Summa Theologica* is obviously not an arbitrary matter. Indeed, in the *Secunda Secundae* in which the external acts of religion are discussed, Thomas already mentions the sacraments but defers their treatment to the *Tertia Pars*, so as first to develop

---

[89] J.M.R. Tillard, "La triple dimension du signe sacramentel," 254: "Le rite sacramentel n'est pas un amalgame de signes, il est un signe unique mais déployé en un certain laps de temps, en certaines étapes dont chacune a précisément pour but de mettre en relief un des aspects du tout."

[90] Does this represent a change in perspective or did St. Thomas actually change his mind from the *Scriptum* to the *Summa*? According to E. Frutsaert, "La définition du sacrement dans Saint Thomas," *NRTh* 60 (1928) 401-409, there is no change from the earlier to the later work. However, H.F. Dondaine, "La définition des sacrements dans *La Somme Théologique*," 213-228, does not agree.

[91] *ST*. III, Q. 60, a. 5.: "...in usu sacramentorum duo possunt considerari, scilicet cultus divinus et santification hominis."

the tracts on the incarnation, death and resurrection of Christ from which the Christian signs derive their power.[92]

2.1.1 The Place of the Sacraments in the "Summa Theologica"

In his *magnum opus*, Thomas faces the challenge of presenting the truths of revelation in a speculative, intelligible order while preserving their inherent historical quality. The then contemporary approaches of the *lectio* or *disputatio* were constrained either by text or controversy. Yet, the innovating approaches hitherto used to classify the truths of the Christian faith in a systematic manner, such as that undertaken by Abelard,[93] seemed to place the historical nature of revelation in jeopardy. Thomas thus chose a *via media* in the neo-platonic scheme of *exitus* and *reditus*: since God is the creator and ultimate end of all reality, he is the efficient and final cause within which all of history unfolds.[94]

This structure is already discernible in the *Scriptum Super Sententiis*. Book 1 reflects on the mystery of God *in se*, that is, on the inter-trinitarian relationship between the Father, Son and Spirit.[95] Book 2 examines the actions of God *ad extra*, that is, the relationship of the Trinity with creation.[96] Since, taken together, these two books constitute the *exitus*, the *reditus* begins with the incarnation in Book 3,[97] and culminates with the *consecutio finis* as presented in Book 4.[98] This *consecutio* takes place in two stages: the *praeparatio* and the *inductio in gloriam.*[99] The sacraments play

---

[92] *ST*. II-II, Q. 89, Prol.

[93] Y. Congar, *A History of Theology,* 70-74.

[94] I *Sent*. D. 2, divisio textus: "Cum enim ... sacrae doctrinae intentio sit circa divina, divinum autem sumitur secundum relationem ad Deum vel ut principium vel ut finem, secundum quod Apoc., XXII, 13 dicitur: 'Ego sum alpha et omega'; consideratio hujus doctrinae erit de rebus secundum quod exeunt a Deo ut a principio, et secundum quod referuntur in ipsum ut in finem. Unde in prima parte determinat de rebus divinis secundum *exitum* a principio; in secunda secundum *reditum* in finem."

[95] See I *Sent*. Prol.

[96] I *Sent*. Prol.: "Secundum quod pertinet ad Dei sapientiam est creaturarum productio. ... Semper enim id quod est primum est causa eorum quae sunt post; [...] unde primus processus est causa et ratio omnis sequentis processionis."

[97] I *Sent*. Prol.: "Tertium, quod pertinet ad Dei sapientiam, est operum restauratio."

[98] I *Sent*. Prol.: "Quartum, quod ad Dei sapientiam pertinet, est perfectio qua res conservantur in suo fine."

[99] I *Sent*. Prol.: "Ad consecutionem enim finis exigitur praeparatio, per quam omne quod non competit fini, tollatur; ita Christus etiam, ut nos in finem aeternae gloriae induceret, sacramentorum medicamenta preaparavit, quibus a nobis peccati

an indispensable part in the *praeparatio*, and are intrinsically linked with the *inductio in gloriam*. Here the sacraments "constitute the penultimate act of the history of salvation."[100] Consequently, their function is essentially eschatological: they are the "*medicina*" which restores (*restauratio*) and repairs (*reparatio*) fallen humanity for resurrection and glory.

In the *Summa*, in which he is no longer constrained by the text of Peter Lombard, Thomas clearly outlines his own *ordo disciplinae*:

> Because ... the fundamental aim of the holy teaching is to make God known, not only as he is in himself, but as the beginning and the end of all things and of reasoning creatures especially, we now intend to set forth this divine teaching by treating, first of God [Part I], second, of the journey to God of reasoning creatures [Part II], thirdly, of Christ, who, as man, is our road to God [Part III].[101]

Parts I and II are the two arms of the one curve which has its point of departure in God, and to whom it returns. The *exitus* grounds the *reditus*: the creation of human beings by God, the efficient cause, provides the ontological foundation for their free return to him, the final cause. Already in the *exitus* of creation, the *reditus* of beatitude is implied. Human life and action, therefore, are neither extrinsic nor accidental, but are the pre-disposed steps by which free beings respond to the deepest reality of their being created out of love by the God in whom they find their fulfillment. Thus, according to M.-D. Chenu,[102] the structure of the *Summa Theologica* indicates that, while dogmatic and moral theology may be studied separately, they are two facets of one single comprehension of truth which is both theoretical and practical.[103]

Turning from Part II to Part III of the *Summa Theologica*, Thomas moves from the order of necessity to that of historical realization.[104] The "*De sacramentis*" is placed in the *reditus*

---

vulnus abstergitur. Unde duo notantur in verbis praedictis; scilicet preaparatio, quae est per sacramenta, et inductio in gloriam."

[100] F. Martinelli, "Collocazione teologica della sacramentaria tomista," *Lateranum* 43 (1977) 1-25, 6.

[101] *ST*. I, Q. 2, Prol.

[102] M.-D. Chenu, "Le plan de la Somme Théologique de S. Thomas," *RThom* 47 (1939) 93-107.

[103] *ST*. I, Q. 1, a. 4.

[104] R. J. Hennessy, *The Incarnate Word*, xvii: "Creation and vocation are already free gifts of God, but the specific economy of salvation, and especially of restoration, are utterly free gifts not included with necessity in the first gift."

between christology and the projected tract on the "last things."[105] Jesus Christ is the way to the Father, and the sacraments extend the benefits of his incarnation, death and resurrection to all humanity. The eschatological import is obvious. If the "grand platonic sweep" of the whole work maps "the *exitus* and *reditus* of creation — the going forth of things from God and their coming back to him, the setting out and returning home, the first birth in which human beings are possessed by God and the second birth in which he is possessed by them,"[106] then, through the celebration of the sacraments, believers turn towards home, are companions with the Son on the journey to the Father, and already possess a foretaste of the glory which is to be fully revealed when they meet with God face to face. Since baptism is the first of the Christian sacraments, it is truly a *signum prognosticum*, the beginning of the end.

2.1.2 The Place of the Sacraments in the Commentators

From the place it occupies in the universal theological project of Aquinas it is evident that baptism has an inherently eschatological dimension. This structural perspective appears to be lost by the commentators of the Counter Reformation period right up to the beginning of the twentieth century. Why was this the case? The overall theological synthesis characteristic of Thomas and the Scholastics, threatened from the mid-sixteenth century, had reached a critical fragmentation by the end of the nineteenth.[107] Dogmatic, moral, spiritual and positive theology ploughed separate furrows without fruitful cross-fertilization. Within dogmatic theology itself, the tendency was more towards an analysis of its parts rather than an appreciation of its integrity. No doubt this trend was in part due to the impoverished historical perspective of Catholic theology of this period.

A.-M. Lépicier provides a pertinent illustration of this tendency. Although his tract on baptism and confirmation is but one tome of a massive twenty-five volume work,[108] he is concerned

---

[105] *ST.* III, Prol.: "... primo considerandum occurrit de ipso Salvatore; secundo, de sacramentis ejus, quibus salutem consequimur; tertio, de fine immortalitas vita, ad quem per ipsum resurgendo pervenimus."

[106] T. Gilby, *Christian Theology*, 43.

[107] See D. Farrell, *The Dogmatic Foundations of Bernard Häring's Thought*, where the author investigates the failure to emphasize the connection between dogmatic and moral theology between the years 1274 and 1954. The earlier date is chosen because "it marks the completion of St. Thomas' mature effort to link sacramental and moral theology" (vii).

[108] See note 1.

more with demonstrating the intrinsic logic and inter-relationship between the questions and articles on baptism than with situating the tract in the context of the returning *iter* of all creation to the God from whom it came. His and many other studies which claim to investigate the plan of the *Summa* merely furnish a synopsis of its teaching rather than an analysis of its fundamental *exitus-reditus* structure.[109] For example, while A. Legendre likens the internal aesthetic unity of the *Summa* to the general harmony of a gothic cathedral,[110] one feels that his appraisal deals more with artistic minutiae and the detailed carvings of angel and gargoyle than with the architectural vision which spans and buttresses the whole. Indeed neo-gothic architecture and neo-scholastic theology seem to have this in common: while both capture much of the detail and form of the original, neither succeeds in retrieving the overall sense of its movement and grace. Perhaps this insight prompted T. Gilby's timely word of caution to the student of the *magnum opus* of the Angelic Doctor:

> Before anatomizing the *Summa* be advised that it composes a living whole pressing forward in a continuous movement which, except for purposes of schematization, should not be arrested in sets of scholastic "stills." Charts have been traced to show its divisions and subdivisions ramifying with all the complications and more of the logic of a genealogical tree: such fixed and flat reproductions are convenient for reference, though they fail to convey the motion and fuller dimension in which human ideas and lives are begotten.[111]

In concrete, whenever the living body of sacramental theology or the *Summa* is dissected into frozen, disjointed parts, a diminution of the eschatological import of the Christian signs is inevitable.

2.2 *The Character of Baptism*

Whenever human beings are deputed to some definite function, argues Thomas, they are commissioned for it by means of some sign.[112] When, in the sacraments, Christians are "deputed for some function in the spiritual sphere pertaining to the worship of

---

[109] See A. Legendre, *Introduction à l'étude de la Somme Théologique de Saint Thomas d'Aquin*; C. Lattey, ed., *St. Thomas Aquinas*; M. Grabmann, *Einführung in die Summa Theologicae des heiligen Thomas von Aquin*.

[110] A. Legendre, *Introduction à l'étude de la Somme Théologique de Saint Thomas d'Aquin*, 16.

[111] T. Gilby, *Christian Theology*, 43.

[112] *ST*. III, Q. 63, a. 1.

God, it naturally follows that as believers they are marked off by some form of spiritual character."[113] In this section, the presentations of baptismal character by the Angelic Doctor and by the twentieth-century commentators are analyzed.

2.2.1 The Character in the "Summa Theologica"

This character is an indelible[114] mark impressed on the soul which configures Christians to the priesthood of Christ.[115] Conferred by the sacraments of baptism, confirmation and order,[116] the characters are either active or passive instrumental potencies.[117] Since all the sacraments, including these three, are protestations of faith, the character resides in the intellect, the cognitive power of the soul in which faith is operative.[118]

Character is the *res et sacramentum* of baptism.[119] Considered *qua res*, it is a distinctive mark which distinguishes believers from unbelievers, marks them for Christ and enables them to exercise certain cultic actions within the Christian community. Since the worship of Christian religion derives from the priestly office of Christ, the character, as the *sine qua non* of the liturgical life of the Church, configures believers to his priesthood, enabling them to worship as instruments or ministers of the risen Lord.[120] The passive character conferred by baptism is the *ianua sacramentorum*, in that it inserts the baptized into the worshipping community and gives them access to the other rites of the Christian religion. Through baptism the believers are inserted by the Spirit of Jesus Christ into the returning movement, the *reditus*, of all creation to the Father.

Considered as sacrament, *qua sacramentum*, the character is a sign of grace. It is not to be confused with grace: "for grace exists in the soul as a certain kind of form having in it an existence that is complete, whereas character exists in the soul as a certain kind of

---

[113] *ST*. III, Q. 63, a. 1.
[114] *ST*. III, Q. 63, a. 5.
[115] *ST*. III, Q. 63, a. 3.
[116] *ST*. III, Q. 63, a. 6.
[117] *ST*. III, Q. 63, a. 2.
[118] *ST*. III, Q. 63, a. 4, ad. 3.
[119] See E. Doronzo, "De Charactere ut est Res et Sacramentum," *RUO* 6 (1936) 243-261.
[120] See T. Marsh, "The Sacramental Character," in *Sacraments*, ed. D. O'Callaghan, 109-138.

instrumental power."[121] As a permanent instrumental power, the sacramental character renders Christians potential instruments of God.[122] In his article "The Configuration of the Sacramental Character."[123] S. McCormack reflects on the implications of character as "instrumental potency." Because the sacraments of the new law cause grace, a disposition or potency is required so as to render the soul capable of receiving such grace.[124] As an instrument, the character is the condition of possibility by which the sacramental rites after baptism produce grace in the soul which receives it by "validating the recipients,"[125] that is, making them capable of the effects that are produced by the external rite. "The function of the character," notes McCormack, "is to produce the works of Christ, works which, properly, are not to be attributed to the character, nor to the one who possesses the character, but to him who works through the character, namely, Christ the Priest."[126] Consequently, "the character can be said to set apart or consecrate its recipients for the sanctification of others as subordinate instruments, just as the Hypostatic Union sets apart the humanity of Christ as the primary instrument."[127]

Baptismal character is therefore an eschatological reality, a *signum prognosticum*: sealed with the Holy Spirit through the waters of baptism, Christians are configured to the priesthood of Christ which enables them to offer praise and worship to the Father until the temporal homage is fulfilled in glory. Furthermore, since the character impressed on the soul is indelible, it persists in eternity. Although external forms of worship no longer have any purpose beyond this life, the end for which liturgical praise is designed does remain. And so, concludes Thomas, "after this life character remains both in the good for their glory and in the evil for their shame."[128]

---

[121] *ST*. III, Q. 63, a. 5, ad. 1: "Nam gratia est in anima sicut quaedam forma habens esse completum in ea; character autem est in anima sicut quaedam virtus instrumentalis."

[122] *ST*. III, Q. 63, a. 2.

[123] S. McCormack, "The Configuration of the Sacramental Character," *Thom* 7 (1944) 458-491.

[124] S. McCormack, "The Configuration of the Sacramental Character," 484.

[125] S. McCormack, "The Configuration of the Sacramental Character," 483.

[126] S. McCormack, "The Configuration of the Sacramental Character," 488.

[127] S. McCormack, "The Configuration of the Sacramental Character," 491.

[128] *ST*. III, Q. 63, a. 5, ad. 3.

2.2.2 Character in the Commentators

St. Thomas' doctrine on sacramental character was to have a profound effect on the subsequent formulation of Church teaching on the matter. His small work *On the Articles of Faith and the Sacraments of the Church* provided the basis for the Council of Florence's "Decree for the Armenians" (1479).[129] This, in turn, grounded Trent's definition that three sacraments, namely baptism, confirmation and order, imprint a character which is a spiritual and supernatural quality inhering in the soul, distinct from divine grace.[130] While Thomas holds that character is a potency residing in the intellect which effects a participation in the priesthood of Christ, these opinions have not been defined by the teaching authority of the Church. Together with the Protestant denial of the existence of character, these open questions provide the parameters for the ulterior discussion on sacramental character which lasted to the middle of this century.

According to B. Leeming, two main questions emerged in this discussion: "Is the character a physical, ontological thing, or is it merely a moral entity, a relationship set up by God's institution? Secondly, granted that the character is an ontological entity, to what category of being is it to be assigned? Is it a habit, or a power, or a kind of figure, or what is it?"[131] In response to the first question, B. Leeming recognizes that there is general agreement among theologians that the indelible mark imprinted on the soul is an ontological entity, more than an extrinsic relationship, as suggested by Durandus of St. Pourcain, and less than a gift of the Holy Spirit himself as claimed by M. J. L. Farine. With regard to the second question, theological opinion varies greatly. Is character a power to do or receive things, or is it a habit or disposition, or a kind of passive quality, or a kind of spiritual figure or shape upon the soul?[132] The answer given is usually influenced by the theory of sacramental causality adopted.

Within this circumscribed context the eschatological aspects of sacramental character fade into the background and many related questions remain undeveloped. The character is a participation in the priesthood of Christ which both deputes and enables the

---

[129] See the introduction to the "Decree for the Armenians" in ND 390.

[130] DS 1609: "Si quis dixerit, in tribus sacramentis, baptismo scilicet, confirmatione et ordine, non imprimi characterem in anima, hoc est signum quoddam spirituale et indelibile, unde ea iterari non possunt: anathema sit."

[131] B. Leeming, *Principles of Sacramental Theology*, 226.

[132] B. Leeming, *Principles of Sacramental Theology*, 228-229.

baptized to participate in the cult of the Church as instruments or ministers of Christ. But, what does Thomas mean by this "cult of the Church"? Is he referring to worship in the strictly liturgical sense or does he intend to embrace the whole of Christian life, acts of service as well as formal liturgy? Here one can detect a development in Thomas' thought. In the *Scriptum*, character referred to the regal and prophetic actions of Christ as well as the priestly actions. However, in the *Summa* character seems to be "confined to the sphere of liturgical priesthood."[133]

Moreover, in the *Scriptum* the character conferred by baptism is viewed as a passive power disposing the recipient to receive the other sacraments, while that conferred by confirmation and orders is perceived as active, enabling the recipient to administer sacraments and to perform other hierarchical actions.[134] In the *Summa*, the character conferred by both baptism and confirmation is considered a passive power disposing the recipient to receive the other sacraments.[135] This confusion is reflected in the theology of the commentators. While E. Doronzo[136] regards the confirmational character as a passive power, A.-M. Lépicier[137] views it as both active and passive, and C. Pesch[138] as solely active. Beyond these comments, this aspect of the theology of sacramental character has received little or no development from St. Thomas until recent times.

3. "... memoria passionis eius recolitur, mens impletur gratia, et futurae gloriae nobis porta reseratur."

The ultimate reality, the *res*, of the sacrament of baptism is justification, the restoration of right relations with God. This justification, according to St. Thomas, is a two-pronged actuality which involves both the remission of sins and the participation in

---

[133] T. Marsh, "The Sacramental Character," 130-131.

[134] IV *Sent*. D. 4, Q. 1, a. 4, ad. 3: "... in spiritualibus est potentia spiritualis quasi passiva per quam homo efficitur susceptivus spiritualium actionum. Et talis spiritualis potentia confertur in baptismo. ... Alia potentia est activa spiritualis ordinata ad sacramentorum dispensationem et aliarum sacrarum hierarchiarum actionum exercitum. Et haec potestas traditur in confirmatione et ordine, ut suis locis patebit."

[135] *ST*. III, Q. 72, a. 5, ad. 2.

[136] E. Doronzo, *De sacramentis in genere*, 350.

[137] A.-M. Lépicier, *Tractatus de sacramentis in communi*, 153-154.

[138] C. Pesch, *De sacramentis*, 228.

new life.[139] The passion and death of Christ is the cause of the remission of sins, and believers share in the benefits of the passion by being sacramentally conformed to him in baptism.[140] The cleansing from sin symbolized by the baptismal washing is effected only because the sacrament truly renders actual the passion of Christ and inserts the recipients into it (*memoria passionis eius recolitur*).

It has already been noted that there is an intrinsic link between baptism and the passion of Christ in the thought of St. Thomas.[141] This link is further accentuated when one considers the impressive coincidence between the effects of the passion (*de effectibus passionis ejus*)[142] and those of baptism (*de effectibus baptismi*)[143] as presented in the *Summa*. Christ's passion frees human beings from sin and releases them from the debt of punishment which is deserved. In baptism sins are taken away without obligation to make satisfaction for them. While the passion of Christ restores the relationship of human beings with God the Father by releasing them from the power of the devil and strengthening them to resist temptation, in baptism grace and virtues are infused into the soul of the recipients so as to assist them in the struggle against concupiscence. The opening of the gates of heaven to humankind in the passion of Christ is extended to individual believers in the sacrament of baptism. From this one can conclude that that which is accomplished "once and for all" for all humanity on the Cross is effected in the life of the Christian through the sacrament of baptism.

Besides linking the passion of Christ and the baptism of believers, Aquinas also perceives an intrinsic correlation between the passion and the baptism of Jesus himself. St. Thomas often expresses the salvation of human beings in terms of the opening of heaven, or of the doors of heaven, to them. This, he states, is caused by the passion of Christ.[144] But how then, he asks, can one account

---

[139] *ST*. III, Q. 56, a. 2, ad. 4: "In justificatione animarum duo concurrunt, scilicet remissio culpae, et novitas vitae per gratiam. Quantum ergo ad efficaciam, quae est per virtutem divinam, tam passio Christi quam resurrectio est causa justificationis quoad utrumque. Sed quantum ad exemplaritatem, proprie passio Christi et mors est causa remissionis culpae, per quam morimur peccato; resurrectio autem est causa novitatis vitae, quae est per gratiam sive justitiam."

[140] *ST*. III, Q. 49, a. 3, ad. 2.

[141] See Section 1.1.

[142] *ST*. III, Q. 49.

[143] *ST*. III, Q. 69.

[144] *ST*. III, Q. 39, a. 5, ad. 3.

for the evangelists' claim that the heavens opened at the baptism of Jesus in the Jordan?[145] In explaining this phenomenon Thomas, quoting John Chrysostom, remarks that "the obstacles which had hitherto hindered the soul of the departed from entering into heaven were entirely removed by the passion, but at Christ's baptism they [the gates of heaven] were laid open."[146] In other words, Thomas infers that the victory won at Christ's passion was initiated at his baptism. In response to the question whether Jesus should have been baptized at all, Aquinas again quotes Chrysostom and notes that, although Jesus did not need baptism for himself, "nevertheless carnal nature in others had need of it."[147] Taken together, these replies suggest that in his baptism Jesus, the innocent and spotless victim, is heralding his ministry of taking on himself the guilt and sin of humanity for the salvation of all. In short, that which is fulfilled on Calvary, Jesus' baptism with blood, is inaugurated in the Jordan, his baptism with water.

If the passion of Christ is the cause of the remission of sins, his resurrection is the cause of the newness of life which is part of human justification. The new life or spiritual regeneration symbolized by the baptismal washing is effected because its recipients, once buried with Christ, rise to fullness of life with him.

3.1 *The Eschatological Dimension of Sacramental Grace in the "Summa Theologica"*

The eschatological dimension of baptismal justification is never far from the surface in the writings of St. Thomas. Baptism, he claims, is a forgiveness of sins and an admittance to the kingdom of God. Both effects are prefigured in the Old Testament: the former by the passing through the Red Sea to freedom, the latter by the crossing through the Jordan into the promised land. This gives rise to the question whether Jesus should have been more fittingly baptized in the Red Sea or in the Jordan. Thomas opts for the Jordan because the principal effect of baptism is not the forgiveness of sins but the opening of the gate to the kingdom of heaven as prefigured in the crossing of the Jordan:

---

[145] Matt 3:16; Mark 1:10; Luke 3:21.

[146] *ST*. III, Q. 39. a. 5, ad. 3: "... dat intellegere Chrysostomus quod obstacula, quibus prius obsistentibus, animae defunctorum introire non poterant coelos, sunt totaliter per passionem Christi ablata; sed in baptismo Christi sunt aperta."

[147] *ST*. III, Q. 39, a. 1: "... pro se baptismate non indegebat, tamen in aliis carnalis natura opus habebat."

> The crossing of the Red Sea prefigured baptism in this — that baptism blots out sin; whereas the crossing of Jordan prefigures it in this — that it opens the gate to the kingdom of heaven: and this is the principal effect of baptism, and accomplished by Christ alone. And therefore it is more fitting for Christ to be baptized in the Jordan than in the sea.[148]

The eschatological implications of this are obvious. In baptism the gates of future glory are opened to believers (*futurae gloriae nobis porta reseratur*). Already the baptized are born again to the new life of righteousness. Illumined by the Spirit they are made the ministers of good works by the infusion of grace.[149] Yet, although the gates of heaven have been flung open by the passion of Christ, Christians have not yet passed through. Again and again, Thomas stresses that baptism is only a beginning: through baptism Christians are initiated to the newness of life and possess the first fruits of the kingdom. While baptism gives them a share in Christ's triumph over death, the fullness of his victory is not yet enjoyed by them. New life has indeed begun, but it will be completed only in beatitude when they meet with God face to face. In the course of history the baptized are "sanctified with a power from heaven,"[150] a light which shines from beyond to dispel the present shadows and illumine the path of *reditus*, the grace of the risen Lord which strengthens and orients them on the journey towards the Father.

Since baptism takes away sin and all the punishment due to it, why, Thomas asks, are its recipients still subject to "death, sickness, bodily weakness and disorders of nature, all of which are seen as the result of original sin and the loss of the state of original justice"[151]? His answer to this question[152] provides further insight into the eschatological tension in the life of the baptized. While baptism could remove these penalties now, it does not yet do so. However, "*by its power* they will be removed from the just at the

[148] *ST*. III, Q. 39, a. 4, ad. 1: "Transitus maris Rubri praefiguravit baptismum quantum ad hoc quod baptismus delet peccata; sed transitus Jordanis quantum ad hoc quod aperit januam regni coelestis, qui est principalior effectus baptismi, est per solum Christum impletus. Et ideo convenientius fuit quod Christus in Jordane quam in mare baptizaretur."

[149] *ST*. III, Q. 69, a. 5.

[150] *ST*. III, Q. 39, a. 5: "... de caetero coelestis virtus baptismum sanctificaret."

[151] This is how J.J. Cunningham, *Baptism and Confirmation*, 129, interprets St. Thomas' "poenalitates praesentis vitae."

[152] *ST*. III, Q. 69, a. 3: "Utrum per baptismum debeant auferri poenalitates praesentis vitae."

resurrection."[153] By virtue of the baptism which they have received, a guaranteed hope of eternal beatitude is given to the Christians who persevere in grace and virtue. Their earthly existence is consequently a time of progressive configuration to Christ. Just as he, albeit full of grace and truth, was tempted, suffered and died before being raised to glory, so too the baptized, full of grace and virtue, are not exempt from struggling with concupiscence, suffering and death before inheriting the crown of eternal glory. It is by being conformed to Christ in his suffering that the baptized become heirs with him in glory.[154]

By undergoing baptism Jesus leaves his followers an example, not merely by acting as the initiator of the lustral rite they will undergo, but also by being the exemplar of the conflictual life they will lead. His baptism is the public declaration of his intention to enter fully into the frailty of the human condition so as to accomplish its definitive salvation. Christian baptism then, is not just an application of the merits of the unique passion to the many individuals, but a challenge to participate in the ongoing eschatological struggle for the redemption of the world which Jesus commenced. Christian life is never a *fuga mundi*, an escape from the present reality. Indeed, St. Thomas states that one of the reasons why the penalties of the present life remain is so that those who approach the sacrament would do so not in the desire to escape the pain of earthly limitation, but in the hope of entering the glory of eternal life by embracing the trials and sufferings which being inserted within history entails.[155] Strengthened by the grace that flows from Christ its head, the Church, the community of the baptized, is truly his ecclesial Body, his instruments in bringing to ever fuller expression the new justice attained by his redemption of the world.

3.2 *The Eschatological Dimension of Baptismal Grace in the Commentators*

L. Billot prefaces his treatment of the effect of the sacraments with the declaration that his interest lies neither with the commemorative nor the prognostic aspects but with the present

---

[153] *ST*. III, Q. 69, a. 3: "... sed ejus virtute auferentur a justis in resurrectione."

[154] *ST*. III, Q. 69, a. 3; II-II, Q. 85, a. 5, ad. 2.

[155] *ST*. III, Q. 69, a. 3, ad. 3.

interior sanctification which the sacraments signify.[156] Immediately the present reality of sacramental grace (*mens impletur gratia*) takes precedence over the past or future dimensions. To this end, his exposition of the theme focuses on those facets of the sacraments which deal directly with their ability to confer here and now the grace they signify.[157]

While the eschatological dimension of baptismal grace is not wholly absent in the neo-scholastic commentators, its manner of being treated has considerably changed. The tension between the "already" and the "not yet," almost palpable in the writings of Thomas, now gives way to what is a fully realized eschatology. The prognostic dimension of baptism is perceived less as the certain beginning of new life, and more as its actual possession. Indeed, while Thomas regards the *poenalitates praesentis vitae* as concrete aspects of this tension, the commentators view them in a secondary, interior manner. Despite the fact that these *poenalitates* exist, they argue, the baptized are truly justified.[158]

Early twentieth-century Catholic dogmatic theologians, in an attempt to refute the errors of Protestant sacramental doctrine, preferred to comprehend baptism as the channel of present grace and its effects as the sure possession of such. This preference severed the form of sanctification from both its cause and its ultimate end, and led to a distortion of the future dimension of the economy of human salvation: Christians do not seem to participate in the passion and resurrection of Christ because they have received the grace of baptism; grace does not seem to be the pledge of the ultimate end of human sanctification, because it is its temporal form. It is more accurate, according to Thomas, to state that, because Christians are inserted into Christ's passion (cause) and united with him in his glory (ultimate end), they are reborn to new life in the forgiveness of sins through infused grace and virtues (form).

---

[156] L. Billot, *De ecclesiae sacramentis,* 50: "Hinc, cum de efficacia sacramentali nunc sermo sit, non amplius considerantur sacramenta ipsa secundum quod sunt rememorativa praeteritae redemptionis, vel prognostica futurae gloriae, sed prout de praesenti significant interiorem sanctificationem, eamque significando conferunt."

[157] Thus questions like the various types of causes, the merits of the different theories of sacramental causality, distinction between *ex opere operato* and *ex opere operantis*, reviviscence, and character as a disposition for grace come to the fore.

[158] See, for example, L. Billot, *De sacramentis*, 169.

Over-emphasis on the form of baptismal sanctification could seem to reduce grace to a mechanical quiddity, classified in its type and species, detached from the person of Christ and the mystery of human redemption. It follows that in this scheme, character is chiefly an ontological reality which identifies believers as members of the Church and which disposes them for future grace. That baptismal character also configures its recipients to Christ as his instruments and ministers in the return of all creation to the Father is certainly of secondary importance from such a viewpoint. And, when the power of baptism to effect remission of sins and rebirth becomes all-important, then the multi-dimensional symbolism of water and of lustral washing throughout the history of salvation is trimmed to the required minimum.

Indeed, C. Lattey's inaccurate contention that Thomas and the Schoolmen "with their sharp eye for scientific precision and the definition of essentials" regard baptism as "a washing, having no thought of it as being sacramentally a burial"[159] is symptomatic of this reduction. This statement fails to perceive the full range of the religious symbolism of washing in medieval theology. Not surprisingly, Lattey views the ultimate reality of baptism in terms of the present effect of the sacramental grace it confers with no reference to the share of Christians in the passion of Christ or in his future coming.[160] Because baptismal grace, even in the early part of this century, was reduced to its formal element, the significance of the lustral washing was correspondingly reduced. To suggest, as Lattey does, that the replacing of "immersion (which offered a closer resemblance to burial) by the pouring of water on the head" is evidence that baptism is a washing as opposed to a burial is clearly untenable. As already mentioned, Aquinas asserts that water is a sign of the "mysteries of Christ by which we are justified" and insists that, while washing is sufficient, the effects of baptism find a fuller expression in the ancient tradition of bodily immersion.[161] Unfortunately Lattey is so preoccupied with the formal aspect of baptismal grace and its principal lustral signification that he risks restricting the sacrament to its demonstrative aspect. It is only when all three aspects — cause, form and ultimate end — are held in balance that such restriction can be avoided. When this equilibrium is upset, both the

[159] C. Lattey, *St. Thomas Aquinas*, 94.

[160] C. Lattey, *St. Thomas Aquinas*, 102: "the infusion of sanctifying grace and of the virtues, together with the actual graces sufficient for perseverance."

[161] See Section 1.1.

commemorative and the prognostic aspects of the sacramental sign of baptism are invariably relegated to presupposed premises, rather than given their proper place as references to the first and the last comings of the Saviour.

CHAPTER 2

Retrieving the Future

The re-emergence of the eschatological dimension of baptism in the liturgical, biblical and patristic studies of the early twentieth century

Within the Roman Catholic Church, the early twentieth century witnessed considerable ferment in the understanding of the sacraments. Liturgical, patristic and biblical research yielded considerable insights into these essential rites of the Church, their celebration down through the ages and their connection with the saving mystery of Jesus Christ.[1] The fruits of this labour, however, did not have an immediate impact on the overly juridical approach to sacramental theology which prevailed in the seminary faculties during this period.[2]

In 1897, Pope Leo XIII (1878-1903) issued the encyclical letter *Aeterni Patris* which encouraged a return to the writings of St. Thomas Aquinas as the basic texts in Catholic faculties of philosophy and theology. Despite the situation described in the preceding chapter, notable advances were made in regaining the notion of sacramentality proper to the Angelic Doctor.[3] The

---

[1] B. Neunheuser, *Baptism and Confirmation,* 225, notes: "There is in the following centuries [after the Council of Trent] nothing special to record with regard to the doctrine of baptism, save perhaps that the frontal opposition to the reformers brought with it a certain narrowing of the field of vision to those portions of doctrine which had been attacked. Only in the modern period has there been an enrichment in baptismal theology. This has come about primarily through a more thorough study of what been handed down with regard to baptism in biblical theology, in the writings of the Fathers, and in the liturgy. Fruitful as well has been the controversy with the comparative religions school and with liberal theology."

[2] See C.E. O'Neill, "I sacramenti" in *Bilancio della teologia del XX secolo*, ed. H. Vorgrimler – R. Van der Gucht, III, 264-269.

[3] J. Wicks, *Introduction to Theological Method*, 25, remarks that "every-day work in Catholic theology in the time between the two Vatican Councils was only rarely marked by the universal quest for wisdom characteristic of St. Thomas. The

sacraments were always defined as signs but, this fundamental concept played no truly determinative role in the theological scheme of many of the commentators of the early twentieth century. Some, however, did manage to withdraw from the controversy surrounding sacramental causality, and to rediscover the emphasis on the ecclesial nature of liturgy and the scholastic understanding of the triple dimension of the sacramental sign as expressed by St. Thomas. Foremost among these is Dom Anscar Vonier.

The influence of the Liturgical Movement on Catholic sacramental theology is widely acknowledged. M.J. O'Connell, for example, enumerates three fundamental facts which this movement "brought home" to the theological reflection on the seven rites of the Church: sacraments are symbolic actions; they are ecclesial acts which are administered by the worshipping community as a profound expression of what the Church is; in these cultic actions Christ himself is the chief Priest.[4] Despite the heated debate which the writings of Dom Odo Casel often provoked, his works are perhaps the greatest legacy of this period of liturgical renewal.

The first forty years of the twentieth century have been described as "dark days for Catholic biblical scholarship."[5] The initial impetus given to Catholic scriptural studies during the pontificate of Leo XIII[6] was stifled with the emergence of the modernist crisis.[7] Significant critical scholarship was not to emerge until after the encyclical *Divino afflante Spiritu* of Pius XII in 1943.[8] During the earlier part of this century, however, important

---

textbooks of theological instruction used in Catholic universities and seminaries in the first half of the twentieth century were more influences by the principles of Cano than by Aquinas."

[4] M.J. O'Connell, "The Sacraments in Theology Today," *Thought* 30 (1961) 44-45.

[5] This is the judgement of R.D. Witherup, "Modern New Testament Criticism," *NJBC* II, 1142.

[6] See Leo's measured encouragement of scriptural studies in his encyclical *Providentissimus Deus*. The École Biblique was founded in Jerusalem by M.-J. Lagrange in 1890. The Pontifical Biblical Commission was established in 1902, and in 1909, during the reign of Pius X , the Pontifical Biblical Institute was founded in Rome. See M. Gilbert, "New Horizons and Present Needs: Exegesis Since Vatican II" in *Vatican II: Assessment and Perspectives,* ed. R. Latourelle, I, 321-322.

[7] G.P. Fogarty, *American Catholic Biblical Scholarship*, 198, notes that "The state of Catholic biblical scholarship in the United States at the end of the 1930's was bleak. Whatever scholarship there had been at the beginning of the century had either been destroyed in the wake of Modernism or had gone underground."

[8] B. Leeming, "Recent Trends in Sacramental Theology," *IThQ* 23 (1956) 195: "As regards method, all theology has been and will probably continue to be much influenced by the intensive study of words and language characteristic of

contributions to the spiritual sense of scripture and on the typology of the sacraments were made by the French Jesuit, Jean Daniélou.[9]

The purpose of this chapter is twofold. First of all ("Sign, Mystery and Type"), it investigates the contribution which exponents of patristic, liturgical and biblical renewal have made to the retrieval of the eschatological dimension of baptism during the earlier part of this century. Then, it introduces the authors whose works form the central part of this research project ("Source, Emergence, Surge and Course").

1. **Sign, Mystery and Type**

This section presents studies from the first part of the twentieth century which contributed to the retrieval of the eschatological dimension of the sacrament of baptism. From the patristic field, the rediscovery of the triple dimension of the sacramental sign is presented through the writings of Ansgar Vonier. The monumental benefaction of the Liturgical Movement is evaluated in the pioneering, if controversial, *Kultmysterium* theory of Odo Casel. The influence of a re-emerging scriptural scholarship on the understanding of baptism as *signum prognosticum* is viewed through the biblical studies of Jean Daniélou. The overall picture discovered on this triptych is evaluated as the section unfolds.

recent biblical theology. There is a strong revulsion from the older method of citing 'proof-texts'."

[9] J. Crehan, "Baptism and Confirmation: 1945-1955," *TS* 17 (1956) 494, notes that "If one were to select, perhaps the most important single event of the period which has opened up new horizons has been the revival of typological exegesis and the consequent interest in those patristic texts where antiquity was busy with the Old Testament foreshadowings of the two sacraments. In Pesch *Compendium* (in the edition of 1936) the only OT text that is used in the discussion of baptism and confirmation is the passage from Ez 36:25 about the outpouring of clean water. Zwingli (*Corp. Ref.* 4, 171) and Calvin (*Inst* 4, 14 21 and 4, 16, 3) had stood for the substantial identity of the two covenants and the two Testaments, and Catholic theologians were forced for a spell to look studiously away from the Old Testament; but time has brought the opportunity for a more balanced appraisal, and that has begun to be made in our own time." In this text, the failure to view the origins of Christian baptism in the religious experience and scriptures of the Hebrew people is linked with the polemical factor as outlined in the previous chapter.

1.1 *Anscar Vonier: The Triple Dimension of Sacramental Sign*

In *A Key to the Doctrine of the Eucharist*[10] the aim of Anscar Vonier[11] is to express the doctrine on the eucharist in terms of the sacramental theory of the Church.[12] His claim is not to produce an original work but "to reproduce faithfully the mental attitude of the great theological age of which St. Thomas Aquinas is the king."[13]

Vonier identifies three concepts from the theory of the sacraments in general proposed by the Angelic Doctor which underpin the subsequent presentation of the eucharist. First among these is the insight that "it is the very essence of a sacrament to be a sign."[14] Immediately, Vonier goes on to explain the signification proper to the sacraments by citing the "truly classical"[15] passage from the *Summa Theologica.*[16] Every sacrament, he notes, is a sign of the past, the present and of the future.[17] Vonier criticises the narrow definition of a sacrament as an external sign of an internal grace. If external grace refers merely to the actual transformation of

---

[10] A. Vonier, *A Key to the Doctrine of the Eucharist.* References in this study are to the American edition. [Hereafter *KDE.*]

[11] Anscar Vonier was born in Ringschnait, Württemburg, on 15 November 1875. He entered Buckfast Abbey as a boy. After his ordination in 1898 he began his doctoral studies in philosophy at San Anselmo in Rome. In 1905 he was appointed to the faculty of San Anselmo for a five year term. But, the events of the Summer of 1906 were to change everything. While journeying from Spain to Argentina with his abbot, Vonier was shipwrecked. Abbot Natter was drowned but Vonier survived. Six weeks later he was elected second abbot of Buckfast. Besides undertaking a monumental building programme at the abbey, Vonier published several theological works. He died at Buckfast Abbey on 26 December 1938. According to J. Stéphan, "Anscar Vonier," *NCE* XIV (1967) 751, Vonier "possessed the gift of expounding abstruse questions so as to make them intelligible not only to professional theologians but to intelligent lay readers as well." See W. Upson, "Anscar Vonier," *DublR* 206 (April, 1939) 236-246; C. Froehle, *The Idea of the Sacred According to Abbot Anscar Vonier*; S.K. Kujur, *The Eucharistic Theology of Dom Anscar Vonier, O.S.B.*; A. Cincinnati, *Pneumatological Ecclesiology in the Writings of Abbot Anscar Vonier, O.S.B.*

[12] Towards the end of the work, Vonier, *KDE,* 242, expresses the thesis as follows: "that the great Catholic tradition visualises the eucharistic sacrifice from the angle of sacrament."

[13] *KDE,* vii. A monk of Buckfast Abbey (E. Graf, *Abbot of Buckfast: A Study of Anscar Vonier*, 84) noted that "the bible and St Thomas are the twin pillars on which rests the spiritual structure erected by the Abbot's busy pen."

[14] *KDE,* 17. Here Vonier refers to *ST* III, Q. 60, a. 1.

[15] *KDE,* 18.

[16] *ST* III, Q. 60, a. 5, ad. 3.

[17] *KDE,* 20: "Every sacrament, then, announces something; it brings back the past, it is the voice of the present, it reveals the future. If the sacraments did no longer proclaim as a sign something which is not seen, it would not be a sacrament; in every sacrament there is a past, a present, and a future; the death of Christ is the past; supernatural transformation is its present; eternal glory is its future."

the soul, then this verbal formula would represent only "one-third of the sacramental function."[18] In fact, he contends that

> to limit the power of significance of the sacrament to the present moment only, to the transformation of the soul at the time when the sacrament is applied to man, would be an unwarranted minimising of the sacramental doctrine, and would make much of the scriptural language unintelligible.[19]

In the case of baptism, Vonier notes that the reality signified "is not any kind of cleansing of the soul, but it is a cleansing of the soul which is a burial with Christ and which is a resurrection with Christ. Baptism is not only the present, but also the past and the future."[20]

Vonier reiterates the thomistic axiom that a sacrament is always a sensible thing.[21] While an act of the intellect or will could never fulfil the role of sign, the latter can be an external manifestation of the former. Vonier gives a lengthy testimony to the effect the baptismal washing has on his own Christian consciousness:

> When I see the baptismal water poured on the head of the catechumen, and when I hear the words of the priest who does the christening, if I am a man of faith, my mind, roused by these external rites and signs, travels a long way. I go back to the Jordan, where Christ is being baptized; I go back to Calvary, where blood and water issue from the side of Christ; my mind leaps forward to that people who stand before the Throne of God in white robes which have been washed in the Blood of the Lamb; and, more audacious still, my mind gazes right into the innermost soul of the catechumen and distinguishes that soul from all other non-baptized souls, through that spiritual seal which makes it a member of Christ. The sacramental sign is pregnant with all that spiritual vision of my faith.[22]

According to this text, past, present and future events converge in the experience of the baptized. Not only do believers "go back" to the events of Jordan and Calvary but, set apart by that seal which marks them for Christ, they stand before the eschatological Throne of God. But, is this triple sacramental representation solely a

---

[18] *KDE,* 22-23.
[19] *KDE,* 23.
[20] *KDE,* 22.
[21] *ST* III, Q. 60, a. 4.
[22] *KDE,* 24.

spiritual experience in the mind of the Christian? Vonier clearly suggests that it is something more.

The fundamental difference between the rites of the old law and those of the new is that, while both signify, only the latter sanctify *ex operato*.[23] "Signification and causation of the spiritual thing, of the mystery of faith, are indissolubly united in the Christian sacrament."[24] If the sacraments are merely signs, they are no greater than their old covenant precursors; if, on the contrary, the ritual acts of the new covenant are solely causes, they immediately lose their historic value. Vonier concludes that

> Whenever the sacramental doctrine is either falsified or deflected from the traditional concept, the cause has been this, that men, who ought to have known better, ceased in one way or another to visualise at the same time the double concepts of signification and causation. The two concepts are strictly inseparable in this matter of the sacrament. The sacraments must be cause in such wise as actually to represent the past, the present, and the future; and it must signify in such wise as actually to effect the thing to which it points.[25]

In other words, while the sacraments are three-fold signs of the sanctification of humanity, they also are causes of what they signify. The saving gift which is conferred in the sacramental celebration is nothing less than a participation in the past, present and future realities which are signified by the rite. In the case of baptism, then, this means that believers are born again through water and the Spirit (present), because they have died with Christ (past), and already participate in the glory of those washed clean in the blood of the Lamb (future).

Although Vonier stresses all three dimensions of the sacramental sign, he often betrays a preference for the commemorative or demonstrative over the prognostic.[26] In Chapter 1, three factors — internal, polemical and semeiotic — were proposed to explain this trend in the early twentieth-century commentators on St. Thomas. Vonier himself clearly lays the blame for the narrowing of the signification of the sacramental sign on two extreme tendencies: Protestant spiritualising and Catholic

---

[23] See Chapter 1, section 1.2.2.

[24] *KDE*, 30.

[25] *KDE*, 31.

[26] See, for example, *KDE*, 74: "The *sacramentum* is all that we know as the signification, with its divine power and its commemorative affinities."

realism.[27] In the light of the theme of this research project, however, another factor emerges. Put simply, while the sacramental words and actions clearly commemorate some saving action of Christ which finds its fulfilment on the Cross and point to the present effect of the liturgical rite, it is difficult to find something within the ritual celebration which in the same way grounds or guarantees the reality of the prognostic dimension. The central thesis of this present study is to propose that one way to overcome this apparent impasse is to view the sacramental rites of the Church in continuity both with the acts of the Hebrew prophets and with the actions of Jesus, the eschatological prophet. A justification for this approach is to be found in some of the sacramental insights of the Abbot of Buckfast.

Vonier deals at length with the relationship between the Last Supper and the drama of the Cross, and expresses the following conundrum:

> The eucharistic sacrifice was offered up first at the Last Supper, before the natural sacrifice took place. Would not this point to the conclusion that in some way the eucharistic sacrifice is truly the beginning of the whole *processus* of Christ? ... If [the eucharistic sacrifice] were a natural sacrifice, we could not avoid the conclusion that the world was redeemed before Christ shed his first drop of Blood, as the Last Supper would have had infinite value as sacrifice in its own right.[28]

Vonier accepts neither this resolution nor that which would reduce the Supper to the first act of one universal sacrifice.[29] Rather, he proposes that, if the sacramental view of the eucharistic sacrifice is admitted, the difficulty no longer remains. To this end, he makes recourse to "the theology of those wonderful anticipations by

---

[27] *KDE,* 93-94: "I have already exhorted my reader to rejoice in the truth that sacraments are signs, and not to give up any of the glory of sacramental symbolism because Protestantism has distorted the traditional notion of sacramental signification. In the same line of thought let me exhort him now to defend against all comers the spiritual character of our sacraments; although Protestantism again has made of this notion of spirituality an emptying out of the contents of the sacrament. Though the text just quoted from S Thomas refers more directly to the eating of the bread of the eucharist, its spirit applies to the eucharistic sacrifice as well. We are truly dealing with a spiritual sacrifice in the sense that there is no death in it, though there be in it all that reality which is indispensable to the sacrifice."

[28] *KDE,* 141.

[29] *KDE,* 137-138: "A sacrament is not part of the drama, however great that drama may be; a sacrament is essentially the representation of the completed drama. The historic drama must be complete before sacraments are possible. Sacraments are the monuments of the finished thing only, not the introductory scenes or the last acts of some great historic deed."

Christ"[30] as expounded by Aquinas.[31] Applying this doctrine to the eucharistic sacrifice of the Last Supper, Vonier concludes that:

> we may say that it prefigured the sacrifice of the Cross; and the Christ who was to give his own natural Flesh and Blood that power of redeeming mankind, gave to bread and wine the power of representing sacramentally that same Flesh and Blood. We need not even consider the eucharistic sacrifice of the Last Supper as being a final vow of the Son of God to undergo death, a theme beloved of more than one preacher. ... The institution of the eucharistic sacrament of the Last Supper was not so much Christ's vow to die, as Christ's anticipated triumph in his death.[32]

The sacrifice in the Upper Room, then, prefigured the bloody immolation on Golgotha. The natural self-giving of Christ on the Cross is represented sacramentally in the proffering of the eucharistic elements at the leave-taking meal. While the table actions with the bread and wine are "Christ's anticipated triumph in his death," Vonier underlines that both are separate events.[33]

This point is reinforced by Vonier in his commentary on the "Doctrine on the Most Holy Sacrifice of the Mass" formulated at the Council of Trent.[34] "Let me only remark", he concludes, "that the Council [of Trent] makes it quite clear that the Last Supper was a complete act, representative by anticipation of that other complete act, the sacrifice of the first Good Friday."[35] Again Vonier underlines the belief that both the sacrifice of the Cross and the events of the Last Supper are complete acts in themselves. Yet, there is a connection: the unbloody sacrifice is "representative by anticipation" of the bloody oblation.[36] This notion of "representative anticipation" bears striking parallels to the Hebrew scriptural concept of *'ôt* as presented in Chapter 3.

---

[30] *KDE,* 142.

[31] *ST* III, Q. 64, a. 2, ad. 1.

[32] *KDE,* 143-144.

[33] This distinction between the Last Supper and Calvary is also applied to the eucharist and Calvary. See, for example, *KDE,* 140: "The traditional view of the Church ... is that the sacrifice of Calvary was completed and perfect in the genus sacrifice; the eucharist adds nothing to it; but it is truly 'the brightness of its glory and the figure of its substance'."

[34] See *KDE,* 152-177. The text to which Vonier refers is to be found in DS 1740-1743.

[35] *KDE,* 156.

[36] Vonier does not specify the text where this is stated in the documents of the Council of Trent. From the context it would appear that he is referring to DS 1740.

Commenting on the Lord's command "*Hoc facite in meam commemorationem*", Vonier notes that "*hoc* means all that they had seen and witnessed in the Upper Room."[37] When Jesus told his disciples to do this in memory of him, he clearly ordered them to carry out this rite which they had seen him perform, together with its prayer of thanksgiving and blessing. But, Vonier adds, he also commanded them to imitate the "other wonderful circumstances, which must have made such a deep impression on their minds."[38] Vonier does not specify, however, what these "wonderful circumstances" might be. Certainly the representative anticipation of the sacrifice of Good Friday in the ritual breaking of bread and pouring of wine would not have gone unnoticed in the semitic pre-comprehension of the onlookers. As the analysis Old and New Testament prophetic acts in the next two chapters shows, the eschatological favour of God is offered by Jesus to his commensals in his striking gestures at table. To celebrate eucharist is to re-present, in an anamnetic manner, Jesus' ritual anticipation of the saving events of Good Friday. To celebrate eucharist, therefore, is also to inaugurate, in a proleptic manner, that fulness of salvation at the messianic banquet which still lies in the future. In the ritual activity of the ecclesial community, the table fellowship simultaneously re-presents the unique meal in the Upper Room, and pre-presents the eschatological meal in the kingdom.

Central to this research project is the conviction that baptism is also a "representative anticipation" of the fulness of eschatological life. The prognostic dimension of this initiatory rite is guaranteed when it is set in the context both of the symbolic actions of the Hebrew prophets and of the eschatological signs of fulfilment which Jesus accomplished and, in turn, commanded his followers to perform until he comes again.

1.2 *Odo Casel: Mystery Presence*

While the Liturgical Movement[39] had a long and contested pre-history,[40] its beginnings are normally associated with the

---

[37] *KDE*, 248.

[38] *KDE*, 247.

[39] M. Augé, "Movimento liturgico - Riforma liturgica - Rinnovamento liturgico," *EO* 6 (1989) 302: "Per movimento liturgico intendiamo il fenomeno storico-culturale che affonda le sue radici nell'epoca dell'Illumenismo, ha le sue prime tangibili manifestazioni in campo liturgico nel rinnovamento del monachismo benedettino di Solesmes nel sec. XIX ad opera di don Guéranger, si espande poi per l'Europa centrale (Beuron, Maredsous), e diventa una forte corrente

Congrès International des œuvres catholiques held at Malines on 23 September 1909.[41] Dom Odo Casel,[42] a benedictine monk at the Abbey of Maria Laach, stands out as one of the most interesting and controversial figures of the entire movement[43] whose contribution to the more recent development of sacramental theology cannot be denied.[44] B. Neunheuser claims that "important aspects of Casel's theory became pretty much universally accepted,

---

ecclesiale di dottrina e di spiritualità, sopratutto all'inizio del nostro secolo."; J. A. Jungmann, "Liturgical Movement," *SM(E)* III (1969) 319-320; R. C. D. Jasper, "Liturgical Movement," *NDCTh* 335-336; R. W. Franklin, "Response: Humanism and Transcendence in the Nineteenth Century Liturgical Movement," *Worship* 59 (1985) 345 n. 2, claims that the term "liturgical movement" was first used in France and associated with the work of the Benedictine abbey of Solesmes in the 1840's and the 1850's. He makes reference to works by Dom Guéranger, Abbé Jouve and M.-D.-A. Sibour where the term can be found during this period. See also G. Oury, "Aux origines du mouvement liturgique," *EeV* 86 (1976) 120-126; 139-143; 157-160.

40 On the origins and the pre-history of the Liturgical Movement, see O. Rousseau, *Storia del movimento liturgico*; B. Neunheuser, "Les conceptions liturgiques fondamentales des premiers maîtres du mouvement liturgique" in A.M. Triacca – A. Pistoia, ed., *Liturgie, Spiritualité, Cultures*. Conferences Saint-Serge. XXIXe Semaine d'études liturgiques, 221-230; F. Brovelli, "Storia del movimento liturgico nel nostro secolo: dati, attese e linee di approfondimento," *EL* 99 (1985) 217-238; T.F. O'Meara, "The Origins of the Liturgical Moviment and German Romanticism," *Worship* 59 (1985) 326-342.

41 This is the opinion of B. Neunheuser, "Movimento Liturgico" in D. Sartore – A. M. Traccia, ed., *Nuovo Dizionario di Liturgia* (Roma: Paoline, 1984) 904-918. L. Bouyer, *Life and Liturgy*, 58, describes this conference which was organized by Dom Lambert Beauduin as "a decisive turning point for the Liturgical Movement."

42 Odo Casel was born in Koblenz on 27 September 1886. He entered the Abbey of Maria Laach and was professed on 24 February 1907. His initial studies were carried out in Rome and at Maria Laach. In 1913 he was awarded a doctorate in theology for a thesis on the doctrine of the eucharist in the writings of Justin Martyr. In 1919 he graduated from the university of Bonn with a doctorate in philosophy entitled *De philosophorum Graecorum silentio mystico*. During the following years he published widely on the liturgy and on its "mystery character." In 1922 Casel became chaplain to the benedictine nuns at Herstelle in Westphalia. He remained there until his sudden death on Easter Morning, 28 March 1948. See B. Neunheuser, "Odo Casel," *NCE* III (1967) 176-177. A list of Casel's works may be found in O. D. Santagada, "Dom Odo Casel: Contributo monografico," *ALW* 10/1 (1967) 7-77. See also A. A. Häussling, "Bibliografie Odo Casel O.S.B. 1967-1985," *ALW* 28 (1986) 26-42.

43 A. M. Triacca, "Odo Casel e il movimento liturgico," *EL* 101 (1987) 153-181. Triacca, 165, n. 43, records that Casel reviewed Vonier's *A Key to the Doctrine of the Eucharist* in *LiZs* 3 (1930-31) 340-347; 375-380. He also calls for further study on the "axial link (asse di raccordo)": Thomas - Vonier - Casel.

44 See D. Bridgehouse, "Dom Odo Casel: A Short Appreciation and a Translation from his Works," *DR* 75 (1957) 140-148.

even if they were to some extent modified or corrected in the process."[45]

In 1932, Casel published the first edition of *Das christliche Kultmysterium*[46] in which he outlines his understanding of the Christian life as the participation in the saving mystery of Jesus through the liturgical activity of the Church. Arraigning any attempt to present Christianity as a collection of doctrinal statements, Casel stresses that

> The Christian thing, in its full and primitive meaning of God's good Word, or Christ's, is not as it were a philosophy of life with religious background music, nor a moral or theological training; it is a *mysterium* as St Paul means the word, a revelation made by God to man through acts of god-manhood, full of life and power; it is mankind's way to God made possible by this revelation and the grace of it communicating the solemn entry of the redeemed Church into the presence of the everlasting Father, through perfect devotion; it is the glory that blossoms out of it.[47]

Here, the threefold sense of *mysterium* which lies at the heart of Casel's presentation is manifest. Mystery is not primarily a truth beyond human reason but is, as in the Pauline scheme, the hidden yet communicated reality of the saving design of God. This gradual

---

[45] B. Neunheuser, "Odo Casel in Retrospect and Prospect," *Worship* 50 (1976) 491. The author continues: "This last statement applies especially to Casel's idea of the 'presence' of Christ's saving acts in the sacred action of the liturgy, an idea that plays an important role in the Second Vatican Council's Constitution *Sacrosanctum Concilium* on the Liturgy. Relevant here is the important concept of the 'paschal mystery' as the epitome of Christ's saving acts and the content of the liturgical actions during the church year. Moreover, the designation of the sacrifice of the Mass as 'Eucharist'; the division of the Eucharist as a whole into two main parts ...; the insistence on the Mass as the action of the local Church with the active participation of the whole people of God; the restructuring of the liturgical year around the main festal cycles of Easter and Christmas-Epiphany; the new appreciation of Sunday as the weekly feast of the resurrection - all these already played a central role in Casel's vision. Even his attempt to throw light on the essential Christian content of mystery as a cultic type (*Kulteidos*) through analogies with the cultic celebrations of non-Christian religions is drawing new attention today (not lessened by disagreement on details), especially after the statement of Vatican II about the elements of truth to be found in the great world-religions." See B. Neunheuser, "The Mystery Presence: Dom Odo Casel and the Latest Research," *DR* 76 (1958) 266-273; J. G. Hart, "The Cult-Mystery Revisited," *DR* 91 (1973) 141-153; A. M. Triacca, "Odo Casel e il movimento liturgico," *EL* 101 (1987) 153-181.

[46] O. Casel, *Das christliche Kultmysterium*. References in this work are to the English translation of the fourth edition which was expanded and edited by B. Neunheuser in 1960: *The Mystery of Christian Worship*. [Hereafter *Mystery*.]

[47] *Mystery*, 12-13.

unveiling of the divine purpose finds its fulfilment in the mystery of the passion and death of the incarnate Son. According to Casel, being a Christian entails an actual sharing in these saving acts of Christ. For this purpose, the Lord has given the Church "the mysteries of worship" which bring the participants into immediate contact with God.

The most controversial aspect of the argumentation provided by Casel in this work is his insistence upon the analogy between the Christian mysteries and non-Christian rituals which were also introduced into the Roman Empire in the first century A.D.[48] Certainly, the nature of the historical relationship between these pagan mysteries and the emerging ritual activity of the first believing communities could not be ignored in the light of the comparative religious studies of the earlier part of this century. While some authors used the striking parallels as an excuse to dismiss the claim of Christianity to distinctiveness, others, like Casel, acknowledged that, while both forms of religious cult are independent, the analogy with the pagan rites provides an important insight into the origin and development of the liturgy of the early Church. According to Casel, all the mystery religions were formed on a similar pattern. L. Bouyer describes the correspondence as follows:

> Each of them was a "dromenon", that is, a kind of religious drama, a liturgical representation of the death and resurrection of a god. By being associated, in the actual performance of this representation, with the saving act of the deity, the initiates or "mystes" were to be saved. They were to be born again to a new and divine life, the life of the god himself triumphing over death.[49]

The mystery, therefore, is primarily a memorial, ἀνάμνησις or *commemoratio*. The ceremonial performance presents some actions of the gods which lie at the very core of the existence and belief of the religious community. The cult establishes union not merely among the members of the worshipping assembly who co-exist in the natural world, but also between the ritual assembly and the godhead which it honours as the guarantor of life after death.[50]

The substance of Casel's thought is captured in his well-known definition of the mystery:

---

[48] See T. Filthaut, *La théologie des mystères. Exposé de la controverse. Dossier complet de la controverse.*

[49] L. Bouyer, *Life and Liturgy,* 87.

[50] See, for example, *Mystery,* 32 and 54.

> The mystery is a sacred ritual action in which a saving deed is made present through the rite; the congregation, by performing the rite, takes part in the saving act, and thereby wins salvation.[51]

The ritual memorial of the divine action brings the participants into fellowship with God. This, according to Casel, is the profound meaning of the saying of St. Ambrose: "I find you in your mysteries: *te in tuis invenio sacramentis.*"[52] In the sacrament of baptism,[53] then, the Christian comes into immediate contact with the paschal mystery of Christ.[54] Quoting at length from the second mystagogical catechesis of Cyril of Jerusalem,[55] Casel concludes that the mystery which in time was completed in the death and resurrection of Jesus is now fulfilled in the believer "in representative, symbolic forms, not purely external ones, but rather images filled with the reality of the new life which is communicated through Christ."[56] As Christ was crucified, buried and raised up at the first Easter, the baptized not only receive "remission of sins and acceptance to sonship, but communion with the real sufferings of Christ by imitation of them."[57]

---

51 *Mystery,* 54.

52 *Apologia propetae David*, 58. See *Mystery,* 7, 65 and 104.

53 For a critique of Casel's view of the rite of baptism see R. Schnackenburg, *Baptism in the Thought of St. Paul*, 127-133. Schnackenburg, 123, concludes that "Casel's interpretation of 'symbol' represents an exaggeration of Paul's teaching. The Apostle establishes an inner connection between Christ's act of salvation and the salvation-event in baptism, but he does not regard it as apportioned in individual phases present in the 'symbol'. However noteworthy Casel's 'symbol' theory may be for later times, it is hardly authenticated for Paul. It can only stimulate a more careful investigation into the significance of the sacramental sign and rites." A. Warnach, a disciple of Casel, answers Schnackenburg's criticism in "Taufe und Christusgeschehen nach Römer 6," *ALW* 3 (1954,2) 284-366. Schnackenburg replies in "Todes- und Lebensgemeinschaft mit Christus. Neue Studien zu Röm 6:1-11," *MThZ* 6 (1955) 32-53.

54 See *Mystery,* 132: "In this liturgy the death of Christ is portrayed in image, as when a man is plunged under the water and thus killed 'in figure'. Here is the presentation of the first act of our salvation, and not merely in words but in gestures too."

55 See *Mystery,* 15-16. Note the following quotation (*Mystery*, 15) in particular: "O rare and paradoxical fact: we did not die as things of nature die; we were not buried in the fashion of them, nor risen after crucifixion in that way; rather it was a likening in image; but the salvation was a fact. Christ was really crucified, really buried, really rose; all this he has given us, so that we might win a real share in the likening of his sufferings."

56 *Mystery*, 16.

57 *Mystery*, 16. See also *Mystery*, 132: ."..the ceremonies of ritual ... are the translation of a myth into action... This is a most important thesis for us, and we should not forget it in the celebration of our Christian liturgy. In this liturgy the death of Christ is portrayed in image, as when a man is plunged under the water and

In the sacramental celebration the participants come into contact with the whole Christ: passion, death, resurrection and glory. These new covenant rites are the means by which the believers are conformed to the Christ who suffered and died, who lives in glory and who acts through the divine *Pneuma*. Baptism, Casel recognizes, is first of all a sharing in the death of the Lord. But, it is also a participation in eternal life: "By baptism, man is made a partaker in the new age, and so is given certainty that he will be taken up in the *parousia*, which is yet to come."[58] Casel insists, however, that this "union with Christ at the level of being"[59] which is established by the initiatory rite "is not finally secure in this age."[60] The Christian, then, is called to enact over and over again the death of Christ in the eucharist so as to strengthen the life of the risen Lord which dwells within. In the caselian scheme, baptism is an eschatological reality which is meaningful only for life on earth. Now it raises the believers "into the sphere of being which belongs to the Spirit"[61]; with the future entry of the Church into the life of heaven the lustral rite will pass away.

In many of the primitive religions which Casel examines the primary aim is to return to the primeval mythical reality which gives identity to the group. On the island of Ceram, for example,

> the ceremonies which accompanied, or better still carried forward and promoted the whole of life were in fact repetitions of the mythical events of the first age: thus the events of the present was brought into contact with the mythical first deed. This means that life is being returned to its proper place; it is being re-placed in the order of the world's course, set into the primeval act in which the gods themselves take part. What took place then is made presence in the rite for the worshippers; the rite returns to the first age and binds men to it.[62]

In other words, by means of a ceremonial repetition of the mythical events which give identity to the ethnic or tribal group, the participants pass, through death, to a share in original blessing. "What was done in the first age, in the *arche*, every generation must repeat; this is the aim of worship."[63] According to Casel, a

---

thus killed 'in figure'. Here is the presentation of the first act of our salvation, and not merely in words but in gesture too."

58 *Mystery*, 149.
59 *Mystery*, 147.
60 *Mystery*, 148.
61 *Mystery*, 149.
62 *Mystery*, 123.
63 *Mystery*, 161.

similar pattern is to be found in Christianity. "Worship is the means which brings back the Origin; in it the new Beginning is made present for the Christian."[64] Here a word of caution must be sounded. Christian worship is not primarily an attempt to return to some mythical Eden. It is not merely a memorial. Rather, in the ritual activity of the Christian community, memorial and anticipation coalesce in the present experience of the believers. In another context, Casel notes that the command of Jesus at the Last Supper to "do this in memory of me" is tantamount to saying "this act of sacrifice done once and for all time on the cross is here being anticipated in image, and you are to imitate it afterwards in image."[65] Notice how Casel presents the farewell meal as an anticipation of the salvation which would be won by means of the sacrifice of the cross. Imitating this ritual action, then, necessarily entails anticipation. In celebrating the eucharist, the Christian community not only recalls the sacrificial self-giving of the leave-taking Lord, but also anticipates the salvation which finds completion in his return in glory.[66]

When the ecclesial community celebrates a sacrament, it comes into contact with the entire saving work of Christ: "there is neither past nor future, only present. What is past in history, the death of Christ, for example, and what is in the future of history, his *parousia*, are present in the mystery."[67] Casel goes on to explain the modality of this mystery-presence:

> Christian worship is no longer bound to time but to eternity; it does not have to keep days and hours; it is always in the new age, the *aion*. When we worship we step out of time. ... We celebrate feasts in the Spirit which are connected with signs in nature; yet these are signs of things in heaven. In the Spirit we are in heaven; in the body we are in time still.[68]

When believers worship they encounter the full Christ because they enter the sphere of God. They "step out of time": they embrace "things which go beyond the 'historical' realm, and reach into the

[64] *Mystery*, 128.
[65] *Mystery*, 104.
[66] Indeed, Casel intimates as much in *Mystery*, 142: "Thus it is the feast which we shall one day celebrate in heaven; in the liturgy we anticipate this feast. Yet for all that we are not, as we celebrate the mystery, already in the moment of this heavenly reality."
[67] *Mystery*, 142.
[68] *Mystery*, 144.

immediate sphere of the Spirit of God."[69] They are no longer "bound to the mesh of time,"[70] but are secured to eternity. Behind this approach, however, lies a certain dualism. Worship becomes a *fuga mundi*; the created world is reduced to a platonic shadow of a spiritual reality. Liturgical activity raises humankind to the timeless sphere of the divine. The ongoing drama of history is relativized in its fulfilment.

In his positive evaluation of the pagan mystery religions, Casel overlooks the significance of the Jewish provenance of the ecclesial rites.[71] Indeed, on one occasion he remarks that:

> it is ... a historical truth that the Hellenes sometimes found it easier to grasp and to grasp more deeply the truth of the gospel than did the Jews with their purely Semitic, imageless, legal thinking. The Christianity of the ancient world appears to us as the fulfilment and glorification of what Greco-Roman antiquity was.[72]

Such a judgement on the "imageless, legal thinking" of the Jewish people is harsh. Fundamental to the religious consciousness of the Israelites is the belief that the saving events of history are re-experienced in the liturgy. By re-presenting in word and action these foundational episodes of their saving story, the chosen people discover that their past is re-experienced.[73] This encounter takes place neither in a primeval past nor in an utopian future, but in the reality of the present which emerges from an interplay of grace and sin and which propels history towards its eschatological *terminus*.

The notion of *anamnesis* or commemoration is central to the sacramental theory of Casel. Assessing the ongoing influence of his writings "in retrospect and in prospect," B. Neunheuser[74] notes that this notion has become commonplace in modern sacramental theology. In fact, he contends that this intuition, which was articulated by the monk from Maria Laach as early as 1918,

---

[69] Casel (*Mystery*, 109) uses this phrase in connection with the celebration of the eucharist.

[70] *Mystery*, 144.

[71] B. Neunheuser, "Odo Casel," 177, notes that, in the course of the controversy which ensued upon his earlier presentation of the mystery religions, "Casel perfected his conception of the liturgy, especially through the inclusion of scriptural teaching and a more positive evaluation of Old Testament worship."

[72] *Mystery*, 35.

[73] For example, D. Cox, *The Psalms in the Life of the People*, 6, notes that: "The recitation of a psalm was more than an act of remembrance. It inserted the reader into the reality of a divine act of liberation."

[74] B. Neunheuser, "Odo Casel in Retrospect and in Prospect," 496.

has become more significant in recent years in connection with the study of the Old Testament concept of memorial (*zikkārôn*) and of its literary form, the *berākā*.

In his comment on the eucharistic actions of Jesus as an anticipation in image of the sacrifice of the cross,[75] Casel inadvertently alludes to another Old Testament category, namely, prophetic act or *'ôt*. The central thesis of this research project is that the New Testament sacramental rites derive from the prophetic actions of Jesus Christ. By examining the concept of *'ôt* found in the Hebrew scriptures one can forge a link between remembrance and anticipation in ritual celebration. Further, in the light of this semitic category, baptism is not a timeless encounter with the Eternal One. Rather, through the ritual action of the Church, the eschatological favour of God bursts into the concrete historical experience of the believer.

1.3 *Jean Daniélou: Baptismal Typology*

Central to the "typological exegesis" of Jean Daniélou[76] is his concept of salvation history. The bible, he notes, is the account of the *mirabilia Dei* which express the unity of the creative and redemptive plan of God. This, in turn, guides his approach to biblical research:

> The aim of exegesis is to explain this language of [salvation] history, to establish the correspondences which link events and

---

[75] Quoted above. See n. 65.

[76] Jean Daniélou was born in Neuilly-sur-Seine (Paris) in 1905. At the age of 24, he entered the Jesuit novitiate at Laval (Mayenne). From 1931-34 he studied philosophy in Jersey. This was followed by two years of teaching in a Jesuit secondary school at Poitiers. Daniélou studied theology at Lyon-Fourvière from 1936-39. He was ordained a priest on 24 August 1938. With the outbreak of World War II, Daniélou was conscripted into the reserves and worked as a guard at airports and at other military installations. During this period he composed a short work which was later published as *Le Signe du Temple ou de la Présence de Dieu* (Paris, 1942). Having completed his tertian year, Daniélou undertook doctoral studies on Gregory of Nyssa at the Institut Catholique in 1941. In collaboration with H. De Lubac, in 1942, he founded *Sources Chrétiennes*, a series which translated the works of Greek and Latin Fathers. In 1943 he completed his thesis and was appointed a professor in the faculty. His thesis was presented at the Sorbonne the following year. In 1961 Daniélou was appointed Dean of the Faculty of Theology. He was a *peritus* at the Second Vatican Council. Having been ordained bishop on 19 April 1969, he was made cardinal by Pope Paul VI on 28 April 1969. He died unexpectedly on 20 May 1974. See P. Lebeau, *Jean Daniélou*. An extensive bibliography is to be found in D. Veliath, *Theological Approach and Evaluation of Religions*.

> institutions over the centuries. It seeks to explain the symbolism which links successive historical events.[77]

Within the Hebrew Bible, Daniélou recognizes that certain events in the history of Israel are employed as a "type" (τύπος) to interpret the present and the future. The prophets, for example, announced that in the future God would perform deeds analagous to, and even greater than, those of the past. Daniélou acknowledges that "these prophecies constitute a primary typology that might be called eschatological, for the prophets saw the future events as happening at the end of time."[78] The Christian scriptures develop this typological exegesis by presenting Old Testament figures and events as realized in the life of Jesus Christ and in the sacramental ministry of the ecclesial community.[79] This tendency is deployed even further in the Fathers of the Church who preserve and elaborate the ancient tradition.

In *Sacramentum Futuri*, Daniélou presents a number of types from the Hebrew scriptures which are prominent in the patristic exegesis of the second and third centuries. First of all, however, he sketches the pre-history that each type has in the Old and New Testaments and in the Jewish milieu of this period. The aim of such a study is to distinguish between those writings which faithfully reflect ecclesiastical tradition and are properly designated typological, and those which are influenced by external factors and are more correctly termed allegorical. Among the baptismal types which Daniélou mentions are creation, the flood, the crossing of the Red Sea, Elijah, the Jordan and the figure of Joshua.

In 1951, Daniélou published *Bible et Liturgie*[80] which examined the biblical character of the patristic presentation of the sacraments and the feasts of the liturgical year. Among the insights which Daniélou brings to bear in this work, three are particularly relevant to the present study. First of all, he recognizes that in the earlier part of the twentieth century, Catholic sacramental theology

---

[77] Jean Daniélou, "Traversée de la mer Rouge et Baptême aux premiers siècles," *RSR* 33 (1946) 429: "Le but de l'exégèse est d'expliquer ce langage de l'histoire, d'établir les correspondances qui relient les événements et les institutions à travers les siècles. C'est d'expliquer le symbolisme qui relie entre eux les événements historiques successifs."

[78] J. Daniélou, *The Bible and the Liturgy*, 5.

[79] J. Daniélou, *Sacramentum Futuri*, 11: "L'Ancien Testament nous donnait une typologie eschatologique; l'Évangile nous la montrait réalisée dans le Christ; saint Paul nous la montre se continuant dans le chrétien." [Hereafter *SF*.]

[80] J. Daniélou, *Bible et Liturgie*. The reference for the English translation, *The Bible and the Liturgy*, is given in n. 78 above. [Hereafter *BL*.]

had focused on the efficacious causality of the sacraments to the detriment of their nature as signs.[81] Secondly, Daniélou calls for a reappraisal of the origins of the Christian sacraments, not in Hellenistic culture, but in the liturgy of Judaism to which they are directly related.[82] Thirdly, Daniélou asserts that, in the first Christian centuries, the sacraments were considered the symbolic prolongations of the great works of God in the Old and New Testaments. These rites "inaugurated a new creation which introduced the Christian even now into the kingdom of God."[83] Together, these presuppositions uncover semitic characteristics of the lustral rite, and allow aspects of the eschatological dimension of the sacramental sign to emerge. The more important of these are listed below.

The enrolling of candidates for baptism and their remote preparation for the sacrament abound with allusions to the eschatological dimension of the rite. To inscribe for baptism is to write one's name in the register of the elect in heaven (Gregory of Nyssa).[84] To renounce Satan and his pomps is to break with Hades and to approach Paradise (Cyril of Jerusalem).[85] The profession of faith, the *redditio symboli*, was normally made facing the East (Cyril of Jerusalem; Methodius of Olympia; Ambrose). This, Daniélou notes, underscores its eschatological significance: the catechumen turns to face the Christ who returns from the East.[86]

The entrance into the baptistry marked the beginning of the immediate preparation for the rite of initiation. Again the eschatological portent is striking. The baptistry was decorated with trees and flowers which suggest the return to paradise from which Adam was driven out, and to which the baptized are restored (Cyril of Jerusalem).[87] The octagonal shape of the building was a reminder of the eighth day, a memorial of the resurrection and a prophecy of the world to come. "Into this eighth day, inaugurated by Christ, the Christian enters by baptism."[88] However, Daniélou

---

[81] *BL*, 3.
[82] *BL*, 6.
[83] *BL*, 17.
[84] *BL*, 22. Note: The full patristic references are not given here. Some names are inserted parenthetically in the text. For further details the reader is referred to the relevant pages in Daniélou's writings.
[85] *BL*, 30.
[86] *SF*, 17; *BL*, 31-33.
[87] *BL*, 36.
[88] *BL*, 37; Daniélou also mentions another tradition (Justin), based on the First Letter to Peter, which links the octagonal shape with the eight people in the Ark (Noah, his wife, his three sons and their wives). Noah's salvation through

insists, this life which is anticipated in baptism finds fulfilment only after death. Christian life is a return to paradise. It is not a flight from this world to some atemporal existence. Rather, it is the active realisation of the new world which will emerge at the end of time.[89]

The baptismal rite is essentially an immersion and an emersion, accompanied by the trinitarian invocation. Commenting on a text taken from the writings of Justin,[90] Daniélou claims that baptism is not merely a preparation for eschatological judgement. Rather,

> because of its symbolism of immersion, baptism appears as a sacramental anticipation by imitation of the final judgement which is a baptism of fire. Because of this [sacramental anticipation] Christians will escape the final judgement, since they are already judged. ... Thus, as well as being an efficacious memorial of the death and resurrection of Christ baptism, considered as baptism by Christ himself, is also an efficacious prophecy of death and eschatological resurrection.[91]

In other words, the water rite not only recalls the death and resurrection of Jesus but also proleptically anticipates, in the present experience of Christians, their future life. This notion of "efficacious prophecy" is close to the Hebrew concept of *'ôt*, or prophetic act, as will be shown in Chapter 3.

The post-baptismal clothing in the white garment also has an eschatological referent (Ambrose; Theodore of Mopsuetia; Gregory of Nyssa). Among the different aspects of the symbolism of this action, Daniélou lists "the prefiguring of future glory, anticipated in this present life."[92]

In his initial writings on baptismal typology, Daniélou is accused of focusing on the "entry into paradise" theme to the detriment of the "earlier idea that baptism was a crossing the Jordan and an entry into the promised land."[93] In subsequent

---

water and the wood is a figure of baptism (*BL*, 77-80). See also, J. Daniélou, "Le dimanche comme huitième jour" in *Le Dimanche*, ed. B.Botte.

[89] *SF*, 18-20.

[90] *Dialogue*, CXXXVIII, 2-3. Quoted in *SF*, 74-75.

[91] *SF*, 78: "Le baptême, par son symbolisme d'immersion, apparaît comme une anticipation sacramentaire, par une imitation, du jugement final qui est un baptême de feu, grâce à laquelle le chrétien échappera à ce jugement, puisqu'il est déjà jugé. ... Ainsi, mémorial efficace de la mort et de la résurrection du Christ, considérés comme baptême par le Christ lui-même, le baptême est aussi prophétie efficace de la mort et de la résurrection eschatologique."

[92] *BL*, 53.

[93] See J. Crehan, "Baptism and Confirmation: 1945-1955," 495. Crehan refers directly to two articles by Daniélou, "Le symbolisme des rites baptismaux,"

work, however, Daniélou does treat Elijah, Joshua and the Jordan as figures of baptism.[94] Interestingly, since Daniélou claims that the typology of the Jordan stems from a later tradition than that of the Red Sea, he cautions against presenting the two in parallel.[95] While, the crossing of the Jordan does represent a traditional catechetical theme, it comes to the fore as a baptismal type only with the writings of Origen.[96] The Alexandrian opposes the Red Sea and the Jordan: the former is a figure of the first covenant with Moses; the latter is a symbol of the second covenant with Joshua-Jesus.[97]

While the Exodus typology underlines the destruction of sin in the sacramental rite, the Jordan cycle accentuates the entry into the promised land through the purifying waters. "The Jordan", Daniélou quotes Gregory of Nyssa, "is exalted because it regenerates humanity and plants it in the Paradise of God."[98] Indeed, the Jordan typology also embraces another event which might well be termed eschatological. The *Second Book of Kings* (2: 1-18) records the ascension of Elijah after crossing the river. This, Daniélou records, inspires both Gregory Nanzianen and Gregory of Nyssa to refer to the Christian rite as "what carries us to heaven."[99]

"The tradition of the Church," Daniélou remarks, "which sees in the crossing of the Red Sea the figure of Baptism is too strong to be overcome by the idea of its being the figure of the Old Testament or of the catechumenate. The tradition of the Church has kept faithful to the symbolism of Origen by interpreting the theme of the crossing of the Jordan as the symbol of Baptism. This figure is not opposed to that of the crossing of the Red Sea, but coexists with it."[100] In the previous chapter, the predominance of the

---

DViv 1 (1945) 17-43, and "Traversée de la mer rouge et baptême aux premiers sieclès," *RSR* 33 (1946) 402-430.

94 See, for example, *BL*, 99-113.

95 According to Daniélou's analysis, the creative, yet destructive waters of Genesis and the Flood are the first type of baptism in the most ancient catechesis. This patristic interpretation, he notes, is "fundamentally biblical," with its foundation in the eschatological typology of the Old Testament and with its fulfilment in the Christ event in the New. Within the Hebrew scriptures, the crossing of the Red Sea is a symbol of the future victory of Yahweh over the powers of evil. In the Christian canon and in the writings of the Fathers this escape from slavery through water is seen as a type of the salvation which comes through the pool of ritual initiation.

96 *SF*, 233.

97 *BL*, 104.

98 *BL*, 103.

99 *BL*, 108.

100 *BL*, 105.

demonstrative over the eschatological dimension of the sacramental sign in post-Tridentine Catholic theology was noted. Such an emphasis betrays a preference for the typology of the Red Sea over that of the Jordan. Any attempt to retrieve the eschatological dimension of baptism, then, must give due consideration to the latter. This is implicit in the treatment of the lustral rite in the following chapters.

2. Baptismal Washing: Source, Emergence, Surge and Course

The central part of this thesis proposes the Hebrew scriptural concept of *'ôt*, or prophetic act, as a key category for appreciating the eschatological dimension of the sacrament of baptism. The writings of two biblical exegetes — Samuel Amsler and Heinz Schürmann — and two systematic theologians — Karl Rahner and Edward Schillebeeckx — are analyzed. Chapter 3 ("The Source of Baptism") proposes Amsler's presentation of Old Testament prophetic actions as the primary interpretative category for the lustral activity of John the Baptist. In Chapter 4 ("The Emergence of Baptism"), the insights of Heinz Schürmann on New Testament "eschatological signs of fulfilment" are used to investigate the baptism of Jesus, the eschatological prophet. Chapter 5 ("The Surge of Baptism") presents the baptismal theology of Rahner and shows how his understanding of this initiatory rite is enriched when the insights gleaned from the biblical *'ôt* are taken into account. Chapter 6 ("The Course of Baptism") claims that the notion of baptism as symbolic act of eschatological salvation emerges as a unifying concept between the earlier and later sacramental theory of Schillebeeckx. The four authors are now introduced in the concluding part to this first section.

2.1 *Samuel Amsler: Prophetic Acts*

From the very beginning of his academic career, Samuel Amsler is concerned with the place of the Old Testament in the life of the Church.[101] Two extremes are immediately rejected: the

[101] Born in Savigny, Switzerland, on July 18, 1925, Amsler chose the theme "La typologie de L'Ancien Testament chez Saint Paul" (extract published in *RThPh* n.s. 37 [1949] 113-128) for his licentiate thesis at the University of Lausanne in 1949. He completed his doctoral thesis (published as *L'Ancien Testament dans l'Eglise. Essai d'herméneutique chrétienne*) at the University of Neuchâtel under the guidance of Professor Robert Martin-Achard. A full bibliography is to be found in

Marcion-inspired Christian position which recognizes that, while relatively interesting as a preamble, the Hebrew Scriptures have virtually nothing to do with an authentic Christian understanding of the New Testament[102]; and the naive Christian view that attempts to suppress faith in Jesus Christ as Messiah and Lord, and to read the ancient texts solely from a Jewish perspective.[103] Amsler insists that both Synagogue and Church must read the Old Testament as it is, recognizing its central intention of witnessing to the unfolding covenant relationship which God has established with his people. Within these texts is found a concept of history which is open to the future and looks forward to its eschatological fulfilment.[104] While the Chosen People continues to hope for this consummation, the New Israel proclaims that, in Jesus Christ, the end has already been inaugurated. How then, Amsler asks, should the Old Testament be read in the Church? From 1949 to 1961, this question was to dominate his thought and to characterize the nature of his theological output.[105] Since he considered that neither an allegorical nor a symbolic reading accounted for the link between the literal meaning and historical events recorded in the texts, Amsler proposed a typological hermeneutic.[106] In recent years, however, he expressed certain reservations about the limitations inherent in this approach, and moved to what he terms a *situational analogy (l'analogie des situations)*.[107]

---

his collection of essays *Le dernier et l'avant-dernier. Etudes sur l'Ancien Testament.* He died in Lausanne in February, 1995.

[102] *L'Ancien Testament dans l'Eglise* 10: "Séparer Jésus de l'Ancien Testament, ou le placer dans un autre contexte historico-théologique que celui où il est venu, c'est rendre incomprehéensible le sens particulier de son œuvre et ouvrir la porte aux hérésies christologiques et théologiques. *Jésus est le Christ promis par l'Ancien Testament*, telle est la foi de l'Eglise primitive et la raison dernière de l'usage qu'elle fait de l'Ancien Testament." See also "L'Ancien Testament et la prédication de l'Evangile," 131-132 in *Pratique et Théologie*, ed. P. Gisel, 131-139.

[103] "Lecture juive et lecture chrétienne de L'Écriture sainte," *Jud* 17 (1961) 23-38.

[104] *L'Ancien Testament dans l'Eglise* 118: ."... l'histoire dont ils témoignent n'est pas close, achevée en elle-même. C'est au contraire une histoire ouverte sur l'avenir, tendue vers un temps où elle doit s'achever, en sorte que chaque événement de cette histoire est en relation plus ou moins directe avec son achèvement eschatologique."

[105] See "Où en est la typologie de l'Ancien Testament?," *ETR* 27 (1952) 75-81; "Typologie et prophétie," *RThPh* 3 (1953) 139-148; "Problèmes d'herméneutique de l'Ancien Testament," *ÉeT(O)* 24 (1961) 23-38.

[106] See *L'Ancien Testament dans l'Eglise,* 153-228.

[107] See "Le dernier et l'avant-dernier. Le rapport entre le Nouveau et l'Ancien Testament," *RSR* 63 (1975) 395; "L'Ancien Testament et la prédication de l'Évangile," 137-138.

In 1962 Amsler was appointed professor at the Faculty of Theology of the Free Evangelical Church of the Canton of Vaud, a post he held until 1966 when, following the merger of the two reformed Churches of Vaud, he was nominated professor at the Faculty of Theology at the University of Lausanne. There, together with Professor P. Bonnard, he founded the *Institut des Sciences Bibliques*. Besides various articles on *Deuteronomy*, *Wisdom* and general studies in biblical theology, the Old Testament prophets were to be Amsler's chief preoccupation in the subsequent years, as is indicated by his commentaries on *Amos*[108] and on *Haggai-Zechariah* 1-8.[109] In 1964, he described the prophet as a seer of what was hidden, an intercessor for the people before God, and, above all, as a messenger who transmits, in word and action, the divine communication of which he is a sign in the midst of the community.[110] Already, Amsler focuses, not only on the oracles of the prophet, but on the gestures which accompany their proclamation.[111]

In an article published in 1977, Amsler lists "prophetic act" as a typical means of expression that strikes the imagination and provokes a response. Such acts "so totally engage the person of the prophet... that they establish him as a striking warning of the direction in which Yahweh is leading the events of history."[112] With the publication of his essay "Les prophètes et la communication par les actes"[113] three years later, Amsler presents his initial investigation of the literary genre and communicative functions of the prophetic act. His subsequent work *Les actes des prophètes*[114] represents a considerable development of the ideas

[108] "Amos" in E. Jacob – C. Keller – S. Amsler, *Osée*, *Joël*, *Amos*, *Abdias*, *Jonas*.

[109] "Aggée - Zacharie 1-8" in S. Amsler – A. Lacocque – R. Vuilleumier, *Aggée*, *Zacharie*, *Malachie*.

[110] "Les ministères de l'ancienne alliance: rois, prêtres et prophètes," *VC* No 71/72 (1964) 29-41.

[111] "Les prophètes et la politique," *RThPh* 23 (1973) 31: "Ils [les prophètes] ne parlent pas de ce règne d'une manière générale et abstraite,... ils le font de la parole, mais aussi du geste de l'action prophétique."

[112] "La fonction prophétique de l'Eglise et dans l'Eglise. Remarques à partir de l'Ancien Testament" in J. Panagopoulos, ed., *Prophetic Vocation in the New Testament and Today*, 45: "Non seulement ils frappent l'imagination et donnent à penser; ils engagent totalement la personne du prophète dans son message et font de lui un signe dressé, que plus personne peut ignorer, et à qui YHWH lui-même donne sa caution en conduisant les événements dans le sens indiqué par ce signe."

[113] "Les prophètes et la communication par les actes" in R. Albertz, ed., *Werden und Wirken des Alten Testaments*. [Hereafter "La communication."]

[114] *Les actes des prophètes*. [Hereafter *Les actes*.]

already present in the seminal article. The *exposé* of Amsler's treatment of prophetic act in Chapter 3 concentrates primarily on these two writings.

2.2 *Heinz Schürmann: Eschatological Signs of Fulfilment*

Many works exist on the prophetic identity of Jesus and on his relationship with his Old Testament counterparts. Few, however, provide a detailed reflection on the relationship between the symbolic acts of Jesus and the dramatic actions of the Hebrew prophets. In 1930, C.H. Dodd[115] presented an impressive list of those aspects of the ministry of Jesus "which caused men to rank him with the prophets."[116] Among the "external" or "more obvious" traits, Dodd includes "symbolic actions." These events, not only proclaimed the divine word but, also played a part in the actual fulfilment of God's design.[117] The table actions at the Last Supper, the cursing of the fig tree and the feeding of the multitude are listed as examples of symbolic actions.

In the immediate post-war years, A.J.B. Higgins[118] briefly alluded to symbolism as one of three distinctive features of the Hebrew prophets which impressed Jesus' contemporaries with his prophetic identity. The choice of the twelve disciples to sit upon thrones judging the twelve tribes of Israel, the entry into Jerusalem, the table actions at the Last Supper and, perhaps, the feet-washing which preceded it are enumerated as examples of symbolic actions. Writing in the same journal, H. McKeating[119] lists "enacted prophecy" among four characteristics common to Jesus and the Old Testament prophets. The "blasting" of the fig tree, the cleansing of the Temple and the anointing of Jesus by the woman who was a sinner all qualify for inclusion in this category. McKeating's classification also incorporates the miracles of Jesus. While these have "no predictive content," they may be considered as "attestations of a verbal prophecy, assertions of power, or demonstrations of truth."[120] In Jesus, word and action become one as prediction and anticipation creatively coalesce. It is in this context that McKeating presents the sacraments of baptism and

---

[115] C.H. Dodd, "Jesus as Teacher and Prophet" in *Mysterium Christi*, ed. G.K.A. Bell - A. Deismann, 53-66.

[116] C.H. Dodd, "Jesus as Teacher and Prophet," 57.

[117] C.H. Dodd, "Jesus as Teacher and Prophet," 65.

[118] A.J.B. Higgins, "Jesus as Prophet," *ExT* 57 (1945-46) 292-294.

[119] H. McKeating, "The Prophet Jesus," *ExT* 73 (1961-62) 4-7; 50-53.

[120] H. McKeating, "The Prophet Jesus," 53.

eucharist as enacted prophecies which the Lord "has ordained should be with us still."[121] This link between the prophetic actions of Jesus and the sacraments of the Church is mentioned by R. Otto,[122] J. Dupont,[123] N.A. Beck,[124] S. Amsler,[125] E. Schillebeeckx,[126] J.L. Espinel,[127] and P. Rosato,[128] to name a few.

The German exegete Heinz Schürmann[129] represents one of the first attempts by a Catholic scholar to systematically identify prophetic acts in the gospel narratives and to differentiate them from those found in the Hebrew Scriptures. In 1970, he published "The Symbolic Actions of Jesus as Signs of Eschatological Fulfilment,"[130] a two-part article in which he identified prophetic acts in the gospel accounts. In 1975, Schürmann published *Jesu ureigener Tod,*[131] a collection of essays which investigates Jesus' own attitude to his death. Contrary to the claim of R. Bultmann, Schürmann argues that Jesus approached the Cross in the spirit of "pro-existence" which characterised his saving mission. This definitive *being-for-others* is manifested in the prophetic actions with the bread and wine at the Last Supper. Chapter 4 examines the

---

[121] H. McKeating, "The Prophet Jesus," 53.

[122] R. Otto, *The Kingdom of God and the Son of Man*, 299-30.

[123] J. Dupont, "'Ceci est mon corps', 'Ceci est mon sang'," *NRTh* 80 (1958) 1025-1041.

[124] N.A. Beck, "The Last Supper as an Efficacious Symbolic Act," *JBL*, 89 (1970) 192-198.

[125] S. Amsler, *Les actes*, 89.

[126] E. Schillebeeckx, *Jesus: An Experiment in Christology*, 136-139.

[127] J.L. Espinel, *La cena del Señor, acción profética.*

[128] P. Rosato, "The Prophetic Acts of Jesus, the Sacraments and the Kingdom," in *Gottes Zukunft - Zukunft der Welt*, ed. H. Deuser, 59-67.

[129] Born in Bochum in 1913, Schürmann studied philosophy and theology in Paderborn and Tübingen. He was ordained in 1938, and gained his doctorate in theology at Münster in 1950. In 1953, following a year at the Biblical Institute in Rome and a brief period in Münster, he was appointed to teach New Testament exegesis at the recently established seminary in Erfurt, a post which he held until becoming emeritus professor in 1978. He was present as a peritus at the Second Vatican Council and served on the International Theological Commission from 1969 to 1984. The festschrift in honour of his sixty-fifth birthday (R. Schnackenburg - J. Ernst - J. Wanke, ed., *Die Kirche des Anfangs*) lists a bibliography of 132 books and articles. This has been revised and updated to 1985 by Theresia Ehrhardt.

[130] H. Schürmann, "Die Symbolhandlungen Jesu als eschatologische Erfüllungszeichen. Eine Rückfrage nach dem historischen Jesus," *BiLe* 11 (1970) 29-41; 73-78. [Hereafter referred to as "DSJ."] An updated version of this article is published in a new edition of Schürmann's articles and essays, K. Scholtissek, ed., *Jesus - Gestalt und Geheimnis: gesammelte Beiträge*, 136-156.

[131] H. Schürmann, *Jesu ureigener Tod. Exegetische Besinnungen und Ausblick.* [Hereafter *JuT.*]

presentation of the New Testament symbolic actions, or "eschatological signs of fulfilment", in the writings of Schürmann.

2.3 *Karl Rahner: Categorising the Experiential*

Although Karl Rahner has written on sacramental theology in general and on penance and orders in particular, baptism is indeed presented but not fully developed in his writings.[132] Initially, then, the choice of Rahner as a theologian whose thought can contribute to furthering this present study is curious.[133] There is yet another, even more substantial, reason for this incipient judgement. While Chapters 3 and 4 of this study analyse the lustral rite of John the Baptist and the eschatological sign of fulfilment of Jesus in the Jordan as the foundation of Christian baptism, Rahner advises against such attempts to locate any of the seven sacramental actions of the New Israel in a specific word or action of the Saviour. Instead, he favours an ecclesiological starting point whereby the liturgical rites of Christianity are viewed as implicitly instituted in the explicit foundation of the new covenant community by Jesus.

Yet, Rahner's influence on twentieth-century sacramental theology is undeniable and tributes to his achievement abound[134]: "the most brilliant theologian since Thomas Aquinas,"[135] "the Holy Ghost writer of Vatican II."[136] In a recent overview of literature in Roman Catholic sacramental theology since 1980, Rahner is acknowledged as still exerting such a "strong influence" on this field that differing contemporary approaches are

---

[132] Biographical accounts of Karl Rahner (1904-1984) also abound. See the two books by H. Vorgrimler, *Understanding Karl Rahner: An Introduction to His Life and Thought* and *Karl Rahner: His Life, Thought and Works*.

[133] One bibliography of Rahner's works updated by P. Imhof - E. Meuser, in E. Klinger - K. Wittstadt, ed., *Glaube im Prozeß. Christsein nach dem II. Vatikanum*, 854-871, lists 3998 titles. See also the analytic bibliography of Rahner's work in English: C.J. Pedley, ed., "An English Bibliographical Aid to Karl Rahner," *HeyJ* 25 (1984) 319-365; 26 (1985) 310. This lists 38 primary texts on sacraments: 15 items refer directly to penance; there is no specific entry listed under baptism or under the sacrament of the sick.

[134] See, for example, T. Hovarth, "After Rahner What? A Tribute to His Memory and Achievement," *Thom* 49 (1985) 157-167; W.V. Dych, "The Achievement of Karl Rahner," *ThDig* 31 (1984) 325-333.

[135] T. Sheehan, *New York Review* (Feb 4, 1982) 13.

[136] K. Rahner, *I Remember: An Autobiographical Interview with Meinhold Krauss*, 82. See H. Vorgrimler, "Karl Rahner: The Theologian's Contribution" in *Vatican II By Those Who Were There*, ed. A. Stackpoole, 32-46.

characterised as either rahnerian or non-rahnerian formulations.[137] Thus, it seems justifiable to treat the eschatological dimension according to his perspective, and to compare and contrast it to the exegetical insights which are examined in the second section of this study.

At the core of Rahner's theology lies the "conviction of faith"[138] that the God who wills the salvation of humanity[139] must offer his life to everyone. Human life, as Rahner explicates it, with the help of categories drawn from existential phenomenology and from transcendental thomist philosophy,[140] is marked by a "supernatural existential"[141]: "existential" because life is necessarily experienced as freedom to be exercised in history; "supernatural" because, despite the autonomy of existence, human freedom is God's unmerited gift to all.[142] Consequently, "as the horizon of every person's entire existence, God's self-communication as grace and revelation is present at least unthematically in all human knowledge and freedom, and is accepted or rejected in all human choices."[143]

Because grace, as the active orientation of all created reality towards God, is everywhere,[144] a "Copernican revolution"[145] in the

---

[137] R.A. Duffy, "The Post-Rahnerian Formulation" in "Sacramental Theology: A Review of Literature," *TS* 55 (1994) 665-675.

[138] K. Rahner, "The Hiddenness of God," *TI* 16, 235. See W.V. Dych, *Karl Rahner*, 39.

[139] See J. Kerketta, *Jesus Christ, the Universal Saviour*.

[140] See G.A. McCool, "Philosophical Pluralism and an Evolving Thomism," *Cont* 2 (1964) 3-16; K. Baker, "Rahner: The Transcendental Method," *Cont* 2 (1964) 51-59.

[141] K. Rahner, "Concerning the Relationship between Nature and Grace," *TI* 1, 298.

[142] K. Rahner, "Concerning the Relationship between Nature and Grace," 311-313.

[143] W.V. Dych, *Karl Rahner,* 45. Note that Rahner's doctrine of the Trinity emerges from his concept of the two modes of the self-communication of God in the *logos* and in the *pneuma*. The Trinity is the condition for the possibility of human subjectivity. See K. Rahner, *The Trinity*, 120; W. Kasper, *The God of Jesus Christ*, 300-303.

[144] K. Rahner, *Meditations on the Sacraments*, xiii: "Whenever the human being as a totality experiences himself in freedom and choice, whenever in hope he takes on an obligation which really demands more than he can give and which cannot be justified from a worldly point of view, whenever he hopes against all hope, whenever he dares to love in a way that is too costly, whenever he believes in the light although everything is dark and in meaning although everything seems to be losing its meaning, wherever he surrenders and believes this surrender to be his final victory, he experiences the radicalized transcendentality of man into the incomprehensible mystery of God. He experiences grace, even though perhaps it cannot be reflected upon and verbalized and thus made into an object of thematic conceptuality. Grace is everywhere, and it is experienced, though usually not under

understanding of the Christian sacraments is demanded. Traditional theology views these sacred rites as isolated events through which human beings leave the realm of time and space in order to enter into a "sacral sphere, a *fanum* or a temple"[146] where sanctifying grace is conferred and grasped as a reality beyond human experience and consciousness. Rahner calls for a new perspective within which the Christian rites are perceived as manifestations of that holiness which penetrates every level of secular existence.[147] But what is the relationship between these two modalities of the divine self-communication, between universal and sacramental grace? Does baptism confer a not yet experienced "increase" of divine grace, or, more accurately, does it furnish a heightened outer expression of an already extant inner reality? These issues are dealt with in Chapter 5.

2.4 *Edward Schillebeeckx: Anticipating the Future*

Edward Schillebeeckx has been described as the "most influential and controversial of modern theologians."[148] From his first publication[149] to his most recent writings,[150] he is concerned to present the intelligibility of Christian faith in a world in which belief in the transcendent God revealed by Jesus Christ is either rejected as unscientific nonsense or is dismissed as unreasonable self-abasement. While Schillebeeckx has dialogued with a pluriformity of philosophical and cultural models, one question is axial within his many writings. Put simply, Schillebeeckx is preoccupied with the age-old dilemma of how one can speak meaningfully of the universal or the absolute in terms of the

---

that name." See also K. Rahner, "Reflections on the Experience of Grace," *TI* 3, 86-90.

[145] See K. Rahner, "Considerations on the Active Role of the Person in the Sacramental Event," *TI* 14, 161-184; "A Copernican Revolution: Secular Life and the Sacraments I," *Tablet* 225 (March 6, 1971) 236-238.

[146] K. Rahner, "Considerations on the Active Role of the Person in the Sacramental Event," 162.

[147] K. Rahner, "The Mass and the World: Secular Life and the Sacraments II," *Tablet* 226 (March 13, 1971) 267-268.

[148] B. Davies, "Editorial Foreword" in P. Kennedy, *Schillebeeckx*, viii.

[149] E. Schillebeeckx, "Schepsel-besef als grondslag van ons geestelijk leven," *TGL* 1 (1945) 15-43. [Note: Many of Schillebeeckx's early publications appear under his religious name Henricus. In this study all publications are listed under his baptismal name Edward.]

[150] A bibliography of Schillebeeckx's works until 1983 is to be found in R.J. Schreiter, ed., *The Schillebeeckx Reader*, 297-321.

particular or the limited.[151] At the nucleus of his thought lies a philosophico-theological constant, namely, that the world is created by God.[152] Furthermore, this ontological presupposition leads to an epistemological principle that human beings may come to know or experience this Creator God as a result of the divine manifestation in the world.[153] However, the choice of the particular human experiences which disclose the transcendent has varied in Schillebeeckx's writings over the years. In his early works the human search for God found its fullest expression in the sacraments of the Church. In later years, Schillebeeckx speaks of praxis as the anticipation of the reality of God.

Schillebeeckx's formative years have been well documented both in autobiographical interviews[154] and in other studies.[155] From his childhood in a Flemish Catholic family and his early education in a Jesuit boarding school in Turnhout, the events in the personal history of Schillebeeckx have determined the development of his theology to a significant degree. In 1934 he entered the Order of Preachers, and he has continued to live in a Dominican community ever since. At Ghent he began the course of spiritual, philosophical and theological training which was prescribed for candidates for the Catholic priesthood at that time. The young scholastic's philosophical studies were supervised by D. De Petter[156] who was

---

[151] P. Kennedy, *Deus Humanissimus: The Knowability of God in the Theology of Edward Schillebeeckx*, 14, notes that Schillebeeckx "once defined theology as a matter of describing how the absolute appears within the relative. His entire body of theological writings has been devoted to explaining what it *means* to say that the absolute ('God') can appear to be known through the contingent facticity of human history."

[152] In E. Schillebeeckx, *I am a Happy Theologian*, 47, Schillebeeckx declares that "I regard the creation as the foundation of all theology."

[153] *ST* I, Q. 1, a. 7, ad. 1.

[154] See, for example, H. Oosterhuis – P. Hoogeveen, ed., *God is New in Each Moment*; E. Schillebeeckx, *I am a Happy Theologian*.

[155] See J. Bowden, *Edward Schillebeeckx: Portrait of a Theologian*; R. J. Schreiter, "Edward Schillebeeckx: An Orientation to his Thought" in *The Schillebeeckx Reader*, 1-24; P. Kennedy, *Deus Humanissimus*, 29-78.

[156] John [Dominic Mary] De Petter was born in Louvain in 1905. In 1923 he joined the Order of Preachers in Ghent. He received a doctoral degree in philosophy (1926) from the *Institut Supérieur de Philosophie* in Louvain on the French philosopher Louis Lavelle (1883-1951) and the Dominican degree Lector in Theology (1930) for his study on "The Epistemological Dynamism of J. Maréchal." In Ghent he was appointed professor of philosophy (1931) and *Magister fratrum studentium* (1934). In 1939 he became *proregens studiorum* in Louvain. Because of opposition to his thought, he was dismissed from his administrative functions in the Dominican house of studies in 1942. His publications include *Begrip en werkelijkheid*; *Naar het Metafysische*. He died in 1971.

to exert a considerable sway over his early thought.[157] This influence was significant for a number of reasons. First of all, De Petter encouraged his pupils to read philosophical works that had been placed on the *Index of Forbidden Books*. Secondly, when Schillebeeckx found little to enthuse him in his early studies of dogmatic theology at Louvain, De Petter, then professor at the Dominican theologate, generated his interested in the sacred science by introducing him to the work of Karl Adam.[158]

Although Schillebeeckx spent just one year in France (1946-47), its significance in his overall academic development cannot be overestimated. At *Le Saulchoir d'Etiolles* he was instructed in the science of *ressourcement*, the study of historical texts in the light of the context which produced them.[159] At the *Ecole des Hautes Etudes* Schillebeeckx came in contact with M.-D. Chenu[160] who, as a driving force behind the French worker-priests movement at that time, attempted to fuse his theological research with socio-political engagement.

In 1947 Schillebeeckx returned to Louvain where he was appointed Professor of Dogmatic Theology in the Dominican *studium generale*. His proposed doctoral thesis on the relationship between the natural and supernatural, which he had planned to write under the direction of Chenu, was abandoned. Instead, because he was required to teach in that area, Schillebeeckx turned to a

---

157 E. Schillebeeckx, *I am a Happy Theologian*, 7: "I began the study of philosophy under the guidance of De Petter. Rooted in tradition, his teaching was extremely open to the modern world. At Louvain he had studied phenomenology. He attempted a synthesis between Thomism and the phenomenology of Husserl. He was above all an anthropologist and was able to construct a synthesis between ancient and modern achievements. I was truly taken with his lessons."

158 E. Schillebeeckx, *God is New in Each Moment*, 12: "When I read Karl Adam's books, however, I began to realize that it was certainly possible to form a solid link between philosophy and theology, with its references to the religious question. As soon as I had discovered that possibility, I began to study theology in a really personal way."

159 E. Schillebeeckx, *I am a Happy Theologian*, 8: "At *Le Saulchoir* I learned to tackle problems from a historical perspective. In my courses, in succession, I went through the Old and New Testaments, the teaching of the Fathers, of St Thomas and the post-Tridentine era. I was convinced that faith and reflection on the faith should be in close connection with the tradition."

160 E. Schillebeeckx, *I am a Happy Theologian*, 8: "I met the greats there [in Paris]: Chenu, Congar... Chenu above all had a great influence. He was a professor at *École des Hautes Études* at that time because in February 1942 he had been dismissed from his teaching post on the orders of the Holy Office... Under the guidance of Chenu I read St. Thomas from a historical perspective and not just literally, in the context of the philosophy of the time." See also, E. Schillebeeckx, "In Memory of Marie Dominique (Marcel) Chenu O.P. (7 January 1895 - 11 February 1990)" in *I am a Happy Theologian*, 89-92.

sacramental theme. In 1951, he was awarded the degree of Doctor in Theology at *Le Saulchoir*. A year later, he published the first part of his dissertation as *De Sacramentele Heilseconomie*.[161] While the second half was never published, he did manage to produce a simplified summary of the entire project.[162] This was later revised and published as *Christus sacrament van de Godsontmoeting*.[163] A modified English translation of this edition appeared in 1963 as *Christ the Sacrament of the Encounter with God*.[164] This work brought Schillebeeckx to the attention of the wider theological world.

In 1957, at the age of forty-three, Schillebeeckx was promoted to the chair of Dogma and the History of Theology at the Catholic University of Nijmegen in the Netherlands, a post he held until his retirement in 1982. His primary responsibility was to lecture post-graduate students in theology. His publications during his early years in Nijmegen include a volume on marriage,[165] and a series of "Theological Soundings" reproduced in five books.[166] Two works, *Vatican II: A Struggle of Minds*[167] and *Vatican II: The Real Achievement*,[168] provide an insight into Schillebeeckx's assessment of the theological debate which took place before, during and after the Second Vatican Council.[169]

1966 is considered to be a turning point in Schillebeeckx's life. In this year which saw the publication of the controversial Dutch *A New Catechism*,[170] Schillebeeckx made his first visit, a lecture tour, to the United States. At Nijmegen, he taught his first course in hermeneutics, and he entered into a discussion on christological method with his colleagues A. Hulsbosch and P.

---

[161] E. Schillebeeckx, *De Sacramentele Heilseconomie: Theologische bezinning op S. Thomas' sacramentenleer*. A review of this work may be found in J. Gaillard, "Chronique de Liturgie," *RThom* 47 (1957) 510-551.

[162] E. Schillebeeckx, *De Christusontmoeting als sacrament van de Godsontmoeting*.

[163] E. Schillebeeckx, *Christus sacrament van de Godsontmoeting*.

[164] Hereafter *CSEG*.

[165] E. Schillebeeckx, *Marriage: Human Reality and Saving Mystery*.

[166] The corresponding English translations of these works are: *Revelation and Theology*; *God and Man*; *World and Church*; *The Mission of the Church*; *The Understanding of Faith*.

[167] E. Schillebeeckx, *Vatican II: A Struggle of Minds*.

[168] E. Schillebeeckx, *Vatican II: The Real Achievement*.

[169] Schillebeeckx remained in Rome during all of the sessions of the Council as theological adviser to Cardinal Alfrink.

[170] The English translation was published as *A New Catechism. Catholic Faith for Adults*.

Schoonenberg.[171] This was to be a period of upheaval and crisis for Schillebeeckx as he searched for a solution to the problems which he knew were facing modern believers. To this end, his attention turned to a variety of intellectual disciplines which served as new dialogue partners.[172] His studies in hermeneutics, biblical exegesis, Critical Theory and eschatology are particularly relevant to the argument of this research project. The fruit of much of Schillebeeckx's research in this period was to appear in 1974 in his book *Jesus, het verhaal van een levende.*[173] This was to be the first of three volumes in his christological trilogy. In this work, Schillebeeckx presents the earthly Jesus as "the eschatological prophet," and refers to his baptism by John as "Jesus' first prophetic act."[174] The second tome appeared in 1977 with the title *Gerechtigheid en Liefde: Genade en Bevrijding.*[175] The overall project was only completed in 1989 with the publication of *Mensen als verhaal van God.*[176]

The later Schillebeeckx does not undertake any explicit study either of sacraments in general or of baptism. A glance at *Church: The Human Story of God*, for example, suggests that both themes are minor concerns in the thought of the author at this stage. This is not to suggest, however, that the recent writings of Schillebeeckx have nothing to contribute to the present research project. In fact, the claim of Chapter 6 is that the notion of baptism as symbolic act of eschatological salvation emerges as a unifying concept between the two phases of his work. Furthermore, it is argued that baptism,

---

[171] This exchange is presented in a full issue of the review *Tijdschrift voor theologie*: A. Hulsbosch - E. Schillebeeckx - P. Schoonenberg, "God's heilspresentie in de mens Jezus Christus," *TTh* 6 (1966).

[172] P. Kennedy, *Schillebeeckx*, 37, catalogues eighteen sources which he considers to be significant for understanding the change in Schillebeeckx's theology after 1966. These are listed in Chapter 6.

[173] E. Schillebeeckx, *Jesus, het verhaal van een levende*. While a direct translation of the Dutch title would be rendered as "Jesus, the Story of the Living One" the English edition appeared as *Jesus: An Experiment in Christology*. [Hereafter *Jesus.*]

[174] *Jesus*, 136-139.

[175] E. Schillebeeckx, *Gerechtigheid en Liefde: Genade en Bevrijding*. The title translates directly as "Justice and Love: Grace and Liberation." In English translation, this work has appeared as: *Christ: The Christian Experience in the Modern World*; *Christ: The Experience of Jesus as Lord* [Hereafter *Christ.*]

[176] E. Schillebeeckx, *Mensen als verhaal van God*. [Reprinted with corrections in 1990.] While the original title translates as "Human Beings as God's Story," the English translation appeared as *Church: The Human Story of God*. [Hereafter *Church.*]

presented in this light, provides a much-needed sacramental axis in his recent praxis-oriented theology.

PART II

THE WATER OF BAPTISM

CHAPTER 3

The Source of Baptism

Old Testament prophetic acts as proleptic anticipations of the future in the writings of Samuel Amsler

The Christian rite of initiation derives from the lustral washing of John the Baptist[1] in the River Jordan (Matt 3:1-12; Mark 1:1-8; Luke 3:1-17). The New Testament writers readily deem John a prophet (Matt 11:9; Mark 11:32; Luke 1:76): his call (Luke 3:2),[2] his food, his dress (Matt 3:4),[3] and his message firmly establish him in line with the great prophetic figures of Israel's past. John is presented as the eschatological prophet; in fulfilment of Isa 40:3 and Mal 3:1, it is he who heralds the coming of the Messiah. Clearly, then, a study of the acts of the Old Testament prophets in general and of the baptismal activity of John in particular provide an appropriate starting point for any attempt to retrieve the eschatological dimension of this sacrament.

The purpose of this chapter is twofold. First of all it investigates the notion of *prophetic act* as presented in the writings of Samuel Amsler, the Old Testament exegete and biblical theologian. His presentation of this semitic category is analysed under three headings: the act itself, the reaction it provoked, and the ultimate end of the act. The baptism of John *as prophetic act* is then examined, applying the results of each section to this initial action.[4] The division which arguably evokes the traditional presentation of sacrament as *sacramentum tantum* (the prophetic act alone), *sacramentum et res* (the act and the reaction to it), and

---

[1] The bibliography on John the Baptist is vast. As well as the works cited in this chapter, see the bibliography given in J.P. Meier, *A Marginal Jew: Rethinking the Historical Jesus*. Vol. 2: *Mentor, Message, and Miracles*. [AncBRL], 63-64.

[2] Luke 3:2 recalls the call of Jeremiah (Jer 1:1-4).

[3] See, also, 2 Kgs 1:8; Zech 13:4.

[4] The baptism of Jesus by John the Baptist is treated in Chapter 4.

res tantum (the final end of the act) already prepares the reader for the closing part of this study which investigates the enhanced eschatological perspectives on baptism which are opened up by contemporary exegesis.

Amsler begins *Les actes des prophètes* by drawing attention to the curious inversion in the names attributed to biblical books. While the sermons and discourses of the first Christian communities are preserved in a document which is traditionally called the "Acts of the Apostles," the accounts of the activity of the Old Testament prophets bear such names as "Words of Amos," "Words of Jeremiah," "The Word of the Lord through Hosea" or "The Word of the Lord that came through Micah." Immediately the impression is given that the prophets were men of words and not of actions. However, Amsler claims that a more faithful translation of the Hebrew title *debārîm*, which refers not only to the specific words but to the whole event of communication, suggests that the prophetic books be called the "Acts of the Prophets."[5]

Within the prophetic books certain actions, recorded by the prophet himself or by one of his disciples, merit special attention. These were studied and identified as "prophetic symbols" by H.W. Robinson[6] and as "symbolic acts" by G. Fohrer.[7] Although Amsler used this second term in an earlier period,[8] he later found it inadequate, because the specific nature of prophetic actions surpasses the conventional understanding of symbol.[9] While the term "significant act"[10] is viewed by him to be something of an improvement, the description "acts of power"[11] has magical

[5] *Les actes*, 7.

[6] H. W. Robinson, "Prophetic Symbolism" in *Old Testament Essays*, 1-17.

[7] G. Fohrer's term is *symbolischen Handlungen*. See *Die symbolischen Handlungen der Propheten*; "Die Gattung der Berichte über die symbolischen Handlungen der Propheten," *ZAW* 64 (1952) 101-120.

[8] "Amos, prophète de la onzième heure," *ThZ* 21 (1965) 318-328.

[9] *Les actes*, 16-17: "S'il est vrai que l'acte prophétique exploite une 'correspondance analogique' qui est fondamentale dans le symbole, il fait plus qu''évoquer par sa forme ou sa nature une association d'idées 'naturelle' (dans un groupe social donné) avec quelque chose d'abstrait ou d'absent', car il est inédit, surprenant, non-conventionnel, et surtout il entend signifier l'action de Dieu lui-même, telle qu'elle va effectivement se manifester sur la scène de l'histoire."

[10] Both C. Uehlinger, "'Zeichne eine Stadt ... und belagere sie!' Bild und Wort in einer Zeichenhandlung Ezechiels gegen Jerusalem (Ez 4f)" in M. Kücher - C. Uehlinger, ed., *Jerusalem. Texte - Bilder - Steine...* , 111-200, and W. Zimmerli, *Ezekiel*, speak of "Zeichenhandlungen."

[11] See T. W. Overholt, "Seeing is Believing. The Social Setting of Prophetic Acts of Power," *JSOT* 23 (1982) 3-31.

overtones and is consequently open to misunderstanding. Amsler prefers to use the term "prophetic act"[12] for the thirty one "speaking-acts" or "words-in-acts" which he identifies in the *corpus propheticum.*[13] Four of these appear in the historical books; twenty-seven are recorded in the later prophets.[14]

1. The Act

There is no single Hebrew word that functions as a *terminus technicus* for the sign-actions of the Old Testament prophets. Of the symbolic actions recorded in the Hebrew Scriptures, just three (Isa 8:18; 20:3; Ezek 4:3) or four (Isa 7:3) are explicitly designated by the term *'ôt*, sign.[15] Two of these (Isa 8:18; 20:3) are also described by the term *môpēt*, wonder.[16] Others (Ezek 12:6, 11; 24:24; 24:27) are characterized as *môpēt* only. A large number of prophetic acts are not identified by any generic term at all.[17] Nevertheless, the similarities between the symbolic actions which

---

[12] *Les actes*, 17: "...il nous semble préférable de parler des *actes prophétiques*, en donnant à cette appellation un sens restrictif et en la réservant à cette type d'actes-parlants ou de paroles-en-actes." Since the publication of *Les actes* a comprehensive work on prophetic actions has appeared in English, W.D. Stacey, *Prophetic Drama in the Old Testament* [Hereafter *Prophetic Drama*.] Stacey identifies a total of 48 "prophetic dramas" which include all of those listed by Amsler. He also catalogues other terms for these word-actions which include (*Prophetic Drama*, 20, n. 9): "symboles" (D. Buzy; A. Regnier), "sign" (R.B.Y. Scott), "symbolic act" (M. Greenberg), "symbolic action" (W.L. Holladay).

[13] *Les actes*, 70: "Il est probable que les prophètes ont accompli d'autres actes de ce genre, dont le souvenir n'a pas été gardé."

[14] In canonical order these are listed as follows: 1 Kgs 11:29-39; 19:19-21; 22:11; 2 Kgs 13:14-19; Isa 7:3; 8:1-4; 20:1-6; Jer 13:1-11; 16:1-9; 19:1-15; 27:1-22; 28:1-17; 32:6-44; 35:1-19; 43:8-13; 51:59-64; Ezek 4:1-3; 4:4-8; 4:9-17; 5:1-17; 12:1-16; 12:17-20; 21:11-12; 21:23-29; 24:1-14; 24:15-24; 24:25-27 (cf. 3:26s; 33:21s); 37:15-28; Hos 1:2-9; 3:1-5; Zech 6:9-15. This resembles Fohrer's list in *Die symbolischen Handlungen der Propheten* with only minor changes, most notably the inclusion of Jer 35:1-19.

[15] According to F.J. Helfmeyer, "אוֹת *'ôth,*" *TDOT* I, 167-188, the word *'ôt* appears 78 times in the Old Testament; in 75 cases it is translated in the Septuagint by sēmeîon. The most frequently used synonyms include *môphēt* ("wonder") and *zikkārôn* ("memorial"). The function of a sign is not to excite or to terrify, but "to mediate an understanding or to motivate a kind of behaviour" (171). Helfmeyer, in fact, groups the Old Testament signs into seven categories: signs imparting knowledge; signs of protection; signs producing faith; signs that bring to remembrance; signs of the covenant; signs of confirmation; and, symbolic signs.

[16] The term occurs 36 times in the Hebrew scriptures, about half of which are linked to *'ôt*.

[17] W.D. Stacey, *Prophetic Drama*, 18, notes that "*māšāl* ['parable'] provides a pointer to the interpretation of some prophetic actions, even though the term *māšāl* is not used to describe them."

are designated as *'ôt* or *môpēt* and those which are not described by any specific term are striking.[18] In this study, the terms prophetic sign/act/action, symbolic act/action, and the Hebrew word *'ôt* are used interchangeably to refer to these sign-actions of the Old Testament prophets.

1.1 *The Act of the Prophet*

The words and actions of the Old Testament prophets exist today thanks to the narratives which record them.[19] Studies reveal that these texts are a complex web which consists of: 1) works written by the prophet or by a disciple; 2) interpretation and re-interpretation by the actual witnesses and by subsequent adherents to the message; and 3) acceptance and rejection by theological editors and by the wider religious community. And yet, because of the link between literary genre and the original *Sitz im Leben* of the event, it is possible, Amsler claims, not only to attempt a reconstruction of the underlying happening, but also to investigate the effect it had on its audience.[20] To this end, he accepts Fohrer's[21] classical thesis that these written accounts are made up of three basic motifs: 1) the order (*Befehl*); 2) the account of the execution (*Bericht*); and 3) the subsequent explanation (*Deutung*).[22] These motifs are now examined in turn.

1.1.1 The Order

First of all, the narratives record the order given by God to the prophet to carry out the act.

> All the accounts which the prophets themselves give of their acts begin by affirming that they carry them out to obey a precise order of the Lord, and not in virtue of a power which might belong to them. The order given to the prophet is not only a conventional literary genre motif. Its purpose is to inscribe the

[18] W.D. Stacey, *Prophetic_Drama*, 18-19, notes a number of "parallels between the meaning of *'ôt* or *môpet* and the thought world of prophetic actions."

[19] *Les actes*, 69.

[20] "La communication," 195.

[21] G. Fohrer, "Die Gattung der Berichte über symbolische Handlungen der Propheten," 103.

[22] W.D. Stacey, *Prophetic Drama*, 63, is critical of Fohrer's attempt to categorize the actions of the prophets by critical-form methods because he claims that (i) the central motifs which Fohrer identifies are not always present, (ii) a concentrated study of literary forms tends to exclude detailed study of the content and (iii) the selection of a particular number of passages isolates these actions from other related actions in the Old Testament.

> prophetic act in the mission of the prophet. The efficacy of the action derives from the power of God's word which directs it, and not from a power which the prophet might possess.[23]

While the divine command to accomplish the action is missing in all four accounts from *Kings,*[24] it is present in all of the remaining narratives, except when Hananiah takes it upon himself to break the yoke of wood which Jeremiah is wearing (Jer 28). Amsler notes that the presence of the order motif at the beginning of the account is an assurance that the prophet is responding to a divine initiative rather than acting on his own impulse. In the case of Hananiah, the absence of the order distinguishes the true from the false, the prophet from the magician.[25] Even in those cases where the prophetic act is carried out by a third party, the form is respected: the order is given by the prophet who, in this case, portrays the role of God, and is executed by the proxy who acts on behalf of the prophet.[26]

The similarity between prophetic actions and mimetic, magical acts is often underlined.[27] Fundamental to distinguishing the two is accepting the belief that the prophet is called by Yahweh to speak and act on his behalf. Unlike the magician, he is not the source of the power or authority which his words and actions display.[28] But, as Amsler stresses, the word of God which directs the action makes it efficacious.[29]

---

[23] *Les actes*, 51: "Tous les récits que les prophètes font eux-mêmes de leurs actes commencent par affirmer qu'ils les exécutent pour obéir à un ordre précis du Seigneur, et non en vertu d'un pouvoir qui leur appartiendrait. L'ordre donné au prophète n'est pas seulement un motif conventionnel du genre littéraire. Il a pour but d'inscrire l'acte prophétique dans la mission du prophète. L'efficacité du geste découle de la puissance de la parole de Dieu qui le dirige, et non d'un pouvoir que le prophète détiendrait."

[24] Amsler, *Les actes*, 46-47, explains the absence of the order from these accounts by noting that they come from the Deuteronomic tradition which held that all of history is directed by the Lord.

[25] *Les actes*, 76. See "La fonction prophétique de l'Église et dans l'Église," 40: "Notre manière commode d'appeler les uns 'prophètes' et les autres 'faux-prophètes' n'a pas d'appui dans les textes."

[26] K.W. Schmidt, "Prophetic Delegation: A Form-Critical Inquiry," *Bib* 63 (1982) 217: "The symbolic action is not divested of its power when it is delegated: it is as though the prophet were there performing it."

[27] See, for example, H.W. Robinson, "Prophetic Symbolism," 2-5; G. Fohrer, *Die symbolischen Handlungen der Propheten,* 94-95; C. Uehlinger, "'Zeichne eine Stadt... und belagere sie!'," 123-125.

[28] See G. Fohrer, *Die symbolischen Handlungen der Propheten,* 114.

[29] See also *Les actes*, 76.

How does the prophet receive the order to act in such a way? Is it a specific call, constraining the prophet to some pre-determined words and actions? To this Amsler replies:

> The originality of each one of these acts and the particularity of the accounts with respect to each prophet allow us to see that the divine order precludes neither the imagination nor the personal language of the prophet. Beyond that, the order to accomplish a particular act or to pronounce a particular oracle is a communication phenomenon which unfolds in the intimacy of the relationship between the prophet and God. In the texts this communication is known only by its effects.[30]

In this text, Amsler convincingly insists that each prophetic act is not a prescribed ritual, but a unique event, desired by God and shaped by the prophet so as to address a specific situation.[31] The prophet is neither a neutral mouthpiece nor a transmitter of a message which leaves him unmoved. Rather, the whole prophetic *persona* is involved in communicating the divine word of judgement or of consolation which is received in the depths of his personal relationship with God. The immediate concern of the prophet is not to analyse the modality of the divine communication or to reveal the nature of this relationship, but to surrender his entire self in transmitting God's word to the people. Consequently, the very existence of the prophet is a sign for the people:

> by his acts, the prophet himself becomes a sign (Hebrew: *môphēt*), set-up by God in the midst of his people. In him, word and act are one reality: even his life is an act through which God speaks, or, if one prefers, a word through which God lives in the middle of his own.[32]

The prophet does not simply set-up signals as the advertiser erects a bill-board; he is an integral part of the sign. In naming his children and by walking naked like a prisoner, Isaiah is aware that

---

[30] *Les actes,* 77: "L'originalité de chacun de ces actes et la particularité des récits se rapportant à chaque prophète laissent entrevoir que l'ordre divin ne met à l'écart ni l'imagination ni le langage personnel du prophète. Pour le reste, l'ordre d'accomplir tel acte ou de prononcer tel oracle est un phénomène de communication qui se déroule dans l'intimité de la relation du prophète avec Dieu, dont les textes ne nous laissent connaître que les effets."

[31] *Les actes*, 84: "... l'acte prophétique est unique, parce qu'il est lié à une situation particulière du dialogue que Dieu poursuit avec son peuple."

[32] *Les actes*, 16: "... par ses actes, le prophète lui-même devient un *présage* (hébreu: *môphēt*), dressé par Dieu au milieu de son peuple. En lui, parole et acte ne font qu'un: sa vie même est un acte par lequel Dieu parle, ou, si l'on veut, une parole par laquelle Dieu vit au milieu des siens."

he is a "sign, *'ôt*, and portent, *môpēt*," (Isa 8:18; 20:3) in the sight of the people. Similarly, Ezekiel's physical condition, his dumbness and his forgoing of the customary rites of mourning establish him as a sign, pointing to the God of Israel (Ezek 24:24, 27). It should be noted that Amsler avoids the debate about the psychological condition of the prophet. For him, it suffices to assert that the order to accomplish the act is a "communications phenomenon" between God and the prophet; he is not interested in probing this "intimacy" so as to investigate the possibility of ecstasy or trance.[33] Indeed, whether the prophet experienced the divine order before or after the particular event is of secondary importance. That the prophet undertook the act as a response to Yahweh is what concerns Amsler here.

1.1.2 The Execution

Having experienced the command to dramatize the action, the prophet then proceeds to describe the execution of the order, as is exemplified by the words of Ezekiel:

> And I did as I was commanded. I brought out my baggage by day, as baggage for exile, and in the evening I dug through the wall with my own hands; I went forth in the dark, carrying my outfit upon my shoulder in their sight. (Ezek 12:7)

Despite the clarity of this text, Amsler observes that the description of the performance of the divine order is rarely as clear or as explicit and it is often missing from the written accounts.[34] Does this suggest that some actions were never really accomplished by the prophets? While the actions are generally simple and could be performed by anybody,[35] certain prophetic acts appear to have been

[33] "La fonction prophétique de l'Eglise et dans l'Eglise," 41-42: "On s'est beaucoup interrogé, à propos des prophètes d'Israël, sur le phénomène de l'inspiration prophétique. On a abondamment analysé notamment leurs récits de vocation. Ces récits se sont généralement montrés réfractaires à ce genre d'analyse psychologique, car leur intention première est de nature théologique. Ils servent à accréditer le prophète auprès de ses auditeurs, et non à décrire les états d'âme d'un homme touché par l'inspiration. Dans une large mesure, le mécanisme de l'inspiration prophétique, si j'ose m'exprimer ainsi, reste insaisissable à notre analyse."

[34] Clear descriptions of the execution of the prophetic act are found in Isa 8:1-4; Jer 13:1-11; 32:6-15; Hos 1:2-9; 3:1-5. There is no explicit account of the performance in Ezek 5:1-17; Jer 16:1-9; 27:1-12; 51:59-64.

[35] *Les actes*, 82: "Ce n'est pas qu'ils requièrent un pouvoir extraordinaire, comme l'exigeraient des actions miraculeuses. Non, en eux-mêmes, ce sont des actes simples, au pouvoir de n'importe qui."

particularly difficult, almost impossible, to execute.[36] Should they be understood, therefore, as accounts of images or as parables, rather than as descriptions of something which really happened? Amsler replies with three points. First of all, he argues that "the presence or absence of the literary motif of execution cannot constitute a criterion for distinguishing two groups of stories, one group consisting of acts which were performed, the other of acts which were merely related."[37] Secondly, the primary purpose of the written accounts was not to reconstruct an historical episode, but to communicate the message of the prophet to subsequent readers. Amsler then remarks that, insofar as this is accomplished without actually describing the execution of the act, the narrative has achieved its purpose.[38] Finally, a particular text does not intend to give an objective account of the prophetic act. In fact, the subsequent explanation of the event colours the written report of execution, often giving it an unreal, exaggerated or "baroque aspect." Amsler notes, however, that this does not allow the conclusion that the action never took place.[39]

1.1.3 The Explanation

The words of explanation are usually presented by the prophet as an oracle to be delivered either when the act is carried out or, often times, shortly afterwards.[40]

> The prophetic act is always accompanied by a saying which explains its meaning. Generally, this word intervenes after the

---

[36] See, for example, Ezek 4:1-3; 5:1-17.

[37] *Les actes*, 75: "La présence ou l'absence du motif littéraire de la mise à exécution ne saurait constituer un critère pour distinguer deux groupes de récits, les uns relatant des actes réalisés, les autres des actes seulement racontés."

[38] *Les actes*, 75-76: "... la disparition fréquente de la mise à exécution de l'ordre par l'objectif principal du récit: celui-ci veut faire entendre aux lecteurs ultérieurs le message délivré par le prophète et non reconstituer un épisode historique du passé. La visée homilétique l'emporte sur souci de reconstitution. Ce silence est donc un indice très parlant de la fonction de nos récits."

[39] *Les actes*, 75: "Le récit ne fait pas un compte rendu objectif de l'acte prophétique. Il met en forme sa description en l'orientant vers l'interprétation qui va suivre. Ainsi certains traits de l'explication pénètrent-ils déjà dans la description de l'acte sans qu'ils reflètent exactement ce que le prophète a réellement fait. Cela ne veut pas dire que le prophète n'a rien fait!"

[40] Amsler, *Les actes*, 73, recognizes that words of explanation are missing in two accounts: 1 Kgs 19:19-21 and Isa 7:3. In the former, Elijah's act of placing the cloak on Elisha's shoulders was already sufficiently clear to the spectators; in the latter, the text betrays considerable editorial activity and remains ambiguous.

> action, to unravel in some way the *suspense* created by the enigmatic aspect of the act.[41]

The actions in themselves can be confusing, ambiguous. Breaking a jar, tearing a robe, boiling a cauldron of meat, all of these gestures could signify many things, but, thanks to the words of explanation, which are often provoked in the written account by the question of a confused witness,[42] they take on a precise meaning.[43] In this relationship between word and action the power of the prophetic act lies. There is, however, a link between the event and the explanation. Amsler speaks of an analogy between word and gesture in the narrative, between the "act which the prophet claims to perform on the basis of the order he has received, and the word which he is given to make the audience understand."[44] On the literary level, this analogy can be established by the verb which describes the act reappearing in the text of the oracle.[45] So, the narrative of Jeremiah's action records: "You shall *break* the flask in the sight of the men who go with you, and you shall say to them, 'Thus says the Lord of hosts: So I will *break* this people and this city, as one *breaks* a potter's vessel' (Jer 19:10-11)." Numbers, too, can reinforce the parallelism between the act and the word. The prophet Ahijah, for example, *tears* his cloak into *twelve* pieces, and then uses the same words to describe the subsequent execution of the act (I Kgs 11:29-31).

1.2 *The Act of John the Baptist*

The baptism of John has been categorized as a prophetic act by scholars such as W.F. Flemington,[46] G.W.H. Lampe,[47] J.

---

[41] *Les actes*, 83: "L'acte prophétique est toujours accompagné d'une parole qui en explicite le sens. Le plus souvent, cette parole intervient après le geste, pour dénouer en quelque sorte le *suspense* crée par l'aspect énigmatique de l'acte."

[42] *Les actes*, 77-80.

[43] "Parole de Dieu et paroles des hommes," *CProt* (1981/3) 10: "Il faut au geste l'accompagnement de la parole pour éliminer toutes les significations possibles du geste, au profit d'une seule qui est pertinente."

[44] "La communication," 196: "Ces récits, se caractérisent par une analogie entre l'acte que le prophète dit avoir reçu l'ordre d'accomplir et la parole qu'il est chargé de faire entendre à ses auditeurs."

[45] S. Amsler, "La parole visionnaire des prophètes," *VT* 31 (1981) 359-363, also notices this analogical element within the written narratives of the 22 vision accounts found in the later prophets.

[46] W.F. Flemington, *The New Testament Doctrine of Baptism*.

[47] G.W.H. Lampe, *The Seal of the Spirit. A Study of the Doctrine of Baptism and Confirmation in the New Testament and the Fathers*.

Delorme,[48] M.D. Hooker[49] and J.P. Meier.[50] This classification immediately suggests a problem: while the latter is usually a particular event, conceived to address a concrete situation in the relationship between God and the chosen people, the former is a repeated rite, administered indiscriminately to all who confess their sins (Matt 3:5-6). Yet, within this discontinuity lies a remarkable continuity: although repeated, John's baptism was a unique prophetic act as far as each individual convert was concerned[51]; and, while particular, each prophetic washing was directed towards the building up of the community of God's people.[52]

The New Testament narratives of the baptismal activity of John differ substantially in form and in content from the Old Testament records of the prophetic acts. Yet, certain common characteristics are discernible. Even though the accounts of John's activity do not mention any explicit *order* to baptize, there is no doubt but that he is acting in accordance with God's will in his prophetic mission to "prepare the way for the Lord" (Matt 3:3; Mark 1:3; Luke 3:2), and to bring "Jerusalem and all Judea and all the region about the Jordan" (Matt 3:5) to repentance. Since a prophetic act precludes neither the imagination nor the language of the perpetrator, the part played by the Baptist's personal intuition[53] and his sense of prophetic mission is paramount.[54] Like the prophets of old, John was a "sign and portent" of the imminent intervention of God: his

---

[48] J. Delorme, "The Practice of Baptism in Judaism" in A. George, ed., *Baptism in the New Testament*, 25-60.

[49] M.D. Hooker, *The Signs of a Prophet: The Prophetic Actions of Jesus*, 12: "When John appeared in the Jordan valley, preaching repentance and baptizing men and women in the river, he was seen as a prophet, and his baptism would have been understood as a prophetic action."

[50] J.P. Meier, *A Marginal Jew*, II, 49.

[51] J.P. Meier, *A Marginal Jew*, II, 51, notes that commentators universally affirm that John's baptism was conferred once only. Yet, neither the New Testament nor Josephus explicitly states this. Meier concludes that "the once-and-for-all character of John's baptism is a legitimate inference from the data, but it is only an inference."

[52] See G.W.H. Lampe, *The Seal of the Spirit*, 22-24.

[53] J.P. Meier, *A Marginal Jew,* II, 52: "Certain great religious figures stand out in history precisely because they take the raw material of traditional religious vocabulary and forge something new out of the old; such is the case with the man whose water ritual was so strikingly singular that he was called the Baptist."

[54] J. Delorme, "The Practice of Baptism in Judaism," 59: "In the last analysis we must look to the prophetic consciousness if we wish to discover the real originality of John and his baptism. The last days had come. His task was to preach, and to bring about conversion once again, acting in God's name."

austere lifestyle, his preaching, his whole existence were so tied to his message that he became synonymous with its dramatization.[55]

The *execution* of the baptismal ministry of John is affirmed by all four Gospels (Matt 3:5-6; Mark 1:5; Luke 3:3,16; Jn. 1:24-26.); the baptism of Jesus is recorded in the three Synoptics (Matt 3:13-15; Mark 1:9; Luke 3:21). The similarities and differences between proselyte baptism of the first century B.C. and John's rite have been widely studied and firmly established.[56] Although both entailed a public immersion in flowing water, the former was self-administered by a pagan who wanted to become a Jew, while the latter was dispensed to a Jew or to a Gentile by John himself for "the forgiveness of sins" (Mark 1:4). The Lucan account (Luke 3:7-9) bears witness to the confusion provoked by John's action and to the *explanation* which he subsequently provided. The Baptist's mission had a moral and eschatological aim, appealing for repentance and a turning back to God in the light of the dawning Kingdom (Matt 3:2). This message was reinforced by a parallel, almost analogical, strategy of word and action: his preaching called the hearers to repent, his baptism was performed with "water for repentance" (Matt 3:11; Mark 1:4; Luke 3:3), his words assembled the eschatological community, his lustration was the rite of entry into this holy remnant.[57]

2. **The Reaction**

What was the function of these striking word-actions which were performed under the divine impulse by the Old Testament prophets? Within Amsler's analysis, it is possible to distinguish two levels in the effect of these bizarre actions: the immediate impact that they had on those who witnessed them; and, the final purpose that they served in the unfolding theological drama. The

---

[55] J.P. Meier, *A Marginal Jew,* II, 91, notes that "like the prophets of old, John incorporates his message into his life even as he stakes his life on his message." In fact, Meier suggests (n. 143) that those symbolic actions which significantly effect a prophet's existence, such as Jeremiah's celibacy (Jer 16:1-4) or Isaiah's three-year nakedness (Isa 20:1-4), provide a clear example of how John's behaviour is significantly altered by his message.

[56] See F. Gavin, *The Jewish Antecedents of the Christian Sacraments*; W.F. Flemington, *The New Testament Doctrine on Baptism*, 3-12.

[57] M.D. Hooker, *The Signs of a Prophet*, 10: "[The account of Josephus] tells us that John exhorted the Jews 'to join in baptism'. We might have expected him to say simply 'to be baptized', but instead he uses a verb which signifies 'to come together'. Here is a hint, at least, that John's baptism was seen as creating a new community, and thus had some kind of eschatological role."

former is discussed in this present section; the latter is investigated in section three.

2.1 *The Reaction to the Prophetic Action*

From the writings of Amsler, it emerges that the immediate effect of a prophetic act, together with its concomitant explanation, was (1) to scandalize the witnesses, and (2) to provoke them into a reaction for or against the divine self-communication in a situation where words alone would have failed. Both of these points are now investigated in turn.

2.1.1 Shocking the Witnesses

The immediate effect of a prophetic act was to shock and appall those who witnessed it. Commenting on Ahijah's gesture (1 Kgs 11:29-39), Amsler remarks that:

> The action of the prophet is always shocking. This is not an era prone to waste, and one would not allow oneself the luxury of changing one's clothes every year! A brand new cloak is expected to provide many years' service for its owner....[58]

On the phenomenological level, then, the action was contrary to the normal expectation and common sense of the Hebrew. To tear a new cloak into strips, or to bury a new waist-cloth, was downright waste. The people could only be outraged at such extravagant behaviour. Other actions cut more deeply into the conventional psyche and social fabric of the Jews. Celibacy, for instance, was regarded as an unfortunate, cursed condition; family and progeny not only conferred identity but were the hallmarks of blessing and success.[59] Funeral rites and mourning custom were governed by an established, binding code which did not suffer infringement.[60] Adultery was a serious crime, demanding the death penalty.[61] That Jeremiah should voluntarily remain celibate (Jer 16:1-9), that Ezekiel would abstain from mourning his dead wife (Ezek 24:15-

---

[58] *Les actes*, 11: "Toujours est-il que le geste du prophète est choquant. L'époque n'est pas au gaspillage, et l'on ne peut pas se permettre de changer chaque année de vêtement! Un manteau tout neuf est destiné à servir de longues années à son propriétaire..."

[59] *Les actes*, 39-40.

[60] *Les actes*, 54-55.

[61] *Les actes*, 24.

24), or, indeed, that Hosea should marry an adulteress (Hos 3:1-5)[62] was bound to attract adverse comment and reaction.[63]

On a theological level, however, the action of the prophet was outrageous, almost blasphemous. As Amsler explains, it was extraordinary enough that Jeremiah would shatter a new vase, but the interpretation given to this heedless gesture was unthinkable:

> The action is not only shocking because the prophet goes to buy this vase, therefore destroying a useful object. It is particularly shocking because it announces the destruction of the city at whose heart stands the temple, considered to be the absolute guarantee of the inviolability of Jerusalem.[64]

In breaking the vase and pronouncing the oracle of explanation, the prophet attacked the very heart of the old covenant, announcing rejection and despair to a people who expected salvation and hope. Here, within the written accounts, Amsler identifies an analogy between the action of the prophet and the action of God. This analogy is *direct* when the prophetic act prefigures the future work of God: as Hosea loves his adulterous wife, so Yahweh loves the people of Israel. It is *indirect*[65] when the prophetic act is used to "evoke the effects of God's action in the destiny of the people"[66]: as Ezekiel shaves his hair to burn one third, beat a second third with a sword and scatter the final third to the wind, so too, Yahweh will subject a third of the people to famine, a third to extinction and a third to dispersion to the ends of the earth (Ezek 5:1,2,11,12).[67] It is noteworthy that, in this account, the prophet is both "actor and

---

[62] Scholars are divided on the relationship of Hos 1 to Hos 3. See F.I. Andersen - D.N. Freedman, *Hosea* [AncB 24]. Amsler understands them as two events in the one relationship, *Les actes*, 23: "... la femme adultère du chapitre 3 n'est autre que Gomer, fille de Divlaïm, celle que le prophète avait pris pour femme et qui lui avait donné trois enfants. Mais l'épisode du chapitre 3 se situe plus tard dans la vie du prophète...."

[63] C. Uehlinger, "'Zeichne eine Stadt ... und belagere sie!'," 125, n. 57, disagrees with Amsler's characterization of prophetic actions as "non-conventionnel": "nur mit Einschränkung, da die Zeichenhandlung ja verständlich sein soll und insofern mit Konvention und Stereotyp arbeitet." But, Jeremiah's celibacy, Ezekiel's abstention from mourning, and Hosea's marriage to an adulteress shatter all conventional stereotypes.

[64] *Les actes*, 26: "Le geste n'est seulement choquant parce que le prophète vient d'acheter ce vase, détruisant ainsi un objet utile. Il est surtout choquant parce qu'il annonce la destruction de la ville au cœur de laquelle s'élève le temple, tenu comme la garantie absolue de l'inviolabilité de Jérusalem."

[65] In "La communication," 198, Amsler uses a different terminology. Here he speaks of "active" and "passive" analogies.

[66] *Les actes*, 26.

[67] See *Les actes*, 29; "La communication," 196-197.

victim."[68] Ezekiel shaves his body to establish a direct analogy between the action of the prophet and the impending act of God. Yet, stripped of his hair and beard, Ezekiel also points to the destruction and the loss of dignity which await Jerusalem. Here, the "word-bearer of God does not appear on the Lord's side...; he stays with the people to signal in advance the fate which awaits them."[69]

In contrast to previous exegetes, Amsler does not seek to explain away or to ignore the shocking aspect of the prophetic act. Writing in the latter half of the nineteenth century, P. Fairbairn regarded prophetic acts to be physically or morally impossible; if they really did take place, they would have been dismissed as "puerile and ludicrous" by the audience.[70] A.B. Davidson echoed these judgements and concluded that the dramatic actions were "merely imagined"; the prophet "went through the actions in his phantasy, and they appeared to him to carry the same effect as if they had been performed."[71] Such explanations resulted both from the imposition of contemporary standards of social propriety and ethical behaviour on the Old Testament prophets, and from the attempt to shield hearers from having to believe that such inappropriate and potentially embarrassing situations were decreed by God. In so doing, these authors follow the medieval Jewish writer M. Maimonides who argues: "God forbid that God would make his prophets appear an object of ridicule and sport in the eyes of the ignorant, and order them to perform foolish acts."[72] Contrary to this position, however, Amsler stresses that the prophets do not set themselves up as examples of moral conduct. Although they observe the precepts of the mosaic law, they do not claim to be models of ethical conduct.[73]

2.1.2 Communicating a Divine Message

According to Amsler, the scandalous nature of the prophetic acts is not, however, an end in itself:

---

[68] *Les actes*, 28.

[69] *Les actes*, 29.

[70] P. Fairbairn, *Ezekiel and the Book of his Prophecy: An Exposition.* [Quoted from W.D. Stacey, *Prophetic Drama*, 226-227.]

[71] A.B. Davidson, *Ezekiel*, xxix.

[72] M. Maimonides, *The Guide for the Perplexed*, 246. [Quoted from B. LANG, "Street Theater, Raising the Dead, and the Zoroastrian Connection in Ezekiel's Prophecy" in J. Lust, ed., *Ezekiel and His Book*, 209.]

[73] *Les actes*, 55: "L'acte du prophète transgresse outrageusement la morale. Il s'agit en effet de tout autre chose que d'un exemple à suivre."

> They are nothing less than a process of communication destined, if possible, to unblock the dialogue between God and his people: the act reinforces the provocative character of the word and shows that Yahweh wishes to make himself understood, whatever the cost. This is because it is easier to refuse to listen to a word than to see an action, especially when this action comes from the ordinary and takes on an abnormal or shocking aspect.[74]

Through his preaching and the oracles which he delivers, the prophet seeks to proclaim God's word to Israel and, on occasion, to the surrounding peoples. At times, the hearers can either fall victim to misunderstandings or can remain indifferent or obdurate, rendering further verbal communication both impossible and ineffective.[75] It is in such a situation that the prophetic act comes into play. Because of its startling aspect, the action commands attention and the spectator is more exposed to the impact of the divine word. In this way, potential barriers are overcome and lines of contact are restored.[76]

Amsler's thesis rests on the communications theory of P. Watzlawick, J.H. Beavin and D.D. Jackson.[77] All human communication, he claims, takes place, to a greater or lesser extent, on two levels: the "digital" level of the transfer of information, and the "analogical" level of the interaction between the transmitter and the receiver.[78] While those passages which contain the words of the

---

[74] "La communication," 199-200: "Elles ne sont rien moins qu'un procédé de communication destiné, si c'est possible, à débloquer le dialogue entre Dieu et son peuple: l'acte renforce la portée provocatrice de la parole et manifeste la prétention de YHWH de se faire entendre, coûte que coûte. Car il est plus aisé de refuser d'écouter une parole que de refuser de voir un geste, surtout lorsque ce geste sort de l'ordinaire et prend une allure anormale ou choquante."

[75] *Les actes*, 62.

[76] S. Amsler, "Le thème du procès chez les prophètes d'Israël," *RThPh* 24 (1974) 116-131; "La fonction prophétique de l'Eglise et dans l'Eglise," 265, sees juridical process or *rîb* as another literary form which aims to overcome conflicting situations and to call the people to correct their behaviour in the light of the imminent intervention of God.

[77] P. Watzlawick - J. H. Beavin - D. D. Jackson, *Pragmatics of Human Communication*.

[78] "La communication," 195: "Les récentes théories de la communication mettent précisément en évidence ces deux niveaux: tout processus de communication opère à un premier niveau: qu'on appellera 'digital' dans la langue de l'informatique, et qui consiste à désigner par des mots et des constructions du code sémantique les réalités à percevoir. Mais en même temps, toute communication opère toujours aussi à un second niveau, qu'on peut appeler 'analogique', parce qu'elle met en oeuvre divers moyens non-verbaux visant à produire un certain effet sur les destinaires, mis en demeure de réagir à leur tour."

prophets operate primarily on the digital level, the accounts of the prophetic actions have a high "analogical coefficient."[79] In the so called "blockage situations" between God and his people, Amsler suggests that:

> It is no longer a matter of clarifying the message on the digital level, a message which is already well known thanks to the numerous oracles of the prophets themselves. Rather, it is a matter of giving the message, by means of a spectacular act, a greater efficacy on the analogical level, so that the resistance of the hearers is broken down and they are, despite themselves, obliged to listen.[80]

While all communication elicits some response, prophetic acts are, by their very nature, more provocative than words.

W.D. Stacey arraigns any attempt to interpret prophetic dramas as communication events.[81] Such an explanation, he argues, accounts neither for those acts which were not performed before an audience (Jer 13:1-11; Ezek 51-17), nor for the lack of clarity, indeed the increased confusion, that arises on the performance of others (2 Kgs 13; Jer 27-28).[82] But, can one justifiably deduce that "an action not recorded as having taken place before an audience"[83] took place in private? Referring to "the book Jeremiah wrote, or is said to have written, concerning the doom of Babylon," Stacey concludes that "there is no mention of anybody being told."[84] In the case of the waist-cloth which was buried and which subsequently rotted (Jer 13:1-11), he notes that it was "never exhibited to Israel."[85] "This is a drama," he writes, "that Jeremiah works through, that he understands himself, but that he never communicates to Israel."[86] Although the text makes no explicit

---

[79] *Les actes*, 61.

[80] *Les actes*, 63: "Il ne s'agit plus d'expliciter le message au niveau 'digital', bien connu grâce aux nombreux oracles des prophètes eux-mêmes. Il s'agit de donner à ce message, par un acte spectaculaire, une efficacité plus grande au niveau 'analogique', afin de percer la résistance des auditeurs et de les obliger à écouter, malgré eux."

[81] *Prophetic Drama*, 264-268.

[82] This is also the opinion of G. von Rad, *Old Testament Theology,* II, 97: "Even if we do not adopt the extreme position that the prophet [Isaiah] himself was, to begin with, ignorant of the significance of what he was ordered to do, it is quite certain that for a long time the people did not understand his behaviour; and this completely rules out the idea that the function of the symbolic actions was to teach and illustrate."

[83] *Prophetic Drama*, 265.

[84] *Prophetic Drama*, 223.

[85] *Prophetic Drama*, 222.

[86] *Prophetic Drama*, 222-223.

reference to witnesses, it is unreasonable to conclude that none was present. If the historical objectivity of the nucleus of the accounts is assumed, as both Stacey and Amsler do, then the very existence of the narrative suggests that either witnesses were present or that Jeremiah himself later described the act.[87] Stacey remarks that the act was "important in itself."[88] The fact of its inclusion in the canon suggests that it had a relevance beyond its mere existence. The written account of the act made the will of God known, and challenged the original spectators as well as the subsequent readers to react accordingly. Indeed, Amsler notes that, even if the act failed to provoke any reaction among the spectators, it still testified to the perseverance of Yahweh and to the hardness of heart of those who chose to ignore him.[89]

Behind Stacey's critique lies a concept of communication which remains on the digital level, that is, which concerns the transfer of information. Amsler, however, recognizes that prophetic acts also operate on the analogical level. They are not mere gimmicks to facilitate a smoother, clearer acceptance of some divine deposit, but are public demonstrations of the present intention and imminent activity of the transcendent God which, by their dramatic aspect, engage their audience and provoke a decision for or against the One who saves.[90]

2.2 *The Reaction to John the Baptist*

The shocking aspect of John's action in the Jordan should not be underestimated. The spectacle of the only son of a priest who had reneged on his solemn duty to follow his father and to ensure the continuity of the sacerdotal line, in order to preach an anti-establishment message and to undermine the cultic order, would

---

[87] Even if no witnesses followed Jeremiah as he buried and retrieved the waist-cloth, he could at least have presented the spoiled cloth to the representatives of the "house of Israel and the house of Judah" as he subsequently delivered the explanation of his action. J. Thondiparambil, *Prophesy as Theatre: Symbolic Acts in Jeremiah*, 46-50, argues that witnesses were present at this and all the other prophetic acts performed by Jeremiah.

[88] *Prophetic Drama*, 223.

[89] *Les actes*, 64.

[90] While Stacey, *Prophetic Drama*, 265, acknowledges this provocative character in B. Lang's presentation of prophetic act as street theatre, he fails to recognize this in the writings of Amsler: "To be fair to Lang, he does not think of 'street theater' purely in terms of visual aid. For him, the prophet is a political activist, not simply bringing news, but calling for decision and action; his aim is not simply to communicate, but to shock, to stir, to move. Involving onlookers in a piece of drama is a powerful way of furthering this aim."

certainly have been unacceptable to the Jewish authorities.[91] The people were already familiar with the rites of proselyte purification, but now they encountered a new reality, bearing certain formal similarities with it whilst belying radical changes. Only a Gentile needed to undergo the earlier rite, but now, even the "children of Abraham" were subject to John's baptism. Theologically, this suggests that even the chosen people, because of their disobedience and sin, were foreigners before the Lord of the covenant. Only by turning back to God could they, together with repentant social outcasts such as tax-collectors and soldiers, be admitted to the eschatological community which confidently awaited the coming of the Messiah.

The analogy between the act of the prophet and the imminent act of God which it prefigured has already been discussed. Just as John now baptizes with water, the "one who is to come" will baptize with the Spirit. The lustral activity of John points beyond itself to the end-time when all would rejoice in the pneumatic outpouring of God. As J.P. Meier notes,

> John's pouring out of water on the repentant of Israel only prefigures the pouring out of God's spirit upon the true Israel, a pouring out promised in the prophets, the intertestamental literature, and notably at Qumran. While the water of John's baptism naturally symbolized the washing away of sin, that symbolism looked to a past that would soon disappear. The more important aspect of his baptism looked to the imminent future, when those who had accepted John's message and his pouring of water (which gives life to the parched land of Palestine on the natural level) would experience the pouring of the holy spirit, which brings eternal life instead of destruction on the last day.[92]

Does John's baptism play any role in prolonging the divine-human communication? Towards the end of the first century B.C. messianic expectation was high and many "prophets" appeared on the scene pretending to be either the precursors or the epiphanies of the Expected One.[93] From this Babel of claim and counter-claim one voice cried out with a unique appeal, and the people came to the wilderness to hear him preach. Why did John enjoy such prodigal

---

[91] J.P. Meier, *A Marginal Jew*, II, 26.
[92] J.P. Meier, *A Marginal Jew*, II, 39.
[93] See E.P. Sanders, *Jesus and Judaism*; G.S. Sloyan, *Jesus in Focus: A Life in its Setting*.

success where others failed? Surely the answer is to be found in the prophetic act accompanying his proclamation, in the action for which he is primarily remembered. This bizarre spectacle of the ascetic prophet's baptism for the forgiveness of sins had a profound effect on its recipients and on the wider group which witnessed it. The reality of the imminent intervention of God and the urgency of joining the eschatological community is forcibly brought home to all who hear and see. While it was easy to ignore another preacher, who could remain unmoved in the face of such a dynamic manifestation?

3. **The End**

The dramatic actions performed by the Old Testament prophets engaged their audiences and provoked a decision for or against the Lord of Israel (immediate effect). However, this is not all. The symbolic actions, Amsler contends, anticipated in the here and now of the onlookers the future intervention of God which they heralded. The aim of this final section is to examine Amsler's understanding of the final effect of a prophetic action and, then, to investigate the end intended by the baptismal rite of John.

3.1 *The End of the Prophetic Action*

The analysis of Amsler's approach to the ultimate end of symbolic actions unfolds in two steps. First of all, the ability of the words and gestures to graft the future onto the present is investigated. Secondly, the relationship between the prophetic gesture and the presaged reality is explored.

3.1.1 Heralding the Future

Amsler alleges that the mission of the Old Testament prophets consists not of predicting the future or of scrutinizing the natural elements in the hope of penetrating the secret intentions of the divinity, but of erecting revelatory signs:

> Far from searching out annunciatory signs of the future in the present, the prophetic mission is to place the people before the God of its future, and, to that end, to set up, here and now in the present, revelatory signs of this future. That is what the prophet

> does with his oracles. That, in particular, is the role of the acts which support his words.[94]

According to Amsler, the role of the prophet is to confront the people with the God of the future by establishing revelatory signs in their midst. This he normally does by proclaiming oracles in the hearing of the community. On occasion, particularly in the blockage situations, another strategy is called for, and the prophet dramatically confronts his audience with an act which discloses the forthcoming intervention of God. By word and deed, then, in breaking the jar and in proclaiming the explanation, Jeremiah heralded the impending destruction of Jerusalem, and brought the people face to face with God's pronounced judgement on Israel. Here the prophet entered into the tension which exists between the present and future relationship of Yahweh and his people.[95] The future announced by the prophetic act could also be salvific. When Jerusalem was besieged by the Babylonians, and Jeremiah was in prison, the prophet was approached by his cousin Hanamel to buy a family field at Anatoth (Jer 32:6-44). At a time when political pessimism prevailed, Jeremiah's foolhardy act stirred-up hope and revealed, "even through its folly, the future which God is preparing, contrary to all appearances."[96]

The prophetic act not only announces or points to the imminent intervention of God in the history of Israel, but,

> is invested with a force which sooner or later will bring about its effects in the history of the relations of God with his people. More than the word with which it shares this efficacy, the action of the prophet is a sort of time-bomb which will explode the day God himself will intervene.[97]

Amsler's point here is of the utmost importance. The prophet heralds a future intervention of God, but, that is not all. His action,

---

[94] *Les actes,* 34: "Loin de chercher dans le présent les signes annonciateurs de l'avenir, le prophète a pour mission de placer le peuple devant le Dieu de son avenir et, pour cela, de dresser déjà maintenant dans le présent les signes révélateurs de cet avenir. C'est ce qu'il fait par ses oracles. C'est en particulier le rôle des actes qui soutiennent les paroles."

[95] *Les actes*, 33.

[96] *Les actes*, 31: "L'achat du champ d'Anatoth est un investissement de fou, mais qui révèle, par sa folie même, l'avenir que Dieu prépare, contre toute apparence."

[97] *Les actes*, 48: "L'acte prophétique est donc revêtu d'une force qui portera tôt ou tard ses conséquences dans l'histoire des relations de Dieu avec son peuple. Plus encore que la parole avec laquelle il partage cette efficacité, l'acte du prophète est une sorte de bombe à retardement qui explosera le jour où Dieu lui-même interviendra."

in fact, literally anticipates the presaged event. In using the image of a time-bomb, Amsler suggests that, once enacted, the foreshadowed happening is inevitably primed to explode on the stage of history.[98] Nor, according to Amsler, should the present effect of this prolepsis be underestimated:

> At the hour when all is about to end, [buying the field at Anatoth] forestalls the new time of reconstruction by already signalling the resumption of social life, in the country liberated by the sovereign intervention of the God of Israel.[99]

By buying the field at Anatoth, the new order to which Jeremiah alluded had already come about; by breaking the jar, not only was the coming destruction of Jerusalem heralded, but the ramparts of the city were already breached. In short, by the words and gestures which constituted his act, the prophet symbolically grafted the future onto the present. Thus, while Amsler sees the immediate effect of a prophetic act as the communication of a divine message, its final end is nothing less than the proleptic participation in the imminent intervention of God.[100]

---

[98] A.C. Thiselton, "The Supposed Power of Words," *JThS* 25 (1974) 283, notes: "Several modern writers betray a fascination for analogies drawn from military weaponry. Zimmerli, following Grether, compares the word in Old Testament thought to a missile with a time fuse. Eichrodt insists that words, once spoken, remain effective or even dangerous 'for a long time, like a forgotten mine in the sea, or a grenade buried in a ploughed field'. Edmond Jacob speaks of 'a projectile shot into the enemy camp whose explosion must sometimes be awaited but which is always inevitable'. Other writers speak explicitly of bullets, torpedoes, and charges of high explosives. It is alleged, in the words of Procksch, that in Hebraic thought 'the word is *kraftgeladen*, it operates as a power-laden force which irresistibly achieves its end. Gerhard von Rad sees it as 'an objective reality endowed with mysterious power'." Thiselton rejects (296) the thesis which views the power of the word of God as something inherent in the word rather than in the God who inspires it: "Prophetic pronouncements are effective because they are spoken by someone in authority, and may often take the form of a performative utterance."

[99] *Les actes*, 31: "A l'heure où tout va finir, il anticipe le temps nouveau de la reconstruction en signalant déjà la reprise de la vie sociale, dans le pays libéré par l'intervention souveraine du Dieu d'Israël."

[100] W.D. Stacey, *Prophetic Drama*, 171-208, rejects the proleptic power of many of the dramas in Ezekiel. These, he claims (185) are "expressive" of the present situation of Jews still living in Jerusalem but are "in no sense causative." This view finds little support with exegetes who generally see the action as related to the future destruction of Jerusalem. M. Greenberg, *Ezekiel 1-20* [AncB 22], 122: "The explicit aim of the first symbolic act, the siege of the city, is to be a sign for the house of Israel. Like other similar acts...this one represents as a present reality a future but impending event." See W. Zimmerli, *Ezekiel*, I, 63; A. Cody, *Ezekiel* [Old Testament Message], 35; J. Blenkinsopp, *Ezekiel*, 35; B. Vawter - L.J. Hoppe, *A New Heart: A Commentary on the Book of Ezekiel*, 41.

Since acts appeared to have more success than words in bringing about their intended end, the relationship between the oracles which the prophets normally proclaimed and the actions which they occasionally performed must be examined. Amsler readily admits that each is invested with the one divine power which inspires and guarantees its efficacy.[101] Both serve the prophetic mission of setting-up signs of the impending future which God has in store for his people.[102] But, did the act possess a greater objective force than the word? Certainly, there is a connection between the two:

> What the prophets already proclaim in their oracles and in their discourses is that, despite appearances, God is at work. But the word is always likely to lose its efficacy and to find itself thrown into insignificance by unimpressed or incredulous hearers. Because it appears as an event, the prophetic act itself is not an idea or an eternal reality, but a person in the process of acting so as to judge and to save the world. While remaining a completely human gesture, the prophetic act assumes the significant import of a visible act of God, inscribed into the overall harmony of his past, present and future work.[103]

Clearly, then, the prophetic act, is a "visible word"[104] which overcomes audience resistance, which restores and prolongs the divine communication, even when in crisis, and which obliges the witnesses to reflect on their existential circumstances and to respond accordingly. The effective difference, therefore, between oracle and act lies not in some ontological superiority of the latter over the former, but in the enhanced subjective impact which the prophetic word, made incarnate through the act itself, has in the community in which it is received.[105]

---

[101] *Les actes*, 48.

[102] *Les actes*, 17.

[103] *Les actes*, 83: "Que Dieu soit à l'œuvre, malgré les apparences, c'est déjà ce que proclament les prophètes dans leurs oracles et leurs discours. Mais la parole est toujours exposée à perdre son efficacité et à se trouver évacuée dans l'insignifiance par des auditeurs blasés ou incrédules. Parce qu'il se produit comme un événement, l'acte prophétique, lui, manifeste que le Dieu des prophètes n'est pas une idée ou une réalité éternelle, mais une personne en train d'agir pour juger et pour sauver le monde. Tout en restant complètement le geste d'un homme, l'acte prophétique revêt la portée significative d'un acte visible de Dieu, inscrit dans la cohérence de son œuvre passé (sic), présente et à venir."

[104] *Les actes*, 55.

[105] W.D. Stacey, *Prophetic Drama*, 232: "It would be overstating the case to say that the objective drama was qualitatively different from the spoken oracle or even from the vision, but it seems necessary to recognize a difference in vitality between them."

3.1.2 Prophetic Action and Divine Future

Amsler does not dwell on how a prophetic drama actually anticipates the future. However, he does make the point that:

> it is important not to diminish the evidence expressing the efficacy of the words and acts of the prophets: it is not only because the Lord had decided to destroy Jerusalem that Jeremiah destroys the jar; it is also because Jeremiah destroys the jar that the Lord is going to destroy Jerusalem. And it is also because Jeremiah buys his cousin's field that the Lord is going to create a new future for his people, where the buying and selling of fields will start again.[106]

From this text it is clear that the proleptic power of a prophetic act derives not only from the Lord who commands the act, but also, from the gestures and words which accompany it. Note the remarkable tension created by Amsler's understanding: the prophet acts because Yahweh intends to intervene; Yahweh acts because the prophet dramatically prefigures his action. Both statements must be held together.[107] Viewed in isolation, the first affirmation reduces prophetic act to factual demonstration, to the arresting communication of a message about Israel's future before God. In this case, the immediate effect of the act is to shock, to stir, to move the spectators to take account of the prediction and to react accordingly.[108] Taken alone, the second statement reduces prophetic act to mimetic wizardry, to the coercive manipulation of the divinity for egotistical motives. In this case, the direct effect of

---

[106] *Les actes*, 47: "... il importe de ne pas atténuer le témoignage rendu à l'efficacité des paroles et des actes des prophètes: ce n'est pas seulement parce que le SEIGNEUR a décidé de briser Jérusalem que Jérémie brise la cruche; c'est aussi parce que Jérémie brise la cruche que le SEIGNEUR va briser Jérusalem. Et c'est aussi parce que Jérémie achète le champ de son cousin que le SEIGNEUR va créer un nouvel avenir à son peuple, où l'on se remettra à vendre et à acheter des champs."

[107] Amsler sees this as a "both-and" rather than an "either-or" situation, as intimated by R.P. Carroll, *From Chaos to Covenant*, 133.

[108] This is the position of B. Lang, "Street Theater, Raising the Dead, and the Zoroastrian Connection in Ezekiel's Prophesy," 300: "...I argue that these so-called symbolic acts, especially those of Ezekiel, should be understood as public, street-theater like performances. Performed on the eve of an anti-Babylonian revolt, they challenged public opinion by visualizing the inevitable consequences of such an inconsiderate, foolish protest. What Ezekiel wanted to sound was a note of warning to make the king and the people abandon that policy. Only an immediate and radical change of the political course could prevent a national disaster."

the act is to exert control, and so, to remove it from the sphere of divine influence to that of esoteric magic.[109]

Amsler is aware of the reductions inherent in either extreme. On one hand he notes that prophetic acts have an effect beyond communication. W.D. Stacey justly rejects the suggestion that a prophetic drama was an "illustration, a visual aid, whose purpose was to make a difficult message more clear and more memorable."[110] However, suspicious of any hermeneutic which attempts to wish onto the prophets "some very modern notions about the process of communication and persuasion."[111] Stacey misrepresents Amsler's understanding of prophetic act. Certainly Amsler would accept that a prophetic act is "a non-verbal means which would draw the audience into the action and so make more effective communication possible."[112] but this is not all. This is little more than what is implied in the first statement above. The purpose of prophetic acts, according to Amsler, is not only to communicate more effectively, they also have the mission of inaugurating a new divine initiative within history:

> Even if the acts of the prophets did not seem to have received a better welcome than their words ..., the simple fact that they were performed at a particular moment in the life of Israel inscribes them on the level of events determining this history, the consequent unfolding of which they play a part in modelling, and the subsequent culmination of which they prepare.[113]

---

[109] This appears to be the position of R.P. Carroll, *Jeremiah*, 295-296: "Their [symbolic acts'] roots are in the world of magic and they belong to an epistemological framework where a divinization and incantation represent power transmitted through words and gestures. These are not just actions which illustrate with gestures but are part of the creation of the thing itself - they make things happen. The performed action, accompanied by the actualized words and gestures, is causal... The action and the words are bound up together and bring about the thing spoken of. Biblical exegetes prefer a more rationalized account of these matters, and favour treating them as symbolic rather than magical. They also tend to invoke a theological justification for the distinction. However, more sophisticated accounts of the matter, whether from a theological perspective or from an analytic philosophical viewpoint, often fail to allow for the extent to which belief in magic dominated the ancient world... It would be unwise to allow anachronistic systems of explanations to obscure that fact or to rationalize the mantic world."

[110] *Prophetic Drama*, 264.

[111] *Prophetic Drama*, 265.

[112] *Prophetic Drama*, 268.

[113] *Les actes*, 48: "Même si les actes des prophètes ne semblent pas avoir reçu meilleur accueil que leurs paroles ..., le simple fait qu'ils ont été exécutés à un moment particulier de la vie d'Israël les inscrit au rang d'événements déterminants

In other words, these gestures and the accompanying words of the prophets shape the ulterior unfolding of the history of Israel by activating the future in the reality of the present.

On the other hand, Amsler is conscious that, behind the external similarities between magical rites and prophetic acts,[114] lie fundamental differences which make it impossible to confuse the two. This correspondence was recognized by Fohrer[115] who proposed several differentiating criteria, to which Amsler refers: the prophet acts at God's command, whereas the magician operates independently[116]; the prophet acts publicly and on behalf of the community, while the magician divinizes in secret, often for his own benefit[117]; the prophet behaves simply and creatively, while the magician follows a complex ritual[118]; the prophet explains the meaning of his act, whereas the magician generally allows the action to speak for itself[119]; the prophet seeks to submit to God's will, while the magician attempts to control it.[120] According to W.H. Robinson,[121] the prophet and the magician act in the present but with regard to the future, exerting a coercive, effective power on the latter. Prophetic acts, because they are dependent on the will of God and work on his behalf, give magic a new meaning.[122]

Amsler, however, takes a radically different approach:

> Contrary to the magic act which intends to operate from the present on the future, the prophetic act aims to operate from the

de cette histoire, dont ils contribuent à modeler le déroulement et à préparer l'achèvement."

114 Amsler, *Les actes*, 49-50, identifies three: phenomenologically, both appear to exert "a sort of pressure on the powers at work in the world in order to orient them in a determined direction"; both function according to "the principle of similitude" (Frazer), whereby the prophet or the magician performs a limited, immediate act which will later unfold on a grander scale; both prophet and magician play a special role in their respective societies.

115 G. Fohrer, "Prophetie und Magie," *ZAW* 78 (1966) 25-47; *Die symbolischen Handlungen der Profeten*, 94-95.

116 *Les actes*, 51; 76.

117 *Les actes*, 50; 77.

118 *Les actes*, 82.

119 *Les actes*, 84.

120 *Les actes*, 45.

121 H.W. Robinson, "Hebrew Sacrifice and Prophetic Symbolism," *JThS 43* (1942) 132: "The forms of acted symbolism were no doubt derived from a source [symbolic magic], but they were sublimated by the religious faith of the prophets. Magic constrains the unseen; religion means to surrender to it. These acts of prophetic symbolism do not in anyway constrain God; they are performed at his command in order to achieve, or to help to achieve, his own purpose."

122 C. Uehlinger, "'Zeichne eine Stadt ... und belagere sie!'," 124, n. 54, suggests that the distinction between prophetic acts and magic cannot be established from the biblical texts, but from ulterior dogmatic considerations.

> future on the present: the "sign" draws the coming event into the actuality of the prophet's spectators-hearers and instructs them to live their present as a function of the future which awaits them.[123]

Unlike magic which moves from execution to eventual fulfilment, from present to future, the prophetic act reverses direction, and operates from the future on to the present. Consequently, prophetic acts are primarily proleptic, unveiling the future action of God within the present experience of the audience. Faced with this remarkable disclosure, the people become aware of the divine intention and are challenged to change their minds and actions. Notice that by highlighting these three dimensions of the prophetic act — provocation, communication and anticipation — Amsler brings revelation, conversion and eschatology together. By performing the act, the prophet dramatically demonstrates and effectively facilitates the future intention of God, and calls Israel to a radical decision for or against the Lord of the Covenant.

In the light of this proleptic understanding of prophetic act, it is evident that Amsler avoids any simplistic, linear cause and effect scheme. In this context, J.W. Bowker's image of a football kicked towards a window, describing the link between a prophetic act and the impending intervention of God, is misleading, for it suggests that the present act of the prophet (kicking the ball) is responsible for the future action of God (the broken window).[124] For Amsler, however, it is not so simple: the window is already broken in the plan of God; the prophetic act both alerts the spectators-hearers to the new reality and inaugurates it by drawing the coming event into the sphere of the audience's present experience.

Amsler underscores the point that prophetic acts do not occur in a vacuum but, at a precise moment in the dialogue between Yahweh and Israel:

---

[123] *Les actes*, 52: "A l'inverse de l'acte magique qui entend agir du présent sur l'avenir, l'acte prophétique a pour but d'agir à partir de l'avenir sur le présent: le 'signe' amène l'événement à venir dans l'actualité des spectateurs-auditeurs du prophète et les met en demeure de vivre leur présent en fonction de l'avenir qui les attend."

[124] J.W. Bowker, "Prophetic Action and Sacramental Form" in F.L. Cross, ed., *Studia Evangelica*, III/II, 130: "A prophetic action is the realistic release of the energy of God, it is the irreversible setting in motion of His activity. It is as though I kicked a football towards a window: nothing can avert the catastrophe: I might as well say that the window is already broken. And yet I still do have to wait for the actual crash of broken glass, the factual event that my careless boot has made inevitable."

> the prophet does not intervene in the name of an unknown God who addresses his people for the first time. Even the name of Yahweh which opens, punctuates and closes the oracles is enough to evoke all the relations established by God with his people, from the times of the patriarchs and the exodus from Egypt.[125]

Every prophetic word, every prophetic act resonates with allusion to the antecedent history between God and his chosen people. While a prophetic act anticipates the next stage of this historical drama, it also reminds the audience of the previous events which both constitute this history and give it its distinctive character. As Jeremiah shattered the jar and pronounced the oracle of explanation, previous words came crowding into the memory of the people. The Lord who called Israel and bestowed the Promised Land now proposes to scatter the unfaithful and sunder the nation. In the episode recorded in Zech 6:9-14, the prophet was ordered to make a crown of silver and gold and to place it on the head of King Zerubbabel[126] as a sign heralding the re-establishment of the Davidic monarchy and, more importantly, announcing that the era of eschatological salvation had begun in the rebuilding of the Temple in Jerusalem. The narrative concludes, however, with the command to deposit the crown in the Temple, as a reminder of the donors. Commenting on this action, Amsler notes that:

> in a single stroke, the object of salvific anticipation becomes the object of remembrance, re-actualising the past in the succession of moments of the present. Therefore, the prophetic act, at the centre of an ever-new reality where God is at work, becomes the point of convergence for the future and the past.[127]

Implicitly, then, a prophetic act is a memorial: as the future is anticipated in the present experience of the people, the past is tacitly

---

[125] "La communication," 199: "... le prophète n'intervient pas au nom d'un Dieu inconnu qui interpellerait pour la première fois son peuple. Le seul nom de YHWH qui ouvre, ponctue et clôt ses oracles suffit à évoquer toutes les relations établies par Dieu avec son peuple, à travers l'histoire, depuis les patriarches et depuis la sortie d'Égypte."

[126] While the extant biblical text records the crowning of the priest Joshua, Amsler, "Aggée-Zacharie 1-8," 107 argues that this is a subsequent interpolation of the original.

[127] *Les actes*, 44: "Ainsi l'objet d'anticipation du salut devient-il du même coup objet de mémorial, réactualisant le passé dans la succession des moments du présent. L'acte prophétique devient ainsi le point de convergence de l'avenir et du passé, au centre d'une actualité toujours nouvelle où Dieu est à l'oeuvre."

recalled. This inherent connection between anticipation and remembrance, between *'ôt* and *zikkārôn*, is significant.

3.2 *The End of John's Baptism*

The baptism of John heralded the forthcoming era of judgement and salvation which would characterize the advent of the Messiah. But, as a prophetic act, it not only indicated a future intervention of God, but unexpectedly anticipated it in the community of his followers.[128] This means that, in the baptism of John, the day of salvation towards which the action pointed had already dawned: "Even now the axe is laid to the root of the trees" (Matt 3:10). Whether John was aware or not of how soon the Christ would appear, there is a sense in which his action made the coming inevitable. Paraphrasing the comment of Amsler on Jeremiah's gesture of breaking the jar,[129] one can assert that it is not only because the Lord had decided to send the Messiah that John baptizes; it was also because John baptized that the Lord was about to send the Messiah. In fact, the very baptism in the Holy Spirit which John foretold became a reality for one of his audience when Jesus stepped into the Jordan.

As a prophetic act, John's baptism was "an event determining history"[130]: he provided the immediate incarnational context for the beginning of the ministry of Jesus. The Gospel evidence recalls that the Christ voluntarily underwent John's rite, that some of his first disciples, who subsequently conferred a ritual lustration themselves (John 4:1-2), were originally the Baptist's followers (John 1:37), and that many of the associated themes mentioned in the Precursor's preaching were subsequently taken up by Jesus, albeit with a different emphasis. From the Christian perspective, then, John is truly the harbinger of salvation, "the beginning of the Good News" (Mark 1:1).

Prophetic acts operate from the future onto the present. Consequently, the ultimate ground for John's rite is found, not in the recipients efforts to convert, but in the eschatological coming of the Messiah and the promised baptism in the Spirit. In fact, while proselyte baptism demanded an initial period of preparation and

---

[128] M.D. Hooker, *The Signs of a Prophet*, 13: "Like Isaiah's nakedness or Jeremiah's pot, John's baptism is *a dramatic representation of what will inevitably follow*."

[129] *Les actes*, 47.

[130] *Les actes*, 48.

trial, John's washing "means letting oneself be changed by God."[131] *Metanoia*, repentance, is first of all a turning towards the God who comes; only then, in view of the divine approach, is conversion possible. Yet, in his condemnation of "the brood of vipers" (Matt 3:7; Luke 3:7), John makes clear that this rite is not to be abused as an automatic escape from the coming judgment. The conversion demanded by John must bear fruit: food and clothing are to be shared, tax-collectors and soldiers are to conduct their affairs with honesty and dignity (Luke 3:11-14). In short, the messianic era heralded by John was to be marked by an end to exploitation and oppression, and a flowering of integrity and justice.[132]

John's baptism promised the forgiveness of sins (Luke 3:3). As a prophetic act, the lustral washing proleptically realizes that which it heralds. Does this suggest, then, that John's baptism was *sacramentally* effective?[133] The Baptist himself realized that the full remission of sin would only come with the definitive outpouring of the Spirit.[134] Insofar as his rite actually prognosticates this future happening, it effects that which it signified. Its power, however, comes not from the washing but from the decisive event it ushers into history. The baptism of John finds its eschatological fulfilment only when the Just and Sinless One steps out of the Jordan and sets his sight on Calvary.[135] It is from this later baptism that all baptism takes its strength (Mark 10:38-39; Luke 12:50).

The geographical setting of John's ministry was in itself evocative of the great deeds that God had performed in the history of his people: the wilderness was a reminder of the Exodus event; the Jordan was an allusion to Israel's first entry into the Promised

---

[131] E. Schillebeeckx, *Jesus*, 129-130.

[132] Josephus: "... he [John] was a good man and had exhorted the Jews to lead righteous lives, to practice justice towards their fellows and piety towards God and so doing to join in baptism." Quoted from S. Mason, *Josephus and the New Testament*, 152.

[133] R. Bultmann, *Jesus and the Word*, 26, refers to the baptism of John as an "eschatological sacrament."

[134] Council of Trent (DS 1614): "Si quis dixerit, baptismum Ioannis habuisse eandem vim cum baptismo Christi, anathema sit."

[135] J.P. Meier, *A Marginal Jew*, II, 55: "I think it is more likely that John saw his baptism as (1) acting out the candidate's repentance and pledge of new life as well as (2) symbolically proclaiming, anticipating, and assuring the cleansing from sin that the holy spirit would effect on the last day when it was poured out like water on the repentant sinner by the stronger one. If one wants to call this an 'eschatological sacrament' in the sense of a visible ritual symbolising invisible spiritual change and a sure pledge of salvation in the near future, that is fine - provided the later Christian understanding of sacrament is not read into the phrase."

Land. Many of the words and actions of the Baptist harkened back to the messianic expectations of the classical prophets: the recruitment of an eschatological remnant (Isa 10:20-22; Amos 5:15; Zeph 3:11-13); the forgiveness of sins though the rite of washing (Ezek 36:25-27; 42:1; Zech 13:1); the general outpouring of the Spirit as a sign of the end-time (Isa 32:15; Ezek 39.29; Zech 12:10). Thus, while firmly fixed on the not-yet, John's baptism as a prophetic act "becomes the point of convergence for the future and the past."[136]

3.3 *From John to Jesus*

According to Amsler, the mission of the Old Testament prophets is to establish signs of the future intervention of God among his people. This the prophets normally do in proclaiming oracles or recounting visions. Occasionally, however, the Hebrew scriptures record that they dramatize their message by performing prophetic acts. Normally contrary to conventional behaviour, the act has the immediate effect of being communicative. Together with its concomitant explanation, it scandalizes the audience and provokes some reaction in a situation where words alone would have fallen on either deaf ears or hardened hearts. Conceived at a particular moment in the ongoing history between Yahweh and Israel, the act, in its analogical structure, not only heralds, but actually proleptically unveils the future intervention of God, grafting it into the present experience of the community. While always a *prophetic* act, its ultimate power lies with the Lord who commands it: unlike a magician, the prophet does not exert pressure on the future from the present, but unveils the upcoming reality in the here and now of the people; unlike a messenger, he does not merely announce a reality already decided in the overall plan of God, but, by his action, shapes the later unfolding of the theo-logical drama. A correct understanding is found with neither extreme: only by holding both together is the nature of the relationship between present and future, and between God and prophet, properly maintained.

As the greatest of the prophets (Matt 11:9-11; Luke 7:26-28), John is entrusted with the mission to set up signs of the imminent intervention of God in the person of the Messiah. By proclaiming that "the Kingdom of God is at hand" (Matt 3:2) and by calling his listeners to repentance, he gathers a faithful remnant to await the

---

[136] *Les actes*, 44.

decisive event. However, by baptizing in the Jordan, John performs the prophetic act *par excellence* and brings home the urgency of his appeal to Jews and Gentiles alike. Already the eschatological community of justice is formed; in the lustral waters, the pneumatic baptism is presaged. The future which the washing proclaims erupts into the present as the "Greater One" paradoxically undergoes the rite of his own anticipation, while the epicletic hope finds fulfilment in the descent of the dove on Jesus of Nazareth.

Amsler's interest in the place of the Hebrew scriptures within the Church has already been noted. Many of his Old Testament studies are not an end in themselves, but are inspired by the desire to throw light on contemporary issues and to articulate an appropriate Christian response. Even in his commentaries on the prophets, Amsler loses no opportunity to indicate the relevance of his research for ecclesial faith and praxis. *Les actes des prophètes* begins with the relevance-identity dilemma facing local Churches today as they reflect on their apostolic and prophetic missions in the light of various situations of injustice and oppression which they encounter in the world.[137] In the Old Testament, the Christian theologian can hear the voice of Yahweh, the God of Jesus Christ, calling for liberation and peace. Yet, in attempting to re-appropriate this summons, Amsler warns against any simplistic transposition of the old covenant onto the new. One cannot go from Israel to the Church unless one passes through the "cross-roads"[138] which is Jesus Christ.

In his article "Le dernier et l'avant-dernier,"[139] Amsler examines the relationship of the Old to the New Testament once again, this time from the perspective of eschatology. Summarizing his argument he states:

> Jesus is understood as the *final* event, wherein God is "recognized," and the Old Testament may then be "re-read," as indeed it was by the authors of the New Testament, as the *semi-final* event preceding the ultimate manifestation of the Son. God's interventions under the Old Covenant (collectively and individually) are, also, only semi-final: *semi*, because

---

[137] *Les actes*, 5-6; 85-86.

[138] S. Amsler, "Les prophètes et la politique," *RThPh* 23 (1973) 15.

[139] S. Amsler, "Le dernier et l'avant-dernier. Le rapport entre le Nouveau et l'Ancien Testament," *RSR* 63 (1975) 385-396.

> directed to a further end; *final*, insofar as they prepared and anticipated that end.[140]

Here Amsler notes that, according to the apostolic scriptures, Jesus Christ is the "final event" of history: as Son, he is the perfect manifestation of God the Father. The revelatory interventions of God in the history of Israel, then, are only "semi-final"; they converge and find fulfilment in the Anointed One. The Hebrew prophets prepared Israel for the future coming of the Messiah and, by their words and actions, they foreshadowed it. John was to be the last in this line. In him promise knew actualization, as the "one who is to come" mysteriously underwent the rite of his own anticipation. In this lustral washing, the prophetic acts of Israel are subsumed and completed. John's baptism, then, is the *semi-final* prophetic act: *semi* because it was directed towards the ultimate intervention of God in the imminent coming of the Messiah; *final* because it not only effectively set the stage for the decisive drama of salvation but also proleptically grafted this episode into history. Jesus Christ is the *final* event. In undergoing the baptism of John, he authenticates the mission of his precursor and presents himself as the one "wherein God is recognized."[141] This *final* prophetic act is now to be explored.

---

[140] This is the English summary provided at the end of the article. "Semi-final" and "final" are translations of "l'avant-dernier" and "dernier" respectively.

[141] This is an application of Amsler's description (see quotation above) of Jesus Christ as the *final event* to his baptism as a *final prophetic act.*

CHAPTER 4

The Emergence of Baptism

New Testament prophetic acts as eschatological signs of fulfilment in the writings of Heinz Schürmann

Jesus of Nazareth was a prophet.[1] The synoptic gospels refer to him as such, and record an occasion when he compared his fate to that of a prophet (Mark 6:4; Matt 13:57; Luke 4:24).[2] The crowds considered him to be one of "the prophets of old" (Mark 6:15); others are more specific and take him for John the Baptist or Elijah *redivivus* (Mark 8:28). His acclamation as a prophet often follows a miraculous intervention: the raising of the widow's son at Nain (Luke 7:16); the feeding of the five thousand (John 6:14); the healing of the man born blind (John 9:12). Both the Samaritan

[1] The literature on the prophetic identity of Jesus is substantial. As well as the works mentioned in this chapter, others are listed in the bibliographies of F. Gils, *Jésus Prophète d'après les évangiles synoptiques*; F. Schneider, *Jesus der Prophet*, 2; M. Karimattam, *Jesus the Prophet*. M. Goguel, "Pneumatisme et eschatologie," *RHR* 132 (1946) 124-169, concludes that there is no scriptural evidence to suggest that Jesus was considered a prophet. R. Horsley, "'Like One of the Prophets of Old': Two Types of Popular Prophets at the Time of Jesus," *CBQ* 47 (1985) 435, remarks that "The question [for Jesus' contemporaries] is clearly not, 'Does this man fit the model of our expectations?' Nor is it, 'Is prophecy alive again in this man?' Rather, the question is, 'Since this fellow is obviously a prophet, what sort of prophet or which one is he?'"

[2] R.H. Fuller, *The Foundations of New Testament Christology*, 127, remarks that "without using 'prophet' as a direct self-designation, Jesus clearly indicates that he understood his role in prophetic terms in so far as it involved rejection and martyrdom." See also J. Daniélou, "Le Christ Prophète," *VS* 78 (1948) 154-170; O. Cullmann, *The Christology of the New Testament*, 13-50. This is to deny neither the uniqueness nor the universality of Jesus Christ as suggested by R. Mikhael, *Jésus comme prophète dans la cristologie contemporaine de langue française*, 80: "Il ne suffit pas de soutenir que Jésus est le Prophète eschatologique pour définir un caractère essentiel de sa personne et de sa mission; il faut affirmer ce qui fait la nouveauté absolue de la foi chrétienne: croire en un homme qui est Fils de Dieu, Messie et Sauveur."

woman (John 4:19) and Simon the Pharisee (Luke 7:39) positively evaluate Jesus as prophet; others, however, dispute his claim to such a hallowed title.[3]

Like the Hebrew prophets,[4] Jesus uttered promises (Luke 6:20) and threats (Luke 6:24); he communicated his visions (Luke 10:18), auditions (John 12:28) and ecstasies (Luke 10:21); he was gifted with a supernatural knowledge (Luke 7:39) which not only searched peoples' thoughts (Luke 6:8), but which also allowed him to foretell future events (Mark 11:2).[5] On his triumphant entry into Jerusalem, the crowds hailed him as "the prophet Jesus from Nazareth in Galilee" (Matt 21:11). In this capacity he is both revered (21:46) and mocked (Mark 14:65) in the course of the passion. Even after his death and the disappointment which it inevitably entailed for his disciples, the men on the road to Emmaus continued to articulate their belief that Jesus, "a prophet mighty in deed and word before God and all the people" (Luke 24:19), was the "one to redeem Israel" (24:21). It is no wonder then, that both Peter (Acts 3:22) and Stephen (7:37) speak of the risen Lord as if he were a prophet like Moses.[6]

In 1970, Heinz Schürmann published "The Symbolic Actions of Jesus as Signs of Eschatological Fulfilment,"[7] a two-part article which, first of all, identifies prophetic acts in the gospel accounts and, then, uses the insights gained from this preliminary study as a key to understanding the table-actions of Jesus at the Last Supper. That Jesus allowed himself to be baptized by John is "historically not to be doubted."[8] By undergoing the lustral rite, Jesus, places a symbolic action at the beginning of his public ministry. This datum provides Schürmann with a vital link between the prophetic acts of the Old and the New Testaments. In explaining this incipient gesture, "it would be strange," he argues, "if further signs were

---

[3] M.D. Hooker, *The Signs of a Prophet*, 17, notes: "The demand for Jesus to perform ... a miracle indicates that he was seen in the category of a prophet (albeit a false one). But *why* was he being seen as a prophet? The answer to that is apparently that he had already been *behaving* like a prophet."

[4] On the continuity between Jesus and the Old Testament prophets, see G. Friedrich, "*προφηχρης κτλ*. Prophets and Prophecies in the New Testament," *TDNT*, VI, 828-856; D. Hill, *New Testament Prophecy*, 48-69; D.E. Aune, *Prophecy in Early Christianity*, 153-170.

[5] G. Friedrich, *προφήτη,*" *TDNT,* VI, 843.

[6] R.H. Fuller, *The Foundations of New Testament Christology*, 167-173.

[7] H. Schürmann, "Die Symbolhandlungen Jesu als eschatologische Erfüllungs-zeichen. Eine Rückfrage nach dem historischen Jesus," *BiLe* 11 (1970) 29-41; 73-78. [Hereafter "DSJ."]

[8] "DSJ," 36.

not found"[9] in the gospel accounts. This intuition spurs Schürmann to uncover at least seven other prophetic actions in the synoptics.

The purpose of this chapter is to examine the baptism of Jesus as a prophetic act. In a first step, what Schürmann sees as the difference between the Old Testament symbolic actions and the New Testament "eschatological signs of fulfilment" is presented ("From Prophetic Acts to Eschatological Signs of Fulfilment"). Then, his analysis of these new covenant signs before and during the Last Supper is outlined ("From Jordan to Calvary"). Finally, with the help of Schürmann's own exegesis of the Lucan narrative, the insights gained from this review are retrospectively applied to the baptism of Jesus ("From Calvary to Jordan"). This leads to the conclusion that not only did the Nazarene submit to the prophetic action of John but, by stepping into the Jordan waters, Jesus is the protagonist of a new symbolic act in which he reveals himself as the Obedient Son who restores right relations between God and Israel. Endowed with the gift of the Holy Spirit as an anticipation of the universal, end-time pneumatic descent, Jesus, the fulfilment of all promises, is then sent by the Father on his salvific mission of being the definitively just and self-giving servant which finds fulfilment in the Cross.

1. From Prophetic Acts to Eschatological Signs of Fulfilment

The writings of Schürmann disclose four characteristics of the New Testament prophetic signs. These are presented below. In a first section, two criteria which establish a certain continuity between the new covenant symbolic actions and their Old Testament antecedents are presented. In a second section, two further aspects which betray a clear discontinuity between them are indicated.

1.1 *Pointing Beyond*

Schürmann recognizes that "the symbolic actions of Jesus are not essentially different from those of the Old Testament prophets"[10] as described by G. Fohrer.[11] The actions recorded in

---

[9] "DSJ," 36.
[10] "DSJ," 34.
[11] G. Fohrer, *Die symbolischen Handlungen der Propheten*. See Chapter 1, section 1.

the Hebrew scriptures heralded the future intervention of God in the life of the covenant community.[12] This, Schürmann claims, immediately suggests an initial criterion for identifying the prophetic acts of Jesus:

> Only those parabolic actions which stand in the tradition of the Old Testament prophetic actions should be taken into consideration, those that are of a *prophetic nature*; better or more limiting — we will see the reason later on — those in which the *eschaton* reveals itself.[13]

Immediately, then, those actions which show Jesus' attitude to the law, such as the demonstrative Sabbath healings and the sending of the leper to the priests, are excluded.

Initially, Schürmann agrees with the study of G. Stählin on the "parabolic actions" of Jesus.[14] All of Jesus' activity, Stählin contends, points to a further reality which it illumines. Yet, not every action of Jesus is a deliberate parabolic action: "only those actions, whose meaning goes beyond the individual gesture to a deeper and more general meaning which Jesus knew and intended may be considered."[15] The healings and the exorcisms fit comfortably into this category: they are performed by Jesus as real signs of the in-breaking kingdom of God. Schürmann, however, objects to this broad concept of parabolic action. These acts have their primary sense in themselves, he suggests, and are not parabolic in the proper sense.

This leads him to go beyond the position of Stählin and to postulate a second criterion:

> One must distinguish such symbolic actions [exorcisms and healings] of Jesus from the real symbolic actions as one normally distinguishes exemplary stories from parables. In the case of parabolic actions, what is really intended (the "content half") lies behind the action (the "image half") which is presented not primarily for its own sake. When the primary

---

[12] See Chapter 3, section 3.1.1.

[13] "DSJ," 33: "Es sollten nur solche Gleichnishandlungen in Betracht gezogen werden, die in der Tradition der alttestamentlichen Prophetenhandlungen stehen, die also *prophetischer Natur* sind, besser noch beschränkender — wir werden den Grund noch sehen - solche, in denen sich das Eschaton anzeigt...."

[14] G. Stählin, "Die Gleichnishandlungen Jesu" in *Kosmos und Ekklesia*, 9-22.

[15] "DSJ," 34 [Quoting G. Stählin, "Die Gleichnishandlungen Jesu," 11].

> intention lies in the act itself, as with miracles and exorcisms, one should not speak of "symbolic actions" in a strict sense.[16]

In practice, however, Schürmann acknowledges that it is difficult to determine whether the primary intention of an action lies in or behind its accomplishment.[17]

Schürmann then proceeds to isolate New Testament symbolic actions and to identify their "new covenant quality."[18] The first of these is the baptism of John:

> The Baptist was in a certain way already an eschatological figure of salvation (see Luke 1:13-17; 1:76-79) when he appeared as a herald sent from God calling for a baptism "for the forgiveness of sins" (Luke 3: 21f.). At God's command he presents, in a sign pledging and comforting, what the prophets had promised for the last time: "Then I will pour clean water over you and you will be cleansed" (Ezek 36: 25; cf. Zech 13:1). One must therefore understand this demonstration as an effective assurance in the forgiveness of God and not just as an empty symbolic action. The Baptist, certainly "more than a prophet" (Luke 7:26), undertakes the washing away of sins at God's command; he gives it authority and effectiveness, if, of course, still limited, namely on condition that "fruits of repentance" are produced (cf. Luke 3:7ff.).[19]

Schürmann readily recognizes that the Baptist is in the line of the great prophets of old. In his commentary on the Gospel of Luke,[20]

---

[16] "DSJ," 34: "Man muß derartige zeichenhafte Handlungen Jesu von den eigentlichen Symbolhandlungen ebenso abheben, wie man gewohnt ist, Beispielerzählungen von Gleichnissen zu unterscheiden: Bei Gleichnishandlungen liegt das eigentlich Gemeinte (die 'Sachhälfte') hinter der Handlung (die 'Bildhälfte' ist), die ob ihres Darstellungsgehaltes, nicht primär um ihrer selbst willen, gesetzt wird. Sobald die primäre Absicht wie bei Wundern und Exorzismen in der Handlung selbst liegt, sollte man nicht im strengen Sinn von 'Symbolhandlungen' sprechen."

[17] "DSJ," 34.

[18] "DSJ," 35.

[19] "DSJ," 35: "Der Täufer war in gewisser Weise schon eine eschatologische Heilsgestalt (vgl. nur Lk 1,13-17; 1,76-79), wenn er von Gott her als Herold auftrat, aufrufend zu einer Taufe der Umkehr 'auf Sündenvergebung hin' (Lk 3.2f.). Auf Geheiß Gottes setzt er in einem Zeichen zusprechend und versprechend in Szene, was die Propheten für die letzte Zeit verheißen hatten: 'Dann sprenge ich über euch reines Wasser, damit ihr gereinigt werdet' (Ez 36,25; vgl. Zach 13,1). Dabei muß man dieses In-Szene-Setzen als wirksamen Zuspruch der Vergebung Gottes verstehen und nicht nur als eine leere Zeichenhandlung. Der Täufer, durchaus 'mehr als ein Prophet' (Lk 7,26), nimmt die Sündenabwaschung im Auftrag Gottes vor; er spricht sie autoritativ und wirksam zu, wenn freilich auch noch bedingt: nämlich unter der Bedingung, daß es zu 'Früchten der Umkehr' kommt (vgl. Lk 3,7ff par)."

[20] H. Schürmann, *Das Lukasevangelium. Erster Teil. Kommentar zu Kap. 1:1-9:50.* [Hereafter *Lukas*.]

he draws attention to the striking "intentional parallels"[21] with Jeremiah: called from the very beginning of his existence,[22] the prophet is sent by God[23] to undertake a specific function in a particular time and place.[24] Like many of the Old Testament prophets, John responds to God's command by dramatizing his message. Schürmann freely acknowledges that John's baptism is a prophetic act and, as such, must be willed by God.[25]

John's unrepeatable[26] public washing and its association with the forgiveness of sins, without analogy in the then contemporary proselyte baptisms or purification rites,[27] is rooted in his prophetic consciousness. According to Schürmann, the Baptist takes up what previous generations of prophets had foretold about the "ablution" from sin and the "effusion" of the Spirit as end-time realities and in his lustral act, both "symbolically" and "effectively," represents their "final actualization"[28]: "the Baptist, as eschatological prophet acting on God's command, takes up and fulfils the Old Testament prophecy of the eschatological ablution from sin in a prophetic sign."[29]

Yet, John the Baptist is "more than a prophet." This, Schürmann explains, is emphasized by the historical introduction to John's ministry as presented in the Gospel of Luke (1:1-2a). While the ministry of Jeremiah is synchronized with three kings of Judah (Jer 1:2-3), John's activity is set on a broader stage, with a cast that includes emperor, governor and religious leaders (Luke 3:1-2).[30] This underlines the universal importance of the Christ

---

[21] *Lukas*, 152.

[22] Jer 1:5; Luke 1:13-17, 66, 76-79, 80.

[23] Jer 1:4; Luke 3:3.

[24] Jer 1:2-3; Luke 3:1-2.

[25] *Lukas*, 156: "Daß in der Taufe etwas von Gott her geschieht, machen nicht nur Sendung und die auftragsgemäße Verkündigung des Täufers deutlich, das deutet sich auch in dem beim Taufvorgang überraschend aktiven Handeln des Täufers an."

[26] *Lukas*, 158.

[27] See Chapter 3, section 1.2.

[28] *Lukas*, 157; 158.

[29] *Lukas*, 156-157: "Wenn wir die Zeichensprache dieser Handlung abzuhören versuchen, werden wir zunächst an die prophezeite eschatologische 'Besprengung', 'Abwaschung' denken, die hier zeichenhaft - und auch wohl irgendwie wirksam - in Szene gesetzt wird und diese zuspricht. So verstanden, nimmt der Täufer als der eschatologische Prophet im Auftrage Gottes in einem prophetischen Zeichen die alt. Prophetie von der eschatologischen Sündenabwaschung auf."

[30] *Lukas*, 152: "Wenn hier die *Anadeixis* des Täufers so gewichtig in weltweiten Rahmen gestellt ist, wird es um mehr gehen als um die Berufung eines Propheten (vgl. 7:26f): Es wird ja der *angelos mou pro prosopou sou* gesandt (Mal 3:1), d.h. der Rahmen ist eigentlich der *archē* (3:23; 4:21) zugeordnet, auf die

event heralded by the Precursor. While Schürmann views John within the time of promise,[31] as "pre-kerygma,"[32] he recognizes that his preaching is already an eschatological announcement.[33] His message is closely related to the time of fulfilment: already the scene is set for the arrival of the Messiah and the imminent unfolding of his saving work.[34] Indeed, many of the initial historical and topographical details which introduce John feature shortly afterwards in the life and death of Jesus.[35] The Lucan Baptist is presented as something of a salvific figure.[36] His washing, Schürmann claims, is "an effective sharing in the forgiveness of God."[37] Certainly it is difficult to imagine a non-efficacious symbolic act in the Old Testament sense.[38] But what, then, is the effect of this action which is "not just an empty symbolic action"? This consideration prompts Schürmann to identify two aspects which differentiate the baptism of John and the symbolic actions of Jesus from the Old Testament prophetic acts.

1.2 *Effecting the Future*

The first dissimilarity touches the relationship between the act and the future which it inaugurates. In the prophetic acts performed by John the Baptist and by Jesus

> the future is not prophesied in a dramatic way, but already the future prophesied in the Old Testament is indicated as fulfilled and presented effectively. The baptismal action of John is not a prophetic parabolic action, rather it actualizes the Old Testament prophecy. While the Old Testament symbolic actions are marked with the time of the promise (insofar as they had a real relationship to the *eschaton* itself), the baptismal action of

Johannes hinwies und die mit dem Kommen Jesu (3:16) anhob, so daß für dieses nachher kein Datum mehr genannt zu werden braucht."

[31] *Lukas*, 185.

[32] Schürmann entitles his commentary on Luke 3:1-20 "Das 'Vor-Kerygma' des Täufers" (*Lukas*, 148-187).

[33] *Lukas*, 179.

[34] Schürmann rejects the tripartite division of salvation history as proposed by H. Conzelman, *Die Mitte der Zeit*. See F. Ó Fearghail, *The Introduction to Luke-Acts*, 117-124; D. Hill, *New Testament Prophecy*, 43.

[35] *Lukas*, 151-152.

[36] *Lukas*, 178-179.

[37] *Lukas*, 159: "Die Taufe des Johannes wird ursprünglich freilich als wirksame göttliche Zusage der Sündenvergebung im Gericht verstanden worden sein, wobei man solche verbindliche - wenn auch bedingte - Zusage noch undifferenziert selbst 'Sündenvergebung' nennen mag."

[38] *Lukas*, 159: "Eine wirkungslose Symbolhandlung wäre atl. kaum vorstellbar."

> John is stamped from within with the time of fulfilment. It is better therefore to speak not of a prophetic symbolic action but of an "eschatological sign of fulfilment."[39]

In their dramatization, Old Testament prophetic acts symbolically anticipate the imminent intervention of God. The baptism of John, however, proclaims that the future announced by Ezekiel, Zechariah and the prophets is both fulfilled and effective. The rite of John performed in the Jordan does not ultimately point to some upcoming forgiveness of sins; rather, the one who submits to the rite in a spirit of repentance is saved from the approaching judgement.[40] While the prophetic acts of the old covenant looked forward to the proximate intervention of God, either immediate or eschatological, they belong to the "time of promise." By contrast, the activity of John, particularly the baptism of Jesus, introduces the irruption of the end-time and, as such, is "marked from within by the time of fulfilment."[41] This is why Schürmann introduces the term "eschatological sign of fulfilment."

Schürmann locates the second difference in the link between sign and effect:

> In the baptismal action of John, the efficaciousness does not follow the symbolism, rather, the eschatological gift is incorporated within the symbolic form itself. There appears to be a difference here with the Hellenistic understanding of signs which is also a characteristic of the sacramental theory of scholastic theology. Here the basic statement *sacramenta efficiunt quod significant* is valid — the effect follows the sign. In the case of the "eschatological signs of fulfilment" of the Johannine baptism the direction of movement is fundamental

---

[39] "DSJ," 35: "... ist nicht in drastischer Weise Zukunft prophezeit, sondern bereits alttestamentlich prophezeite Zukunft als nunmehr erfüllt angezeigt und wirksam angeboten. Die Taufhandlung des Johannes ist keine prophetische Gleichnishandlung; vielmehr aktualisiert sie die alttestamentliche Prophetie. Während die alttestamentlichen Symbolhandlungen von der Verheißungszeit her geprägt waren (soweit sie überhaupt einen echten Bezug zum Eschaton schlechthin hatten), ist die Taufhandlung des Johannes innerlich von der Erfüllungszeit her geprägt. Man redet daher besser nicht von einer 'prophetischen Symbolhandlung', sondern von einem '*eschatologischen Erfüllungszeichen*'."

[40] J.D.G. Dunn, *Baptism in the Holy Spirit*, 16, contends that "John's baptism is a prophetic symbol not of present forgiveness, but of the future Spirit-and-fire baptism." This rests on an impoverished understanding of prophetic act. See S. Légasse, *Naissance du baptême*, 43 n. 61.

[41] Is this eschatological stamp traceable to John the Baptist or does it derive from the subsequent interpretation of the evangelists? J.P. Meier, *A Marginal Jew*, II, 52, argues that "the precise nature of John's baptism stems from John's own eschatological vision and message."

> and is in the first instance the opposite. God grants eschatological salvation, which is shared in word and incorporated in a symbolic action — the sign follows the effect. In God's name, the Baptist guarantees the eschatological forgiveness which is then announced in the effusion with water.[42]

Here Schürmann claims that the Old Testament prophetic acts follow the *sign→effect* scheme: it is because Jeremiah shatters the jar that the Lord is going to destroy Jerusalem. Regarding the water rite of John, however, Schürmann notes that this eschatological sign of fulfilment does not effect the forgiveness of sins which it proclaims: it is the Father who "guarantees" the eschatological salvation; the Baptist "represents" this in the pouring of water. While it is valid to argue with Schürmann that here the primary direction is the reverse *effect→sign* scheme, a word of caution must be sounded. The analysis of the previous chapter insists that the converse is also true: because the Lord had decided to reject Jerusalem, Jeremiah breaks the jar.[43] A one-sided, either-or situation does not adequately represent the inter-dependence between the action of the prophet and the intervention of God. If the origin of John's eschatological sign of fulfilment is to be found in the Old Testament prophetic acts, both aspects must be held together: because John baptizes, God forgives the sins of those who undergo the rite in a spirit of repentance; because God guarantees the gift of eschatological forgiveness, the Baptist effectively performs the symbolic washing which represents it. However, Schürmann suggests, this second aspect alone comes to the fore in John's rite.

According to Schürmann, then, John's baptism is not adequately explained in terms of the prophetic acts of the old dispensation. Rather, this episode represents an eschatological sign of fulfilment with four differentiating characteristics: (i) The basic

---

42 "DSJ," 35-36: "Bei der Taufhandlung des Johannes folgt die Effektivität nicht der Zeichenhaftigkeit; vielmehr verleiblicht sich die eschatologische Gabe in die Zeichengestalt hinein. Hier scheint ein Unterschied zum hellenistischen Zeichenverständnis vorzuliegen, das auch die Sakramentenlehre der Schultheologie prägt: Hier gilt der Grundsatz: sacramenta efficiunt quod significant - die Wirkung folgt der Bezeichnung. Bei dem 'eschatologischen Erfüllungszeichen' der Johannestaufe scheint die Bewegungsrichtung grundlegend und zunächst umgekehrt zu sein: Gott gewährt das eschatologische Heil, das sich im Wort zuspricht und in eine Zeichenhandlung hinein verleiblicht - *die Bezeichnung folgt der Wirkung*. Der Täufer gewährt im Namen Gottes die eschatologische Sündenvergebung, was sich in der Übergießung mit Wasser dann anzeigt."

43 S. Amsler, *Les actes*, 47. See Chapter 3, section 3.1.2.

orientation of the action is eschatological; (ii) The primary meaning of the washing lies beyond the deed itself; (iii) The lustral rite, "marked from within by the time of fulfilment," effectively actualizes the Old Testament prophecy; (iv) In contrast with the prophetic acts recorded in the Hebrew scriptures, the fundamental relationship between sign and gift, between the water rite and the forgiveness of sins, is reversed so that, pre-eminently, the sign follows the gift.

2. **From Jordan to Calvary**

Schürmann's primary interest is to investigate the *ipsissima gesta Jesu* in the upper room: all new covenant prophetic acts, beginning with the Baptism of John, converge and find meaning in the mensal activity of the leave-taking Lord. In this section, the exegete's analysis of the symbolic actions of Jesus before and during the Last Supper is outlined.

2.1 *New Testament Signs*

Despite certain historical reservations, Schürmann tentatively chooses from the prophetic actions of Jesus seven eschatological signs of fulfilment[44] which indicate the Nazarene's "conscious will" for symbolism.[45] In (1) gathering a group of disciples which represents all facets of then contemporary Palestinian Judaism — "from tax-collectors and Hellenistic Galileans to strict Pharisees and Zealots"[46] — Jesus sets up a sign for Israel. Here is a group which trusts in the eschatological promise of Jesus "in an exemplary way." Similarly, Schürmann notes, Jesus (2) symbolically constitutes the apostles as a "radical promise to Israel that the prophetic-apocalyptic expectation of the end-time restoration of the twelve tribes of Israel should now become a reality."[47] By (3) accepting invitations to meals with tax-collectors and sinners, Jesus establishes symbols of the eschatological salvation which is offered to the social and religious outcasts with whom he shares table.[48] So too, the (4) feeding of the multitude in the wilderness may be a "symbolic eschatological meal occasion of

---

[44] "DSJ," 37-40.
[45] "DSJ," 37.
[46] "DSJ," 37.
[47] "DSJ," 37.
[48] "DSJ," 37.

Jesus."[49] In these four actions the primary intention lies behind the gesture itself, and both the eschatological and the symbolic aspects are clearly discernible.[50] These characteristics, Schürmann continues, become more pronounced when the action is performed under the threat of growing opposition or of possible failure. "In the face of threatening catastrophe the promise and anticipation of the *eschaton* in symbolic actions become clearer and more emphatic. Jesus' symbolic actions appear to have something to do with his forthcoming death...."[51] This "anticipation of the eschaton" is particularly pronounced in the three remaining eschatological signs of fulfilment: (5) the sending out of the disciples; (6) the ascent to Jerusalem; and (7) the cleansing of the Temple.[52]

2.2. *The Death of Jesus*

In his work *Jesu ureigener Tod* Schürmann seeks to overcome the historical skepticism of R. Bultmann and to investigate the attitude of Jesus as he approached his death.[53] As a working hypothesis, he respects the "critical sorting principle"[54] of E.

---

49 "DSJ," 38.

50 D.E. Aune, *Prophecy in Early Christianity*, 162, remarks that "If we insist that in order to qualify as prophetic acts the actions of Jesus must incorporate a predictive element within them,..., then the feeding of the multitude, the entrance into Jerusalem, the sending of the Twelve, the selection of the Twelve, the giving of symbolic names to the disciples, and the miracle of walking on water cannot be regarded as prophetic symbolic actions." Schürmann, however, insists that, since the *eschaton* is heralded or predicted in these four actions, they should be considered as prophetic acts.

51 "DSJ," 38-39: "Die Verheißung und Antizipation des Eschatons in zeichenhaften Handlungen wird im Angesicht der drohenden Katastrophe immer deutlicher und emphatischer: Jesu Zeichenhandlungen scheinen etwas mit seinem vorausgeschehenen Tod zu tun zu haben...."

52 In outlining Schürmann's presentation of Jesus' awareness of the salvific import of his death, W. Becker, *The Historical Jesus in the Face of His Death*, 131-132, remarks that "Towards the end of his career, then, as Jesus gave up hope of an imminent, powerful intervention of the kingdom, his message came to be characterized by dramatic signs, such as the entry into Jerusalem, his action in the Temple, and his Last Supper." According to Schürmann, however, these "dramatic signs" are not confined to the latter part of Jesus' ministry; they do, however, become clearer and more emphatic as his death approaches.

53 See J.P. Galvin, "Jesus' approach to Death: An Examination of Some Recent Studies" *TS* 41 (1980) 713-744; "The Death of Jesus in Contemporary Theology," *Horizons* 13 (1986) 239-252.

54 *JuT*, 20-21: "Einigermaßen sicheren Boden haben wir nur in einem einzigen Fall unter den Füßen, wenn nämlich Tradition aus irgendwelchen Gründen weder aus dem Judentum abgeleitet noch der Urchristenheit zugeschrieben werden kann."

Käsemann and brackets any controversial sayings of Jesus about his own fate. Instead, he focuses on the entire personality of Jesus, with special emphasis on the insight gained from an analysis of the questions he posed to his disciples.[55]

From the beginning of his public ministry "Jesus could, and really should, seriously count on the possibility of a violent death."[56] He had taken up the announcement of the Baptist concerning the eschatological judgement, and so could reasonably expect to be met with comparable opposition. His kingdom message, and his blatant solidarity with sinners, provoked Romans, Sadducees and Pharisees alike. Consequently, Schürmann concludes, "Jesus could not have lived, worked and preached without the perspective of an eventual violent death before his eyes; this is one point which is widely accepted by contemporary research."[57]

While R. Bultmann claims that Jesus "broke down"[58] in the face of death, Schürmann counters that not only did he accept the eventuality of a violent end but his entire behaviour was substantially influenced by its approach:

> One can say that, beyond a vague calculation on the eventuality of a violent death, the behaviour of Jesus is driven by the awareness of this death, even more so as it approached. The behaviour of Jesus, when observable, confirms the conclusion ... that he had an inner relationship with the possibility of martyrdom. Furthermore, his behaviour allows the recognition of his "attitude" in facing this destiny; it is not possible to perceive only a passive submission there.[59]

In this context Schürmann presents the three remaining symbolic actions. The (5) desperate mission to "every town and place" (Luke 10:1) had little hope of success. Yet, Jesus sends the disciples out on the great final missionary onslaught before the end-time "not as a dreamer who had lost touch with reality,"[60] but

---

[55] *JuT,* 26.
[56] *JuT,* 33.
[57] *JuT,* 33.
[58] Bultmann's own word is "zusammengebrochen" (*JuT,* 33).
[59] *JuT,* 38: "Man wird sagen dürfen, daß über ein vages Rechnen mit der Möglichkeit hinaus Jesu Verhalten - je mehr es dem Ende zuging - von diesem Todeswissen her bestimmt war. Das erkennbare Verhalten Jesu bestätigt den obigen Schluß, den wir aus den Forderungen Jesu glaubten ziehen zu dürfen: Jesus hatte ein inneres Verhältnis zur Möglichkeit des Märtyrertodes. Jesu Verhalten läßt darüber hinaus seine 'Haltung' in diesem Geschick erkennen, die nicht nur als passive Fügsamkeit verstanden werden kann."
[60] *JuT,* 38.

as one who attempts to set up a symbolic event whereby Israel, through this apparently fool-hardy action, is placed before the eschatological decision.[61] Despite the obvious risks involved, Jesus (6) goes up to Jerusalem to provoke a final resolution. This ascent, Schürmann suggests, may well be "an eschatological symbolic action in the face of the awaiting catastrophe."[62] As he enters the Holy City, Jesus is welcomed with a "dangerous messianic ovation" which is echoed in the title "King of the Jews" as he hung on the Cross.[63] While the precise meaning of the (7) cleansing of the Temple is difficult to establish, it certainly gave the enemies of Jesus the opportunity to seize him. This is not the action of a prophet intent on cultic cleanliness, nor is it the project of a political Zealot. Rather, Schürmann contends, this deliberately provocative episode is to be viewed in line both with Jesus' announcement that the fulfilment of the eschatological hope is at hand and with his growing acceptance of the possibility of a violent death.[64]

When the sovereignty and the salvific will of God are taken seriously, Schürmann maintains that it is possible to reconcile the death of Jesus with his mission of proclaiming the kingdom.[65] This is obvious, he suggests, from the Master's exemplary attitude of service, "the fundamental element of Jesus' demands ... which is truly his own."[66] But does this example, together with its concomitant invitation to love one's neighbour as oneself (Mark 9:35 par.), persist in the face of the impending martyr-death of Jesus? "If it is illuminated by the totality of Jesus' activity," Schürmann responds, it is not unreasonable to accept that it does.[67]

---

[61] "DSJ," 39.

[62] "DSJ," 39: "... eine eschatologische Zeichenhandlung angesichts der bevorstehenden Katastrophe."

[63] "DSJ," 39.

[64] *JuT,* 40; "DSJ," 39. See E.P. Sanders, *Jesus and Judaism,* 61-76; C. Evans, "Jesus' Action in the Temple: Cleansing or Portrait of Destruction?," *CBQ* 51 (1989) 237-270. D. Seedley, "Jesus' Temple Act," *CBQ* 55 (1993) 263-283, understands the act as a literary creation by Mark.

[65] For Schürmann's approach to the relationship between the eschatological and the theological dimensions of Jesus' preaching, see "Das hermeneutische Hauptproblem der Verkündigung Jesu" in *Gott in Welt,* 579-607.

[66] *JuT,* 48.

[67] *JuT,* 48.

2.3 *The Pro-existence of Jesus*

At the heart of this issue lies what Schürmann terms, the "pro-existence"[68] of Jesus. This is best exemplified by the radical saying of Luke 6:27: "But I say to you who hear, love your enemies, do good to those who hate you, bless those who curse you, pray for those who abuse you." While most form-critical studies of this and the verses which follow would undoubtedly attribute them to the early Christian community, Schürmann insists that they capture the fundamental attitude of the Servant-Lord.[69] Consequently, the suggestion that Jesus suffered moral collapse at the moment of his death must give way to the supposition that he approached his passion as the means of being faithful to his stance of pro-existence.[70] Nor is this pro-existent stance reserved for enemies; it extends scandalously to embrace sinners. Therefore, in response to the question "Did Jesus see his death as a possible source of salvation?" Schürmann concludes that

> Jesus' willingness to serve, his call to charity, his commandment to love one's enemies, and especially the love which he showed for sinners: all this, together with the offer of salvation which he made until the end, lead to a positive response to this question. Moreover, there is a series of convergent indices which lead to the conjecture that Jesus faced and understood his own death as an offering of love, intercession, benediction and salvation. That this fundamental attitude of pro-existence was subsequently presented in terms of the theological ideas of vicarious representation and expiation for sinners or of any other category is, in the final analysis, less important. If Jesus did not apply the title "servant of God" or any other theological theory of expiation to himself, that does not mean that he had no awareness of being the servant of God, surrendering himself and suffering for the multitude, because all his life is marked by this characteristic.[71]

---

[68] This translates the German term "Proexistenz" which generally means "existing for others." See "Der proexistente Christus - die Mitte des Glaubens von morgen?," in *JuT,* 121-155; "'Pro-Existenz' als christologischer Grundbegriff," in *Jesus. Gestalt und Geheimnis*, 286-315. See also M. Denken, "Pour une christologie de la pro-existence," *RSR* 82 (1988) 265-290.

[69] In fact, Scürmann notes, *JuT,* 48: "Es ist nicht notwendig, den Anteil der Gemeinde an dieser Tradition hier im einzelnen auszusondern; es bleibt eine grundlegende Forderung Jesu."

[70] *JuT,* 49.

[71] *JuT,* 50-51: "Jesu Dienstwille und Liebesforderung, vor allem seine Forderung der Feindesliebe und speziell seine Sünderliebe, verbunden mit seinem Heilsangebot bis in die letzte Stunde, führen an eine positive Beantwortung unserer

Clearly, then, behind a web composed of various theological titles, the gospels portray Jesus as one whose fundamental life-orientation is *existence for-others*. Even as he generates opposition and conflict, and recognizes the likelihood of a violent death, he is depicted as persisting in the sure hope that, despite apparent failure, the eschatological salvation which he proclaimed would be advanced. While there is no evidence that Jesus ever spoke publicly about his imminent death or its salvific import, Schürmann is convinced that he would have broached the subject within the restricted circle of his disciples.[72] With this tenet in mind, Schürmann analyses the words and actions of Jesus at the Last Supper as radical expressions of his self-giving attitude.

2.4 *The Table-actions of Jesus*

Schürmann's attempt to establish a link between the Last Supper and the Christian eucharist extends back to the 1950's when he published a series of articles which were summarized in a trilogy based on Luke's supper account.[73] While J. Jeremias[74] had previously argued that the Markan-Matthean version, with its discernible semitic traces, represented the most primitive tradition, Schürmann champions the priority of the Lucan-Pauline account.[75] Schürmann is convinced by the evidence which suggests that the Passover meal provided the original *Sitz-im-Leben* of the Last Supper. His own research concludes that it is more prudently understood as a farewell meal.[76]

Frage heran, mehr noch: sie konvergieren zu der Vermutung, daß Jesus seinen eigenen Tod liebend, fürbittend, segnend und heilseffizient durchgestanden und verstanden hat. Ob man eine derartige proexistente Grundhaltung dann durch den theologischen Stellvertretungs- und Sühnegedanken oder wie immer sonst artikuliert, ist letzlich nicht so wichtig. Wenn Jesus weder den Titel 'Gottesknecht' noch eine theologische Sühnetheorie auf sich selbst angewendet hat, dann besagt das nicht, daß er sich nicht als den für die Vielen dienenden und leidenden Gottesknecht gewußt hätte, weil sein ganzes Leben eben diesen Charakter gehabt hat."

[72] *JuT,* 54-56.

[73] H. Schürmann, *Eine quellenkritische Untersuchung des lukanischen Abendmahlsberichtes Lk. 22:7-38*, I-II-III.

[74] J. Jeremias, *The Eucharistic Words of Jesus*, 138-203. [Originally published as *Das Abendmahlsworte Jesu.*]

[75] A succinct summary of Schürmann's position is found in J. Kodell, *The Eucharist in the New Testament*, 26-31. The opposing case is defended by R. Pesch, "The Last Supper and Jesus' Understanding of His Death," *BiBh* 3 (1977) 58-75, and by B. Smith, "The More Original Form of the Words of Institution," *ZNW* 83 (1992) 166-186.

[76] *JuT,* 85.

Because the words accompanying the eucharistic gestures vary in all four accounts, Schürmann approaches them by a road less travelled, that is, by examining the *ipsissima facta Jesu*. The double action with the bread and the wine is undoubtedly of Palestinian origin, involving the juxtaposition of two meal rites. At the beginning of a Jewish festive meal

> [the host], in the name of the assembly, would pronounce over the bread, a prayer of praise to which all would respond "Amen." Then, he broke a little piece of the bread for each participant and had it distributed. Already in the Jewish world this "breaking of bread" was a gesture of great importance, one which was carried out according to a fixed, stylized ritual.[77]

Likewise, the second action, the blessing of the cup, can be explained only in the light of Palestinian banqueting mores. In this context Schürmann notes that

> *towards the end* of the meal, the seated *pater familias* was presented with a cup which he took in his right hand; he held it up, a hand's breath above the table, and pronounced the prayer of thanks to which all responded "Amen." Then, according to the custom, he who had said the prayer of blessing lifted the goblet to his lips; this was a sign inviting the other participants to drink from their own cups.[78]

This peculiar fusion of two previously separated acts can, Schürmann argues, find its inspiration only in the unique actions of Jesus at the Last Supper:

> The eucharistic double action at the end of the primitive Christian "Lord's Supper" ... had its origin in the action performed by Jesus on the occasion of his Last Supper: in the "breaking of bread" which opened the meal and the "eucharist" over the cup which closed it, two rites which after

---

[77] *JuT,* 72: "Dann sprach er darüber im Namen aller einen Lobspruch, den alle mit 'Amen' beantworteten. Danach brach er für jeden Mahlteilnehmer ein Stückchen Brot ab und teilte aus. Schon im jüdischen Raum war dieses 'Brotbrechen' ein bedeutsames Tun in verfestigter, stilisierter Form."

[78] *JuT,* 72-73: "[Beim jüdischen Gastmahl] nahm *gegen Ende* des Mahles der Hausvater einen ihm kredenzten Weinbecher sitzend in die Rechte, hielt ihn eine Hand breit über den Tisch und sprach darüber für alle das Tischdankgebet, das alle mit "Amen" beantworteten. Nach der üblichen Sitte trank dann der Sprecher des Tischgebetes aus seinem Becher, was dann für die Tischgenossen das Zeichen abgab, aus ihrem eigenen Becher zu trinken."

> Easter were brought together are imitated because of their significance.[79]

The "significance," Schürmann contends, lies in "two departures from what was customary in what Jesus did."[80] Firstly, instead of the usual practice of individual participants drinking from their own cups, Jesus passed his goblet to all. Given the firmly established rubric, this departure from the norm must, like the symbolic acts of the prophets of Israel, have surprised the onlookers, and arrested their attention. Secondly, the presentation of the eucharistic elements is subsequently, as in the case of Old Testament symbolic actions, accompanied by words of explanation. These gestures already had a particular significance within their cultural context. By adding a commentary to them, Jesus takes pains to clarify the new meaning which they now assume.

The passing of the one cup finds a parallel in the custom whereby the father of the family could "send his cup to a guest at the meal who was to be specially honoured."[81] By proffering the bread and wine to his disciples, Jesus is extending or sharing a blessing with them.[82] But what exactly is the nature of this gift? Given the overall thrust of Jesus' preaching, Schürmann suggests "that also by offering the bread and the cup, Jesus wished to announce the promise of eschatological salvation or to give it already under the form of a promise."[83]

Attributing an eschatological significance to Jesus' actions is supported, Schürmann notes, by the reference to the "new covenant"[84] in all the scriptural accounts. Given the context of the farewell meal, he adds that "by presenting (the bread and) the cup, Jesus refers not only to the eschatological salvation but also to his

---

[79] H. Schürmann, "Jesus' Words in the Light of His Actions at the Last Supper," *Conc* 4/10 (1968) 63. [Hereafter "Jesus' Words."]

[80] "Jesus' Words," 63.

[81] "Jesus' Words," 63.

[82] A.-L. Descamps, "Cénacle et Calvaire: Les vues de H. Schürmann," *RTL* 10 (1979) 343: "Il est question d'un geste de *don*. La louange prononcée était probablement porteuse de bénédiction, et le pain distribué a pu être considéré comme porteur d'une certaine vertu salvifique; celui qui reçoit un fragment de pain reçoit donc l'*effet* de la prière de bénédiction, et n'en est pas réduit à participer simplement à la prière même."

[83] *JuT,* 84: "… daß auch Jesu Brot- und Becherdarbietung das eschatologische Heil verheißend anzeigen oder zusprechend geben wollte."

[84] *JuT,* 84.

imminent death."[85] Indeed, Schürmann continues, despite the total failure of his preaching and activity, Jesus chooses the moment when he faces death in a spirit of radical pro-existence to perform a sign promising the gift of eschatological salvation. Thus, the subsequent words of explanation, with their references to the expiatory fate of a martyr (Luke 22:22a) or to the vicarious death of the suffering servant (Luke 22:19; Mark 10:45), are already implied in this final symbolic action of Jesus.

The table actions of Jesus stand firmly in the tradition of the Old Testament prophetic acts as they have been outlined by Samuel Amsler. Comprising a surprising departure from the normal Jewish meal customs, the gestures and their subsequent explanation radically communicate the prefigured sufferings of Jesus as the act by which the Father offers definitive salvation to all. In their analogical structure, the breaking of the bread and the pouring of the wine proleptically prefigure the self-giving of Jesus on the Cross.[86] In this way, Holy Thursday and Good Friday can be viewed as a single event in the redemptive activity of the pro-existent Lord: because Jesus proffers the broken bread and the outpoured wine as saving food and drink the *via crucis* has already begun; because the *being-for-others* is to be consummated in the bloody immolation on Golgatha, the bloodless sacrifice in the Upper Room is truly an offer of eschatological salvation.

Yet, Schürmann's analysis goes further. In the eucharistic gestures Jesus enacts an eschatological sign of fulfilment which points beyond the present to the end-time (Luke 22:16.18). The table-actions take on a symbolic meaning greater than the deeds themselves. Confronted by his approaching death, and faced with the evaporation of any hope for the conversion of Israel, Jesus "renews the eschatological promise and incarnates it in the gestures of presentation which express his existence-for-others."[87]

---

[85] *JuT,* 85: "... daß Jesus die Darreichung (des Brotes und) des Bechers in Beziehung gebracht hat nicht nur mit dem eschatologischen Heil, sondern auch mit seinem bevorstehenden Tod."

[86] W.D. Stacey, "The Lord's Supper as Prophetic Drama," 89, sums up the similarities between an Old Testament prophetic act and the events of the Last Supper as follows: "We have in the upper room, an acknowledged prophetic figure, a movement of intense crisis, a commonplace action, a sense of divine compulsion, the involvement of other people, a material substance, an obvious mimetic element, a verbal formula which deepens rather than explains. Taken together these factors show that the disciples could not have avoided the conclusion that they were involved in a prophetic dramatic action and this would have effected their understanding of what was going on."

[87] *JuT*, 94.

The future prophesied in such a dramatic way is already presented as fulfilled and effective.[88] The superiority of the signs of Jesus over the symbolic acts of the Hebrew prophets lies primarily in the ability of the former to actualize the future which they announce. Schürmann regards this "more" as justifying the ecclesial repetition of the prophetic actions of Jesus in the sacraments of baptism and eucharist.[89] Further, Schürmann notes that, in contrast to the Greek conception of sacrament, the primary direction of the symbolism is reversed.

> Jesus' distribution of bread and wine signify something by doing and giving something. The sign is in the gift; the gift is not the effect of the sign. The effected gift signifies something; the sign does not primarily effect something. The disclosure of such symbolism does not exclude a realist conception of the Eucharist; on the contrary it presupposes it. The words which accompany the distribution are intended to signify and set forth predictively what kind of nourishment is actually being given with the bread and wine which in so unusual a way is distributed to all. Bread and wine are certainly not distributed as food and drink in order to represent Jesus' death as salvific in a purely symbolic manner (=*sacramentum tantum*), but because they are salvific gifts. And the explanatory words are not merely intended to identify what is proffered with "body" and "blood" (=*sacramentum et res*) but, in different ways, are emphatically concerned to characterize them as saving gift (=*res sacramenti*).[90]

Although the post-paschal celebration of the Christian eucharist is guaranteed by the presence of the risen Lord, Schürmann insists that, while of an inferior quality, the efficacious character of Jesus' actions at the Last Supper cannot be denied.[91]

In the prophetic acts of Jesus the eschatological orientation is emblematic. As his death draws closer "the promise and anticipation of the eschaton in symbolic actions become clearer and more emphatic."[92] These new covenant signs culminate in the

---

[88] "Jesus' Words," 65: "... by his double action at the Last Supper, Jesus would have effectively proffered eschatological salvation as the fruit of his death, and by so doing also represented it symbolically."

[89] *JuT,* 92: "In diesem 'Mehr' scheint auch die Möglichkeit einer applizierenden Wiederholbarkeit begründet zu liegen, wie sie der Taufe und Jesu Abendmahlshandlung - im Unterschied zur prophetischen *ôt* - von Anfang an eignete."

[90] "Jesus' Words," 65.

[91] *JuT,* 93.

[92] "DSJ," 38.

gesture enacted by means of the eucharistic elements at the Last Supper. By proffering the gifts of bread and wine, Jesus gives his companions a share in his eschatological victory over sin and death. Here, the pro-existent attitude of Jesus, his constant awareness of being the suffering servant of God on behalf of the multitude, finds its definitive expression. Since all the signs of eschatological fulfilment performed by Jesus "appear to have something to do with his forthcoming death."[93] they reveal much of their significance only when viewed retrospectively through the prism of Calvary. This, then, is the purpose of the next section which applies the insights gleaned from Schürmann's treatment of the Last Supper and death of Christ to his baptism. This incipient symbolic action reveals the Son and his proclamation of the kingdom motivated by pro-existence. This water rite ultimately seeks completion in the baptism of blood on the Cross.

3. **From Calvary to Jordan**

According to Schürmann, the baptism of Jesus is situated by Luke within the unit 3:21 - 4:44.[94] While the "beginning" took place after the Precursor's announcement of baptism, Schürmann recognizes that, for the third evangelist, *ἀρχή* is a kerygmatic term which designates the inauguration of the kingdom with the preaching of Jesus in the synagogue at Nazareth (4:16-30). Yet, Schürmann stresses that

> the "today" (4:21) of the "time of fulfilment" (16:16) has its foundation in two events which are strictly linked with each other: a) the notification of Jesus as "Son" (and anointed by the Spirit)(3:21-22, taken together with 3:23-38) and b) the testing [of his true identity] in the temptation (4:1-13).[95]

Note that Schürmann views the baptism account as primarily an announcement of the sonship of Jesus; the messianic anointing is

---

[93] "DSJ," 39.

[94] This section (*Lukas*, 187-259) is entitled "Der Beginn der Basileiaverkündigung Jesu."

[95] *Lukas*, 188: "... die Begründung dieses 'Heute' der messianischen Heils- und Erfüllungszeit, indem er zwei (eng zusammengehörende) Geschehnisse voranstellt: a) die Kenntlichmachung Jesu als 'Sohn' (und seine Geistalbung - 3:21-22) (ergänzt um 3:23-38) und b) seine Bewährung in der Versuchung (4:1-13)." See also "Jesu Aufbruch zum Jordan - Beginn der ureigenen Basileia-Verkündigung Jesu," in *Jesus - Gestalt und Geheimnis*, 31-44.

secondary.[96] This filial identity is subsequently put to the test in the temptation story.

3.1 *The Baptism of Jesus*

In his "succinct"[97] baptismal account, Luke deliberately underlines the objectivity of the revelatory event: the heavens opened and the Holy Spirit descended in an "externally visible form"[98]; the voice of the Father was heard by all the onlookers. But what, according to Schürmann, is the meaning which underlines this scene?

> The text, in its sobriety, does not say that the Holy Spirit which descended had an effect in or on Jesus: it is enough to say that it comes down (and "remains") on Jesus to make the believer understand who Jesus is. Here it is neither a question of endowment with a pneumatic power nor of a new creation which would bring about the conditions for the messianic era. The verb "descend," the definite article and, particularly, the figure of the dove, evoke the notion of a personal being whose descent seems primarily to demonstrate rather than to effect something. This divine demonstration affirms: You are the one who was announced in 3:16 and who will now be baptizing with the Holy Spirit. The Spirit who descends indicates the One who will be the baptizer in the Spirit. As the "Son of God" — through the power of the Spirit from his mother's womb (1:35) — Jesus now needs only a revelation of his identity.[99]

---

[96] *Lukas*, 196: "Nach unserer Analyse des Taufberichtes müßte die ihn prägende Sohnes-Christologie das Motiv der Geistsalbung an sich gezogen haben; nicht aber erklärt sich umgekehrt die Sohnes-Christologie aus jedem Motiv."

[97] This is Dibelius' description (*Lukas*, 189).

[98] *Lukas*, 190.

[99] *Lukas*, 191-192: "Der schweigsame Text sagt aber nicht, daß der herabgekommene Geist in oder an Jesus etwas bewirkt habe; es genügt das Faktum der Herabkunft (und sein 'Verbleiben auf' Jesus, weil dieses schon dem Glaubenden zur Genüge sagt, wer Jesus ist. Nicht eine Begabung mit pneumatischer Kraft wird geschildert, auch nicht eine eschatologische Neuschöpfung, die Bedingungen der messianischen Ära erstellt. Das Verbum 'niedersteigen', der bestimmte Artikel, mehr noch die Taubengestalt rufen die Vorstellung eines personalen Wesens hervor, dessen Herabkunft aber zunächst eher etwas zu demonstrieren als eigentlich zu bewirken scheint. Diese göttliche Demonstration besagt: Du bist der 3:16 Angekündigte, der mit heiligem Geist taufen wird; der herabkommende Geist bezeichnet hier den, der Geisttäufer sein wird. Als der 'Sohn Gottes' — schon im Mutterschoße geistgewirkt (1:35) — bedarf Jesus eigentlich ja nur noch der Offenbarmachung."

The descent of the Spirit publicly identifies Jesus as the Promised One of Israel.[100] Here, the one who already bears the Spirit (Luke 1:35) and who, after Pentecost, will bestow the eschatological gift on others, is revealed.[101] Since Jesus is already the "Son of God" from the moment of his conception, any adoptionistic reading of the paracletic descent is precluded. Nor, Schürmann claims, should it be interpreted as the messianic out-pouring which would usher in the new creation. The heavenly voice explicates in words what has already been eloquently expressed in action[102]: "You are my beloved Son in whom I am well pleased" (3:22). Once designated Son according to the Spirit, Jesus' filial relationship with the Father is also established according to the flesh by the genealogy account which follows (3:33-38).[103]

There is a significant difference between the baptism which John confers on the repentant crowd and the rite he performs with Jesus. In the baptism of the multitude the Spirit was promised, not given. When the Sinless One undergoes the Johannine washing, however, the pneumatic gift which later empowers his public mission (Luke 4:1) is bestowed, and the promise made at the general baptism is now fulfilled. How is this difference to be explained? Could the answer lie in the intention of Luke to present the baptism of Jesus not just as a lustral act to which he passively submitted, but as an eschatological sign of fulfilment in which he is the deliberate subject?

Schürmann does stress that Jesus subscribed to the Baptist's eschatological sign of fulfilment

> in so existential a manner that it became a turning point in his life. He left house and occupation in Nazareth and began with his preaching of the kingdom (cf. Mark 1:14f.). Jesus had also subscribed to the baptism of John in such a way that he — after John — made John's baptismal action his own (John 3:22; 4:2), that in any case, after Easter, his disciples carried on the baptism

---

[100] I. de la Potterie, "L'onction du Christ," *NRTh* 80 (1958) 239: "A la théophanie du Jourdain, Jésus est désigné comme le prophète qui va annoncer la bonne nouvelle, comme le Serviteur de Yahvé, comme le Fils même de Dieu."

[101] The Lucan interpretation of the descent of the Spirit differs from that found in Mark 1:10. Its primary purpose in Luke is to reveal publicly the identity of the Son who already bears the gift of the Paraclete. Mark (who has no infancy narrative) recounts his anointing with the Spirit at this point.

[102] *Lukas*, 194.

[103] F. Ó Fearghail, *Introduction to Luke-Acts*, 23, notes that "The genealogy complements the epiphany of 3:22 with respect to the mission of Jesus, for while the symbolism of the epiphany points towards a mission in Israel's favour, the genealogy points towards a mission of universal significance."

of John — with a new Easter understanding and a new action. This is hardly comprehensible if they did not know that it was the intention of Jesus. One can say therefore that Jesus subscribed to the eschatological symbolic action of the Baptist existentially, but also in word and deed. And from Mark 11:27-33 it follows that Jesus indicated the baptism of John as the key to understanding himself, and consequently valued it.[104]

Clearly, Jesus is revealed as Son at his baptism. However, according to Luke, since he is both Son of God and bearer of the Spirit from the very moment of his conception, it seems unlikely that this event constituted for Jesus himself a revelation of his filial identity. Rather, the baptism represents the public manifestation of the Son and, as the beginning of his messianic mission at the request of the Father, marks a "turning point in his life." Yet, it is unreasonable to suggest that the Sinless One would undergo the rite of purification as did the others who flocked to the desert. Certainly, he submits to the rite of John in order to validate and fulfil it, but that is not all. When Jesus steps into the Jordan, he actively appropriates the Baptist's ritual, and thus "makes it his own." Jesus is far more than the passive participant in the prophetic action of the Baptist, he deliberately becomes the "protagonist" of another.[105]

While the Old Testament symbolic acts are rooted in the intimate relationship of the prophets with Yahweh, the descent of Jesus into the Jordan emerges from his maturing filial consciousness. The dramatic portrayals of Jeremiah and Ezekiel generally shocked the onlookers, often dramatically overcoming a blockage in the divine-human communication and provoking a decision before the imminent intervention of God. The symbolic

---

[104] "DSJ," 36: "… in so existentieller Weise bekannt hat, daß das für ihn zur Lebenswende wurde. Er verließ Haus und Beruf in Nazareth und begann mit der Basileiaverkündigung (vgl. Mk. 1:14f.). Jesus hat sich auch in der Weise zur Taufe des Johannes bekannt, daß er - nach Johannes - die Taufaktion sich zu eigen gemacht haben soll (Jo. 3:22; 4:2), daß jedenfalls nach Ostern seine Jünger die Johannestaufe — dann mit neuem österlichen Verständnis und neuartiger Wirkung — weitertrugen, was kaum verständlich zu machen ist ohne das Wissen um eine Intention Jesu. Man wird also sagen dürfen: Jesus bekennt sich zu der 'eschatologischen Zeichenhandlung' des Täufers existentiell, aber auch in Wort und Werk. Und aus Mk. 11:27-33 geht hervor, daß Jesus die Johannestaufe als Schlüssel zum Verständnis seiner selbst bezeichnet und demzufolge geschätzt hat."

[105] *Lukas* 196: "Der Tradition aber ist — trotz der heilsgeschichtlich periodisierenden und schematischen Notiz Mk. 1:14 — geschichtlich glaubwürdig, daß Jesu wort- und wirkmächtiges Auftreten seit der Johannestaufe datiert, und die Kunde ist überzeugend, daß dieser wichtige Anfang in einem Offenbarungsgeschehen an Jesus gründete."

action of Jesus caused consternation for John,[106] and for subsequent believers,[107] placing them before the radical offer of salvation made by the God-man. And, while the Hebrew symbolic act always requires an explanation by the prophet, that given as Jesus comes out of the river is provided by the heavenly voice: "You are my beloved Son in whom I am well pleased."[108] Whereas the baptism enacted by John both fulfilled the eschatological hope regarding the forgiveness of sins expressed by the Hebrew prophets and heralded the future coming of the Spirit-Giver, the act performed by Jesus is quite distinct. It is indeed continuous with the prophetic actions of old and with that of John, but is nevertheless the actualization of all the promises inherent in them. In other words, by stepping into the Jordan, Jesus himself is effecting an eschatological sign of fulfilment.

Herein lies a decisive point, often overlooked.[109] While not explicitly stated by Schürmann, it is clear that the prophetic act initiated by Jesus himself satisfies the four criteria for an eschatological sign of fulfilment as identified by the author: (i) The action is in "the service of the preaching of the eschaton." While the Hebrew prophetic actions looked to a future, often intermediate, divine intervention, this new rite unveils the final eschatological enterprise. Here the Son is revealed by the Father as the one who has received the Spirit-filled mission to proclaim to all the in-breaking kingdom. (ii) The primary purpose of the baptism of Jesus lies beyond the action itself. As a washing "for the forgiveness of sins," the lustral rite of John is meaningless for the Innocent One. In his resolve to stand in the waters of the Jordan, the pro-existent Lord demonstrates his solidarity with the repentant crowd and inaugurates the mission that brings the future redemption expected by John and the prophets. (iii) By stepping into the river, Jesus "effectively actualizes" the promise of the

---

[106] The Matthean account of the baptism records John's astounded protestation that he should baptize Jesus (3:14). Luke does not record any exchange between the two. M. Karimattam, *Jesus the Prophet,* 142, suggests that this allows Luke to maintain Jesus' superiority over John.

[107] Christians have always been faced with the question "Why did Jesus allow himself to be baptized by John?" See, for example, St Thomas Aquinas, *ST* III, Q. 39, a. 4.

[108] Matthew (3:17) records "*This* is my beloved Son with whom I am well pleased." Luke (3:22) and Mark (1:11) report the saying in the second person: "You are my beloved Son; with you I am well pleased." See *Lukas*, 192-194.

[109] P.J. Rosato, *Introduzione alla teologia dei sacramenti*, 59-68, and E. Schillebeeckx, *Jesus*, 136-139, are among the few who regard the baptism in the Jordan as a prophetic act performed by Jesus himself.

Precursor: not only does the Greater One take part in the rite which was meant to anticipate him, but the presaged Spirit-baptism is also achieved in the descent of the dove. (iv) Note too, that the "sign follows the gift": the Father sends the Paraclete not primarily because Jesus readily undergoes the washing by John; rather, the Son forges his way into the water because the Father has already poured-out the messianic gift on him.

3.2 *The Temptation of Jesus*

Any treatment of Luke's temptation narrative must take both text and context into account. Schürmann remarks that

> In itself, the story has a fundamentally "christological" interest; telling, especially with the help of Deut 6-8, what the truth is regarding this Son in whom God is so pleased. Moreover, in the overall plan of the gospel, it has an important and well defined position: before the beginning of the public activity of Jesus, it gives a preview of a fundamental "victory" of Jesus over Satan: as a fundamental action of Jesus it forcefully introduces all his *ποιεῖν τε καὶ διδάσκειν* (Acts 1:1).[110]

While the baptism reveals Jesus as the beloved Son, the temptation discloses the nature of this filial relationship in which the Father rejoices. Within the third gospel, this narrative recounts the initial encounter with Satan. Jesus is presented as "full of the Holy Spirit," the protopneumatic,[111] who, like Israel of old, is led into the desert. There, in this demonic habitat, he is assailed three times. Two of the provocations begin with a direct reference to the recent baptismal proclamation: "If you are the Son..." (vv.3 and 9). Each time Jesus refutes the devil by quoting from the Torah, and thus the former disobedience of Israel is now contrasted with the filial obedience of the Anointed One.[112] Jesus neither struggles nor disputes with the Tempter; he simply remains inaccessible to his promptings.

---

[110] *Lukas*, 205: "In sich ist die Erzählung grundlegend 'christologisch' interessiert; erzählend — vor allem mit Hilfe von Dt. 6-8 — demonstriert sie, was es um jenen gottgefälligen "Sohn" ist. Im Zusammenhang des EvLk bekommt sie darüber hinaus aber einen bestimmten wichtigen Stellenwert: Vor dem öffentlichen Auftreten Jesu läßt die Erzählung einen grundlegenden 'Sieg' Jesu über den Satan ahnen; als grundlegende Tat Jesu steht sie allem *ποιεῖν τε καὶ διδάσκειν* (Apg. 1:1) machtvoll voran."

[111] *Lukas*, 207.

[112] *Lukas*, 209.

The first offensive urges Jesus to change stones into bread (4:3), to place his power as Son "at the service of his own sustenance."[113] In rebuking the evil one, however, Jesus witnesses to his absolute trust in God, a fundamental disposition which is contrasted with the "arbitrary and egocentric attitude"[114] of Satan. By refuting the second temptation to bow down and worship the prince of this world (4:7), Jesus acknowledges that, as Son, he will receive all power and glory from the Father: to God alone belongs honour; from God alone Jesus derives his filial identity and authority.[115] While the first two devilish strategies are designed to make Jesus do evil, the third is directed toward his relationship of trust with the Father: "If you are the Son of God, cast yourself from this pinnacle of the Temple ... and the angels will bear you up lest you strike your foot against a stone" (4:9-11). But again, with reference to Deut 6:16, Jesus dismisses his adversary and reaffirms his relationship with the Father (Luke 4:12).

Jesus' prophetic actions, Schürmann claims, have "something to do with his forthcoming death."[116] The Lucan baptismal account already introduces some of the *dramatis personae* who feature in the passion: Pontius Pilate is mentioned in the historical introduction to John's baptismal activity[117]; Herod Antipas has the Precursor imprisoned as the Son moves to centre stage. This implicit link is accentuated in the temptation narrative. After the final rout, Satan leaves Jesus. Schürmann notes, however, that he will reappear at a later stage:

> After the last rejection, Satan leaves Jesus. His action is provisionally suspended; but he does not yet give up defeated. In Jerusalem, where [Satan] stopped [tempting Jesus], he will try again (cf. 22:3.53; John 14:30): he will respond to Jesus' refusal to worship Satan with the ultimate killing of Jesus himself (cf. 22:3). In the temptation route from the desert to Jerusalem the "journey of Jesus" is reflected. Jerusalem is in fact the city of the assassins of the prophets (13:34s.), in which

---

113 *Lukas*, 209.
114 *Lukas*, 210.
115 *Lukas*, 212.
116 "DSJ," 39.
117 M. Karimattam, *Jesus the Prophet*, 146 n. 93, notes that the verb (*anakraxo*) used to describe the cry of the people before Pilate (Luke 23:18) is used in only two other places in Luke's gospel (4:33; 8:28) where it denotes the shouts of demons at the sight of Jesus.

the destiny of Jesus must also be fulfilled; it is therefore the goal of Jesus' journey.[118]

While in the temptation narrative the Evil One cannot subvert the just resolve of the Son, he is far from vanquished. The conflict is resumed at the beginning of the passion (22:3.53) when Satan returns "not to tempt Jesus, but to ensnare him."[119] Notice, too, how the geographical unfolding of the temptation episode foreshadows the route from Jordan, through the desert, to Jerusalem.

The pro-existent attitude of Jesus, so clearly demonstrated at the Last Supper and on Calvary, can be discerned from the beginning of his public ministry. Though sinless, Jesus stands with the repentant crowd on the river bank and undergoes John's rite of purification. In this way, the radical *being-with* which underlines his fundamental *being-for* others is revealed. The paracletic descent which identifies Jesus as the anointed Son launches him on the mission "to preach the good news to the poor" (Luke 4:18). By refusing to change the stones into bread, Jesus declines to manipulate the transcendent power of his words and actions to selfish advantage. To do otherwise, Schürmann observes, would constitute a devilish "fundamental perversion"[120] of the trustful relationship that the Son has with the Father. Jesus accomplishes his saving work by walking the path of service and self-giving, a path which begins at the Jordan and culminates on the Cross.[121]

---

[118] *Lukas*, 214: "Nach der letzen Abweisung läßt der Satan von Jesus ab; er stellt seine ganze Aktion einstweilen ein. Endgültig geschlagen gibt er sich freilich noch nicht. In Jerusalem, wo er endete, wird er dereinst wieder einsetzen (vgl. 22:3.53; Joh. 14:30): Die Verweigerung der Satansanbetung 4:8 wird der Satan am Ende mit der Tötung Jesu (vgl. 22:3) beantworten. In dem Versuchungsweg von der Wüste nach Jerusalem spiegelt sich so schon der 'Weg Jesu': Jerusalem ist ja die Stadt der Prophetenmörder (13:34f.), in der auch Jesu Geschick sich vollenden muß und die darum das erklärte Ziel des Wanderns Jesu ist."

[119] *Lukas*, 216.

[120] *Lukas*, 209.

[121] F.X. Durrwell, "La transfiguration de Jésus," *VS* 85 (1951) 123: "Dans le baptême de Jésus fut joué, en symbole et comme prélude à la réalité, tout le drame de la mort et la résurrection." A. Feuillet, "La personnalité de Jésus entrevue à partir de sa soumission au rite de repentance du précurseur," *RB* 77 (1970) 47: "...ce n'est pas seulement le Calvaire que l'événement mystérieux du Jourdain permet de pressentir c'est aussi, et même tout d'abord, le ministère public du Christ pris dans son ensemble, en particulier l'attitude de Jésus, toute de miséricorde et de condescendance, à l'endroit des hommes pécheurs, attitude qui s'accompagne de la conviction d'être le médecin messianique envoyé par Dieu pour guérir ces malades spirituels."

This is the cup that he must drink; this is the life-long baptism with which he must be baptized (Mark 10:39; Luke 12:50).

3.3 *The Emergence of a New Symbolic Act*

When Jesus of Nazareth undergoes the water rite of John a new reality is born. Spurred on by his growing filial awareness, he completes the rite of the Precursor and becomes the protagonist of another eschatological sign of fulfilment. In this dramatic action the Promised One is revealed as the pro-existent Son of God, who is anointed by the Spirit to bring the "good news to the poor." In the temptation story which follows, the sonship of Jesus is put to the test.

The writings of the Hebrew prophets contain many references to Israel as the Son of Yahweh.[122] In *Hosea*, chapter 11, Israel is the beloved son whom the Lord calls out of Egypt (11:1). The Father "took the people up in his arms" (11:2) and "bent down to feed them" (11:3), while they kept "sacrificing to Baals and burning incense to idols" (11:2). Notice the similarities between this and the temptation story, between the two sons, Israel and Jesus: the former abandons the doting Father to worship false gods and to rely on his own power; the latter rejects Satan's temptations and displays his absolute trust in the Father (Luke 4:12) by his refusal to bow down before the devil (4:8) and by his insistence that one does not live "by bread alone" (4:4). The obedient Son in whom the Father is well-pleased, then, stands in stark contrast to the rebellious Israel. Indeed, this opposition between the infidelity of Israel and the loyalty of Jesus is intensified by the Matthaean interpretation of the return from Egypt (Matt 2:15) as the fulfilment of Hos 11:1. Jesus is the symbol of the New Israel who faithfully adheres to the Word of God.

Earlier this century, R. Otto[123] noted a parallel between the words accompanying the table-action of Jesus at the Last Supper and the explanation which followed the prophetic acts of Ezekiel and Jeremiah.[124] When Ezekiel shaved his body hair and scattered

---

[122] See, for example, Jer 3:19; Ezek 63:16; 64:8; Mal 1:6; 2:10.

[123] R. Otto, *The Kingdom of God and the Son of Man*, 299-301.

[124] See C. Vollert, "The Eucharist: Quests for Insights from Scripture," *TS* 21 (1960) 420: "Grammatically, 'This is Jerusalem' corresponds to 'This is my body', 'This is my blood'. In Ezekiel the hairs represent Jerusalem by what happens to them: the lot of these hairs symbolizes the lot of Jerusalem. By the prophetic action performed at the Supper, Jesus showed the apostles in figure what was to happen on the morrow: the bread which he breaks and distributes signifies His body

it to the wind, he pronounced the warning "This is Jerusalem." When Jesus blesses the bread and wine and gives them to his disciples to share, he adds: "This is my body/blood." In the former, the imminent destruction of the city was effectively presaged; in the latter, the fruit of his eschatological victory over death is communicated to those at table.

The Father's voice at the Jordan could well be understood in a similar vein. The parallel between the Matthaean version of the heavenly voice, "This is my beloved Son" (Matt 3:17), and all three synoptic accounts of the words accompanying the bread gesture, "This is my body" (Mark 14:22; Matt 26:29; Luke 22:19), is particularly striking. So, when the Spirit descends on the baptized Jesus as he emerges from the river and the voice from heaven proclaims "This is my Son," the eschatological favour of God is made known to those who witnessed this symbolic action. But the celestial voice also echoes Isa 42:1[125]:

> Behold my servant, whom I uphold,
> my chosen, in whom my soul delights;
> I have put my Spirit upon him,
> he will bring forth justice to the nations.

When this reference is taken into consideration, it is clear that Jesus, the symbol of the new People of God, is presented not only as the Promised One but, as the Just One in whom right-relations between Yahweh and Israel are restored.[126] In the descent of the Spirit on the obedient Son, the bearer and future dispenser of the divine power of justice is unveiled, and the post-paschal pneumatic baptism of the New Israel is anticipated.

While Schürmann distinguishes between the baptism of John and the symbolic actions of the Old Testament prophets, he does

which is to be delivered up for them; the wine in the cup is the sign of the blood He will shed on the cross to establish the alliance God wishes to conclude with men." This parallel is also taken up by R.H. Strachan, *The Fourth Gospel*, 264; J. Dupont, "'Ceci est mon corps', 'Ceci est mon sang'"; N.A. Beck, "The Last Supper as an Efficacious Symbolic Act." Significantly, the Old Testament exegete, W.D. Stacey, "The Lord's Supper as Prophetic Drama," 88, notes: "The use of bread, therefore, in the upper room is entirely in line with the traditions of prophetic drama. It is common to identify the object with some other reality for the purpose of the drama. Jeremiah's pot stands for Jerusalem; his loincloth stands for the pride and privilege of Judah. In Ezek 5:5 Ezekiel's shorn hair is Jerusalem. So there is nothing unusual about the upper room formula, 'This is my body'. The bread is identified with the person of Jesus for the purpose of the drama."

125 See *Lukas*, 192-193.

126 P.J. Rosato, *Introduzione alla teologia dei sacramenti*, 62, comes to a similar conclusion based on the Matthaean text (Matt 3:14-15).

not differentiate between the act performed by the Precursor and that accomplished by the Promised One. Since John had baptized the repentant crowds with a rite for the remission of sins, his symbolic act looked forward to the coming of the Messiah who would definitively confer the justice of the Spirit. His washing effected, to a certain extent, the end-time forgiveness promised by the Hebrew prophets. In this sense it is proper for Schürmann to speak of John's action as an eschatological sign of fulfilment. Yet, this sign had another function, namely that of foretelling the upcoming baptism with the Holy Spirit which was to be realized only by the action of the Stronger One. *With respect to the conferral of the Holy Spirit*, then, it is necessary to go beyond Schürmann's position and to distinguish between the efficacy of the prophetic action performed by John and that enacted by Jesus. By stepping into the Jordan, the Son unleashes the presaged gift of the Paraclete, and thus enacts a symbolic gesture which fully deserves the designation "eschatological sign of *fulfilment.*" Since the Johannine washing only announces the future descent of the Spirit, but cannot confer it, his ritual is more appropriately termed an "eschatological sign of *promise*."

Neither the gesture of John nor the pre-Easter washing by the disciples can confer the Spirit. The universal reception of the Paraclete can take place only when the baptism of Jesus is complete, that is, when the journey to Calvary is accomplished.[127] This gift, unexpectedly anticipated in Jesus' eschatological sign of fulfilment, is imparted by the post-paschal celebration of the sacrament of initiation. Schürmann alludes to the "superior quality"[128] of the sacramental rites of the Church over the prophetic acts performed by Jesus in the Jordan and at the Last Supper. This superiority seems to be attributed to the presence of the Spirit of the risen Lord in the later ecclesial celebrations. There is, therefore, a qualitative difference between the various symbolic acts in question: those performed by the Old Testament prophets, by John the Baptist, by Jesus himself before Calvary, by the disciples before Easter, and by the Christian community since

---

[127] On Matt 10:38-39, where Jesus refers to his death as the completion of his baptism, see V. Howard, "Did Jesus speak of his own death?", *CBQ* 39 (1977) 515-527; A. Feuillet, "La coupe et le baptême de la passion," *RB* 74 (1967) 356-391.

[128] *JuT,* 93; *Lukas*, 159-160.

Easter and Pentecost.[129] The liturgical repetition of the prophetic act of Jesus in the Jordan is now examined.

[129] Did Jesus administer baptism during his public ministry? This question is discussed by J.P. Meier, *A Marginal Jew,* II, 116-130. Meier concludes, 129, that: "So strong was the impact of John on Jesus that, for a short period, Jesus stayed with John as his disciple and, when he struck out on his own, he continued the practice of baptizing disciples."

CHAPTER 5

The Surge of Baptism

The sacrament of baptism as prognostic sign of the form of eschatological life in the writings of Karl Rahner

The justification for the present exposition of Rahner's theology of baptism arises from a number of converging indices which emerge as this chapter unfolds. First of all, the role of the prophet in Rahner's fundamental theology is examined ("Categorizing the Divine Self-Communication"). This reveals the profile of biblical figures who authentically expressed in word and action the universal transcendental divine self-communication within the concrete history of a particular religious community. According to Rahner, this prophetic role, as it is developed in Israel, is taken up by Jesus of Nazareth in his proclamation of the kingdom of God. Since the Church, as the basic sacrament of the triumphant mercy of God, is the ongoing presence of Christ in the world, his identity as the eschatological prophet permeates its entire existence. In a second section ("Actualizing the Eschatological Victory of Christ"), the relationship between the socio-historical manifestation of victorious grace, which is called Church, and Jesus Christ, the fundamental sacrament of salvation, is examined. Rahner's presentation of the individual sacraments as concrete actualizations of the redemptive grace of Christ in the life of an individual is then analysed. Here, the correspondence between Rahner's understanding of these ritual actions and the Amsler-Schürmann analysis of Old and New Testament prophetic acts is underlined. In a third step ("Baptism as Symbolic Act of Eschatological Salvation"), Rahner's baptismal theology is exposed, and the motif of baptism as symbolic event of eschatological salvation is employed so as to further illumine the prognostic dimension of this lustral rite.

1. Categorizing the Divine Self-Communication

To appreciate the role of the prophet in Rahner's theology, the correlation between the supernatural, transcendental experience of the self-communication of God and the categorical, particular history of revelation and salvation must be explored. In his *Grundkurs des Glaubens*[1] Rahner suggests that this can find a satisfactory explanation only when two considerations are taken into account:

> First, the categorical history of man as a spiritual subject is always and everywhere the necessary but historical and objectifying self-interpretation of the transcendental experience which constitutes the realization of man's essence. Secondly, this realization of man's essence does not take place alongside the events of historical life, but within historical life.[2]

In other words, the transcendental experience of God, by its very nature, must be made concrete in the particularities of each human life. This "realization" neither parallels nor overlays historical existence: it is precisely within the joy and pain of human living that the infinite mystery is encountered, recognized and expressed. Since the unthematic experience of the divine self-communication has always been present everywhere, there necessarily have been, are, and will be various attempts to interpret it explicitly. Moreover, given the reality that the human situation is conditioned by sin and guilt, such attempts will be fraught with confusion and error. Some, however, will be more successful than others and these constitute the categorical history of revelation:

> the history of revelation in the usual and especially the full sense of the term is found where this self-interpretation of God's transcendental self-communication in history succeeds, and where with certainty it reaches its self-awareness and its purity in such a way that it correctly knows itself to be guided and directed by God, and, protected by him against clinging tenaciously to what is provisional and to what is depraved, it discovers its own true self.[3]

---

[1] K. Rahner, *Grundkurs des Glaubens: Einführung in der Begriff des Christentums*. The English translation by W.V. Dych is entitled *Foundations of Christian Faith: An Introduction to the Idea of Christianity*. [Hereafter *FCF*.]

[2] *FCF*, 153.

[3] *FCF*, 155.

Within this process of the history of transcendental revelation finding an authoritative expression, the prophet plays a key role.

1.1 *The Role of the Prophet*

Between 1967 and 1969 Rahner collaborated with Adolf Darlap in compiling the theological encyclopaedia *Sacramentum Mundi.*[4] In an article entitled "Prophetism,"[5] Rahner remarks:

> There is a general, genuine grace-given history of revelation, co-extensive with the history of mankind in general because given with the perpetual and universal self-communication of God in grace, by virtue of his universal salvific will. And this "transcendental" revelation is inconceivable without being in some way consciously objectivated in words, a process which is necessarily the history and mediation of this "transcendental" revelation itself. Thus the phenomenon of prophecy must occur again and again in this general history of revelation.[6]

Within the general history of revelation, then, there is a phenomenon known as prophecy which strives to translate the primordial transcendental experience of God's self-communication into specific words and symbols. Prophets are found, beyond the realm of the Old and New Testaments, whenever a religion is convinced that it is established by a divine historical revelation.[7] There are no inherent criteria for distinguishing "false" from "true" prophets. Neither is there any immediate guarantee that a concrete prophetic actualization of the unthematic revelation is free from error or contains any validity beyond a particular time and circumstance.[8]

Fundamental, however, to the prophetic office in all religions is the experience of vocation or call:

---

[4] The English edition in six volumes is *Sacramentum Mundi*. [Hereafter *SM(E)*.]

[5] *SM(E)* V, 110-113.

[6] "Prophetism," 111.

[7] "Prophetism," 111.

[8] *FCF,* 157: "In Jesus Christ, the crucified and risen one, then, we have a criterion for distinguishing in the concrete history of religion between what is a human misunderstanding of the transcendental experience of God, and what is the legitimate interpretation of this experience. It is only in him that such a discernment of spirits in an ultimate sense is possible."

> The prophet is the "bearer of revelation." He claims to be the envoy sent directly by God, the *legatus divinus* of Catholic fundamental theology, with a primordial relationship to the word of God. He is convinced that what he proclaims is the word of God himself. He feels himself the instrument not of a numinous power but of a personal, "living" God who freely reveals himself.[9]

Through the intimacy of a personal relationship with God, prophets come face to face with the divine word which they are charged to communicate to others. This activity is neither abstract nor general: the prophet is "the envoy sent directly by God" to address a people existing in a definite cultural, socio-political situation. This enables the listeners of prophets to determine whether these envoys, in offering a meaning to the events of their history, provide an authentic response to, or a fundamental perversion of the transcendental divine self-communication within a particular religious community.[10]

Although the prophet is neither a clairvoyant nor a soothsayer, Rahner states the following:

> since he creates a new and forward-looking situation in the history of salvation by his criticism of society, he is essentially associated with promises and the future.[11]

By objectifying the unthematic self-communication of God for other members of the group, or in other terms, by facilitating the historical discovery of transcendental religious experience for them, the prophet unveils a silently desired future in which social injustice and oppression are to cease, in which worship and praxis are to correlate, and the pre-conceptual experience of God and its subsequent historical articulation are to be expressed more perspicaciously. In this history of categorical revelation, then, one prophet succeeds and exceeds another, while the primary, "unreflexive" and "non-objective" revelation is more adequately explicated in words and signs. In this way, propheticism enables the concrete history of the religious community to speak more clearly of the pre-existent mystery which underlines it. According to Rahner, then, prophets are called to voice authentically for the group in which they live God's transcendental self-communication. By word and action they point beyond the limitations of the

---

[9] "Prophetism," 111.
[10] *FCF*, 160.
[11] "Prophetism," 111.

present, and herald a new situation where the divine-human drama continues to unfold.[12] This description is not far from Amsler's understanding of the Old Testament prophet as outlined in Chapter 3.

1.2 *The Eschatological Prophet*

Rahner then proceeds to present Jesus Christ as a prophet. Like his precursors, the Nazarene is compelled by his awareness of a privileged relationship with the word of God to speak and to act. He categorically expresses the transcendent divine self-communication for a people living in a particular time and place, and proclaims an unexpected future of the history of God with the chosen people. But, as Rahner points out, in the case of Jesus this is not all:

> Jesus Christ is *the* great prophet, the absolute bringer of salvation.... He is the eschatologically final prophet, *the* prophet as such, who cannot be surpassed in the further history of revelation and salvation, not because God arbitrarily decided that no prophet (to surpass him) should be sent, but because his task and his person are identical (though he explains himself in the light of the presence of the kingdom of God rather than vice versa). He brings the absolute immediacy and self-communication of God, not just a particular message and promise, couched in ordinary categories and addressed to this nation or that age.[13]

Jesus is the "eschatologically final prophet" who can never be surpassed or exceeded because "his task and his person are identical." By means of a singular relationship of sonship with God whom he calls "Father," Jesus is aware that the divine closeness to all humanity has arrived at a point of existing in a novel and irrevocable way. The pre-resurrection Jesus experiences

---

[12] K. Rahner – H. Vorgrimler, "Prophet" in *Concise Theological Dictionary,* 383-384: "In fundamental theology a man can be called a prophet in a general sense if he is the accredited witness of God's revelation in such a way that he not only experiences God's gracious self-communication to man but declares it correctly, that is without error, with divine guidance and attestation, expounds it in a manner appropriate to the concrete situation facing himself and his environment, and in obedience to a divine impulse proclaims it to this environment. In so far as an estimation of one's religious situation necessarily involves looking into the future, though not an advance report on it, the prophet has the ability (more or less explicitly) to interpret the present in the light of its dynamism for the future."

[13] "Prophetism," 112.

this advent of God, the dawning of the kingdom, as grounded in his own person.[14] His is not a provisional utterance, but the final, unsurpassable word of the self-disclosure of God in history, the "absolute immediacy and self-communication of God" to all.[15] This claim, Rahner continues, is validated in the resurrection:

> Through his death, the elimination of all intramundane goals, his entry, by the resurrection, into full immediacy to God, he created and manifested the situation in which "*after* him" there could only come the consummation of history by the absorption into the immediate presence of God. When God responded to his prophetic destiny with the resurrection from the dead, he became the final prophet, the one real prophet in the full sense of the word, and was manifestly revealed for what he was. All other prophetic words either point to the (unanswered) question of death or to a coming prophet, and so remain "precursors."[16]

According to a thomistic maxim, the human person is a being with a natural desire for the beatific vision (*desiderium naturale in visionem beatificam*).[17] Given the intrinsic connection between transcendental reality and categorical expression, Rahner insists that this *desiderium* awaits a definitive appearance in history.[18] In the events of the life, death and resurrection of the prophet from Nazareth, then, "all intramundane goals" are eliminated as Jesus

---

[14] *FCF,* 254: "According to his own self-understanding he [Jesus] is already before the resurrection the one sent, the one who inaugurates the kingdom of God through what he says and what he does in a way that it did not exist before, but now does exist *through* him and *in* him."

[15] *FCF,* 280: "In his word a genuine prophet must allow God in his unlimited possibilities to be greater, and he speaks his word to a definite situation which presently exists, but then gives way to a new and different situation. He must experience and proclaim his word essentially as a promise reaching out into an open and unlimited horizon. Hence Jesus is a prophet who surpasses and subsumes the essence of a prophet with the claim of his word."

[16] *FCF,* 279-280: "By the resurrection, then, Jesus is vindicated as the absolute saviour. We can say more cautiously at first: as the *final* 'prophet'. For on the one hand the self-interpretation of Jesus in his message which was vindicated by the resurrection makes him a 'prophet', that is, one who brings a word of God to concrete historical existence over and beyond all 'eternal truths', and calls one to decision. But this prophet holds that his word is final and unsurpassable. ... It is the final word of God that is present in Jesus because there is nothing to say beyond it, because God has really in a strict sense offered *himself* in Jesus."

[17] See K. Rahner, *Nature and Grace*, 10.

[18] Behind this statement lies "a proposition from metaphysical anthropology: man as subject and as person is a historical being in such a way that he is historical precisely *as* a transcendent subject; his subjective essence of unlimited transcendentality is mediated *historically* to him in his knowledge and in his free self-realisation" (*FCF,* 140).

enters into "full immediacy with God." The human orientation towards beatitude is affirmed "in and through his absolute, irreversible and 'eschatological' offer of himself."[19] In other words, the protagonist of this eschatological event of salvation is none other than the absolute saviour of humanity. Jesus Christ, "*the* great prophet," is "the absolute bringer of salvation."[20] In him the gratuitous self-communication of God and the free acceptance of it on behalf of humanity become irrevocably one, and the history of the whole human race reaches its goal. "After him" the history of the world, and the role of prophecy in it, is no longer open the way it was beforehand. While the question of individual salvation is still to be decided, the definitive word of divine grace has been spoken, and the fulness of time and of salvation has dawned.[21]

According to Rahner, then, prophets authentically categorize the transcendental self-communication of God within a particular religious community. By word and action, they bear witness to the ineffable mystery at the core of history, and herald a new reality in the ongoing divine-human relationship of salvation. As the final prophet, Jesus Christ proclaims the desired yet unimagined nearness of the kingdom in a manner which can never be surpassed. Through his life, death and resurrection the eschatological victory of God is guaranteed as a permanent offer of salvation within human history. The present actuality of this victorious grace, Rahner continues, is found in the Church. This aspect of the ecclesial body is to be investigated in the following section.

2. **Actualizing the Eschatological Victory of Christ**

In *Kirche und Sakramente*[22], Rahner challenges what he considers the "superficial," almost "accidental"[23] relationship between the Church itself and the sacraments which it continually dispenses. Rahner divides this monograph into two parts. In the

---

[19] *FCF,* 298.

[20] Rahner's ascending christology then goes on to show that "the absolute event of salvation and the absolute mediation of salvation by a man mean exactly the same thing as Church doctrine expresses as Incarnation and hypostatic union" (*FCF,* 299).

[21] See *FCF,* 169-170; 194-195.

[22] K. Rahner, *Kirche und Sakramente,* Quaestiones Disputatae 9. All references are to the English translation by W.J. O'Hara, *The Church and The Sacraments*. [Hereafter *CS*.]

[23] *CS,* 9-10.

first, he proceeds from an understanding of the Church as the fundamental sacrament [*Ursakrament*[24]] to a consideration of the individual Christian rites. In the second part the direction is reversed since Rahner treats the seven symbols of the new covenant as indispensable realizations of the very nature of the Church.

2.1 *Church and Sacrament*

Rahner's theological approach in *Kirche und Sakramente*, although it does not deny the anthropological presupposition that human beings enjoy a transcendental orientation to the divine mystery, has a christological starting-point: "Christ is the historical real and actual presence of the eschatological victorious mercy of God."[25] From the moment of the incarnation, the fate of the world has been decided in this ultimate word of grace, reconciliation and eternal life which has been spoken, not "steeply down from on high"[26] but, from within the concrete events of the life, death and resurrection of the itinerant preacher and prophet from Nazareth. In his earthly existence, Christ is both "reality and sign, *sacramentum* and *res sacramenti*,"[27] of the redemptive grace of God. This triumphant victory of saving grace is not a fleeting reality but "is permanently in the world in tangible historical form."[28] The ongoing presence of the eschatological victory of Christ is found in the Spirit-filled community of believers:

> Now the Church is the continuance, the contemporary presence, of the real, eschatological triumphant and irrevocably established presence in the world, in Christ, of God's salvific

---

[24] In later writings, particularly after 1966, Rahner reserves the designation *Ursakrament* for Jesus Christ and refers to the Church as the *Grundsakrament*. L. Leijssen, "La contribution de Karl Rahner (1904-1984) au renouvellement de la sacramentaire," *QuLi* 75 (1994) 92-93, suggests that this deliberate change reflects Rahner's growing appreciation of the Church as the bearer of the word of God for the world and, consequently, as the present appearance of grace and as the efficacious sign and instrument of salvation within a history which finds its fulfilment in the kingdom of God. One notable exception is found in two instances in *Grundkurs des Glaubens*, 402 & 408 where Rahner refers to the Church as the *Ursakrament* to underline the origin of the seven sacraments in the Church (L. Leijssen, "La contribution," 94). In *FCF*, *Ursakrament* is rendered as "primordial sacrament" and *Grundsakrament* as "basic sacrament." See also E. Vacek, "Development within Rahner's Theology," *IThQ* 42 (1975) 36-49; L.J. O'Donovan, ed., "A Changing Ecclesiology in a Changing Church: A Symposium on Development in the Ecclesiology of Karl Rahner," *TS* 38 (1977) 736-762.

[25] *CS*, 14.

[26] *CS*, 15.

[27] *CS*, 15.

[28] *CS*, 15.

> will. The Church is the abiding presence of that primal sacramental word of definitive grace, which Christ is in the world, effecting what is uttered by uttering it in sign. By the very fact of being in that way the enduring presence of Christ in the world, the Church is truly the fundamental sacrament, the well-spring of the sacraments in the strict sense.[29]

Jesus Christ is the "primal sacramental word [*sakramentales Urwort*] of definitive grace"; the Church is the continuation, the perpetual presence of his message and function in the economy of salvation. Because the Church is the spatio-temporal embodiment of the eschatological victory of the grace of God in the world, it is never an empty symbol. Rather, as the fundamental sacrament [*Ursakrament*], it unfailingly actualizes the grace of the risen Lord by expressing it in diverse signs. In relation to the sacraments, therefore, the Church is not some "spiritual welfare establishment"[30] but is the "well-spring" from which these rites derive both their meaning and their power. It should be noted that, as the legitimate expression of the eschatological mercy of God, the Church plays a prophetic role in the history of salvation. While the whole of creation is penetrated by the transcendental offer of grace, the ecclesial community alone objectifies it for the world in a manner which can neither be exceeded nor surpassed.

In order for a group or a society to exist, Rahner notes, it has to fulfil its nature by actually functioning.[31] As the socially and juridically organized people of God, the Church is no exception. Precisely when this community teaches, witnesses to Christ's truth, bears the cross, loves God in its members and presents its saving grace in the eucharistic sacrifice, does it exist in the full sense.[32] In this context, Rahner introduces his understanding of the sacraments:

> when the Church in her official, organized, public capacity precisely as the source of redemptive grace meets the individual in the actual accomplishment of her nature, there we have sacraments in the proper sense, and they can be seen to be the essential functions that bring into activity the very essence of the Church herself. For in them she herself attains the highest degree of actualization of what she always is: the presence of redemptive grace for all, historically visible and manifest as the

---

[29] *CS,* 18.
[30] *CS,* 11.
[31] *CS,* 20.
[32] *CS,* 20.

> sign of the eschatologically victorious grace of God in the world.[33]

In the sacraments, the Church actualizes its "very essence" as the victorious mercy of Christ in the life of individual believers. Rahner then proceeds to present selected aspects of traditional sacramental theology within this restored ecclesiological framework.[34] Three of these, the institution of the sacraments, the meaning of *opus operatum* and the nature of sacramental causality are of particular interest and are treated in the next sections. From the outset it must be noted that, in *Kirche und Sakramente*, Rahner mentions neither prophets nor prophetism. Yet, as his understanding of the ritual actions of the Church unfolds, there are striking parallels with the prophetic acts as described by Samuel Amsler and by Heinz Schürmann. These correspondences are highlighted in what follows.

2.2 *Word and Sacrament*

Preliminary to any such attempt, however, mention must be made of Rahner's notion of the relationship between word and sacrament. In 1971 Rahner, together with E. Jüngel, explored an ecumenical approach to the sacraments.[35] In his contribution, Rahner took as his point of departure "the distinctive theological character of the word of God uttered in the Church as the eschatological presence of God."[36] Like profane words, the ecclesial word exists on various levels and in different degrees: catechetical information, kerygmatic proclamation and sacramental absolution are listed as particular instances.[37] Given the theory of

---

[33] *CS,* 22.

[34] K. Rahner, "Introductory Observations on Thomas Aquinas' Theology of the Sacraments in General," *TI* 14, 151-152: "It must be remembered that the *Summa Theologica* of Thomas Aquinas does not include any developed ecclesiology, and that the treatise on sacraments which follows immediately upon that of christology, is itself included at a relatively late stage. In view of these facts it is of course impossible for there to be any really effective treatment of the Church as 'basic sacrament' as a distinct theme. This inevitably has a damaging effect on the doctrine of the sacraments in general too, for the connecting member, so to say, is missing. Or to put it in other terms: the truly ecclesiological dimension of the sacraments is not taken into consideration."

[35] K. Rahner, "What is a Sacrament?," *TI* 14, 135-148. This article originally formed the text of a guest lecture delivered at the Faculty of Catholic Theology of the University of Mainz on 21 January 1971. It was subsequently published in *StZ* 188 (1971) 16-25.

[36] "What is a Sacrament?," 136.

[37] "What is a Sacrament?," 140.

Rahner concerning a necessary categorical expression of a transcendental reality, the eschatological presence of God in the word must assume an exhibitive character in history as an event of saving grace. Whenever this word is proclaimed through the Church in existentially decisive moments in the life of an individual, the irreversibly victorious promise of God is assured. Moreover, since this is how Rahner defines a sacrament, it is clear that he makes a doctrine of the word the basis for an inter-Church approach to the Christian rites. Therefore, he states that a "sacrament is understood as one quite specific word-event within a theology of the word."[38] The intrinsic link between prophetic words and gestures has already been underlined in the presentation of the thought of Amsler.[39] While both word and gesture efficaciously place the people of Israel before the Lord of its future,[40] the latter, as the word-in-symbol, "assumes the significance of a visible act of God"[41] in a particular time and place. Prophetic acts and Christian sacraments, then, have a common ground in the symbolized and dramatized proclamation of the divine word to God's people.

2.3 *The Institution of the Sacraments*

Rahner dissuades from any attempt to locate the institution of the individual sacraments in specific statements of the pre- or post-resurrection Jesus.[42] Such an endeavour faces an uphill, nigh impossible struggle, particularly in the case of ministry or of the anointing of the sick. Even when such proof-texts appear to exist, as with baptism, eucharist and penance, problems abound. Rahner prefers an ecclesiological point of departure:

> The institution of a sacrament can (it is not necessarily implied that it must always) follow simply from the fact that Christ founded the Church with its sacramental nature. It is clear too that, properly understood, the treatise *De sacramentis in genere*

---

[38] "What is a Sacrament?," 138. Note the comment of Pope Paul VI in his Apostolic Exhortation *Evangelii Nuntiandi* 47 (ND 1336): "Evangelization exercises its full capacity when it achieves the most intimate relationship, or better still a permanent and unbroken inter-communication, between the Word and the Sacraments."

[39] See Chapter 3, Section 1.1.3.

[40] S. Amsler, *Les actes,* 34.

[41] S. Amsler, *Les actes,* 83.

[42] *CS,* 41-46.

> is not an abstract formulation of the nature of the individual sacraments, but a part of the treatise *De ecclesia*.[43]

By explicitly instituting the *Ursakrament* as the historical form of eschatologically victorious grace, Christ implicitly instituted the seven[44] sacraments. Whenever the ecclesial community, in a decisive situation for an individual's salvation, performs an act which truly involves its nature as the eschatological presence of redemptive grace, then, *ipso facto*, there is a sacrament.[45] This, Rahner warns, does not imply that the sacraments and their number can be deduced *a priori* from the nature of the Church. Without falling victim to an epistemological vicious circle, Rahner methodologically insists that, precisely in the process of self-actualization the Church comes to recognize *a posteriori* what exactly the acts of its own realization are.[46]

The seven Christian rites, then, are essential symbols in which the Church actualizes its nature as the fundamental sacrament. Remember that Rahner posits the sacramental structure of the Church, not from some "vague borrowing of the concept"[47] from sacramental theology, but from reflecting on the historical perceptibility of the Christ-event. To make this clearer, Rahner acknowledges that "Christ's own rôle in the mystery of redemption must be considered more closely."[48] In other words, while asserting that an implicit institution of the sacraments is to be intuited in Christ's explicit institution of the Church, Rahner claims that the ecclesiological focus of the individual rites must not obscure their fundamental christological origin.

In *Kirche und Sakramente*, Rahner's declared purpose is to articulate the connection between the Church which actualizes itself and the sacraments which it celebrates. Consequently, the connection between the individual rites and the symbolic gestures of Jesus of Nazareth is not treated in any detail. Yet, the relationship between sacraments and Jesus as the eschatological

---

[43] *CS,* 41.

[44] Rahner (*CS,* 56-57) recognizes that "what is essential about the definition that there are seven sacraments, is not the number, but the affirmation that the ecclesiastical rites comprised by this number are in fact of sacramental efficacy, all these and only these." Consequently, if the three grades of orders can each be considered a sacrament the number becomes nine; conversely, if baptism and confirmation are reckoned as one there are only six.

[45] *CS,* 41.

[46] *CS,* 68-72.

[47] *CS,* 23.

[48] *CS,* 13-14.

prophet is clearly discernible when several strands of Rahner's thought are brought together.

Rahner repeatedly affirms that the Church, as the community of those who believe in Jesus, is the historical continuation of his eschatological triumph.[49] In his *Grundkurs des Glaubens*, Rahner notes that first among the "minimal historical presuppositions of an orthodox christology,"[50] is the thesis that Jesus viewed himself as "the *eschatological* prophet, as the absolute and definitive saviour."[51] The Church, then, is not the ahistorical promulgation of a myth or an ideology, but is the perpetual presence of a word and a gesture of Jesus the prophet in the economy of salvation. Rahner admits that, while it is not necessary to trace back the more concrete structures of the Church, as it has been constituted in history, to any explicit sayings of its founder, exegetically it is possible to uncover "acts of Jesus which founded the Church."[52] First among these is the gathering of the twelve apostles, the significance of which Rahner assesses as follows:

> For precisely by their number the twelve were to represent symbolically the whole of Israel, the eschatological Israel which Jesus had in mind. Therefore they were sent out by Jesus to preach, and they participated in the healing power of Jesus which was a sign for him that the eschatological kingdom as a present and pressing reality was operative here and now in him.[53]

As has already been shown, Schürmann listed this gesture as one prophetic act of Jesus.[54] Notice how Rahner's description satisfies the exegete's criteria for an eschatological sign of fulfilment[55]: in the constitution of the twelve the end-time community of salvation is represented (the basic orientation of the action is eschatological and its primary meaning lies beyond the deed itself); the disciples already participate in the mission of the messianic Lord (it is marked from within by the time of fulfilment); the very existence of

---

[49] In *CS,* this assertion is widespread. See, for example, pages 13; 18; 19; 21-24; 39; 63; 74; 76-77; 86; 94; 100.

[50] *FCF,* 245.

[51] *FCF,* 245-246: "Jesus saw himself not merely as one among many prophets who in principle form an unfinished line which is always open towards the future, but understood himself rather as the *eschatological* prophet, as the absolute and definitive saviour."

[52] *FCF,* 332-335.

[53] *FCF,* 333.

[54] See Chapter 4, section 1.2.

[55] See Chapter 4, section 1.2.

the group points to the power presently at work in Jesus (pre-eminently, the sign follows the gift). Not only does the new covenant community derive from the intention of Jesus, but the concrete symbolic action of the eschatological prophet underpins its very foundation. To be true to its own nature, then, it is essential that its prophetic roots be appreciated.

In *Sacramentum Mundi*, commenting on prophetism and the Church, Rahner remarks:

> the Church itself is the permanent presence of the word of *the* prophet, Jesus Christ. It is the Church in which the word effects what it signifies and is therefore a prophetic word. For the sacraments of the Church are also the supreme actuation of the efficacious word, both as regarding the ministering Church and the recipients of grace.[56]

In other words, while a sacrament is the realization of the very nature of the Church as the permanent presence of redemptive grace in the life of the individual, it is also "the supreme actuation of the efficacious word" of *the* prophet, Jesus Christ. In another context Rahner maintains that the sacraments must be understood as "Christ's gestures, as the real physical appearance of his action."[57] In performing these ritualized actions the Christian community has always believed that the recipient encounters Christ and shares in the grace of his victory over sin and death. This, however, does not suggest that the ecclesial rites come from Christ in the precise manner in which the Church now celebrates them. Yet, it does indicate that they are in some way rooted in his proclamation of the kingdom, particularly in his words and actions which, as the Spirit-filled prophet, he employed to announce the absolute immediacy and the self-communication of the Father.[58] Rahner does not deny this claim. His contention is that, given the nature both of the Church as the ongoing presence of the triumphant victory of God and of the sacraments as its actualization in the existential situation of the individual, such a demonstration, even if it were possible, is wholly unnecessary. While each

---

[56] "Prophetism," 112.

[57] K. Rahner, "Personal and Sacramental Piety," *TI* 2, 124.

[58] To this end P.J. Rosato, *Introduzione alla teologia dei sacramenti*, sees the seven sacraments as rooted in specific actions and attitudes of Jesus: baptism in the Jordan washing and in Jesus' ministry of justice (59-68); confirmation in the prophetic mission of hope (69-73); eucharist in the self-giving of Jesus at the Last Supper (82-92); penance in Jesus' ministry of peace and reconciliation (73-76); anointing in Jesus' ministry of compassion (76-79); orders in Jesus' call to serve (94-99); matrimony in the fidelity of Jesus (99-104).

sacrament is implicitly instituted in the explicit foundation of the Church, there is a vital link between a particular ecclesial gesture and the prophetic actions of the Promized One. In this way, christology, ecclesiology and sacramental theology come together as the eschatological victory of God in Jesus Christ is communicated through the Spirit to the believer.[59]

With regards to the sacrament of baptism, then, Rahner is not concerned to root the institution in explicit words or deeds of Jesus, or in his appropriation of the rite of the Baptist. In *Kirche und Sakramente* he asks how Jesus could have spoken of ritual acts in such a way that grace could be recognized as their effect. While despairing of a resolution in the case of either matrimony or orders, Rahner notes that

> with baptism, for instance, the matter is easy to understand. It is expressly called re-birth, forgiveness of sins, because without these designations it can hardly be intelligibly described even in externals.[60]

But this is of little consequence for Rahner.[61] In his attempt to establish an intrinsic link between the sacraments and the Church he is content with the conclusion that "the sacraments in general have been instituted by Christ because and to the extent that the Church as such derives from him."[62] As this study shows, however, this does not mean that baptism is not rooted in the life and mission of the eschatological prophet, particularly in the drama which unfolded between Jesus and John in the River Jordan.

2.4 Opus operatum *and Prophetic Act*

Given that the Council of Trent expressly taught the necessity of an inner disposition and of a faithful appropriation for a fruitful

---

[59] W.A. Van Roo, "Karl Rahner's 'Kirche und Sakramente'," *Gr* 44 (1963) 497, sees a *via media* between institution as an explicit word about sacramentality and Rahner's approach of implicit institution in the foundation of the Church: "Christ instituted this sacrament, because Christ ordered His apostles to exercise *this* kind of function and to produce *this* grace. *Indeterminate, obscure, implicit* as such a word may have been in comparison with later explicit conceptualization of the sacramental teaching, still it was a word concerning a rite, not just a word instituting a Church, and it was the necessary indication to the Church that this *is* one of her basic acts."

[60] *CS*, 42.

[61] Indeed, sometimes Rahner appears to doubt it. See "What is a Sacrament?," 146; *FCF*, 413.

[62] "What is a Sacrament?," 146.

reception of a sacrament by an adult,[63] Rahner recognizes that, as in the case with *opus operantis*, there is an element of uncertainty about the grace conferred *opus operatum*. Unimpressed by traditional theology's explanations of the latter[64] and convinced that God has attached the unconditional promise of grace to instances of the former,[65] Rahner questions the difference between the two. In response, he claims that

> the answer can only be that in the first case [*opus operantis*] the sign ... to which God has attached his grace, is itself intrinsically fragile, vulnerable, capable that is of becoming invalid of itself, and of being for its own part deprived of the character of visible expression of God's promise of grace. In the second case [*opus operatum*] the sign has an irrevocable eschatological validity; in itself it is the sign of the eternal irrevocable covenant of God with men, a sign which so shares in the eternity and irrevocability of God's salvific will, that the sign itself can never lose the quality of being the visible expression of God's consenting answer to man.[66]

In the case of *opus operantis*, then, a doubt always remains. Such a sign (a prayer, for example) may be empty (it may not be a prayer). A sign which is placed *opus operatum*, however, can never be evacuated of its ability to communicate divine grace.[67] As an action which expresses "the eternal irrevocable covenant of God" with humanity, it is none other than the self-actualization of the Church as the historical presence of the victorious mercy of God to the individual concerned. Indeed, Rahner suggests, the difference between *opus operantis* and *opus operatum* becomes clearer in the light of the distinction between the sacraments of the old covenant and those of the new.[68] Like *opus operantis*, the Old Testament and its associated signs were inherently "fragile," "temporary,

---

[63] DS 1525; 1559; 1606.

[64] *CS,* 26: "The idea of *opus operatum* in fact current, contains an element of what one might almost call physical certainty of functioning, which does not belong to it in more accurate theology." W.A. Van Roo, "Karl Rahner's 'Kirche und Sakramente'," 465, is unhappy with Rahner's characterisation of *Schultheologie*.

[65] *CS,* 26: "If someone prays in the name of Jesus for saving grace and for nothing else ..., he knows with infallible certainty that God hears him, even if the precise mode of the answer remains hidden and must be left in God's hands."

[66] *CS,* 28.

[67] Even when this communication meets a human refusal, it still remains a word of grace, God's "yes" to the world. See *CS,* 28-29.

[68] *CS,* 29-32.

replaceable and destructible."[69] Even now, superseded by the sealing of the eternal covenant, they continue to persist outwardly but are no longer guarantees of grace. Since the new covenant and its signs are the "visible manifestations of the final power of God,"[70] they are permanently assured to communicate divine life. In other words, as ecclesial actions, as infallible realizations of the eschatological triumph of God with respect to the believer, New Testament signs are posited *opus operatum*; as expressions of a covenant which is partial and which is open to future fulfilment, Old Testament signs are inherently threatened actions and consequently do not unfailingly confer the grace they signify.[71] This difference parallels Schürmann's distinction between prophetic acts and eschatological signs of fulfilment. The former belonged to the time of promise: they heralded a proximate intervention of God and they looked forward to a future fulfilment in which they would be superseded. The latter, by contrast, belong to the time of fulfilment: they introduce the irruption of the end-time and, consequently, they can never be annulled or surpassed.

2.5 *Symbolic Causality and Prophetic Acts*

That "sacraments produce grace" is axiomatic in Catholic theology.[72] However, within the many attempts to explain the relationship between sign posited and grace conferred, Rahner detects a fundamental flaw.[73] Spurred on by the traditional postulate *sacramenta significando efficiunt gratiam*, Rahner proposes the notion of "symbolic causality" [*Symbolursächlichkeit*], developed earlier in his article "The Theology of Symbol."[74] Attempting to determine the first principle of "an ontology of symbolism," Rahner claims that "all beings are by their very nature symbolic, because they necessarily 'express'

---

[69] *CS*, 31.

[70] *CS*, 31.

[71] W.A. Van Roo, "Karl Rahner's 'Kirche und Sakramente'," 487, argues that this is only a partial explanation which ignores the traditional teaching of the Council of Florence (DS 1310): "[Sacramenta Antiquae Legis] enim non causabant gratiam, sed eam solum per passionem Christi dandam esse figurabant: haec vero nostra et continent gratiam, et ipsam digne suscipientibus conferunt."

[72] See, for example, DS 1310; 1451; 1606-1608; 3489.

[73] According to Rahner (*CS*, 37) the basic defect which leads these theories into difficulty is "in tacitly laying down the pattern of transitive efficient causality, in which one factor adequately distinct from another must produce the latter." See D.A. Tappeiner, "Sacramental Causality in Aquinas and Rahner: Some Critical Thoughts," *SJTh* 28 (1975) 243-257.

[74] K. Rahner, "The Theology of Symbol," *TI* 4, 221-252.

themselves in order to attain their own nature."[75] The symbol is constituted by what is symbolized, yet it remains distinct from it.[76] Furthermore, as its external manifestation, the symbol not only reveals the underlying reality, but also facilitates its self-realization in time and space.[77] Immediately Rahner applies this concept to the Trinity,[78] christology,[79] ecclesiology,[80] and sacramental theology.[81] As the symbol of the final victory of Christ, the ecclesial community, then, is the visible and outward expression of grace,

> not in the sense that she subsequently announces as it were the presence of something already there without the announcement, but in the sense that in the Church God's grace is given expression and embodiment and symbolized, and by being symbolized is present.[82]

The Church exists because it announces grace, it exists *as* it embodies the eschatological mastery of God in the world. Grace persists in history because it is announced and finds spatio-temporal perceptibility in the Church. The ecclesial rite is, therefore, the cause of the grace of Christ, being the manner in which grace realizes itself. There is an inner and mutual causal relationship between the symbol and the symbolized, between the Church and the grace of Christ.

Being actualizations in the life of the individual of the essential nature of the Church as the presence of the victorious grace of Christ, sacramental signs are efficacious. Their power is neither that

---

[75] "The Theology of Symbol," 224.

[76] "The Theology of Symbol," 247.

[77] "The Theology of Symbol," 231.

[78] "The Theology of Symbol," 236: "... the Logos is the 'symbol' of the Father, in the very sense which we have given the word: the inward symbol which remains distinct from what is symbolized, which is constituted by what is symbolized, where what is symbolized expresses itself and possesses itself."

[79] "The Theology of Symbol," 238: "...the humanity of Christ is really the 'appearance' of the Logos itself, its symbolic reality in the pre-eminent sense, not something in itself alien to the Logos and its reality, which is only taken up from outside like an instrument to make its own music but not strictly to reveal anything of him who uses it."

[80] "The Theology of Symbol," 241: "The Church...really constitutes the full symbol of the fact that Christ has remained there as triumphant mercy."

[81] "The Theology of Symbol," 241: "The teaching *on the sacraments* is the classic place in which a theology of symbol is put forward in general in Catholic theology. The sacraments make concrete and actual, for the life of the individual, the symbolic reality of the Church as the primary sacrament and therefore constitute at once, in keeping with the nature of this Church a symbolic reality." See C.A. Callahan, "Karl Rahner's Theology of Symbol: Basis for his Theology of the Church and the Sacraments," *IThQ* 49 (1982) 195-205.

[82] *CS,* 34.

of a transient efficient causality nor that of a subsequent notification of a pre-existent reality. Rather, Rahner remarks,

> Their efficacy is that of intrinsic symbol. Christ acts through the Church in regard to an individual human being, by giving his action spatio-temporal embodiment by having the gift manifested in the sacrament. This visible form is itself an effect of the coming of grace; it is there because God is gracious to men; and in this self-embodiment of grace, grace itself occurs. The sacramental sign is cause of grace in as much as grace is conferred by being signified.[83]

The sacramental sign, then, is the visible, tangible, ecclesial communication of divine life to the believer concerned. The sign does not produce grace. The sign has its concrete form because grace exists and wishes to express itself. Rahner's thought is not adequately represented by the linear *sign→grace* relation; nor is it amply portrayed by the inverse *grace→sign* relation. Since the sign effects grace, because the latter produces the sacrament of the sanctification effected, Rahner's symbolic causality is more accurately illustrated by the compenetrating *grace↔sign* relation. In it the starting point is found in neither term, but with the Gracious One who wishes to share the divine life with humanity.

The parallels between *grace↔sign*, as expressed in Rahner's theory of symbolic causality, and *prophetic act↔notified reality* are striking. This is particularly the case when one considers the correlation between the symbolic action of the prophet and the presaged intervention of God, on the one hand, and between the positing of the sacramental sign and the conferral of grace, on the other. Because Jeremiah shatters the jar, the Lord is going to destroy Jerusalem; because the sacramental sign is posited, the Lord bestows grace. Similarly, because the Lord had decided to reject Jerusalem, Jeremiah breaks the jar; because the Lord has decided to communicate his saving love to individual believers, the sacramental rite is performed in their favour. Notice too that, while always a prophetic act, its ultimate power lies with the God who commands it; while always a sacramental rite, its ultimate efficacy is found in the Lord who guarantees the gift of eschatological life. Amsler is careful to distinguish between magic and prophetic act[84]: the former attempts to exert a coercive power on God; the latter unveils a future divine action within the present experience of the

---

[83] *CS,* 39.

[84] See Chapter 3, section 3.1.2.

audience. With his understanding of the inner-dependence between *opus operatum* and *opus operantis*,[85] and with his presentation of symbolic causality, Rahner avoids any impression of the Christian sacrament as a magic rite. He notes that

> Always and everywhere men have had the conviction that in gestures and rites and figurative representation, what is signified and pointed to, is in fact present, precisely because it is "represented," and this conviction should not be rejected off-hand as "analogy magic." This rejection is false because it fails to recognize the primarily ontological nature of symbol.[86]

In fact, because of the "ontological nature of symbol," a sacrament is neither an efficient cause nor a mere sign of a pre-existent situation. This point is developed in the next section.

3. **Baptism as Symbolic Act of Eschatological Salvation**

Within Rahner's writings, then, there is a series of converging indices which justify the present consideration of a sacrament as a symbolic prophetic act. Rahner's baptismal theology is now exposed in the first part of this section. Particular emphasis is placed on the effect of this lustral rite on non-baptized adults who, even prior to the liturgical event, are already justified by the indwelling of divine grace through faith, hope and love. In a second movement, the category of symbolic act is employed to highlight the prognostic dimension of baptismal grace.

3.1 *Rahner's Theology of Baptism*

Traditionally, Catholic theology has never insisted on the absolute necessity of water baptism for salvation: catechumen baptism of desire, and martyr baptism of blood, have always been recognized as salvific.[87] This, together with Rahner's doctrine of the transcendentality of the divine self-communication, raises as a matter of urgency the question of the relationship between sacramental and universal grace.

---

[85] *FCF*, 414: "And insofar as the *opus operatum* of the sacraments encounters the *opus operantis* of the believer or the person who accepts God's act, it is clear that sacraments are only efficacious in faith, hope and love. Hence they have nothing to do with magic rites. They are not magic because they do not coerce God, and because they are God's free act upon us."

[86] *CS*, 36.

[87] See *CCC* 1257-1259.

3.1.1 Ecclesial embodiment of universal grace

In an essay "Baptism and the Renewal of Baptism,"[88] published towards the end of his life, Rahner articulates the problem as follows:

> When adults are baptized they must, in order to receive the sacrament worthily, bring to baptism faith, hope and love.... When these conditions are fulfilled, the common doctrine of the Church and of theologians holds that these adults come to baptism already "justified"; they have accepted the divine life offered to them; they are, through the indwelling of the Holy Spirit, children of God. In such a case at least those who are baptized already possess what baptism is supposed to give them, the grace of justification.[89]

If the believer is justified through the indwelling of the Holy Spirit before actually receiving baptism, what, then, is the specific effect, or indeed, the point of the sacramental celebration? Certainly, the liturgical rite makes explicit that which is already implicit. It is the sign of the divine reality which is already at work in the life of the person. This corresponds to the *grace→sign* relation described above. But, if this is all that happens, the causality of the sacrament as defined by the Council of Trent is difficult to maintain.[90]

Rahner responds by analysing how a human phenomenon such as inter-personal love must find an outward embodiment in affectionate behaviour on the part of two lovers.[91] Words of love not only manifest the inner emotion, but also concretize its historical actualization. These words, then, are both the sign of the love, and its cause. In applying this insight to baptism, Rahner notes that the already justified candidates

> bring to their baptism the grace of God that has already freely been accepted. But through this ceremony of baptism this very grace wants to make itself visible historically (in space and time, in body) and socially (in the Church). And by becoming visible in this way it becomes present also in the bodily and social dimensions of the baptized person. Baptism is an effect of grace

---

[88] Originally published as "Warum man trotzdem beichten soll," *Entschluß* 37 (9/10/1982) 6-11. ET: "Baptism and the Renewal of Baptism" *TI* 23, 195-204.

[89] "Baptism and the Renewal of Baptism," 199.

[90] DS 1606: "Si quis dixerit, sacramenta novae Legis non continere gratiam, quam significant, aut gratiam ipsam non ponentibus obicem non conferre, quasi signa tantum externa sint acceptae per fidem gratiae vel iustitiae, et notae quaedam christianae professionis, quibus apud homines discernuntur fideles ab infidelibus: anathema sit."

[91] "Baptism and the Renewal of Baptism," 199.

> in such a way that through it this grace itself assumes full reality. And to that extent baptism is also the cause of grace.[92]

In baptism the pre-sacramental gift of grace "wants to make itself visible." The ritual activity, however, is not merely the subsequent notification of the antecedent indwelling of the Holy Spirit, or of the grace "that has already been freely accepted." Here another dimension is added. This grace, in the very act of positing itself (baptism as justification), attains its full historical and social nature in the pouring of the water (baptism as ritual). Behind this explanation lies Rahner's theory of symbolic causality as already exposed. In this sense, by eschewing any quasi-quantitative conception of the supernatural gift, Rahner recasts the traditional notion that the baptism of an already justified adult candidate leads to an "increase" in sanctifying grace.[93] Here, then, the question "what does baptism cause in its celebration?" receives a two-pronged response. First of all, the pre-sacramental indwelling of the Spirit finds a socio-historical embodiment in the lustral drama and thus achieves a concrete actualization. Secondly, the recipient is visibly incorporated into the ecclesial community which has established the ritual words and gestures as its own initiation rite.

Baptism is "concrete becoming-visible of the divine life, insofar as this life is also a Christian and therefore an ecclesial life."[94] The precise manner in which this embodiment of the divine life takes place in the culturally determined existence of the individual is not an arbitrary phenomenon. In fact, Rahner notes, the candidates

> must shape it in *the way* that is prescribed to them by this ecclesial community. And this way is precisely baptism with water and the invocation of the triune God. When somebody wants to state a juridically effective intention to bequeath an estate to a freely chosen heir, his intention, in order to be effective, must be stated in a will that is valid according to the laws of society. Something similar is true for baptism with water.[95]

In other words, because baptism is a rite of ecclesial initiation, the specific form of the ceremony which is used is not a question of personal choice but of liturgical norm. Here Rahner seeks to

---

92 "Baptism and the Renewal of Baptism," 200.
93 "Baptism and the Renewal of Baptism," 200.
94 "Baptism and the Renewal of Baptism," 198.
95 "Baptism and the Renewal of Baptism," 198.

explain how it is possible to conjoin a gift of the triune God to a categorical action of the Church. The sacraments are implicitly instituted in the explicit foundation of the Christian community. Consequently, the particular words and gestures which constitute each ecclesial act are stipulated by this pneumatic group. The analogy with the procedure involved in making a legally effective will, however, could be misleading. Rahner does not intend to suggest that the water rite is a whimsical detail which could be changed with the consensus of the legitimate authority. While a legal system could devise another means of bequeathing property to a chosen heir, it does not follow that the Church could devise willy nilly a totally different means of formally admitting new members. Insofar as either a juridical will or a lustral rite is presently valid according to the respective societal or ecclesial norms, this procedure is what must be observed by lawgivers or ministers.

But, the Church can and indeed has changed the matter and form of a Christian sacrament.[96] Such a prerogative, however, is not an arbitrary power. If Rahner's principle is to be upheld that "the sacramental sign is cause of grace in as much as grace is conferred by being signified,"[97] any alteration in the liturgical rite should ensure a more perspicacious relationship between the words and/or actions which constitute the symbol and the underlying self-communication of God which it represents. The lustral rite is not an arbitrary Church norm. In fixing this dramatic action, the People of God not only recall the decision of Jesus to be washed in the Jordan, but also attempt to symbolize the divine life which is imparted in its celebration. The relationship between the baptismal symbol and symbolized reality is developed later in this chapter.

3.1.2 "What *happens* in baptism?"

Rahner's book *Meditations on the Sacraments*[98] brings together a series of homilies and reflections on the Christian rites. Although the baptismal entry focuses on the practice of

---

[96] In *Divinae consortium naturae*, *AAS* 63(1971) 657-664, Pope Paul VI approved the revised rite of confirmation proposed by the Sacred Congregation for Divine Worship. The traditional form of the sacrament (the laying on of hands) was replaced by the anointing with chrism. This Byzantine gesture was considered as more expressive of the meaning of the sacrament.

[97] *CS*, 39.

[98] K. Rahner, *Meditations on the Sacraments*. [Originally published as *Die siebenfältige Gabe*.]

administering the sacrament to infants, Rahner is faced with the question: "But what *happens* in baptism?" He formulates his answer as follows:

> baptism is the act by which a human being joins the visible company of the members of the Church of Jesus Christ, crucified and restored to life and, in serving the one living God who has revealed Himself in one Lord, seeks to find perfection in the Second Coming of Christ.[99]

Initially this response reiterates the view, outlined in the previously analysed essay, that baptism is the gateway into the Church. Even when membership in the Church is forfeited by a Christian through unbelief or schism, Rahner acknowledges that he remains bound to the community of the Lord by virtue of the "everlasting spiritual title to share in the Holy Spirit of the Church and in the grace of righteousness bestowed upon him at his baptism."[100] In this way Rahner presents the traditional doctrine of baptismal character in an ecclesiological perspective.[101]

To be incorporated into the ecclesial community is the first effect of baptism.[102] Full membership brings other effects,[103] provided no obstacle is placed in the way of the pneumatic gifts: "This permanent spiritual seal is therefore his everlasting spiritual title to share in the Holy Spirit in the Church, and in the grace and righteousness bestowed upon him at his baptism."[104] Belonging to the Church, then, is both *sacramentum et res* of this lustral rite of initiation. Notice how the triple dimension of the sacramental actions is implicit in Rahner's answer which is quoted above. Through membership in the Church, the initiated receives a share of grace, that is, in the self-communication of the Holy Spirit (*signum demonstrativum*), in the life of the crucified and risen Lord (*signum rememorativum*), and in the future "Second Coming of Christ" (*signum prognosticum*).[105] Rahner develops this

---

[99] *Meditations on the Sacraments,* 6.

[100] *Meditations on the Sacraments,* 7.

[101] See *CS,* 87-90.

[102] *Lumen gentium* 11: "Incorporated into the Church by baptism, the faithful are appointed by their baptismal character to Christian religious worship: reborn as sons of God, they must profess before men the faith they have received from God through the Church." [Flannery, 361.] See *FCF,* 415.

[103] All grace, according to Rahner, is both christological and ecclesiological. See, for example, *CS,* 21.

[104] *Meditations on the Sacraments,* 7.

[105] Rahner often refers explicitly to the triple dimension of sacramental sign. See, for example, K. Rahner, "Introductory Observations on Thomas Aquinas' Theology of the Sacraments in General," *TI* 14, 154; *FCF,* 428-429.

eschatological dimension of the baptismal gift as he seeks to come to a clearer understanding of what is meant by sanctifying grace.

As is often the case, Rahner takes an anthropological starting point in his attempt to understand "this sublime gift"[106] which God bestows in the rite of baptism. The human person, he notes, experiences life as a journey into infinite mystery. But how this voyage will end can only be known from the gospel of Jesus Christ which reveals "a two-fold truth":

> this fulfilment is the boundless love of God Himself, which is shared with us and through which we are born again. It makes us sons and heirs with His Son, and pours the Spirit of God into our hearts, thus enabling us to share in the divine nature. And this perfection is not merely a verbal promise which must find its fulfilment in the future. The fulfilment is already here, but still remains hidden, believed in but not yet enjoyed. The future is already here, the life of God is already within us, the Holy Spirit is already poured out upon us, and we are already sons of God, so that we need only to receive the revelation of what we already are. And this fulfilment of our infinite longing comes with the life of God Himself, already given to us, although it is known only to faith. We call it saving grace.[107]

The destiny of the human person is the participation in the life of the triune God: through the power of the Spirit each one is called to be a son or daughter with the Son to the eternal glory of the Father. This potentiality comes to completion in the beatific vision when God will be seen face to face.[108] In the meantime the individual can glimpse this fulfilment in advance through justifying grace.[109] In the sacrament of baptism the candidate, by virtue of reception into the Church, is born again to the new life of Christ. Through the ritual washing, the future which the eternal God has in store for the believer is "already here": the eternal life of God is symbolically manifested and proleptically imparted. Beyond the ecclesial embodiment of pre-sacramental grace, the baptized "already enjoys a foretaste of the eternal glory in which he now has a right to share."[110] A consideration of the sacramental event as a prophetic act brings this *novum* of baptismal grace into sharper focus.

---

[106] *Meditations on the Sacraments,* 7.

[107] *Meditations on the Sacraments,* 8.

[108] See K. Rahner, "Some Implications of the Scholastic Notion of Uncreated Grace," *TI* 1, 326.

[109] K. Rahner, "Concerning the Relationship between Nature and Grace," *TI* 1, 302-303.

[110] *Meditations on the Sacraments,* 9.

3.2 *Baptism as Prophetic Act*

In the light of the baptismal theology of Rahner, then, what contribution does the biblical category prophetic act make to this study of the eschatological dimension of the lustral rite? This question is addressed in this concluding section.

3.2.1 Establishing a new relationship

When Jeremiah broke the jar, the onlookers became aware of the disaster which lay in store for them. The prophetic action not only gave notice of divine intent, but also unleashed the impending historical activity of God in the there and then of the audience. In order words, what would come to pass was already a reality determining the contemporary situation of the community. If Jeremiah had refrained from performing his scandalous action, the divine-human relationship would have been different; because of the shattering scene, however, all was changed. The very identity of the group was overturned: once a people of hope and promise, they were now under the threat of menace and destruction. What if a member of the covenant community were unaware of the prophetic action? Clearly, such a person would have been ignorant of the altered situation before God, and oblivious to the immediate unfolding of the divine self-communication in the history of the chosen people. However, it would not simply have been a matter of a lack of information about a present or future eventuality. Rather, unconscious of the impending divine intervention, the self-understanding of the individual and his very identity before God would have been inherently false.

A candidate who comes forward to be baptized is cognisant of the saving design of God in his life. The lustral action not only averts the recipient to the divine plan to confer eternal beatitude in some heavenly time and place, but also assures him that, in the midst of the ecclesial community, this fulfilment is already at hand. In other words, the gracious gift of eternal life with God is already a reality determining the present circumstances of Christian existence. Because of the ritual action the self-awareness of the candidate and his singularity before God are transformed: once a child bound by time and death, the recipient now lives on the threshold of everlasting life.

3.2.2 Word and sign

Old and New Testament prophetic acts reveal an analogical structure between the gesture and the word of explanation, on the one hand, and the presaged activity of God, on the other: Ahijah tears his cloak into twelve pieces as an anticipation of the scattering of the twelve tribes of Israel; Jesus calls twelve disciples to announce the formation of the community of the new covenant. The relationship between the action of the prophet and the future intervention of God has already been discussed.[111] In the case of New Testament eschatological signs of fulfilment, Schürmann argues that primarily "the sign follows the effect"[112]: the divinely guaranteed end-time gift of salvation is represented by the prophetic action. Notice the similarity between this and Rahner's notion of symbol. "The grace of God," Rahner contends, "constitutes itself actively present in the sacraments by creating their expression, their historical tangibility in space and time, which is its own symbol."[113] Applied to the sacrament of baptism, then, this intimates that the lustral washing together with the trinitarian invocation (the gesture and words which constitute the prophetic symbol) is brought about by the grace of justification (the symbolized activity of God) which finds actualization through it. This saving gift necessarily creates its own symbol which expresses its deepest sense. The sacramental sign, therefore, is not an arbitrary factor which could be changed by ecclesiastical decree. Through the enactment of the lustral rite something comes to be in the concrete existence of the individual which otherwise would not be realized.[114]

---

[111] See Chapter 3, section 3.1.2.

[112] See Chapter 4, section 1.2.

[113] "The Theology of Symbol," 242.

[114] In "Personal and Sacramental Piety," 110, Rahner asks if there are "'sacramental' graces which can be received only through the sacrament?" He answers as follows: "There are, of course, *effects* of the sacrament which cannot be received otherwise than through the sacraments, such as our allotted place in the order of the hierarchico-visible Church, given to us by Baptism, Confirmation and Holy Orders, or the sacramental character, and the marriage bond. But our question is not concerned with such matters. The question is rather: is there some *grace* which can be acquired only through a sacrament, be it the grace of the state of justification and sanctification and its growth, or be it (actual) grace to help us to continue in the truly Christian life of oneness with Christ and to fight against sin, face the trial of death, profess the Faith, fulfil our vocation to the priesthood, matrimony, etc? This may well be doubted." If each rite is truly a symbol of grace, Rahner's own ontology of symbol suggests that any difference between sacramental and extra-sacramental grace, or indeed between the grace conferred by different sacraments, is not just confined to the effects but actually impinges on the

There is a difference then between the justified non-baptized and the initiated Christians. In the liturgical rite the pre-sacramental offer of divine life is celebrated as a socio-ecclesial event. The words and gestures do not merely explicate that which is already an implicit reality; rather, by constituting a symbol which facilitates a tangible actualization of the underlying mystery, they categorically express the transcendental divine self-communication. This takes place for particular members of the believing community and proclaims a new future in God's ongoing relationship with them. The prophet, according to Rahner, authentically objectifies in word and deed the unthematic self-communication of God and heralds a new situation in the unfolding divine-human drama.[115] As the solemn embodiment of the innermost grace operative in the believer and as the harbinger of his eschatological life, baptism has an inherently prophetic function.

3.2.3 Character as indelible delegation

As has already been noted, Rahner considers baptismal character from his overall ecclesiological viewpoint: incorporation into the *ekklesia* is the first effect of baptism; as a *signum indelibile* it expresses the Church's "enduring claim to the baptized person."[116] The immediate effect of the Old Testament prophetic act was to shock the spectators, provoking them into taking a stance for or against the transcendent reality announced by the inspired messenger. Those who accepted the dramatic action as the anticipated divine intervention, took on a new identity before God and among the people. Such an altered consciousness must correspond to something more than a changed existential situation before the Lord of life. Through the prophetic action, God has spoken in the history of a specific people. As a public declaration which can never be repealed, the relationship between Yahweh and this group is radically changed.

In addressing the extrinsicism which he saw in "the average teaching on grace in the last few centuries,"[117] Rahner offers an insight into the nature of the effect the divine intention has on the human person:

---

grace itself, on the very nature of the divine self-communication associated with each sacrament.

[115] See above, section 1.1.

[116] *CS,* 89.

[117] "Concerning the Relationship between Nature and Grace," 298.

> *must* not what God decrees for man be *eo ipso* an interior ontological constituent of his concrete quiddity "terminative," even if not a constituent of his "nature"? For an ontology which grasps the truth that man's concrete quiddity depends utterly on God, is not his binding disposition *eo ipso* not just a juridical decree of God but precisely what man *is*, hence not just an imperative proceeding from God but man's inward depths?[118]

Here Rahner notes that the human race is utterly dependent on God and takes its name from this relationship; this orientation towards the divine determines not just the accidental characteristics of human persons, but also their inner reality. Each unfolding of the divine *mysterion* has profound implications for humanity: as God unveils the eternal plan of salvation in the history of the covenant people, their self-understanding and group identity change. This transformation is explained satisfactorily neither by extrinsic nor existential considerations. Since the very reality of the human condition before God is radically modified, it is necessary to speak of some ontological change in the individuals or in the community concerned.

When, for example, Jeremiah shatters the jar in the sight of the people of Israel, their relationship with Yahweh is substantially altered in the light of the anticipated disaster. Once a people of promise, they now live under the impending threat of irrevocable destruction, and the very identity of each witness is essentially changed before God. As the irreversible offer of the eschatological life of Christ to the individual by means of incorporation into the Church, baptism can never be repealed or superseded. Through the ecclesial rite, the triune God intervenes in the lives of the candidates so as to change radically their identity. No matter what baptized persons may do in the future, no matter how vehemently they may subsequently renounce the faith which was once ritually celebrated, God has spoken in their lives and the effect of this intervention can never be obliterated. Having undergone the unrepeatable and irrevocable prophetic rite of washing, the baptized are ontologically changed and stand as reminders of what God has already accomplished, and has yet to complete, in their lives.

---

[118] "Concerning the Relationship between Nature and Grace," 302.

3.2.4 Conferring the form of eschatological life

While the indwelling of the Holy Spirit may precede any sacramental celebration, there is a specific grace which can only be conferred by the initiatory action.[119] This grace creates its own symbol; by being symbolized the underlying divine gift finds its actualization in the personal history of the candidates. The liturgical cleansing with water in the name of the Father, Son and Spirit frees them from sin, and imparts the justice of God which it represents. Rahner's theology highlights the essential continuity between the beatific vision and grace.[120]

> the life of glory is the definitive flowering (the "manifestation," the "disclosure") of the life of divine sonship already possessed and merely "hidden" for the moment. Hence grace, as the ontological basis of this supernatural life, is also an inner entitative principle (at least a partial principle) of the vision of God. According to scripture the possession of the Spirit is the earnest and firstfruits of the definitive beatifying bestowal of God's grace and mercy; thus it is not just its "pledge" and legal title, but a commencement of glory, still hidden, no doubt, only present to consciousness in faith, but really and entitatively given already.[121]

The future life of glory, therefore, is the "definitive flowering" of the current dispensation of grace; the present indwelling of the Spirit is the "ontological basis" of the impending life with God. While traditional Catholic theology focused on created grace in terms of efficient causality, that is, as an effect wrought by God on the human soul, Rahner accentuates the actuality of uncreated grace in terms of quasi-formal causality, that is, as the indwelling of God in it.[122] The justified non-baptized already possess this pneumatic gift of "the life of divine sonship" in a hidden way. Now, in the midst of historical existence, they enjoy not just a "pledge" or a "legal title," but also the entitative commencement of glory.

---

[119] See B. Leeming, *Principles of Sacramental Theology*, 94-125.

[120] "Some Implications of the Scholastic Concept of Uncreated Grace," 319-346.

[121] "Some Implications of the Scholastic Concept of Uncreated Grace," 326.

[122] P. De Letter, "Divine Quasi-Formal Causality," *IThQ* 27 (1960) 225: "The *quasi-* ... does not mean to suggest that the union of the divine quasi-form with the human quasi-matter is not immediate. Nothing stands between. It only means to exclude all shadow of mutual causality, such as it exists of necessity between matter and form when taken in the proper sense of the terms." See G. Vandervelde, "The Grammar of Grace: Karl Rahner as a Watershed in Contemporary Theology," *TS* 49 (1988) 445-459.

Baptized Christians, however, are explicitly the definitively justified people whom all hope to become. The sacramental rite specifies and imparts the form of future life: washed free from sin in the regenerating waters of the Spirit, they come face to face with the will of the Father to save, and are incorporated into the eschatological community of the Son. They now live neither out of the past nor out of the present but out of the future which God now communicates to those who journey towards the fulness of everlasting life.

While universal grace which all the justified enjoy is a veiled inception of eternal life, "a new eschatological intervention of God who is still ... concealed"[123] is required for the unfolding of definitive glory. In the prophetic washing of baptism, this intervention is proleptically unleashed into the present of the recipients. Just as the broken jar not only apprized the chosen people of the destruction of Jerusalem but also grafted the divine action into their history, so too the ecclesial water-rite is the *signum prognosticum* which both adverts Christians to eternal life with God and ushers them into the epoch of perpetual beatitude. This entrance will be prolonged without end, once the new creation takes hold of the old.[124] In baptism, then, through water and the invocation of the triune God, the form of eschatological life is foreshadowed. This gift which non-baptized justified persons are to receive in the *visio beatifica*, is bestowed on believers through the lustral rite.

---

[123] "Some Implications of the Scholastic Concept of Uncreated Grace," 335.

[124] L. Leijssen, "La contribution de Karl Rahner," 102: "Dans la vision de Rahner les sacrements sont de manière évidente des signes eschatologiques, des signes précurseurs du salut encore imparfaitement réalisé. Ils sont des *signa prognostica*, pré-connaissance et pré-célébration de l'achèvement à la fin des temps. Ils sont des expressions de la force de l'Esprit qui est actif dans la dynamique vers la destination finale (*entelechie*)."

CHAPTER 6

The Course of Baptism

Baptism as the prophetic act of ecclesial commitment to the praxis which anticipates a new world in the writings of Edward Schillebeeckx

In 1952, Edward Schillebeeckx published *De Sacramentele Heilseconomie,*[1] a re-worked edition of the first part of his doctoral dissertation which he had presented the previous year at *Le Saulchoir.* An impressive study of almost seven hundred pages, it situated the thomistic doctrine on sacraments within the overall platonic scheme of *exitus-reditus,*[2] and then offered an overview of the sacramental theology of a number of patristic and medieval authors. From 1947, Schillebeeckx had been Master of Students at the Dominican house of studies in Louvain. This book, written for students of theology, advanced an alternative to the manuals of neo-scholasticism which were the staple diet in seminary faculties at that time. The subtitle of the work — "A theological reflection on St. Thomas' teaching on the sacraments in the light of tradition and the current sacramental problematic" — immediately reveals two notable influences on the early Schillebeeckx, one transcendental, the other liturgical. At Ghent, in the course of his philosophical training, the young Dominican not only read the usual works by Aquinas, but also, under the direction of D. De Petter, he became familiar with the writings of modern philosophers, such as E. Kant, G. Hegel, E. Husserl and M. Merleau-Ponty, then forbidden to aspirants for the Catholic priesthood. In dialogue with the ideas proposed by these authors, Schillebeeckx came to an heightened awareness of certain limitations of neo-scholastic philosophy and

---

[1] The full title is *De Sacramentele Heilseconomie: Theologische bezinning op S. Thomas' sacramentenleer in het licht van de traditie en van de hedendaagse sacramentsproblematiek.*

[2] *De Sacramentele Heilseconomie,* 2-18.

of the "current sacramental problematic" which were made evident by contemporary modes of thought. Moreover, by returning to primary theological sources and by situating scholastic texts within the historical and philosophical contexts of the twelfth and thirteenth centuries, Schillebeeckx learned to go beyond the summary digests of the early twentieth-century commentators on St. Thomas, and to study the original writings of the latter "in the light of tradition."

Numerous studies exist on the sacramental theology of Schillebeeckx.[3] This chapter is not intended as one more. Rather, in conformity with the overall thrust of this research project, it seeks to investigate how the writings of this theologian further the understanding of baptism as prophetic act of eschatological salvation. It has already been noted in Chapter 2 that two distinct phases can be identified within Schillebeeckx's theological *corpus*. His explicit treatment of sacraments derives from the first period, which has been dated from 1945 until 1966. No significant publication on a sacramental theme comes from the later stage of Schillebeeckx's academic career.

This chapter unfolds in three steps. First of all the role of baptism in the early sacramental theory of Schillebeeckx is investigated ("Initiating Encounter"). In this section the broad strokes of his sacramental theory, as presented in *Christ the Sacrament of the Encounter with God*, are outlined before focusing on selected texts which throw light on his understanding of baptism at this early stage. A second movement ("From Chalcedon to Galilee") centres on the presentation of the prophetic actions of Jesus in *Jesus* and *Christ*, the first two volumes of the christological trilogy. Finally, a third section ("Anticipating Future") analyses the place of the sacrament of baptism in the later praxis-oriented thought of Schillebeeckx as portrayed in *Jesus Christ in our Western Culture*[4] and in *Church*, the conclusion to his christological project. The underlying thesis of this chapter is that baptism viewed as symbolic act of eschatological salvation not only provides a key insight into Schillebeeckx's work on this

---

[3] See J.M. Powers, *Symbolic Instrumentality in the Sacramental Theology of Edward. H. Schillebeeckx*; C. G. Bruno, *Il concetto di sacramento in Schillebeeckx*; S. M. Ross, "Salvation in and for the World: Church and Sacraments" in *The Praxis of Christian Experience,* ed. R. J. Schreiter – M. C. Hilkert, 101-115.

[4] E. Schillebeeckx, *Jesus Christ in our Western Culture*. [Hereafter *JWC*.] This book contains the texts of the Abraham Kuyper lectures which Schillebeeckx delivered in Amsterdam in the Spring of 1986.

sacrament but, understood in this vein, it is an architectonic concept which unites the earlier and later periods of his thought.

1. **Initiating Encounter**

From the outset, Schillebeeckx declares that his intention in writing *Christ the Sacrament of the Encounter with God* is "to arrive at the insight that the sacraments are the properly human mode of encounter with God."[5] The fruits of Schillebeeckx's two-strand, philosophical and historical, approach are condensed in the concept of "encounter" which he includes in the title of this summary volume. In the foreword, C. Ernst acknowledges the dependence of Schillebeeckx on the phenomenological anthropology of writers such as M. Merleau-Ponty, F.J.J. Buytendijk and L. Binswanger. While pre-phenomenological philosophy conceived of all knowledge on the model of the human comprehension of physical realities, Ernst argues that this model has been abandoned so that "'knowledge-of-things' is derived from a fundamental being-in-the-world."[6] The concept "encounter," then, underlines the "preordained openness to our fellows which releases our being into the fellowship of a *we*."[7] Within a sacramental theology it reinforces the fact that the self-giving of God is fulfilled in the incarnation, "God addressing man as man amongst men."[8] Schillebeeckx himself claims that "encounter" is simply a modern word for that "theological, personal relationship to God in virtue of grace,"[9] which has always been recognized in religious experience. In this way, Schillebeeckx uses the tools of historical *ressourcement* to retrieve the fuller sense of a scholastic concept which he then expresses with the help of phenomenological analysis.[10]

1.1 *Encounter in Jesus Christ*

In *Christ the Sacrament*, the starting point chosen by Schillebeeckx is the dogmatic definition of the Council of

---

[5] *CSEG,* 6.
[6] C. Ernst, "Foreword," in *CSEG,* xv.
[7] C. Ernst, "Foreword," xv.
[8] C. Ernst, "Foreword," xvi.
[9] See "De zin van het mens-zijn van Jesus, de Christus," *TTh* 2 (1962) 128. [Quoted in C. Ernst, "Foreword," xvi, n. 4.]
[10] See C. Ernst, "Foreword," xvi, n. 4.

Chalcedon which affirms that Christ is "one person in two natures."[11] This implies that

> one and the same person, the Son of God, also took on a visible human form. Even in his humanity Christ is the Son of God. The second person of the most holy Trinity is personally man; and this man is personally God. Therefore Christ is God in a human way, and man in a divine way. As a man he acts out his divine life in and according to his human existence. Everything he does as man is an act of the Son of God, a divine act in human form; an interpretation and transposition of a divine activity into a human activity. His human love is the human embodiment of the redeeming love of God.[12]

In other words, the earthly acts of Jesus Christ are divine actions in visible form. To come into contact with Jesus of Nazareth is to approach the divine offer of grace. The human actions of Christ not only "interpret" and "transpose" the saving love of the Father, but they also "possess"[13] and "bestow"[14] the divine salvation which they actually manifest. According to Schillebeeckx, since a "sacrament is a divine bestowal of salvation in an outwardly perceptible form which makes the bestowal manifest,"[15] the man Jesus is the primordial[16] sacrament of God. His human actions as "the divine bestowal of grace itself realized in visible form"[17] are sacraments.

In Jesus the divine offer of salvation and the human acceptance in faith converge. Therefore, as Schillebeeckx comments,

> Jesus is not only the divine offer of love to man made visible but, at the same time, as prototype (or primordial model) he is the supreme realization of the response of human love to this divine offer: "in our place" and "in the name of us all," as Scripture repeatedly says. Whatever Christ does as a free man is not only a realization in human form of God's activity for our salvation; it is also at the same time the positive human acceptance, representative for all of us, of this redeeming offer from God.[18]

---

[11] DS 302.

[12] *CSEG,* 13-14.

[13] *CSEG,* 14.

[14] *CSEG,* 15.

[15] *CSEG,* 16.

[16] Schillebeeckx uses the term "primordial sacrament" with reference to Jesus and to the Church. See *CSEG,* 115, where he refers to both as primordial sacrament.

[17] *CSEG,* 17.

[18] *CSEG,* 18.

In the mystery of the incarnation, the descending motion of the divine approach (*exitus*) and the ascending motion of human response (*reditus*) converge. While the former corresponds to salvation from God and the latter to praise by humankind, together they constitute in Christ "one mystery of saving worship."[19] This unity is the linchpin in the author's early sacramental construct.

Schillebeeckx identifies four phases in the redemption established by Christ.[20] Firstly, within the eternal life of the Godhead, there is the initiative of the Father through the Son in the Holy Spirit. Secondly, during the historical duration of the incarnation, the intra-trinitarian self-giving of the Son is expressed as the obedient human response of Christ.[21] Thirdly, this loving attachment of Jesus to the Father finds an initial response in the resurrection and is brought to fulfilment in the ascension. Finally, the gift of the Holy Spirit is sent by the *Kyrios* existing in his glorified or consummated humanity. The "mystery of saving worship" which began in the incarnation, life, death and resurrection of Jesus continues in the glorified humanity of the Exalted One. The activity of the Lord in heaven is still a filial and reverent intercession of the Father, and a continual sending of the Holy Spirit upon humankind.[22] The one who was sanctified by the Spirit now sanctifies through the same pneumatic gift. The result of the "redeeming incarnation, as an enduring reality,"[23] is that all human beings are adopted in Christ as children of the Father.

Within the divine plan of salvation, an encounter with God remains bound up with a personal encounter with the man Jesus.[24] Now that he has ascended to the Father, Christ must still make his presence felt in a sensate way in his body, the Church, and in the sacraments. As Schillebeeckx remarks:

> Christ makes his presence among us actively visible and tangible too, not directly through his own bodiliness, but by extending among us on earth in visible form the function of his

---

[19] *CSEG*, 19; 37.

[20] See *CSEG*, 20-21.

[21] *CSEG*, 31: "For however much the Son of God is pure self-giving to the Father, on the divine level it is nevertheless not possible for this to be in the mode of a giving-up, a dispossession of self or a sacrifice, as certain Russian Orthodox theologians (Bulgakov, Lossky) have wanted to suggest. Only in his human existence can the Son's eternal giving of himself to the Father be realized in the true form of a sacrifice and of self-dispossession."

[22] *CSEG*, 37.

[23] *CSEG*, 39.

[24] *CSEG*, 40.

> bodily reality which is in heaven. This precisely is what the sacraments are: the earthly extension of the "body of the Lord." This is the Church.[25]

Since all grace derives from the personal action of Christ himself[26] it follows that, unless redemption would no longer be communicated to humanity, an encounter with him who is living in glory must be possible. This necessary meeting, according to Schillebeeckx, takes place in the ecclesial body through the economy of the sacraments.

Within this understanding there is a strong eschatological emphasis. At the heart of Christian faith lies the promise of eternal glory with God in heaven. As an existence between *pascha* and *parousia*, the present life of believers is a waiting in hope for that encounter which has yet to come. However, Schillebeeckx insists, this is not all. Any expectation of the ultimate, perfect encounter can be understood, he claims, only because the living, glorified Christ is already experienced in the Church which is his body and in the sacraments which are its visible worldly extensions. Christian life in the world, then, is "markedly eschatological."[27] Moreover, this end-time quality is decidedly sacramental.

1.2 *Encounter in Baptism*

In his presentation of Christ as the sacrament of the encounter with God and of the ecclesial rites as its visible signs in the world, Schillebeeckx makes two notable baptismal references. In the first, he explains that the mystery of the saving worship of Christ is founded both on his humiliation and on his glory. The mystery of the love of the Son for the Father is the foundation of the unfailing gift of grace. In the humiliation of the Incarnate One, the redemptive worship of the Father comes to the fore; in the glorification of the Crucified One, the gracious out-pouring of the Spirit is clearly pronounced. Yet, as Schillebeeckx remarks, there is no contradiction between these two inseparable aspects of Christ's activity:

> for though Christ before his glorification had still to realize actual redemption, and was not yet in reality a sender of the Holy Spirit, even in his humiliation, he was nevertheless the Son always beloved by the Father. In this we see how encounter with

---

[25] *CSEG,* 41.
[26] *CSEG,* 43. See *ST* III, Q. 8, a. 5 ad. 1.
[27] *CSEG,* 41.

> the earthly Jesus was already a grace. For in his heart Jesus already bore his sacrifice, with which, in anticipation, the Father was well pleased: "Thou art my beloved son. In thee I am well pleased." But this does not eliminate the fact that the great "pouring forth" of grace could take place only after the resurrection from the dead. So therefore we must say that, on the foundation of his earthly mystery of worship, the Lord himself does in fact bestow the grace of redemption on us, at the same time not forgetting that his earthly mystery of worship had already touched hearts with grace and that the heavenly sending of the Spirit is founded upon the heavenly liturgy of Christ, who in his worship of the Father "is always living to make intercession for us."[28]

According to Schillebeeckx, then, the heavenly voice at the baptism of Jesus witnesses to the pleasure of the Father at the self-giving of the Son. While Jesus already bore his sacrifice "in his heart," this being-for the Father is expressed and affirmed in the river rite. The sacrifice of Jesus which is fulfilled on Calvary is already acknowledged "in anticipation" at the Jordan. A clear connection is established, therefore, between the baptism of Jesus and his death on the Cross. The pro-existence of the incarnate Son, which is manifest from the outset of his public ministry, culminates in the event of the passion. Although the "pouring forth" of grace could take place only after the resurrection from the dead, Schillebeeckx recognizes that it is already operative in the earthly encounter with the self-giving Son. In fact, when the voice of the Father rejoices in the sacrificial love of the Beloved, the content of that love is revealed in the descent of the Spirit. According to Schillebeeckx, then, the baptism of Jesus is at once a proclamation of his ceaseless self-giving, and an anticipation of its consummation on the Cross. It is also both an acknowledgement of the One who can confer grace and a revelation of the universal gift which is yet to be outpoured.

In the second baptismal reference, towards the end of the same chapter, Schillebeeckx argues that:

> From the moment that, by his ascension, the "primordial sacrament" leaves the world, the economy of the "separated sacraments" becomes operative in consequence of the incarnation and as its prolongation. From Scripture we learn that while none of the twelve Apostles who enjoyed immediate contact with the "primordial sacrament" himself was baptized,

[28] *CSEG*, 37-38.

> St. Paul, the "thirteenth Apostle," who had not encountered the earthly Christ in faith, was in fact baptized. Sacramentality thus bridges the gap and solves the disproportion between the Christ of heaven and unglorified humanity, and makes possible a reciprocal human encounter of Christ and men even after the ascension, though in a special manner. A permanent sacramentality is thus an intrinsic requirement of the Christian religion.[29]

Here the reality of the sacramental encounter between Christ and the post-apostolic believers is underlined. While the apostles and those who enjoyed "immediate contact" with Jesus were not baptized, Paul and others who had not "encountered the earthly Christ in faith" underwent the lustral rite. Since Schillebeeckx states that the sacraments "bridge the gap" and "solve the disproportion between the Christ of heaven and unglorified humanity," it is obvious that Schillebeeckx envisages baptism as the first step in this "reciprocal human encounter" between them. Moreover, whereas all seven rites of the Christian dispensation facilitate this meeting with the Risen One, baptism is the initiation of this life-giving encounter.

1.3 *Encounter in Sign*

In formulating a "general definition" of the sacraments, Schillebeeckx states that:

> Each sacrament is the personal act of the risen Christ himself, but realized in the visible form of an official act of the Church ... To receive the sacraments of the Church in faith is therefore the same thing as to encounter Christ himself.[30]

According to this text, the sacraments are institutional acts of the Church. Yet, they are also the personal actions of Christ who prolongs his saving activity in time through the ecclesial body. Here the author asserts the ecclesiological dimension of the sacraments without detaching them from their christological foundation. In this context Schillebeeckx takes up and adapts the notion of *Mysteriengegenwart* or "presence in mystery" proposed by O. Casel.[31] Since the sacrifice of the Cross and all the mysteries of the life of Christ are personal acts of the God-man, they are

[29] *CSEG,* 44.
[30] *CSEG,* 54.
[31] For O. Casel on "mystery presence" see Chapter 2, section 1.2.

"eternally actual and enduring."[32] These historical actions of Christ possess a "perennial," "trans-historical element" which endures forever in the mode of glory.[33]

This inevitably raises the question of the relationship in the sacramental event between the past, historical actions of Christ and his eternal, heavenly presence. In this context, Schillebeeckx refers to the threefold orientation of the sacramental sign as presented by St. Thomas.[34] A sacrament is a *signum rememorativum*, an *anamnesis* or commemoration of the saving events of the life of Jesus Christ. But, Schillebeeckx warns, to say that the sacraments are extensions of the earthly life of Christ is an "insufficient statement of the case."[35] After the events of the passion and the resurrection of the Incarnate Son, the modality of his presence in the world has changed. The Church is a "prolongation primarily of the heavenly Christ" and, insofar as the sacraments bestow the grace they signify (*signum demonstrativum*), they are actions by which he "is reaching out to humanity here and now."[36] As Schillebeeckx remarks, treatises on the Church fail to explain that the glorified Christ is at the centre of primitive Christian faith. While recognizing that what Christ has achieved in the past is the indispensable foundation of his spiritual presence in the community, the early Christians focused more on the latter than on the former. In this way, Schillebeeckx underlines that the long neglected eschatological dimension of the sacrament as *signum prognosticum* is a datum of Christian faith from the first centuries. The sacraments, he notes,

> are a pledge of eschatological salvation and a herald of the *parousia*, because the sacraments are the sacramental presence of Christ, the *Eschaton*. ... Hence a visible intervention in our lives of the *Eschaton* himself takes place in the sacraments. Sacramental encounter with the living Christ in the Church is therefore, in virtue of the historical mysteries of Christ's life, the actual beginning of eschatological salvation on earth.[37]

Notice again how eschatology and sacraments are linked by the author: through the ritual actions of the Church, the end-time

---

[32] *CSEG,* 57.
[33] *CSEG,* 58.
[34] *ST.* III, Q. 60, a. 3. See Chapter 1, section 1.1.
[35] *CSEG,* 63.
[36] *CSEG,* 62.
[37] *CSEG,* 62-63.

encounter with the glorified Lord takes root in the life of the believers.

The unity of the descending and ascending motions both in the mystery of the incarnation of the Son (the divine offer of salvation and the human response to it) and in his eternal glorification (the adoration of the Father and the sending of the Spirit) finds a parallel in Schillebeeckx's understanding of the ecclesial celebration of the sacraments. In these ritual actions, the Church, together with Christ its Head, pleads with the Father for the bestowal of grace on the recipients of the sacrament (ascending motion) and, at the same time, it performs a saving act by conferring the pneumatic gift on them (descending motion).[38] This twofold aspect of the sacraments highlights their essential trinitarian structure: through the power of the Holy Spirit, the believing community is united with the eternal glorification of the Father by the Son, while effecting, in turn, the "salvation-through-worship" which it expresses.[39] Schillebeeckx contends, therefore, that "the substance of a sacrament always includes a twofold element," namely,

> an *epiclesis* in the form of a request (*in forma deprecativa*) that is to say, a prayer in which we plead with the Father by the power of the Spirit and together with Christ; and a definitive bestowal (*in forma indicitiva*). Both elements are always present, even when they no longer appear, as was formerly the case, in two separate ritual moments in the Liturgy.[40]

Here, Schillebeeckx charges that the western liturgy has often concentrated on the "indicative formula" to the detriment of the epiclesis or "deprecatory formula" of the sacramental event. Indeed, this downplaying of the pneumatic liturgical moment is closely connected with the eclipsing of the eschatological dimension of the sacramental sign as outlined in Chapter 1. By emphasizing the indicative aspect, the western tradition has accented the demonstrative and, to a lesser extent, the commemorative dimensions of the sacramental sign.[41] By insisting on the

---

[38] *CSEG,* 66.

[39] *CSEG,* 67.

[40] *CSEG,* 72.

[41] The indicative sacramental formulae are normally couched in a commemorative framework. The indicative of the formula of absolution used in the sacrament of penance ("Through the ministry of the Church may God give you pardon and peace and I absolve you from your sins, in the name of the Father and of the Son and of the Holy Spirit.") is preceded by a concise reminder of the salvation won for humanity by the Triune God ("God, the Father of mercies, through the death

complementarity between the pneumatic deprecation and the christic formula, Schillebeeckx retrieves the eschatological perspective, and restores the equilibrium between *epiclesis* and *anamnesis* in the liturgical action.

As personal acts of the glorified Christ in visible form, sacraments bestow the grace they signify. On the relationship between sign and grace, Schillebeeckx notes that:

> The sign itself makes the actual gift of grace here present. It is not of course as if the sign, as sign, could have an actual effect, but rather the other way about; the gift of grace comes in its own visibility; it makes itself here present visibly (thus "in a sign") and therefore "works" in visible presence. Certainly the gift of grace makes itself present in an embodiment borrowed from this world or, more precisely, in a human act of the ecclesial minister.[42]

This approach is similar to that of Rahner in *Kirche und Sakramente.*[43] It also reflects the interdependence between the performed action and the signified reality both in the Old Testament prophetic acts[44] and in the New Testament eschatological signs of fulfilment.[45] Grace is conferred not just because the minister performs a ritual action; the sacramental sign comes into being because of the approach of divine grace. Again, the interpenetrating *grace↔sign* relation provides an adequate representation of Schillebeeckx's position.

In his discussion on the institution of the seven sacraments, Schillebeeckx attempts to hold christological and ecclesiological considerations together. While the Church as "primordial sacrament and community of worship already is the fundamental institution of the seven sacraments by Christ,"[46] this theory of implicit institution "is not entirely sufficient."[47] Schillebeeckx reasons as follows:

> It does not suffice because in the seven sacraments the actual saving act of the *Kyrios* takes a hold on us in a direction indicated by the outward sign. So Christ himself must have had some immediate part in directing the meaning, since this implies

---

and resurrection of his Son, has reconciled the world to himself and sent the Holy Spirit among us for the forgiveness of sins.").

[42] *CSEG,* 74.

[43] See Chapter 5, section 2.5.

[44] See Chapter 3, section 3.1.2.

[45] See Chapter 4, section 1.2.

[46] *CSEG,* 115.

[47] *CSEG,* 116.

> directing his own redemptive grace to a specific need of Christian life. This further implies that Christ ... must himself have established the sevenfold direction of grace, of which a visible action of the Church is the medium.[48]

So, while Christ laid down the sevenfold direction of the sacramental acts of his ecclesial Body, the institution of the Church remains an essential factor in the determination of the individual rites. Therefore, Schillebeeckx argues, since positive studies reveal that both the matter and the form have undergone considerable alteration and modification over the centuries, the immutable substance of the sacraments must lie behind these external aspects.[49] It may be possible, then, for the post-apostolic Church to "redetermine the embodiment of its own symbolic sacramental acts"[50] as long as the intended meaning or signification[51] instituted by Christ is still manifested in the chosen representation. According to Schillebeeckx, such an approach to the institution of the new covenant rites underlines that they are not "things, but rather spiritual and religious symbolic acts of the Church."[52]

1.4 *Encounter in Liturgy and Life*

Catholic theology recognizes that a sacrament has a double effect: the intermediate *signum et res* and the final *res tantum*. According to the Councils of Florence[53] and Trent[54] the intermediate effect of baptism, confirmation and orders is the conferral of an indelible character which makes these sacraments unrepeatable. Yet, Schillebeeckx maintains, the conciliar documents, beyond describing character as "a spiritual mark on the soul," indicate nothing about what it really is.[55] Only in recent decades, he claims, has the ecclesial dimension of character emerged as a "constant tradition"[56] within the history of theology. This permits

---

[48] *CSEG,* 116.
[49] *CSEG,* 119.
[50] *CSEG,* 125.
[51] For Schillebeeckx's understanding of "*significatio* as the essence of the *sacramentum*," see J.M. Powers, *Symbolic Instrumentality in the Sacramental Theology of E.H. Schillebeeckx.*
[52] *CSEG,* 132.
[53] DS 1310.
[54] DS 1609.
[55] *CSEG,* 159.
[56] *CSEG,* 158.

Schillebeeckx to assert that "the character relates one to the visible community of the Church."[57]

Schillebeeckx's notion of the twofold mystery of the saving worship of Christ embraces both his self-giving within history and his establishment in power as the source of the Holy Spirit. This mystery is prolonged in the Church through its ministry of perpetual praise and through its bestowal of the pneumatic gift. Initiation into the Church is clearly related, therefore, to these "two fundamental mysteries of Christ's life: his passover or religious sacrifice for brotherly love, with which the Father is well pleased, and his establishment as *Kyrios* whereby, in his humanity, he is the sender of the Spirit."[58] The believers are incorporated into the paschal mystery through baptism, and into the pentecostal mystery through confirmation. So, while the two rites are clearly distinct and may be separated in time, together "they form the sacramental representation of the one redeeming mystery of Christ perfected to the full."[59] But, if the pneumatic gift is already given in baptism, how can confirmation rightly be understood as the sacrament of the Spirit? Schillebeeckx resolves the difficulty as follows:

> even before Christ was "established in power" he lived his life of service to the full, even to death, in the power of the Holy Spirit. Baptism, by the same power of the Spirit, gives us a participation in the service which the Son of God rendered to the Father through the *invisible* mission of the Spirit. In baptism and in the person baptized, that which becomes visible, though in the power of the Spirit of Christ, is the mystery of passover; death to sin and life unto God in Christ Jesus. But in confirmation and in the person confirmed it is the mystery of Pentecost that receives a visible manifestation, a visible witness to the fact that we are "established in power" by the Spirit of Christ.[60]

The Spirit of God was already operative in the earthly Jesus, empowering a life of self-giving which was fulfilled on the Cross. At baptism, the believers participate, through the Spirit of Christ, in the "service which the Son of God rendered to the Father." After the ascension the risen Lord is "established in power" as the principle of saving grace. In confirmation the recipients share in the

---

[57] *CSEG,* 158.
[58] *CSEG,* 160.
[59] *CSEG,* 161.
[60] *CSEG,* 162.

pneumatic fulness which the Church possesses and in the ministry of the bestowal of the Paraclete to others.

Schillebeeckx arraigns any attempt either to envisage baptism as related to an inward spiritual life or to construe confirmation as indicative of a situation which already exists. Both sacraments sanctify the recipients, and confer a character or a commission to carry out specific activities within the priestly people of God.[61] While confirmed Christians take their place in the public life and mission of the Church by actively and visibly sharing in the sending of the Spirit by Christ, this, Schillebeeckx stresses, is not their "first investiture with the apostolate." For,

> the grace of baptism, as life-out-of-death, and the commission given in baptism are apostolic realities. It is not possible to conceive of a Christian grace or a Christian task in the Church which, while being a service to God, would not at the same time be an apostolic work. Yet the fulness of the messianic power is lacking in Christians who are not confirmed; the situation is more or less parallel to that of the earthly Christ who, though he was the Messiah, could not visibly unfold the full force of his messianic purpose among us through the sending of the Spirit until he had entered into his heavenly Pentecost mystery.[62]

Through the character conferred in baptism, the recipients already bear the ecclesial status of laypersons within the priestly people of God. The baptized are initiated into "Christ's mystery of saving worship," a term that refers equally to religious cult and to apostolic service.[63] Through the water rite, the Spirit-filled believers participate in the mystery of the self-giving of the Son to the Father, in the *doxa* offered in the liturgical assembly and in the *diakonia* rendered in the wider human family. Unless the initiates personally and positively oppose it, this commission includes the "conferring of a corresponding messianic sanctity."[64] The character of baptism, then, is also the *sacramentum* of all the further graces flowing from this rite: incorporation into the visible Church entails entrance into its inner mystery. From the moment of sacramental washing, "throughout the rest of [the Christian's] life, the character of baptism keeps exercising its infallible function."[65]

---

[61] *CSEG,* 166-167.
[62] *CSEG,* 164.
[63] *CSEG,* 37; 159.
[64] *CSEG,* 172.
[65] *CSEG,* 173.

From the ecclesial incorporation proper to the sacramental character, the final effect, or *res*, of baptism is derived: "the forgiveness of original and all personal sins, the sealing with Christian faith, and union in grace with the heavenly Father, with all the other consequences of being a child of God."[66] Sacramental grace is the gift of redemption itself. It is

> sanctifying grace which comes to us visibly in the Church, in the fulness of its power, specifically aimed and ordered to the particular ecclesial needs of life and to the particular commission of a Christian. A certain grace can be present apart from the sacraments, but this is an incipient grace which reaches its full development only in them, for there communion in grace with God is achieved in the sanctifying context of the Church as the fulness of Christ, in the visible Mystical Body.[67]

Believers may be justified without receiving the sacrament of baptism (of desire, for example). However, according to Schillebeeckx, this extra-sacramental grace "reaches its full development" only in that encounter with God which takes place in the sacramental event. While baptism of desire does cleanse believers from original and all personal sin, it does not give the character and, hence, it effects neither their visible incorporation into the Church nor their ability to receive other sacraments.[68]

Schillebeeckx concludes *Christ the Sacrament* with a reflection on Christian life as a sacrament of encounter with God.[69] In essence, this is a heartfelt appeal to the members of the Church to give visible witness to the salvation they profess in their present-day encounter with the world. Not merely a call to the hierarchy to exercise its teaching and governing authority in an exemplary manner, it is a plea to the people to activate the commission given through the characters of baptism and confirmation, that is, to be a sign of the victorious presence of Christ in human history. People have had "a bellyful of sermonizing."[70] Schillebeeckx exclaims. Today, men and women are brought to faith through the mediation of the Church only when they "discover a genuine holiness truly incarnate in the Christians they meet."[71]

---

[66] *CSEG,* 173.

[67] *CSEG,* 182.

[68] *CSEG,* 143.

[69] See "The Christian Life itself as Sacrament of the Encounter with God" in *CSEG,* 200-214.

[70] *CSEG,* 208.

[71] *CSEG,* 206.

> Incarnate love, the love of God transposed into brotherly love for our fellow men, is the irresistible motive of credibility for the Christian faith. It is this that confronts men with the reality of salvation in the midst of daily life. In the course of their life men can discover grace visibly present in such a way that they cannot avoid it, but must decide for or against.[72]

In other words, Schillebeeckx underlines the fact that, through the sacraments of initiation, the Christian community is called to be a prophetic sign in the world. By virtue of its acts of worship and service, when words no longer seem to have any value, it draws the attention of contemporary men and women to the eschatological presence of Jesus Christ, and challenges them personally to opt for or against the divine salvation offered to all.

1.5 *Encounter in the* Eschaton

The early work of Schillebeeckx on sacraments has rightly been described as an exercise in *ressourcement*. By returning to the sources and by situating the texts of St. Thomas within the historical context from which they emerged, a number of traditional insights are retrieved. In particular, the eschatological dimension of the sacramental sign is highlighted, together with an appreciation of the mutuality of the epicletic and anamnetic moments in the liturgical event. Schillebeeckx also links his sacramental theory to the universal yearning for interpersonal encounter as expressed by the phenomenological and existential philosophies of the time. In baptism this necessary meeting between the glorified Lord and the latter-day believer is initiated. The connection between sacraments and eschatology has been noted: through these ritual acts of the Church the believers encounter the *Eschaton* himself, the glorified humanity of Jesus Christ.

From 1947 until 1957 Schillebeeckx lived in the relatively sheltered environment of a seminary theologate in Catholic Belgium. Despite the immediate intra-ecclesial background to his writings during this period, he did betray an awareness of a wider audience for whom, after the devastation of World War II, the relevance of Christian faith and practice is called into question. Within this context Schillebeeckx is keen to stress that the sacraments are not isolated, mechanical means of individual sanctification. They are communal actions of the Church by which believers encounter the glorified Lord and are strengthened to give

---

[72] *CSEG,* 206-207.

public witness, in their graced service of humanity, to the faith, hope and love that they celebrate liturgically. By virtue of the sacramental character, the baptized are commissioned to serve the Church and the broader human family. The Christian community is called to be a prophetic sign of the salvific presence of the eschatological Lord in its social ambience.

2. **From Chalcedon to Galilee**

In *Deus Humanissimus*, P. Kennedy charts the interplay of philosophical and theological factors which led to the shift in the thought of Schillebeeckx after 1966.[73] In a later publication on the thought of Schillebeeckx, he catalogues eighteen sources which he considers to be significant for understanding this change.[74] Previously the writings of Schillebeeckx represented an historico-critical reading of patristic and thomistic texts which is coupled with the phenomenological anthropology derived from his mentor D. De Petter. Following his lecture tour to the United States, Schillebeeckx was struck both by the growing secularization of modern society, and by the philosophical pluralism which accompanied it. He speaks of undergoing something of a Copernican revolution from the cosmocentrism of neo-scholasticism to the anthropocentrism associated with secularization.[75] Such a turn necessarily led to new emphases in the systematic theology, and especially in the doctrine of God, espoused by Schillebeeckx. The insights which he gleaned from the experience of secularization were consolidated by his studies in hermeneutics, Critical Theory and eschatology. Against this background, he embarked on an extended historico-critical study of the scriptures.

Kennedy claims that Schillebeeckx was "the first Roman Catholic dogmatician this century to incorporate thoroughly into the mainstream of Catholic dogmatic theology results culled from

---

[73] See P. Kennedy, *Deus Humanissimus,* 143-216.

[74] P. Kennedy, *Schillebeeckx,* 37. These sources are listed as: North American and Dutch philosophical pragmatism; philosophical hermeneutics of the humanities; historico-, form-, and redaction-critical biblical studies; religious sociology; practical-critical hermeneutics; universal pragmatics; the Critical Theory of the Institute for Social Research (Frankfurt); theoretical linguistics; semeiotics; philosophies of language and linguistics, including phenomenological and logical linguistic analysis; secular eschatology (Ernst Bloch); psychology; anthropology; cultural historiography, structuralism; post-structuralism; postmodernism and; the philosophy of Emmanuel Lévinas.

[75] See P. Kennedy, *Deus Humanissimus*, 157-159.

scientific exegesis. He was certainly not alone in this, but he was pre-eminent."[76] From about 1969 to 1974 Schillebeeckx devoted himself almost exclusively to biblical exegesis in preparation for his work on christology.[77] The purpose of this section is to investigate the understanding of the prophetic acts of Jesus, particularly his baptism in the Jordan and his death on Calvary, which emerges from *Jesus* and *Christ*, the first two volumes of this ambitious project.

2.1 *Jesus: The Story of One Alive*

In *Jesus*, the overriding theological concern of Schillebeeckx to speak of the universal in terms of the particular receives a fresh impetus. In his earlier work the problem of the universal and unique revelation of God in the man Jesus Christ found a ready response in the credal statement of Chalcedon. Now, however, having acknowledged in his hermeneutical studies the historicity of all human knowledge and the inaccessibility of the dogmatic formulae to contemporary believers,[78] Schillebeeckx takes another approach. He turns from Chalcedon to Galilee, from the credal Christ of dogmatic statements to the historical Jesus of first century Israel. Schillebeeckx envisages this volume as a *manuductio*[79]: taking Christians by the hand, he leads them through the maze of historico-critical scholarship to Jesus of Nazareth; then, he accompanies them, bolstered by this exegetical process, on the return journey as they attempt to formulate what faith in Jesus Christ might mean today.[80]

---

[76] P. Kennedy, *Schillebeeckx*, 101

[77] E. Schillebeeckx, *God is New in Each Moment*, 20-22.

[78] *Jesus*, 567: "I have no trouble at all with any of this [the creed of Chalcedon], seen from within a Greek intellectual outlook and the questions posed by it at that time: it is straight gospel; but ... within a nexus of philosophical problems which is no longer in all respects entirely ours and indeed presents us nowadays with certain difficulties."

[79] See P. Kennedy, *Schillebeeckx,* 108.

[80] *Jesus,* 258-259: "...our purpose is along with his disciples, as it were, to follow the way of Jesus from Nazareth right up to his death so far as in that way ... to trace for ourselves how the faith-inspired interpretation of Jesus as the Christ came into being. Secondly, we are looking for traces in the life of Jesus that, for us as for the disciples, could constitute an invitation to assent in faith to what is indeed God's great work of salvation in Jesus of Nazareth. The result is not to 'legitimize' our faith; but it does mean that we can keep a critical watch on the legitimate 'emergence' (or persistence) of distinctively Christian belief."

2.1.1 Baptism in the Jordan: the first prophetic act

Central to the christology of Schillebeeckx is the interpretative category of eschatological prophet. Before his death, both Jesus himself and his disciples understood his mission in this light. The first "historically firm fact"[81] about Jesus is his baptism by John in the Jordan. This, Schillebeeckx notes, is the initial step in the prophetic ministry of Jesus. John the Baptist was the eschatological penitential preacher who announced in advance the imminent judgement of God.[82] This threat of divine retribution was not directed towards the enemies of Israel, but towards its chosen ones who had forsaken the ethical and religious demands of Sinai.[83] For John the Baptist the covenant sign of circumcision was not a guarantee of salvation; only a penitential baptism would suffice.[84] Consequently, Schillebeeckx states that, the baptism was practised by John as a "prophetic sign intended to bring about the latter-day repentance and conversion of Israel."[85]

It is certain, not only that Jesus was baptized by John but also, according to Schillebeeckx, that this historical action is "a primary hermeneutical key"[86] in understanding his life and mission. Against any attempt to interpret this somewhat embarrassing and problematic Gospel event as a call-narrative, he proposes that it can properly be explained only by the awareness of Jesus that the eschatological preaching of *metanoia* by the Baptist was of crucial significance for his own public ministry. In fact, Schillebeeckx insists that the decision of Jesus to undergo the baptism offered by John "cannot have been done by him just to 'set an example,' as though he were really above it all. John's message about the baptism of repentance must have been a 'disclosure experience' for Jesus, a revelatory event or source experience, an orientation of his own life."[87] While there is no textual evidence to suggest that the ritual washing affords the Nazarene the "first breakthrough of his prophetic awareness,"[88] Schillebeeckx contends that his "public activity as a prophet is in fact quite evidently connected with his

---

[81] *Jesus,* 115.
[82] *Jesus,* 127.
[83] *Jesus,* 133
[84] *Jesus,* 130.
[85] *Jesus,* 135.
[86] *Jesus,* 137.
[87] *Jesus,* 115.
[88] *Jesus,* 138.

baptism."[89] This leads Schillebeeckx to the conclusion that, "in view of the course taken subsequently by the life of Jesus and its plainly prophetic character,"[90] the baptism in the Jordan was his very first act as a prophet.[91]

Schillebeeckx then goes on to explain what he means by a prophetic act. As he lists the Old Testament precedents of this New Testament event,[92] he refers to the seminal study of the symbolic actions of the Hebrew prophets by G. Fohrer.[93] He argues that

> Jesus' baptism in the Jordan, in what is for us its revelatory character, as a fact of history does indeed assume a compact theological quality. It is Jesus' first appearance as a prophet: a symbolic prophetic action or prophecy in action, through which he intimates that Israel as a whole does indeed require a change of heart and must return once more to God, as indeed the Baptist demands. As a prophetic act, whereby Jesus submits to 'the Baptism of John', his baptism is confirmation of Israel's apostasy, yet at the same time of Israel's repentance and thus of salvation. Fundamentally, this goes a great deal further than what John himself intended with his baptism.[94]

By receiving baptism, Jesus concurs both with the dramatized message of John concerning the need for conversion and with its concomitant "moral-cum-religious"[95] appeal in the face of eschatological judgement. However, by heralding "Israel's repentance and salvation" Jesus goes "a great deal further." The salvation which was presaged in the prophetic action of John is offered to humanity in the ministry of the Anointed One. So, although he submits to the rite of the Precursor, Jesus is the protagonist of something greater. By stepping into the Jordan, Jesus fulfils and appropriates the act of the Baptist. Far from simply searching for a way of confirming his moral message, Jesus

---

[89] *Jesus,* 138.

[90] *Jesus,* 138.

[91] In *Jesus*, as well as the baptism in the Jordan, Schillebeeckx identifies four other prophetic actions in the public ministry of Jesus: the calling of his disciples (221); the meals he shared with tax-collectors and sinners, as well as with his own disciples (218); the cleansing of the Temple (243-248); and his death on the Cross (318-319).

[92] As Old Testament examples of prophetic actions Schillebeeckx lists Jeremiah's carrying the yoke (Jer 28:10; 27:2); Hosea's marriage to Gamer (Hos 1:1-9); Jeremiah's celibacy (Jer 16: 1-4). [The English translation (138) mistakenly mentions Isaiah's celibacy.]

[93] *Jesus,* 138, n. 56.

[94] *Jesus,* 138.

[95] *Jesus,* 135.

asserts "in that very gesture, his own independent, prophetic role." To use the terminology introduced by Schürmann, the prophetic act of John becomes the first eschatological sign of fulfilment of Jesus.

Schillebeeckx recognizes that the gospel accounts surround the baptism of Jesus "with explanatory visions, setting them within the aura of paschal glory."[96] In Part III of *Jesus*, Schillebeeckx considers what he terms the "Christian interpretation of the Crucified-and-Risen One."[97] Within this framework the significance of the voice from heaven at the baptism of the eschatological prophet is treated. According to Schillebeeckx, the divine proclamation forms part of the growing reflection on the identity of Jesus on the part of the primitive Christian community which is found within the traditions of the New Testament. Each of the four evangelists links the mysterious gratuitous proclamation of Jesus as Son of God with the baptism by John.[98] The words attributed to the heavenly voice echo a number of Old Testament texts, and they cannot be accurately traced to any one of them. While certain allusions to the messianic and royal anointing are present, Schillebeeckx stresses that "the main emphasis in all of this falls on Jesus' appointment as eschatological prophet."[99] Again Schillebeeckx refutes any attempt to interpret the voice, or the descent of the Spirit as a vocation narrative. Instead he proposes that

> the models employed and the style point rather to an 'interpretative vision': Jesus' baptism is interpreted as the start of the saving activity of God in his 'beloved Son', who, being filled with the Spirit, has been sent to Israel: by getting himself baptized Jesus accepts that God is at work in John the Baptist; and at the same time he himself performs (according to the interpretation already mentioned) his first prophetic act. Thus the vision functions as an element of a faith-motivated interpretation of a historical process; in the account given and word spoken is articulated what has been transmitted in the living tradition concerning the historical effect of what took place at the Jordan.[100]

---

[96] *Jesus*, 139.
[97] *Jesus*, 399-571.
[98] *Jesus*, 552.
[99] *Jesus*, 553.
[100] *Jesus*, 553.

The heavenly voice and the pneumatic descent present the prophet from Nazareth as the fulfilment of the expectations of Israel.[101] In Chapter 3, it was noted that the biblical narratives of the symbolic actions of the Hebrew prophets normally contain a subsequent explanation of the act.[102] In his examination of the voice at the Jordan, Schillebeeckx proposes a similar reading. The account of the proclamation from heaven and of the descent of the Paraclete is a "faith-motivated" interpretation of the historical event in the Jordan.

2.1.2 Signs and works

Schillebeeckx postpones his treatment of the "signs and works" of Jesus which are recorded in the Fourth Gospel until the second volume of his christological trilogy. In *Christ*, of the seven wonders or signs listed,[103] six are referred to as *σημεῖα,*[104] the Septuagint Greek version of the Hebrew *'ôt*. Even though it is never possible to make a precise distinction between the "signs" and the "works" recorded in the *Gospel of John*, Schillebeeckx suggests that, considered separately, each opens a different perspective on Jesus.[105] In another reference to G. Fohrer, Schillebeeckx states that prophetic acts are revelatory signs which creatively anticipate the future. Yet, he notes that, in the Johannine scheme, symbolic actions have a "deeper significance" when Jesus is the protagonist. First of all, Schillebeeckx claims that, compared with the dramatic actions portrayed by the prophets of Israel, "the signs performed by the Johannine Jesus *do not anticipate* but introduce eschatological salvation here and now in Jesus' *present* actions."[106] Secondly, although the Johannine signs "cause

---

[101] *Jesus,* 553: "From his baptism Jesus is the one filled, eschatologically, with God's Spirit: God is with him, just as in Isa. 63-64 the coming of God after the crossing of the Red Sea, is described as the heavens being opened and God's Spirit descending therefrom. In Jesus, after his coming out of the waters of the Jordan, this is now fulfilled. So Jesus' being 'fulfilled' with the Spirit brings to pass Isa. 11:2; 42:1-2; 61:1; Ps. 2:7: he it is who completes all the promises to Israel."

[102] Chapter 3, section 1.1.3.

[103] These are enumerated (*Christ*, 375) as the miracle of the wine at Cana (2:1-11); the healing of the son of an official (4:46-54); the healing of a lame man (5:1-9); the miracle of the loaves (6:1-14); the walking on the water (6:16-21); the healing of the man born blind (9:1-41); the raising of Lazarus (11:1-44).

[104] The exception is the healing of a lame man (5:1-9). [Note: The text mistakenly lists the exception as the walking on the water.]

[105] *Christ,* 376.

[106] *Christ,* 376.

astonishment" and "stimulate reflection,"[107] their primary function is not to make people believe "because they have seen the signs" (John 6:2). Rather, Schillebeeckx contends, the prophetic actions of the Fourth Gospel presume faith and lead the believers to the deeper christological insight that the glory of the divine *Logos* is at work in the flesh of the man Jesus. In other words, these signs (which are limited to the public ministry) constitute an historical expression of the Word made flesh.[108] Since John views the Cross as the ultimate revelation of the glory of the incarnate Lord, Schillebeeckx concludes that these actions are "*preliminary signs* of what will happen at Easter."[109]

The "works" of the Fourth Gospel bear witness to the Incarnate Word as the one sent by God: they arouse faith and put disbelief under judgement. The communities of the beloved disciple had not encountered the historical Jesus. Faith, then, was a matter of "not seeing and yet believing" (John 20:28). Nevertheless, in the Johannine project, reliable witnesses to the divine provenance of Jesus take on a special importance as intermediaries. Schillebeeckx notes that, in the writings of John, three converging witnesses take pride of place: the Spirit, the water and the blood (1 John 5:8). These, Schillebeeckx continues, have an immediate sacramental connection:

> John himself speaks in 19:34 of the flowing of water and blood from the pierced side of Jesus on the Cross. Christian baptism (John 3) and Christian eucharist (John 6:51b-58) are said to be undertaken in 'the Spirit'. For the Spirit is the principle of life from which these sacraments of initiation draw their force (2:6; 6:63). Supported by the Holy Spirit, the sacraments of the Church bring the historical testimony of Jesus to the later communities which did not know the earthly Jesus.[110]

Put simply, through the power of the Holy Spirit, the sacraments of baptism and eucharist bridge the gap between second and third generation Christians and the earthly Jesus. The connection made by the synoptics between the event of the baptism of Jesus (his first prophetic act) and its consummation on the Cross (his final prophetic act) has already been mentioned: the pro-existent attitude

---

[107] *Christ,* 376.

[108] *Christ,* 377: "The signs illustrate what the prologue has said: he is *sarx* and yet Logos. The *sēmeia* have an earthly, *sarkic* form, but they reveal a christological depth."

[109] *Christ,* 377.

[110] *Christ,* 379.

of the Son which finds its initial expression in the River Jordan is brought to its conclusion on the Hill of Golgotha. In the Fourth Gospel the situation is different. Because of the rivalry between the followers of John and the disciples of Jesus,[111] there is no explicit account of the baptism in the Jordan. While all the "signs and wonders" accomplished by Jesus find their climax in the crucifixion,[112] the event of the Cross paradoxically becomes the source of the waters of baptism. So, according to Schillebeeckx's analysis of the *Gospel of John*, the glory of God which was first revealed in the prophetic actions and in the crucifixion of the earthly Jesus is made fully manifest in the ecclesial celebration of the sacraments of baptism and eucharist.

2.2 *The Praxis of the Kingdom*

In keeping with the results of contemporary biblical research, Schillebeeckx locates the core of the public ministry of Jesus in his proclamation of the approaching reign of God. John expected imminent judgement; Jesus announces the advent of universal salvation, wholeness and well-being. This kingdom is associated with the person of Jesus himself. In his "going around, doing good" the end-time rule of God takes hold. As Schillebeeckx remarks:

> In Jesus' conduct of his own life we have not a theoretical but a practical and proleptic realization — explorative and forward-reaching — of the 'new world', of the desiderated new praxis of good and true living, worthy of human kind — even though it be within a very concrete historical contingency which in itself we cannot repeat.[113]

This text is almost epigrammatic of many of the changes in the thought of Schillebeeckx from the mid 1960's onwards. It witnesses both to his concern with orthopraxis as the norm for orthodoxy, and to his acceptance of the primacy of the future over the past. It also touches on the ever-present dilemma of the relationship between the particular ("a very concrete historical contingency") and the universal ("the new world...worthy of humankind"). The first two concerns are treated in what follows; the third is considered later.

---

[111] See J.P. Meier, *A Marginal Jew*, II, 169.
[112] *Christ,* 377-378.
[113] *Jesus,* 153.

Given the multivocity of philosophical presuppositions which abound in the modern, secularized world, Schillebeeckx is critical of any claim to articulate the truth in one metaphysical or linguistic framework. In an article published in 1966,[114] he proposes that a dogma is meaningless ideology if it does not promote the practice of Christian love. In fact, from this early stage, Schillebeeckx criticizes believers who are more concerned with ideological orthodoxy than with Christian orthopraxy, and asks instead if "right doing" is not the best guarantee of "right thinking."[115] In his christology, then, Jesus is not presented as the proclaimer of a new message or teaching. In the person of the eschatological prophet, humanity is confronted with a practical realization of the kingdom which is announced.

According to Schillebeeckx the "practical realization" of the new world, inaugurated by the conduct of Jesus, has a "proleptic" character. This description betrays Schillebeeckx's acceptance of the modern philosophical axiom of the primacy of the future over the past.[116] If God is the "Entirely New"[117] as opposed to the "Wholly Other,"[118] it follows that the Transcendent cannot be known and interpreted on the level of pure theory. Rather than speak of a theoretical participation in absolute meaning and truth, it becomes necessary for Schillebeeckx to speak of a proleptic anticipation of meaning in action.[119] So too, the "new world" which Jesus proclaims is not a total reality: it is "explorative and forward-reaching." It is ushered in by the "praxis of good and

---

[114] "De kerk op drift?," *TGL* 22 (1966) 533-554. The English translation was published in 1973 as: "Is the Church Adrift?" in *The Mission of the Church*, 20-42.

[115] "Is the Church Adrift?" 42.

[116] E. Schillebeeckx, *God the Future of Man*, 35-36, criticizes the so-called "new hermeneutics" for passing over the biblical primacy of the future in silence. "Everything to which the Bible bears witness is directed towards the fulfilment in the future of God's promise, the history of which has been narrated in faith in the Bible. It is possible to express our understanding of the Bible in this way - we should not look back at the Bible, but rather look forward, with the Bible, to a future which is given to us to be achieved - to be achieved, but also *given us* to be achieved." See *God the Future of Man,* 178-186.

[117] See "Zweigen en spreken over God in een geseculariseerde wereld," *TTh* 7 (1967) 337-359. ET: "Secularization and Christian Belief in God" in *God, the Future of Man*, 53-90.

[118] Already in 1961 Schillebeeckx speaks in this manner in his article "De betekenis van het niet-godsdienstig humanisme voor het hedendaagse katholicisme," in *Modern niet-godsdienstig humanisme*, 74-112. ET: "Non-Religious Humanism and Belief in God" in *God and Man,* 41-84.

[119] See *Church,* 175.

true living" which creates an ambience which is worthy of humankind.[120]

Jesus tells parables to scandalize his listeners into acknowledging the inversion of values which lies at the heart of the praxis of the kingdom. But, Schillebeeckx argues, Jesus himself is a parable of God who shocks his audience into adopting a position for or against the salvation which he proclaims.[121] Jesus is the "exegete" of God: he acts as God acts.[122] By liberating people from the oppression of the powerful, the injustice of the ruthless and the de-humanization of the hypocritical, the prophet from Nazareth reveals not only the God whose kingdom is to be sought before all else, but also the "God bent on humanity."[123] In other words, Jesus reveals the cause of God as the cause of humankind and *vice versa*.[124] By reconciling message and conduct in his own life, Jesus overcame the disparity between orthodoxy and orthopraxis which confounded access to the God of the Covenant by means of the Jewish Law.

---

[120] According to P. Kennedy, *Humanissimus Deus*, 282, by "praxis" Schillebeeckx intends "actual conduct."

[121] *Jesus*, 158.

[122] *JWC*, 20.

[123] *Jesus*, 266-267: "All this goes to show that one of the most reliable facts about the life of Jesus is that he broached the subject of God in and through his message of the coming rule of God; and that what this implied was made plain first and foremost through his authentic parables and the issues they raised: namely *metanoia* and the praxis of God's kingdom. And then this message was given substantive content by Jesus' actions and way of life; his miracles, his dealings with tax-gatherers and sinners, his offer of salvation from God in fellowship at table with his friends and in his attitude to the Law, sabbath and Temple, and finally in his consorting in fellowship with a more intimate group of disciples. The heart and center of it all appeared to be the God bent on humanity. Of this God's rule the whole person of Jesus was a 'celebration' and also 'orthopraxis', that is, a praxis in accord with the kingdom of God. The bond between the two - God's rule and orthopraxis - is so intrinsic that in the praxis itself Jesus recognizes the signs of the coming of God's rule. The living God is the focus of his life."

[124] *JWC*, 17: "For Jesus God's cause - the kingdom of God as salvation of and for human beings - was of greater importance than his own life. ... For Christians Jesus (a) is therefore the decisive and definitive revelation of God and (b) precisely through this at the same time shows us what and how we human beings can, need to and really may be. Therefore any definition of the man Jesus in fact has to do with the being of God. In Jesus God reveals his own being by wanting to be salvation of and for human beings in him. To repeat what the church father Irenaeus said: (a) human salvation lies in the living God and (b) God's honour lies in the happiness, liberation and salvation or wholeness of humanity. In the man Jesus the revelation of the divine and the disclosure of true, good and really happy humanity coincide in one true and sane person."

2.2.1 The 'Abba' experience of Jesus

According to Schillebeeckx, the "novel and original experience of God"[125] which made this possible is grounded in the *Abba* experience of Jesus. "In the calamitous and pain-ridden history within which Jesus stood it was impossible to find any grounds or indeed any reason at all which would serve to explain and make sense of the unqualified assurance of salvation that characterized his message."[126] Yet, in his *Abba* experience Jesus is immediately aware of God as

> the benevolent, solicitous 'one who is against evil', who will not admit the supremacy of evil and refuses to allow it the last word. This religious experience of contrast is, after all, what informs his conviction and proclamation of God's liberating rule, which should and can prevail even in this history, as Jesus knows by experience in and from his own praxis.[127]

The "religious experience of contrast" which Schillebeeckx perceives to be at the core of Jesus' proclamation of the kingdom amidst the history of human suffering is closely related to the author's notion of "negative contrast experience." In 1968 Schillebeeckx claimed that within secularized society, faith functions as a "critical negativity"[128]: "a positive power which continues to exert constant pressure in order to bring about a better world, without humanity being sacrificed in the process."[129] This is a double-edged concept[130] with negative and positive moments: it is negative insofar as it is the protest of human beings against the suffering and injustice of history which are unworthy; it is positive insofar as it is their conviction that something more worthy lies in the future. In their indignation at what should not be, because of their hope for what could be, negative contrast experiences give rise to a prophetic voice.[131] By means of the *Abba* experience of Jesus, then, Schillebeeckx welds into his christological construct an insight which he had earlier gleaned from his study of hermeneutics and of Critical Theory.

---

125 *Jesus,* 256.
126 *Jesus,* 267.
127 *Jesus,* 267.
128 "The New Image of God, Secularization and Man's Future on Earth" in *God the Future of Man,* 169-207.
129 *God the Future of Man,* 191.
130 For the origins of this concept in the works of T.W. Adorno and P. Ricoeur, see P. Kennedy, *Deus Humanissimus,* 233-246.
131 *God the Future of Man,* 158.

2.2.2 Death on a Cross: the final prophetic act

Schillebeeckx contends that there is an intrinsic connection between the kingdom proclaimed by Jesus and his death on the Cross. His provocative words and actions, his unrelenting service of justice and love, his association with tax-collectors and sinners and his harsh critique of exploitative religious and social structures inevitably led to conflict and opposition. At the Last Supper, Jesus makes it perfectly clear that he accepts his approaching death as a consequence of his divine mission. In fact, Schillebeeckx, borrowing the central notion of pro-existence from Schürmann,[132] interprets this final moment of table-fellowship as a renewed offer of salvation to his disciples. He notes:

> There is no getting round the historical fact that in the very face of death Jesus offers the cup of fellowship to his disciples; this is a token that he is not just passively allowing his death to overcome him but has actively integrated it into his total mission, in other words, that he understands and is undergoing his death as a final and extreme service to the cause of God as the cause of men, and that he has communicated this self-understanding to his intimate disciples under the veiled sign of extending to them the fellowship-at-table shared with his friends. The 'for you' (*hyper* formula), in the sense of Jesus' whole pro-existence, has been the historical intention of his whole ministry, which his very death now substantiates.[133]

Schillebeeckx does refer to the table-fellowship which Jesus shared with his disciples and with tax-collectors and sinners as "enacted prophecy,"[134] a synonym for a symbolic prophetic act.[135] He does not, however, refer directly to the Last Supper gestures of Jesus in these terms. Nevertheless, it is clear from the above text that Schillebeeckx understands that, in proffering the bread and wine to his disciples, Jesus "actively integrates" his death into his total

---

[132] Schillebeeckx does not acknowledge that the term "pro-existence" comes from Schürmann. Yet, in his treatment of Jesus' attitude as he approaches the Last Supper and his death on the Cross he refers to several of Schürmann's works: *Der Einsetzungsbericht Lk. 22: 19-20*; "Wie hat Jesus seinen Tod bestanden und verstanden?" in *Orientierung an Jesus,* 325-363; *Jesu Abendmahlshandlung als Zeichen für die Welt*; "Das Weiterleben der Sache Jesu in nachösterlichen Herrenmahl," *BZ* 16 (1972) 1-23. See *Jesus,* 300-308, nn.87; 89; 97; 98; 99.

[133] *Jesus,* 311.

[134] *Jesus,* 218.

[135] The terms are interchanged in *Jesus,* 138: "Prophets have a habit of conjoining what they want to say with striking *symbolic actions*. By way of *enacted prophecy* Jeremiah carries a yoke on his shoulders to let all Israel know that it was 'held captive'." [Emphasis added.]

mission. Throughout his preaching of the kingdom, Jesus had identified the cause of God with the liberation of humankind. At the Last Supper, by extending the eucharistic elements to his friends, Jesus heralds the culmination of his life-long attitude of pro-existence. Furthermore, he proleptically enacts the imminent drama of Calvary. By extending table-fellowship to his disciples, the leave-taking Lord has already inaugurated "his last prophetic sign,"[136] his death on a Cross.

2.2.3 Experiencing the Risen Lord

Schillebeeckx's interpretation of the resurrection of Jesus is perhaps the most controversial element of his christological project.[137] In brief, his claim is that, after the death of Jesus, his disciples underwent an experience of forgiveness and conversion. Since a dead person cannot forgive, the argument unfolds, the logical conclusion is that he is alive.[138] Whatever the merits or demerits of this approach, the study of the appearance narratives which Schillebeeckx conducts clearly underlines such an identification of Jesus of Nazareth, "experienced as a sheer act of grace on God's part,"[139] as ground and source of the Church's mission.

In the course of his analysis of the credal statements of the primitive Christian community two baptismal references should be recorded. In the first, the context is the speech of Paul before King Agrippa (Acts 26:2-23) in which he gives an account of his Damascus experience.[140] According to this report, the heavenly voice commissions Paul to be a servant and a witness of the Good News to the Gentiles: "to open their eyes, that they may turn from darkness to light and from the power of Satan to God, that they may receive forgiveness of sins and a place among those who are sanctified by faith" (26:18). In this command, Schillebeeckx recognizes three technical terms linked with conversion: preaching (opening eyes); faith (turning around); and baptism (forgiveness of sins). The overall thrust of the vision is no longer the conversion of Paul, but "the christological affirmation that Jesus of Nazareth is

---

136 *Jesus,* 318-319.

137 For a critique of Schillebeeckx's theory of the resurrection, see the works of G. O' Collins, *Interpreting Jesus,* 120-124; *Jesus, Risen*, 115-117.

138 *Jesus,* 391.

139 *Jesus,* 360.

140 See *Jesus,* 374-377.

'the light of the people and of the gentiles' (26:23)." Then, Schillebeeckx adds,

> The Christian meaning of baptism is also explained: it is an action signifying an ethico-religious reversal, but at the same time a 'light-vision' which mediates knowledge of God and of Jesus Christ whom he has sent, and incorporates the convert into the *ekklesia* from among Jews and Gentiles.[141]

The second reference concerns the difference between Paul and the author of the Deutero-Pauline letters with regard to the relationship between baptism and eschatology,[142] a point which is developed at greater length in *Christ.*[143] As a result of his analysis of Rom 6:4-11, Schillebeeckx suggests that the Apostle differentiates between the conditions of being "dead to sin" and of being "alive to God in Christ Jesus" (6:11):

> For Paul, this formal distinction is...necessary since for him (in contrast to the Deutero-Pauline epistles) baptism is *not* a rising with Jesus. Baptism is only dying and being buried with Jesus, dying to sin (6:3; 6:4; 6:6; 6:7). Jesus himself has been raised from the dead (6:9) but we still have to be raised. ... Therefore Christian baptism means: (a) no longer being servants of sin (6:6), to have settled up with sin (6:10), and therefore to 'live for God' (6:11) - (b) not yet being risen with Christ, but only in the spiritual sense, 'as men who have been brought from death (the death of sin) to life' (6:13), namely to life for God without sin.[144]

In the Pauline view of baptism, then, the believer shares in the death of Christ as an end to sin, and is given the ground for hope in the future resurrection which is not yet enjoyed.[145] The Deutero-Pauline position is that the Christian has already been raised up by virtue of this sacrament. As Schillebeeckx remarks:

> In *Colossians*, baptism is no longer dying with Christ, but above all *rising with him* (Col 2:12; 3:1, though even *Colossians* does not make the addition that we find in *Ephesians*: even now we are sitting with Christ at the right hand of God, Eph 2:6). We still await the manifestation of what we *are* now, hidden in Christ (Col 3:3).[146]

---

[141] *Jesus,* 376.
[142] *Jesus,* 432-435.
[143] *Christ,* 152-157; 187-194.
[144] *Christ,* 155.
[145] *Jesus,* 433.
[146] *Christ,* 191.

According to Schillebeeckx, these references, if taken together, suggest that the early Church understood baptism as the symbolic action of ethical and religious conversion. It brings the recipients closer to Jesus Christ by incorporating them into his ecclesial body, and confers on them the gift of eschatological — whether future or realized — life.[147]

2.3 *From the Particular to the Universal*

Having depicted the historical particularities of the life of Jesus of Nazareth, Schillebeeckx then proceeds to investigate how this specific instance can be considered to be universally significant.[148] In christological terms the problem may be reduced to the quandary that, even if there is a firm historical basis on which to assert that Jesus did many of the things which Christian faith ascribes to him, it cannot be shown that these unique events have any relevance for the contemporary believer.

In response, Schillebeeckx proposes a theory which he designates as a "universality through historically particular mediation."[149] In searching for a means of applying this concept of universality to the life of Jesus, Schillebeeckx determines three criteria: that which is universal in Jesus must reside within the humanity he shares with all men and women; it must find its ground in his history; and it must precede any credal affirmations concerning him as Lord.[150] Given the reality of evil and suffering in the world, Schillebeeckx refutes any thematization of the universal meaning of history on the basis of reason or of theoretical hermeneutics.[151] Against this groundless idealism, Schillebeeckx has recourse to the concept of negative contrast experiences as the key to unlocking the *condition humaine*. Such an experience of having to pronounce a "no" to the world as it exists is pre-

---

[147] *Jesus,* 438.

[148] Schillebeeckx does this by attempting to breach the "broad ditch" which, according to G. E. Lessing, lies between accidental and necessary truths of reason. Schillebeeckx credits Lessing with posing the Enlightenment dilemma of the irreconcilability of truths of reason with facts of history in a new light. According to Schillebeeckx (*Jesus,* 583), "for him [Lessing] what mattered was the antithesis between 'truths from the past', concerning which we can be historically informed, and 'truths lived out' here and now, something that we are going through ourselves." See *Jesus,* 583-594.

[149] *Jesus,* 591-594.

[150] *Jesus,* 611-612.

[151] *Jesus,* 621.

religious, and is consequently accessible to all human beings.[152] This insight spurs Schillebeeckx to postulate the apparent contradiction that the universality of Jesus Christ is to be found in his wholly partisan option for the poor. In fact, Schillebeeckx stresses, unless it is partisan it is not universal.[153]

> Within this as yet unfinished human history of suffering in quest of meaning, liberation and final good, Jesus of Nazareth presented himself, with a message and praxis of salvation, as a fellow human being who nevertheless through his new approach to the conduct of life and his innocent suffering and dying on the Cross gave us a new reading of our old history that is a source also of renewal. Its effect is to reveal that the factor of mediating between the historical person, Jesus, and his significance for us now is in concrete terms the practice of Christian living within our continuing human history. Apart from the churches' solidarity with the sufferers, whoever or whatever they may be, their gospel becomes impossible to believe or understand.[154]

In his praxis based on the nearness of the kingdom, then, Jesus stands in solidarity with the outcast and the oppressed. In his radical protest against marginalization and injustice he opens a new possibility within the human drama of suffering and death. The pro-existence of Jesus which finds its fullest expression in his death on Calvary and its divine ratification in his resurrection, provides a new reading to the whole history of humanity. But, the intermediary factor linking the historical and universal significance of Jesus is the concrete mission of the Church in the world.[155] In other words, the praxis of the values of the kingdom not only refers to the conduct of the prophet from Nazareth, but also comprises the *sequela Jesu*, the way of life of those who follow him.

2.4 *Prophetic Actions: From Jordan to Calvary*

By stepping into the River Jordan, Jesus of Nazareth performed his first prophetic act, and heralded the dawn of the end-time intervention of the just God which had been foretold by the Precursor. In the Synoptic accounts, the action itself, together with the heavenly voice and the pneumatic descent, points to the fulfilment of the hope of Israel in the arrival of the eschatological

---

[152] *Church* 5.
[153] *Church* 178.
[154] *Christ,* 622-623.
[155] *Jesus,* 671.

prophet. This incipient gesture marks the first breakthrough of the prophetic awareness of Jesus. It provides the foundation for the subsequent unfolding of his radical praxis of the values of the kingdom, and it finds its climax in the drama of the Cross. In the person and activity of the Nazarene, humanity is confronted with a proleptic anticipation of the new world of the *Deus Humanissimus.*[156] In Chapter 3 it was noted how the whole person of the Hebrew prophets was involved in transmitting the divine word of judgement or consolation which was communicated to them from the depths of their intimate relationship with the God of Israel.[157] According to Schillebeeckx, the eschatological prophet is himself the sign of the proclaimed in-breaking of the kingdom. This message, in turn, emerges from his extraordinary *Abba* experience. As a protest against the injustice and oppression which dehumanizes men and women, and as a promise of a better world to come, this solitary life takes on a universal significance when the self-giving death on the Cross is vindicated by the resurrection.

According to Schillebeeckx's study of the Fourth Gospel, the "signs and wonders" accomplished by Jesus serve both to unveil the glory of the divine *Logos* at work in him, and thus to bear witness to his divine provenance. Both aspects are fulfilled on Calvary as the astounding mercy of God is revealed on the up-lifted Cross, and as the saving waters of baptism flow from the pierced side of the crucified Jesus. The ecclesial rite of washing springs from the supreme moment of the sacrifice of Christ and assures humankind of his pneumatic presence as history continues to unfold. This mediation between the definitive prophetic existence of Jesus of Nazareth and his unlimited significance for the men and women of subsequent generations is the concrete mission of the Church in the world.

3. **Anticipating Future**

With his appointment to Nijmegen in 1957, Schillebeeckx left the relative isolation of a seminary lectureship in Catholic Belgium for a university professorship in the Protestant Netherlands. Certainly the context of his theologizing had changed. At Louvain Schillebeeckx exercised what could be termed a "service to the Church": the concern was to present the vitality of Catholic faith to an ecclesial audience by re-reading thomistic texts in the light of the

---

[156] *Jesus,* 669.
[157] Chapter 3, section 1.1.1.

insights gleaned from *ressourcement* and from phenomenological existentialism. At Nijmegen, Schillebeeckx was called to offer "a service to the world": the challenge was to justify the relevance and credibility of Christian faith to an increasingly secularized and post-Christian world by dialoguing with a vast array of philosophical and anthropological presuppositions.[158]

All the explicit reflection of Schillebeeckx on baptism and on the other sacraments of the Church come from the initial phase of his theological enterprise. In the later stage there is little mention of either. Yet, from the ecclesiological publications of Schillebeeckx it is possible to construct his understanding of baptism, the sacrament of ecclesial initiation. This section begins with an investigation of the role of the Christian community in *Jesus Christ in our Western Culture* and in *Church: The Human Story of God*, the long-awaited finale to the christological project of Schillebeeckx. Then, it proposes an understanding of baptism as ecclesial commitment to the praxis which anticipates the new world.

3.1 *The Church: Between Memory and Anticipation*

Schillebeeckx highlights the centrality of the Church in all three volumes of his christological trilogy. Throughout history the memory of Jesus (*memoria passionis Christi*) is kept alive by the community which gathers in his name. The Church is "the human face of God"[159]; "people are the words with which God tells his story."[160] The Church survives not just from memory; it is called into existence by the Spirit of the eschatological Lord. As Schillebeeckx writes,

> the power of the *Pneuma* or Holy Spirit puts this community of faith into contact with the life-work and death of Jesus. *Pneuma* and *anamnesis*, both the living recollection of the story, conduct and career of Jesus of Nazareth, handed down through the Church, and the active presence of the Spirit of Christ in the Church community of faith, form two sides of one and the same coin.[161]

---

[158] In his later writings Schillebeeckx recasts the traditional dogmatic statement "No salvation outside the Church" to read "No salvation outside the world." See *JWC*, 8; *Church*, 5-15.

[159] This is the English title of Schillebeeckx's work on the theology of ministry: *The Church with a Human Face: A New and Expanded Theology of Ministry*.

[160] *Church*, xiii.

[161] *Church*, 158.

Through the power of the Holy Spirit, the Christian community comes into contact with Jesus and with the praxis of the kingdom, that is, with the moral example which it seeks to imitate. Without this concrete practice of Christian living within the warp of history, the message of the gospel remains an irrelevant account of a particular life lived almost two thousand years ago: "Jesus' light burns in this world only with the oil of our lives."[162] The memory of the saving mission of Jesus is rendered actual by the Spirit-filled community which anticipates the eschatological reign of God. The Church, then, finds itself between memory and anticipation, between *anamnesis* and *pneuma* or *epiclesis*.

According to Schillebeeckx, the Christian charge to preserve the memory of Jesus is not primarily a matter of speculative orthodoxy or doctrine. It is not a question of "selling Bibles."[163] The salvation that is founded in Christ as a promise for all becomes universal, not through the mediation of an abstract idea, but by the power of its critical and liberating character in and through a consistent praxis of the kingdom of God.[164] Schillebeeckx asserts the primacy of orthopraxis, of following the way of life of Jesus. This *sequela Christi* has two essential characteristics:

> it is the way of the rejection of any power on the basis of a sovereign inner human freedom (the bold human commitment to the poor and oppressed, the solidarity of love, lies in this opposition to oppressive powers), and this way of life implies the *via crucis*, a cross.[165]

The Church is the community of men and women which continues to utter a prophetic "no" to situations of suffering and oppression. Through the praxis that aligns itself with the marginalized and with the poor, it realizes in fragmentary forms that fulness of life which lies in the future of the history of humanity. To be Christian is to be open to the deepest "experiences of conversion, crucifying experiences which evoke *metanoia*, a change of mind, of action and being."[166]

Human beings cannot treat good and evil or justice and injustice on the same footing. That said, Schillebeeckx claims that both the humanist and the believer can perform a "prophetic action

---

[162] *Church,* 846.
[163] *Christ,* 643.
[164] *Church,* 176.
[165] *Church,* 168.
[166] *JWC,* 48.

in the hope of the ultimate triumph of humanity."[167] But, he argues, the humanist cannot know whether reality will eventually prove his ethical conviction of standing on the side of justice to be right.[168] For the believer, however, the situation is different. Schillebeeckx notes that:

> belief in God makes the theoretical connection between the human hope of the victory of the *humanum* and the specific reality of our history. ... Thus belief in God is the basis for a world-renewing prophetic praxis. Believing praxis bears the promise of hope. Ultimately (for Christians) historical mediation is achieved through eschatological reminiscence of the death and resurrection of Jesus which is itself a promise that has not yet been fulfilled for humanity, though it nevertheless has a foundation. Thus the hope of believers is dialectically reconciled with the contradiction of hope in the world as they experience it — reconciled, not in an undialectical model of harmony but through the critical and productive, saving practice of living people and through the belief that there is always a surplus of hope over and above the recalcitrant world as we experience it.[169]

While humanists may make the ultimate sacrifice of surrendering their lives in the service of a better humanity, there is no anthropological historical basis for this hope. Furthermore, while hope based on a purely ethical foundation may offer a perspective on the future of the *humanum*, it forgets not only the many sacrifices which have been made on the way, but also the countless victims who still may fall.[170] But, Schillebeeckx enjoins, the believer who performs the same self-sacrificing gesture for the future of humanity does so not "as a blind fate or as wild chance,"[171] but as a committed praxis supported by the absolute saving presence of God.

Schillebeeckx wants Christians to remember, however, that their social and political praxis in the world should not be severed from their engagement in proclamation, sacramental life and pastoral work by which they explicitly exercise the common priesthood. To break this connection between ecclesial and practico-social involvement, he warns, is to damage the inherent

---

[167] *JWC,* 60.
[168] *JWC,* 61.
[169] *JWC,* 64.
[170] *JWC,* 61.
[171] *Church,* 96.

religious structure of the Church.[172] Christian praxis entails putting into public action the salvific story of Jesus which is told in the liturgy. Just as the eschatological fulness which was anticipated by the praxis of Jesus expressed itself in the symbolic language of parables and metaphors,[173] so too, the ongoing discipleship of the Church in the form of service finds its culmination and new energy in the rituals it celebrates.[174] The Christian community, which is a priestly people, keeps hope alive by proclaiming prophetically, enacting liturgically and serving pastorally the salvation that comes from God.[175]

Alongside the ethical, ecological and socio-political expressions of Christian faith, Schillebeeckx places the mystical. He does not mean by this a *fuga mundi*, a turning inwards which negates all that is finite.[176] Rather, he speaks about a mysticism which is grounded in the experience of God as the creator who loves so as to make all things whole.

> In such mysticism, love for all men and women and all-embracing love for fellow creatures as an expression of love of God can come fully into its own. Within this mysticism there is plenty of room for the struggle for justice and love, for making the creation whole, for all that lives in this finite world.[177]

Schillebeeckx proposes a comparison between the mysticism of Christians and the *Abba* experience of Jesus.[178] The sense of the loving nearness of the Father, which lay at the heart of the prophetic self-understanding of Jesus and empowered his praxis of the kingdom, is reflected in the believers' mystical experience of "dark light"[179] or of "mediated immediacy"[180] which equips them for concrete social and political commitments.

---

[172] *JWC,* 34.
[173] *Church,* 133.
[174] *Church,* 15-16.
[175] *JWC,* 32.
[176] *JWC,* 69.
[177] *Church,* 181.
[178] *Church,* 181.
[179] This term derives from the Flemish mystic Ruysbroeck [also known as Jan van Ruusbroec] (1293-1381) whom Schillebeeckx read as a young novice at Ghent. He is mentioned in Schillebeeckx's first publication from 1945.
[180] This term is coined by Schillebeeckx himself in an attempt to express the nature of the direct relationship the believer can have with God. See *Christ,* 809: "What we have here is not an inter-subjective relationship between two persons - two mortal men - but a mutual relationship between a finite person and his absolute origin, the infinite God. In other words, we are confronted with a unique instance, an instance in which the immediacy does not do away with the mediation but in fact constitutes it. Thus from our perspective there is *mediated immediacy.* Between God

According to Schillebeeckx, then, the Church lives from the eschatological memory of Jesus Christ. Gathered in the power of the Holy Spirit, it is the sacrament of the salvation which the Father of Jesus Christ brings about in the world.[181] The credible conduct of life which accompanied the salvific proclamation of Jesus is mystically continued in the service offered by the ecclesial community to the poor and the oppressed. From the depths of their spiritual encounter with the Creator God, Christians utter prophetic protests against the prevailing forces of repressive domination and dehumanizing control. Moreover, buoyed up by faith in the eschatological victory of Jesus, Christians freely set up in their environment tangible signs of the final liberation which is to be attained at the second coming.

3.2 *From Participation to Anticipation*

In Chapter 2 it was noted that some cardinal points hold pride of place within the theological *corpus* of Schillebeeckx. At the heart of his thought lies the philosophico-theological constant that the world is created by God. Belief in creation provides the ontological presupposition against which all of his subsequent reflections unfold.[182] Closely allied with this is the epistemological principle which holds that human beings may come to know God through experience as the result of the divine manifestation in creation. Throughout his career Schillebeeckx stresses that there is both a positive and negative component in the knowledge of God possessed by humankind. In this earlier phase, the articulation of such a dialectic relies principally on the theory of "implicit intuition" proposed by D. De Petter.[183] This suggests that knowledge of God is possible because of a contemplative, non-conceptual factor of human cognition which links individuals with the absolute Other. This led Schillebeeckx to postulate that human religious knowledge rests on a non-conceptual factor which, ultimately, sustains a more negative conceptual feature. In his

---

and our awareness of God looms the insuperable barrier of the historical, human and natural world of creation, the constitutive symbol of the real presence of God for us. The fact that in this case an unmistakable mediation produces immediacy, instead of destroying it, is connected with the absolute or divine manner of the real presence of God: he makes himself directly and creatively present in the medium, that is, in ourselves, our neighbours, the world and history. This is the deepest immediacy that I know."

[181] *Church*, 15.

[182] See *Church*, 90.

[183] See D. De Petter, "Impliciete Intuïtie," *TPh* 1 (1939) 84-105.

earlier thought, then, Schillebeeckx affirms the possibility of cognitive contact with, or theoretical participation in, a totality of meaning. This human search for God finds its fullest expression in the sacraments of the Church.[184]

Baptism is the sacrament which initiates this privileged cognitive contact with God. It is not a participation in some abstract ontological reality, but an encounter with the glorified Lord. Through the liturgical rite of initiation, the catechumens become members of the Church with all the rights and responsibilities that this entails. From the sacramental character other gifts flow. The early Schillebeeckx is at pains to point out that baptism is neither a sacrament for the moment, nor an isolated rite of personal sanctification. Rather, the baptized live by the sure hope of a better world to come, and this hope orientates the whole of Christian life. The baptized participate in the mystery of the self-giving of the Son to the Father, a diaconal service which begins with the liturgical rite of pouring water, and which finds its fulfilment in glory. The Church, then, is the sign of the victorious presence of Christ in history. By establishing prophetic signs of justice and love, it confronts men and women with the unexpected reality of eschatological salvation which is offered to all through Christ and in the Holy Spirit.

In his later writings Schillebeeckx "breaks" with De Petter,[185] and posits the non-conceptual aspect of the knowledge of God as a mystery of promise which guarantees the identity of faith in its successive reinterpretations.[186] From his studies in linguistic analysis, Schillebeeckx concludes that given "the multiplicity of presuppositions at play in contemporary philosophical discourses, it is impossible to produce a purely theoretical confirmation that contemporary interpretations of Christian faith are either orthodox or heterodox."[187] Orthopraxis must be an inner element of whatever principle is used in order to verify the authenticity of

---

[184] See *CSEG*, 198-199.

[185] In *Jesus*, 618, Schillebeeckx remarks that "...the theologian's 'hypothesis' (the thesis of faith) must be capable in one or another (not apodictic but very significant) way of being tested by and finding support in the reality of man, his world and society, in short, in our historical experience. I long ago realized that this entails a clear break with the 'implicit intuition' of the meaning-totality maintained by classical philosophy like that of D. De Petter, L. Lavelle and the French *philosophes de l'Esprit*." For a further commentary on this text, see P. Kennedy, *Deus Humanissimus*, 213-216.

[186] *God the Future of Man*, 38.

[187] P. Kennedy, *Deus Humanissimus*, 190.

contemporary expressions of Christian faith. Through his confrontation with Critical Theory, Schillebeeckx has come to realize that the only guarantee of an orthodox interpretation of faith is to be found in negative contrast experiences. In asserting this, he has accepted as axiomatic the cognitive primacy of praxis. Humankind, then, no longer participates in a totality of theoretical meaning. Instead, Schillebeeckx suggests that, by embracing the praxis of the kingdom, it is possible to experience proleptically that fulness of meaning which lies in the future.

Christian baptism, then, is the sacrament by which believers express their commitment to live as members of that pneumatic community which seeks to anticipate a new world. For Jesus, the incipient symbolic action in the Jordan provided "the first breakthrough of his prophetic awareness."[188] It also revealed the fundamental pro-existent attitude which underpinned his praxis of the kingdom and which found its ultimate articulation on the Cross. By undergoing the ecclesial rite of washing, Christians embark on a life-long mission of being-for-others. Filled with the Spirit of justice, and confirmed as sons and daughters of the heavenly Father, they announce a prophetic protest to the suffering and oppression which enslave humanity. And, by word and action, they testify to the proleptic in-breaking of the new world whose complete unveiling lies in the future with God. In other words, baptism is the prophetic act of ecclesial commitment to the praxis which anticipates a new world as Jesus did by bringing justice to victory and causing the nations to hope (Matt 12:20-21).

According to Schillebeeckx, Christian faith holds that to come into contact with God one must first encounter Jesus who is met, in turn, in the community which gathers in his name. In his earlier publications, the inter-subjective encounter between God and the believer was experienced most fully, though not exclusively, in the sacraments. Baptism, then, is presented as the rite which initiates encounter between the believer and the glorified Lord, the *Eschaton*, the "Wholly Other." According to P. Kennedy, this encounter could be described schematically as *one-to-One*. Schillebeeckx's more recent writings, however, "stress to a far greater extent that a person's contact with God is mediated primarily through others."[189] This, Kennedy claims, can be represented by the threefold pattern *one-to-others-to-One*. In this later phase, baptism

---

[188] *Jesus,* 138.
[189] P. Kennedy, *Schillebeeckx,* 136.

is envisaged as initiation into the ecclesial community which is the sacrament of the "Entirely New." While the ontological, the existential and the socio-practical dimensions of baptism converge, in this evolution from individual participation to communitarian anticipation, the eschatological sweep of the lustral rite comes to the fore.[190]

[190] For an explanation of the four interwoven approaches to theology in the documents of Vatican II, see P.J. Rosato, "Perché studiare teologia a Roma?" in K.H. Neufeld, ed., *Problemi e prospettive di teologia dogmatica*, 495-520.

PART III

SYMBOL AND ANTICIPATION

CHAPTER 7

Symbolizing the Future

A re-evaluation of baptism as *signum prognosticum* in the light of the dialogue between contemporary biblical and systematic theology

What, then, does this dialogue between biblical and systematic theology uncover about the eschatological dimension of the sacrament of baptism? What insights are yielded by viewing this initiatory rite of the Church as a symbolic gesture that springs from the eschatological sign of fulfilment which Jesus inaugurated in the Jordan, and which, in turn, is rooted in the dramatic actions of the Old Testament prophets? This chapter aims to answer these questions. In a first section ("Invitation to Dialogue"), it reflects methodologically on the response that this study offers to the conciliar invitation to make the study of Scripture the soul of sacred theology. In a second section ("Evaluating the Sources"), it critically considers the contribution of each of the four authors to the unfolding of this understanding of baptism as symbolic act of eschatological salvation.

1. **Invitation to Dialogue**

The precise relationship between exegesis and dogmatic theology is far from clear.[1] In 1961, because of a "certain estrangement" that he perceived between these disciplines, Karl Rahner wrote an essay on the interconnection between the two.[2] Exegetes are reminded that they are Catholic theologians, whose duty it is to make manifest the harmony between the results of their

---

[1]See R.M. Grant – D. Tracy, *A Short History of the Interpretation of the Bible*.

[2] K. Rahner, "Exegese und Dogmatik," *StZ* 168 (1961) 241-262. ET: "Exegesis and Dogmatic Theology," *TI* 5, 67-93.

research and the teaching of the Church. With a more exact knowledge of scholasticism, and with a greater understanding of the principles that govern the correlation between exegesis and theology, they are to bridge the gap from their own field of expertise to the rest of the sacred sciences.[3] Similarly, dogmatists are reminded that they should not just borrow the results of exegetic scholarship; instead they should engage in their own exegetical research which must be convincing to the specialist.[4]

1.1 *"The Soul of Theology"*

According to *Dei verbum*, the dogmatic constitution on Divine Revelation of the Second Vatican Council, "the study of the sacred page should be the very soul of sacred theology."[5] The conciliar document notes that:

> Sacred theology relies on the written word of God, taken together with sacred Tradition, as on a permanent foundation. By this Word it is most firmly strengthened and constantly rejuvenated, as it searches out, under the light of faith, the full truth stored in the mystery of Christ. Therefore, the "study of the sacred page" should be the very soul of sacred theology.[6]

In his commentary on this text, J. Ratzinger[7] identifies three different images which describe the relationship between Scripture and theology. First, a "static" notion is employed: Scripture, "taken together with sacred Tradition," functions as the "foundation" of theology. Just as a house cannot stand without foundations, so too, this image suggests, a theological construct cannot survive without resting on the rock of the sacred page. Second, an "organic" vision is proposed: the Word "strengthens and constantly rejuvenates" theology. "The 'house' of theology is

---

[3] K. Rahner, "Exegesis and Dogmatic Theology," 70-71.

[4] K. Rahner, "Exegesis and Dogmatic Theology," 77.

[5] *Dei verbum,* 24. See E. Hamel, "L'Ecriture, âme de la théologie," *Gr* 52 (1971) 511-535; L. Leloir, "La sainte Ecriture, âme de toute la théologie," *Seminarium* 16 (1966) 880-891.

[6] *Dei verbum,* 24: "Sacra theologia in verbo Dei scripto, una cum sacra traditione, tamquam in perenni fundamento innititur, in eoque ipsa firmissime roboratur semperque iuvenescit, omnem veritatem in mysterio Christi conditam sub lumine fidei perscrutando. Sacrae autem scripturae verbum Dei continent et, quia inspiratae, vere verbum Dei sunt; ideoque sacrae paginae studium sit veluti anima sacrae theologiae." [ET: Flannery, 763-764.]

[7] J. Ratzinger, "Sacred Scripture in the Life of the Church," [Commentary on *Dei verbum*, ch. 6] in H. Vorgrimler, ed., *Commentary on the Documents of Vatican II*, Vol. III, 262-272.

not a building that has been erected once and for all," Ratzinger notes, "it stands only because theologizing continues to go on as a living activity, and so the foundation is also something that is always actively founding and hence the constant starting-point for the possibility of theology's existence." Indeed, while this sentiment had already been expressed in the encyclical *Humani generis*, Ratzinger contends that its concrete realization was stultified by a lack of exegetical work.[8] Third, a biological figure, first suggested by Pope Leo XIII,[9] is proffered: the study of sacred Scripture is the "soul of sacred theology."[10]

In the dogmatic manuals employed in Catholic seminaries before Vatican II, magisterial statements provided the starting-point, while Scripture and Tradition offered proof-texts in the subsequent positive theological synthesis. The result of this approach, Ratzinger claims, was that themes were neither developed from the biblical perspective, nor suggested by the scriptural texts themselves. However, in the conciliar decree on priestly formation[11] the procedural order in dogmatic theology is reversed: biblical themes should have first place; then, the contribution of the Fathers of the Church is to be considered; next, the later history of dogma is to be elucidated; and, finally all aspects of the Christian mysteries and their interconnection are to be presented.[12] Within this

---

[8] E. Rasco, "Biblical Theology: Its Revival and Influence on Theological Formation" in R. Latourelle, ed., *Vatican II: Assessment and Perspectives Twenty-five Years After (1962-1987)*, Vol. III, 344, claims that, until the aftermath of the Second Vatican Council, "the fact remains that the general outline of theological studies remained impervious [to biblical scholarship]. Professors of Scripture certainly changed their outlook within their own fields, and many professors of fundamental and dogmatic theology felt the need for change. But that change did not come. A shock was needed, and that is exactly what the Council provided — Samson brought the edifice down."

[9] Leo XIII, *Providentissimus Deus*, *AAS* 26 (1993-94) 283.

[10] J. Wicks, *Introduction to Theological Method* 61, n 22, notes that the phrase has been traced by J.M. Lera, "Sacrae Paginae studium sit veluti anima sacrae theologiae..." in A. Vargas-Machuca – G. Ruis, ed., *Palabra y vida* (Madrid, 1983), 409-422, to a decree issued by the thirteenth General Congregation of the Society of Jesus in 1687. It was cited by R. Cornely on the opening page of his introduction to the books of the Old Testament in 1885. From here it was taken up by *Providentissimus Deus*.

[11] *Optatam totius, AAS* 58 (1966) 713-727. [ET: Flannery, 707-724.]

[12] *Optatam totius*, 16: "Students should receive a most careful training in holy Scripture, which should be the soul, as it were, of all theology [*Sacrae scripturae studio, quae universae theologiae veluti anima esse debet*]. After a suitable introductory course, they should receive an accurate initiation in exegetical method. They should study closely the principal themes of divine revelation and should find inspiration and nourishment in daily reading and meditation upon the sacred books. The following order should be observed in the treatment of dogmatic theology:

understanding "the Bible must first be seen, considered and questioned on its own terms," and "only then can the development of tradition and dogmatic analysis take place."[13] This understanding of the relationship between exegesis and systematic theology is also to be found in the document of the Pontifical Biblical Commission on the interpretation of the Bible in the Church.[14]

A pertinent example of this method is to be found in B. Van Iersel's article "Some Biblical Roots of the Christian Sacraments."[15] His approach is not to begin with "classical or current notions" of sacramental theory in order to search either for substantiating scriptural evidence or for criteria to judge extant theological opinion. Rather, he is concerned to begin with concepts or facts that are presupposed in the biblical texts and which may shed new light on the understanding of the Christian rites. Van Iersel takes two examples from the Old Testament: the Hebrew idea of *zkr*, or remembrance; and, the Jewish notion which is expressed in the term "corporative person." A similar approach has been adopted in this present study. By beginning with an understanding of the semitic *'ôt*, the enhanced insights which accrue for sacramental theology in general and for the eschatological dimension of baptism in particular are presented.

---

biblical themes should have first place [*themata biblica primum proponantur*]; then students should be shown what the Fathers of the Church, both of the East and West, have contributed towards the faithful transmission and elucidation of each of the revealed truths; then the later history of dogma, including its relation to the general history of the Church; lastly, with the help of speculation and with St. Thomas as teacher, all aspects of these mysteries, and to perceive their interconnectedness ." [Flannery 719.]

[13] J. Ratzinger, "Sacred Scripture in the Life of the Church," 269.

[14] Commission Biblique Pontificale, *L'Interprétation de la Bible dans l'Eglise*. ET: J.A. Fitzmyer, *The Biblical Commission's Document "The Interpretation of the Bible in the Church": Text and Commentary*, 163-164: "Without being the sole *locus theologicus*, Sacred Scripture provides the privileged foundation of theological studies. In order to interpret Scripture with scholarly accuracy and precision, theologians need the work of exegetes. From their side, exegetes must orientate their research in such fashion that 'the study of Sacred Scripture' can be in reality 'as it were the soul of Theology' (*Dei verbum*, 24). To achieve this, they ought to pay particular attention to the religious content of the biblical writings. ... The exegete performs the groundwork for this operation, which the systematic theologian continues by taking into account the other *loci theologici* which contribute to the development of dogma." Note that the appearance of this document coincided with the fiftieth anniversary of the publication of the encyclical of Pope Pius XII, *Divino afflante Spiritu* (1943) and the hundredth anniversary of the publication of the encyclical of Pope Leo XIII, *Providentissimus Deus* (1893).

[15] B. Van Iersel, "Some Roots of the Christian Sacraments," *Conc* 4/1 (1968) 4-11.

The first section of this thesis focused on the eclipsing of the prognostic aspect of the triple dimension of sacramental sign in the commentators on St. Thomas, and on its subsequent retrieval in the patristic, liturgical and biblical studies of the earlier part of this century. The intention in this introductory section, however, was not to search for scriptural roots for this traditional notion, but to justify the subsequent application of the biblical *'ôt* to the thomistic *signum prognosticum*. In this way, the study of Scripture enlivens theological work as, analogously, the soul animates the body. This methodology is more apparent in Chapters 5 and 6. Here, the results of the scriptural analysis are employed to cast new light on the theological understanding of the eschatological dimension of baptism.

Yet, while Catholics and non-Catholics alike are in agreement on the centrality of Scripture in systematic theology, there is an extraordinary divergence of opinion as to how this principle might be achieved concretely.[16] A. Dulles assesses ten approaches to this problem in contemporary theology. In conclusion, he admits that:

> My own present leaning would be toward a method that makes use of historical critical studies to assure a solid foundation in the biblical sources themselves, but does so under the continuous guidance of tradition and magisterial teaching. An adequate theological use of Scripture, I believe, would build also on the achievements of biblical theology and the kinds of spiritual exegesis described above.[17] An interpretation that limited itself to the historical-critical phase would overlook the tacit meanings conveyed by the biblical stories, symbols, and metaphors. A comprehensive approach, combining scientific and spiritual exegesis, does better justice to Catholic tradition and the directives of Vatican II, and better serves the needs of systematic theology.[18]

---

[16] This is attested to by the proliferation of material which has appeared on this subject. See, for example, R.E. Murphy – C.J. Peter, "The Role of the Bible in Roman Catholic Theology," *Interp* 25 (1971) 78-92; D.H. Kelsey, *The Uses of Scripture in Recent Theology*; J. H. Wright, "The Bible and the Hermeneutical Horizon: The Use of Scripture in Theology," *TS* 43 (1982) 651-672; K.J. Becker, "Der Gebrauch der Hl. Schrift in der dogmatischen Theologie," *Gr* 73 (1992) 671-687; H. Küng – J. Moltmann, ed., *Conflicting Ways of Interpreting the Bible* [*Concilium* 138]; J. Ratzinger, "Biblical Interpretation in Crisis: On the Question of the Foundations and Approaches of Exegesis Today" in R.J. Neuhaus, ed., *Biblical Interpretation in Crisis: The Ratzinger Conference on Bible and Church*, 1-23.

[17] Among those surveyed by Dulles in this regard are Henri De Lubac; Hans Urs von Balthasar and Yves Congar.

[18] A. Dulles, "The Uses of Scripture in Theology," 85.

J.A. Fitzmyer, despite certain reservations about the "eisegetical fruits of the so-called spiritual interpretation of Scripture"[19] advocated by some of the proponents cited by Dulles, agrees with the refined approach to the historico-method[20] mentioned above. This too has been the principle guiding this present study.[21]

1.2 *"Integral Christology"*

A Christian approach to the Scriptures demands that both Testaments are considered. As part of the written Word of God, the Jewish Scriptures are also part of the *norma normans* of Christian theology.[22] The Pontifical Biblical Commission, in its document on the Bible and christology, calls for an "integral christology."[23] This is achieved only when the promise and expectation of the people of Israel are given due attention as preludes to their ulterior fulfilment in the person of Jesus Christ.[24] Indeed, this approach is evident in the writings of the four authors which constitute the central part of this thesis. Samuel Amsler insists on the inherent relationship between the two biblical testaments.[25] Even when engaged in the scientific exegesis of the prophetic books, Amsler never fails to highlight the connection between these texts and the Christian Scriptures[26] on one hand, and ecclesial praxis on the

---

[19] J.A. Fitzmyer, *Scripture, the Soul of Theology*, 91.

[20] For a critique of an exclusive biblical-critical method, see J. Wicks, "Biblical Criticism Criticised," *Gr* 72 (1991) 117-128.

[21] This is also in accord with the method adopted by G. O'Collins, *Christology*, 53, who, as he examines the human history of Jesus, "prioritizes a historical approach through the Synoptic Gospels but in no way wishes to exclude the need to complement such an approach with theological, literary, liturgical and spiritual reflection."

[22] J.A. Fitzmyer, *Scripture, the Soul of Theology*, 89.

[23] Commission Biblique Pontificale, *Bible et christologie*, Section 1.3.3, 69-70. An English translation has been published by J.A. Fitzmyer, *Scripture and Christology. A Statement of the Biblical Commission with a Commentary.*

[24] For an outline of what an integral christology would necessarily involve, see J. Dupuis, *Who Do You Say I Am?* 32-36.

[25] See, for example, S. Amsler, "Le dernier et l'avant dernier," *RSR* 63 (1975) 385-396.

[26] Among the many New Testament references that Amsler makes in his commentary on *Amos* (169; 181; 182; 186; 193; 198; 202; 209; 211; 213; 219; 222 236; 237), he notes, for example, 231: "L'affrontement d'Amatsia et d'Amos à Béthel est l'une des pages de l'Ancien Testament qui soulignent le mieux la liberté et l'autorité de la prédication des prophètes, face aux prétentions orgueilleuses des autorités civiles et religieuses d'Israël. De nombreux prophètes auront à affronter les mêmes contestations et à subir les mêmes tentatives d'étouffer leur voix. Leur ministère déjà dans la ligne de celui de Jésus, chassé de Nazareth (Luc. 4.28) et rejeté par les chefs du peuple (Mat. 16.21; Act. 4.11). Disciples, ils partagent le sort de leur maître (Jean 15.20). Mais contestée par les hommes, la parole des prophètes

other.[27] Indeed, Amsler suggests that the Old Testament prophetic actions find their fulfilment in the eucharistic breaking of the bread and in the death of Jesus on the Cross.[28] W.D. Stacey also concludes his study on prophetic drama by calling for an approach to Christian doctrine which acknowledges that Old Testament thought patterns persist in the New. "Perhaps the most interesting of the possibilities in this regard," he speculates, "is the relation to the theology of the sacraments."[29] Similarly, Heinz Schürmann recognizes that his analysis of the Christian Scriptures must be set against the background of their preparation in the Jewish writings,[30] and must inform the subsequent doctrine and life of the Church.[31] Despite his avowed declaration of the important link between exegesis and dogmatic theology, Karl Rahner is often accused of having "a begrudging attitude"[32] towards the Scriptures.[33] From the analysis of Chapter 5, however, it is clear that an adequate biblical scholarship informs the theology of the transcendental thomist.[34] The presentation of the work of Edward Schillebeeckx in the previous chapter attests to his extraordinary competence in biblical and extra-biblical literature.[35] The influence of this research on his later writings has already been noted.

---

tire son autorités de Celui qui les envoie et aux plans duquel les hommes ne sauraient faire obstacle."

[27] In *Les actes,* 6, Amsler notes that "la mission de l'Église est et droit être *prophétique*, c'est-à-dire à l'image de l'activité des prophètes bibliques, du Nouveau et d'abord de l'Ancien Testament."

[28] *Les actes,* 82.

[29] W.D. Stacey, *Prophetic Drama,* 282. See also Stacey's "The Lord's Supper as Prophetic Drama" in M.D. Hooker, *The Signs of a Prophet.*

[30] This is indicated by Schürmann's study of both the continuity and the discontinuity between Old Testament prophetic actions and New Testament eschatological signs of fulfilment as presented in Chapter 4.

[31] In discussing the relationship between symbol and effect of the eschatological signs of fulfilment Schürmann acknowledges that there may be implications for the traditional conception of sacramental causality. In fact, in correspondence with the author of this work, Schürmann acknowledges that this and other insights which derive form his exegetical research need to be considered by dogmatic theology.

[32] This is the judgement of J.A. Fitzmyer, *Scripture, the Soul of Theology,* 84.

[33] See G. C. Kalayil, *The Co-Relation of the Common and Ministerial Modes of Christian Priesthood According to Karl Rahner*, 218-227.

[34] Rahner outlines the methodological principles for a Christian understanding of the Hebrew Scriptures in his essay "The Old Testament and Christian Dogmatic Theology," *TI* 16, 177-190.

[35] See E. Schillebeeckx, "Exegesis, Dogmatics and the Development of Dogma" in H. Vorgrimler, ed., *Dogmatics vs Biblical Theology*, 115-145.

1.3 *The Eschatological Prophet*

Contemporary exegetical research witnesses to the so-called "third quest" for the historical Jesus. The first, or "old quest" emerged from the historical consciousness of the Enlightenment and came to a head with the publication of the work by A. Schweitzer in 1906.[36] This was followed by a period of historical skepticism, exemplified by the writings of R. Bultmann, which despaired of ever finding the Jesus of history. The second, or "new quest" was heralded in 1953 by E. Käsemann[37] who argued that the historical Jesus is important for any understanding of the Christ of faith. The "third quest," which began in the late 1980's, has generally reduced the picture of Jesus to a wisdom teacher or to a "cynic sage" similar to many others of the first-century Mediterranean world. D.A. Lane justly claims that "it is instructive to note how eschatology either positively or negatively has been an area of constant debate in all quests for the historical Jesus."[38] Nevertheless, it should be noted that an awareness of eschatology does not gives rise to the historical search. Rather, each quest attempts to articulate the tension which it uncovers between the present and the future dimensions of the message and the actions of the Nazarene. In fact, within the three quests noted above, D.A. Lane detects four different positions concerning the eschatological of Jesus: the 'consistent' eschatology of A. Schweitzer and J. Weiss; the 'realized' eschatology of C.H. Dodd,[39] the 'inaugurated' eschatology of R.H. Fuller,[40] and the non-eschatological approach of J.D. Crossan,[41] M. Borg,[42] and other members of the "Jesus Seminar."[43] Within the "third quest," however, a number of scholars affirm the presence and importance

---

36 The English translation appeared as J.A. Schweitzer, *The Quest for the Historical Jesus: A Critical Study of its Progress from Reimarus to Wrede* in 1910 (New York: Macmillan).

37 E. Käsemann, "The Quest for the Historical Jesus" in *Essays on New Testament Themes*, 15-47.

38 D.A. Lane, *Keeping Hope Alive. Stirrings in Christian Theology*, 80.

39 C.H. Dodd, *The Parables of the Kingdom.*

40 R.H. Fuller, *The Mission and Achievement of Jesus.*

41 J.D. Crossan, *The Historical Jesus: The Life of a Mediterranean Jewish Peasant* .

42 M. Borg, *Jesus in Contemporary Scholarship*. D.A. Lane, *Keeping Hope Alive*, 81-82, traces a shift in the writings of Borg towards a "more temperate case for a non-eschatological Jesus."

43 See R.W. Funk – R.W. Hoover, ed. *The Five Gospels: The Search for the Authentic Words of Jesus.*

of eschatology in the life of Jesus. E.P. Sanders,[44] for example, insists that Jesus was an eschatological prophet who believed that the promises made to Israel would be fulfilled in the near future. J.P. Meier[45] presents strong evidence of both a future and present eschatology in the life of Jesus.[46]

D.A. Lane concludes his review of eschatology in the historical life of Jesus by noting that to eliminate the former from the latter "would be to remove him from his thoroughly Jewish roots, to sever his connection with John the Baptist, to ignore the Pauline material and to negate a substantial part of the Gospel material."[47] To deny the eschatological dimension to the life of Jesus is to pluck him from the religious matrix of Judaism with its definite eschatological orientation. It is also to repudiate his association with John the Baptist and the prophets of Israel. In continuity with these and on the basis of his own unique religious experience, Jesus is concerned to highlight the action of God which is breaking into the world. In a very real sense, the disciples of Jesus experience the future as glimpsed, anticipated and realized through his ministry. He is the eschatological prophet whose proclamation of the kingdom emphasizes the nearness and the actuality of God as the numinous presence effecting religious, social, political and economic life in this world. While no one title can adequately encompass the originality of the person or penetrate the self-awareness of Jesus, it is widely accepted in christological research that the concept of eschatological prophet, however incomplete, plays an important role in the designation and self-identity of the historical figure from Nazareth. This features prominently in the writings of R.H. Fuller,[48] O. Cullmann,[49] D.A.

---

[44] E.P. Sanders, *The Historical Figure of Jesus*.

[45] J.P. Meier, *A Marginal Jew*, II, 348-351.

[46] For an overview of the Catholic participation in the quest for the historical Jesus, see W.M. Thomson, *The Jesus, Debate*,101-103.

[47] D.A. Lane, *Keeping Hope Alive,* 84.

[48] R.H. Fuller, *The Foundations of New Testament Christology*, 130: "Take the implied self-understanding of his role in terms of the eschatological prophet away, and the whole ministry falls into a series of unrelated, if not meaningless fragments."

[49] O. Cullmann, *The Christology of the New Testament*, 36-37: "We conclude that according to all four Gospels a section of the people expressed their faith in Jesus by the title 'the Prophet' and by the thoughts which were connected with it in the Jewish eschatological hope. But Jesus himself did not identify himself in this way. We should repeat here, however, that the prediction of his own return is at least foreshadowed in the conception of the return of the Prophet."

Lane,[50] W. Kasper,[51] J. Dupuis[52] and G. O'Collins.[53] This is also an important factor of the theological construct of both K. Rahner and E. Schillebeeckx.

1.4 *Baptism and Eschatology*

In the course of the twentieth century the tract on eschatology has moved from the periphery to the centre of theological discourse. "If Christianity be not altogether and unreservedly eschatology," charged K. Barth in 1921, "there remains in it no relationship to Christ."[54] This relocation to the core of systematic theology is marked by a number of shifts: "from the *eschata* to the *Eschaton*; from the future to the present *and* the future; from an individualist approach to a more inclusive one."[55] In other words, the retrieval of the biblical doctrine of the appearance of the *Eschaton* in Christ plays a critical and constructive function with regard to the rest of theology. It is critical insofar as it opposes any attempt to absolutize the present theological or ecclesiological order; it is constructive insofar as it sustains the community of believers in hope and empowers it to build a new future in the present. The traditional study of the "last things" treated eschatology as a theological appendix in which the emphasis was placed on the future destiny of the individual. As such, it was removed from other theological tracts including sacraments in general and baptism. The purpose of this present research project

[50] D.A. Lane, *The Reality of Jesus*, 39: "...it seems most reasonable and historically reliable to hold that Jesus at this stage of his life would have been seen as the eschatological prophet. Not only that, but this category seems to sum up most comprehensively the overall thrust that the ministry of Jesus would have had upon his followers at this point in his life. As eschatological prophet he announced the end of time, he proclaimed the Kingdom of God, he performed eschatological signs (miracles and exorcisms) and he heralded the advent of salvation."

[51] W. Kasper, *Jesus, the Christ,* 69: "Jesus is not just one in the line of the prophets, but the eschatological one: the last, definitive, all-transcending prophet. He brings God's final word, his definitive will."

[52] J. Dupuis, *Who Do You Say I Am?* 49: "We have already noted the surprising way in which Jesus situates himself in relation to the Reign of God. Not only does he herald the coming of the Kingdom as the eschatological prophet. He further claims that the Reign of God - God's self - is breaking through to people in him, in his life and mission, in his preaching and action."

[53] G. O'Collins, *Christology,* 68: "[Jesus] saw his ministry as standing, at least partially, in continuity with the prophets, right down to John, his prophetic precursor from whom he received baptism." See also, G. O'Collins, *Interpreting Jesus,* 60.

[54] K. Barth, *The Epistle to the Romans*, 314.

[55] D.A. Lane, *Keeping Hope Alive,* 3.

has been to focus on the eschatological dimension of baptism by treating the relationship between this initiatory rite and the *Eschaton* himself[56] as opposed to its connection with the various *eschata*.[57]

2. **Evaluating the Founts**

The persistent aim of this study has been to examine the eschatological dimension of baptism, understood as prophetic act, in the writings of two biblical and two systematic theologians. Methodologically it brought representatives of these two theological disciplines into dialogue with regard to the origin of baptism in the prophetic acts of Jesus in the Jordan and on Calvary. The purpose of this section is to appraise, in a "diachronic" movement, the contribution of each of the four authors to the foregoing investigation and to identify areas which could benefit from further research and development.

2.1 *Samuel Amsler: Returning to the Source of Baptism*

Despite the intriguing problems posed by the accounts of Old Testament prophetic actions, biblical scholars have shown limited interest in them. Samuel Amsler's *Les actes des prophètes* represents the first monograph in over thirty years to attempt a systematic treatment of these symbolic acts.[58] Less than a hundred pages in length, the work draws on the author's own previous research on the prophets, and offers an up-date on the seminal studies of H.W. Robinson and of G. Fohrer in the light of the advances in Old Testament scholarship in the later part of the twentieth century.

The core of Amsler's argument has already been presented under three headings: the act; the reaction; and the end. Significant to the present study is his contention that the immediate effect of the prophetic act is communicative: together with its concomitant explanation, the symbolic action scandalized the audience and provoked a reaction where words alone would have failed.[59] As

---

[56] See M. Michel, "Le retour de l'eschatologie dans la théologie contemporaine," *RSR* 58 (1984) 180-195.

[57] This would appear to be the approach of J. Mummadi, *Eschatological Aspects of Baptism*.

[58] The previous book on this subject, G. Fohrer, *Die symbolischen Handlungen der Propheten*, was first published in 1953.

[59] C. Uehlinger, "'Zeichne eine Stadt ... und belagere sie!'," 190, nn. 313 & 314, recognizes that the position of Amsler is more nuanced than that of either

already outlined, W.D. Stacey is wary of any attempt to reduce a prophetic drama to a communication event[60] and, consequently, he is apprehensive of the approach adopted by Amsler. It appears that, on this point, Stacey bases his criticism of Amsler on the ideas expressed in the article "Les prophètes et la communication par les actes."[61] As the title suggests, the concern here is not to present a full *exposé* of prophetic acts, but to deal precisely with their communicative function. Indeed, if Amsler had limited his exposition to this article, Stacey's censure would be valid. However, a more comprehensive treatment of the subject is undertaken in *Les actes des prophètes*. Here the immediate effect and the final end of the symbolic actions are distinguished. In this later presentation, the prophetic act is said not only to herald the future will of God, but also to anticipate the presaged divine intervention in the here and now of the spectators.

Amsler's approach to the relationship between the action executed by the prophet and the reality intended by Yahweh is particularly astute. At once, he avoids reducing the symbolic act either to the performance of a magical rite, on the one hand, or to the unveiling of a reality already foreclosed in the mind of God, on the other. While always a prophetic act, its ultimate power lies with the Lord who commands it: unlike a magician, the prophet does not exert pressure on the future from the present, but unveils the upcoming reality in the experience of the people; unlike a messenger, he does not merely announce something previously decided in the overall plan of God but, by his concrete action, shapes the ulterior unfolding of the theo-logical drama. To dismiss Amsler and other commentators who share this view because they display "a tendency to have it both ways at this point"[62] is invalid. The answer is not to be found with a simplistic *either-or* situation as W.D. Stacey intimates. There is little merit in the "boldness"[63] of a decision in favour of one pole or the other over "an amalgam of Yahwist theology and magical form"[64] when the scriptural texts call for a balance between the two. As outlined in Chapter 3, a correct understanding is found with neither extreme: only by

---

Fohrer or Zimmerli. While the latter understand the prophetic act as a dramatized word, the former insists that the symbolic action also prolongs the divine communication in a crisis situation and provokes a response from the audience.

[60] See Chapter 3, section 2.1.2..

[61] See W.D. Stacey, *Prophetic Drama,* 268.

[62] W.D. Stacey, *Prophetic Drama,* 270.

[63] W.D. Stacey, *Prophetic Drama,* 270.

[64] W.D. Stacey, *Prophetic Drama*, 271.

holding both together is the relationship between God and prophet properly maintained. Herein lies the true worth of the study by Amsler.

Old Testament symbolic acts do not occur in a vacuum, but are enacted at a precise moment in the ongoing historical drama between Yahweh and Israel. A prophetic action implicitly recalls the covenant which the God of Abraham has made with his chosen people. As such, it was at once *zikkārôn* and *'ôt*, memorial and anticipation. In other words, a prophetic action was a *signum rememorativum* of the great actions that God had already performed in Israel's regard; it was a *signum demonstrativum* of a new phase in that relationship; and a *signum prognosticum* of the future that the Lord had in store for the chosen people.

Specific aspects of Amsler's approach need to be nuanced further. First of all, the extent to which the modern communication theory of P. Watzlawick, J.H. Beavin and D.D. Jackson is an appropriate interpretative model for Old Testament prophetic actions certainly demands further investigation which is beyond the scope of this present study.[65] Secondly, while Amsler reiterates the points made by G. Fohrer on the differences between the prophet and the magician, it is evident that, in the light of more recent biblical and anthropological studies, the relationship between the two is not so extrinsic as once proposed.[66] Indeed, this is perhaps the most convincing criticism that W.D. Stacey levels at biblical theologians who have passed over the issue in cursory fashion.[67] Finally, the notion of time and of causation which is presumed by Amsler may owe more to twentieth-century attitudes than to the semitic world from which the prophetic acts emerge.[68] These last two point are developed below as preludes to the ulterior sketching of a new approach to the eschatological dimension of baptism in Chapter 8.

In 1942, H.W. Robinson expressed the difference between magic and religion almost epigrammatically: "Magic constrains the unseen; religion surrenders to it."[69] In this scheme, both the prophet and the magician act in the present but with regard to the

[65] See L–M. Chauvet, *Symbol and Sacrament: A Sacramental Reinterpretation of Christian Existence*, 347-353.

[66] A concise survey of this material is to be found in a chapter entitled "Prophetic Drama and Magic" in W.D. Stacey, *Prophetic Drama*, 234-263.

[67] See W.D. Stacey, *Prophetic Drama*, 236-259.

[68] See, for example, H.W. Wolff, *Anthropology of the Old Testament*, 81-89.

[69] H.W. Robinson, "Hebrew Sacrifice and Prophetic Symbolism," *JThS* 43 (1942) 132.

future, exerting a coercive, effective power on the latter. However, prophetic acts, because they are dependent on the will of God and work on his behalf, give magic a new meaning. While Amsler accepts Robinson's slogan, the analysis of Chapter 3 suggests that he draws a different conclusion as to the ultimate distinction between the magician and the prophet. The former moves from the execution to eventual fulfilment, from present to future; the latter reverses the direction, and operates from the future on to the present. Nevertheless, W.D. Stacey insists that Robinson's widely accepted distinction compares "the crudest and most unsophisticated form of magic with the most refined and selfless expression of religion." Consequently, the expression is not "simply too brief to be helpful; it is so heavily loaded that it is misleading."[70]

Whether the action under consideration is the breaking of a jar outside the gates of Jerusalem or the performing of a dance in the middle of a desert, the enacted ritual and the presaged reality are so intertwined that it is impossible to distinguish the most exalted prophetic act from the most notorious sorcery. Both actions are effective; both articulate a reality that needs to be expressed; both modify the experience and self-understanding of the onlookers; both intimate a future which effects the present situation of those in attendance. Given the similarities and dissimilarities that exist between prophetic drama and magic, W.D. Stacey concludes that the *principium discrimen* is theological: "The history, the ritual form, even, to some extent, the modes of thought, are the same, but different concepts of deity inform them. It is not what prophets actually do, but what they think about what they do that is important."[71]

If, then, the distinction between prophetic action and magic is not to be found among the external factors that constitute the dramatic event but in the subjectivity of the protagonist, further problems arises. First of all, it is impossible to reconstruct the motive of the prophet or to know what went on in his mind. It is feasible to argue that the classical prophets give the impression that they are acting under the divine impulse which is the directing force of history. Such a developed Yahwism cannot be detected, however, in the attitudes and actions of the earlier prophets like Elisha. Secondly, it is possible that *apriori* assumptions will be imposed

---

[70] W.D. Stacey, *Prophetic Drama,* 247.
[71] W.D. Stacey, *Prophetic Drama,* 257.

on the data which emerges. An atheistic anthropologist will conclude most likely that there is no difference between a prophetic and a magical action; an adherent to the Judeo-Christian tradition will not be prone to settle for such a judgement. Indeed, the approach of believers to this problem may well be prejudiced by theological, ecclesiastical or sacramental considerations.[72] If one's theological perspective precludes the activity of God beyond the confines of categorical revelation, then one is unlikely to accept any similarity between the activity of the magician and that of the prophet. However, if one holds that vestiges of the divine self-communication are to be found throughout human history, then some similarity between the two can be allowed.

In keeping with the agrarian world view which they shared, the religions of the ancient east developed a cyclical, primeval understanding of time. The Jews, however, proposed a novel conception of saving history and of time by ascribing their existence to the concrete interventions of Yahweh. G. Von Rad traces the development of this singular biblical conception: the gradual dissociation from the notion of a cultic return to an original state, which was common among the neighbouring nations, is combined with a growing sense of history as a linear series of saving events.[73] The Hebrew language does not have a word which corresponds to the modern concept of abstract or absolute "time." Instead, the idea of time is always tied to a particular historical event. When the people celebrated such an event cultically, they actually participated in the saving reality which they commemorated. G. Von Rad speaks of the "contemporaneousness"[74] which not only united the ritual community with the dramatic enactment of a past event, but also forged a link among disparate saving episodes in the life of the people.

The Jews viewed the relationship between past, present and future in a radically different way from that familiar to the modern world. According to H.W. Wolff, the Israelites perceive the past as a reality before them, and the future as something which lies behind them. According to this viewpoint man proceeds through time like a

---

[72] In 1927, W.H. Robinson, "Prophetic Symbolism," 15-16, recognized that viewing sacraments as prophetic actions overcame the "antithesis" between a "Protestant declaratory" and a "Catholic effective" conception of the Christian rites.

[73] G. Von Rad, *The Message of the Prophets*, 77-94.

[74] G. Von Rad, *The Message of the Prophets,* 82-85.

rower who moves into the future backwards: he reaches his goal by taking his bearings from what is visibly in front of him; it is in this revealed history that for him the Lord of the future is attested.[75] Clearly, therefore, any attempt to impose a simplistic *past cause→ future effect* scheme on Old Testament prophetic actions is blatantly anachronistic. Just as a dramatic action "contemporizes" past events in the present enactment, it also "encompasses" future eventualities in the current portrayal.[76] The baptismal implications of this biblical insight are investigated in Chapter 8.

2.2 *Heinz Schürmann: Tracing the Emergence of Baptism*

As already noted, Heinz Schürmann represents one of the first Catholic scholars who has attempted systematically to identify prophetic acts in the gospel narratives and to differentiate them from those found in the Hebrew Scriptures. The primary intention of Schürmann is to refute the widely-supported claim made by R. Bultmann that Jesus' death on the Cross represents the ultimate collapse of his person and ministry. In formulating a coherent response to this position, Schürmann is aware that the historicity of many of the Gospel texts concerning the attitude of Jesus to his death is disputed. His unique relationship to God as Father and his singular mission as eschatological representative of the kingdom would have opened up prethematic possibilities of interpreting his death in a way far exceeding the range of any categories available in the socio-religious environment of first century Palestine.[77] Against this background, Schürmann strives to uncover whether or not Jesus understood his death as a salvific, vicarious offering of himself to the Father. Schürmann does this by attempting to uncover the *ipsissima facta* which reveal the basis conduct and life-orientation of the historical person. In this manner, Schürmann transcends the contentious linguistic debate which surrounds the search for the *ipsissima verba*, and situates his treatment of the mission and identity of the Nazarene against a broader background.

Schürmann examines the basic orientation which is betrayed by the attitudes and actions of Jesus. His research suggests that

---

[75] H.W. Wolff, *Anthropology of the Old Testament*, 88.

[76] J. Moltmann, *The Crucified God*, 113: "'History as recollection' and 'history as hope', within the 'hope in the form of recollections' which is the determining element of Christian faith, are not contradictory, but must be complementary."

[77] J.P. Galvin, "Jesus' Approach to his Death," *TS* 41 (1980) 718.

> certain fundamental characteristics of Jesus' life — his will to serve and requirement of love, and especially his love for sinners and demand of love of enemy — favour the presumption that he would have seen his own death in a "pro-existent," intercessory, and salvific way, no matter what categories he may have used in this connection. His basic "pro-existent" stance would almost of it itself have produced a corresponding acceptance of death as an act of vicarious love, even if unthematically, and in a way which surpasses all available categories.[78]

In other words, regardless of the categories used to express the fact, Jesus lived as a man for others. The soteriological interpretation of the death on the Cross and the "for" of the words of institution have a solid foundation in the life and death of the eschatological Saviour. This is supported by Schürmann's analysis of the table-actions of Jesus at the Last Supper as eschatological signs of fulfilment.

The advantages of Schürmann's approach for the present study are evident. The continuity and the discontinuity between the actions of John the Baptist and of Jesus and those performed by the Hebrew prophets are acknowledged. The former are distinguished as "eschatological signs of fulfilment" with four defining characteristics: the basic orientation is eschatological; the primary meaning lies beyond the deed itself; the deed is marked from within by the time of fulfilment; and, pre-eminently, the sign follows the reality symbolized. The claim that the eschatological mission of Jesus is marked by his fundamental pro-existent demeanour is also significant. This existential stance is particularly obvious in the events leading up to the passion and death. But, all of his life is characterized by this radical *being-for-others* which is fulfilled on Calvary. This insight is particularly significant when the baptism of Jesus is considered.

According to Schürmann, the Baptist "took up and fulfilled the Old Testament prophecy of the eschatological ablution from sin in a prophetic sign."[79] Yet, while the prophetic acts of the old covenant looked forward to the proximate intervention of God, the activity of John introduced the irruption of the end-time and, as such, is termed an eschatological sign of fulfilment. When Jesus stood in the Jordan to be baptized by John he did so as one who was aware both of his unique relationship with the Lord of Israel

---

[78] J.P. Galvin, "Jesus' Approach to his Death," 719.
[79] *Lukas,* 156-157.

and of his particular mission to proclaim the eschatological nearness of divine salvation. The Lucan Jesus was endowed with the Spirit from the moment of his conception: the paracletic descent at the baptism serves to reveal the protopneumatic existence of Jesus, and to herald his arrival as the one who was presaged by John. The Sinless One is not content to undergo merely the lustral rite of the Baptist. Rather, he appropriates it and becomes the protagonist of a new eschatological sign of fulfilment. On this point, the analysis of Chapter 4 goes beyond the presentation of Schürmann. Yet, it draws this conclusion from this exegete's own criteria for a new covenant symbolic act.

By readily undergoing the ritual washing of the Baptist, then, Jesus performs a prophetic action which reveals him both as the pro-existent one who stands in solidarity with sinners and as the proleptic bearer of the Spirit which all are called to share as members of the post-paschal ecclesial community. Schürmann stresses that not only the prophetic actions of Jesus but also his pro-existent attitude find their ultimate expression in his death on the Cross. Already in his baptism, the incipient prophetic action of Jesus, this essential *being-for-others* is expressed. The Jordan rite, then, stands at the beginning of the public ministry of Jesus as a programmatic declaration of his *being-for-others* which finds its consummation on Calvary.[80] It is also a revelation of the one who has the Spirit-filled mission to proclaim the good news of the eschatological intervention of God in history, and who will ultimately bestow this presaged end-time gift on all creation.

In 1980, the International Theological Commission issued a document entitled "Select Questions on Christology."[81] Two sections of this text were prepared by Schürmann,[82] and they

---

[80] H. Urs von Balthasar, *Mysterium Pasquale*, 69-95, argues that the earlier events of Jesus' life announce the Cross and that his whole existence is an anticipation of the Passion.

[81] International Theological Commission, "Select Questions on Christology" in M.J. Sharkey, *International Theological Commission: Texts and Documents 1969-1985*, 185-295. [Hereafter Sharkey.]

[82] Once a document is approved and issued by the Commission, it does not identify the authors of individual parts. However, in his introduction to the French translation of the present document, P. Delhaye, "Presentation," *EeV* 90 (1980) 610, lists the members of the working group and attributes Chapter VI, B and C, to "a member who has made a special study of the attitude of Jesus to his forthcoming death." Here, he is clearly referring to Heinz Schürmann. Indeed, these two sections of the document are also listed in the bibliography of Schürmann which is edited by Theresia Ehrhardt.

incorporate many of the ideas discussed above. Introducing the earthly life of Jesus, the Commission notes that:

> Jesus was perfectly aware that, in his words and actions, in his existence and Person, the Kingdom and the reign of God were at once a present realization, an expectation, and a coming (cf. Lk. 10:23ff.; 11:20). Accordingly, he presented himself as the eschatological Saviour and gave a direct, albeit implicit, explanation of his own mission. He was ushering in the eschatological salvation, since he was coming after the last of the prophets, John the Baptist. He was bringing God and his reign to presence, and the time of promise to fulfilment (Lk. 16:16; Mk. 1:15a).[83]

The text acknowledges both a continuity and discontinuity between Jesus and the prophets: what the latter had proclaimed as promise, the former announces as fulfilment. The long-awaited eschatological salvation is at once "a present realization, an expectation and a coming" in Jesus' proclamation of the kingdom in words and action, in his very existence and person.

The document goes on to note that the "life and death [of Jesus] grow out of a fundamental attitude that is the will to live and die for God and for others. This is what has been called an existence-for-others, or a pro-existence."[84] This existential disposition, the text insists, must include personal knowledge on the part of the subject who offers himself, and the will to take on the suffering and the sin of humankind as a proxy. This disposition is "a lucid readiness"[85] to conform to the will of God, and it inevitably receives more "vitality and concreteness"[86] as the events of the life of Jesus unfold.

At the core of the life and ministry of Jesus, therefore, from Jordan to Calvary, there is a desire to be *for-others*. At his baptism in the Jordan, Jesus is revealed as the long-awaited bearer of eschatological salvation, as the "one who is to come." By standing in solidarity with sinners he manifests his willingness to undertake the divine mission which he had received from the Father. In the descent of the Spirit, the promise which had been made by John and the prophets are recalled and fulfilled, the pro-existent mission of the Son is revealed to the onlookers, and the general out-pouring of the end-time gift on the New Israel is anticipated. The action of

---

83 ITC, "Select Questions on Christology," IV, B, 2.1. [Sharkey, 197.]
84 ITC, "Select Questions on Christology," IV, B, 2.3. [Sharkey, 197.]
85 ITC, "Select Questions on Christology," IV, B, 2.4. [Sharkey, 198.]
86 ITC, "Select Questions on Christology," IV, B, 2.4. [Sharkey, 198.]

Jesus, then, is at once a *signum rememorativum* of the promises made by the prophets up to and including John, a *signum demonstrativum* of the inauguration of eschatological salvation, and a *signum prognosticum* of the future gift of divine life in which all are called to participate.

Apart form the baptism in the Jordan and the gestures at the Last Supper, Schürmann gives little consideration to other prophetic actions in the Gospel narratives. With certain historical reservations, he individuates seven further eschatological signs of fulfilment from this *corpus*. Following the more restrictive approach adopted by Fohrer and by Amsler in relation to Old Testament prophetic actions, Schürmann immediately excludes parables and miracles which other authors number among the symbolic actions performs by Jesus.[87] Even within the criteria accepted by Schürmann himself the inclusion of some and the exclusion of other actions needs to be re-evaluated. The writings of R. Fisichella,[88] for instance, would suggest that further consideration should be given to the narratives of the cursing of the fig tree (Matt 21:18), Jesus' writing on the ground while the accusers level charges at the woman taken in adultery (John 8:1-11), and his welcoming of a little child as an expression of the greatness of embracing the message of the kingdom.[89]

---

[87] B.F. Meyer, *The Aims of Jesus,* 153, examines the "public actions of Jesus" which "include the call of disciples and the sending of the disciples to Israel; miraculous signs of salvation; table fellowship with sinners; public debates and public formulations of mission; and, finally, the entry into Jerusalem to 'cleanse' the temple." He concludes, 173, that: "From the public traditions it would appear, then, that nothing short of a stunningly, unexpected restoration of Israel defined the historic form of Jesus' career. Symbolic words and actions imaged this restoration as eschatological reversal. 'The twelve' as such evoked restoration motifs that had stamped the hope of Israel since the days of Ezekiel (see Ez. 47:13-48:29). But Jesus did more than call on Israel to accept its rightful destiny of restoration. His exorcisms and his fellowship with sinners effected the restoration they signified. A leading purpose of his parabolic teaching was to heal religious divisions in Israel. The bold stroke of cleansing the temple laid a claim on the whole nation, pressing it to acknowledge the dawning reign of God. These conclusions have a greater specificity than those drawn from our study of the Baptist and Jesus' stance toward him. Otherwise the two sets of conclusions remarkably converge."

[88] R. Fisichella, "Prophecy" in R. Latourelle – R. Fisichella, ed., *Dictionary of Fundamental Theology*, 791.

[89] E. Schüssler Fiorenza, *In Memory of Her: A Feminist Theological Reconstruction of Christian Origins*, 152-153, considers the anointing of the feet of Jesus (Luke 7:36-50) as a "prophetic sign-act." G. O'Collins, *Christology*, 73, describes the cleansing of the temple as a "symbolic action."

In identifying prophetic actions which were performed by Jesus or by other characters in the New Testament, M.D. Hooker adopts the more inclusive[90] approach which was championed by her husband W.D. Stacey in cataloguing Old Testament dramatic actions. Hooker explains what she means by the term 'prophetic sign': "*not* a visual aid intended to *assist* in teaching — rather, the dramatic *equivalent* of the spoken oracle; *not* an efficacious act, which *causes* something to happen — rather, the dramatic *embodiment* of the divine purpose, which otherwise may well be at present hidden."[91] However, in the light of this present study, the double opposition which is proposed by Hooker's definition seems unnecessary. A prophetic action is both a visual aid and a dramatized oracle; it causes something to happen as well as unveiling the divine purpose to the on-lookers.[92] In any case, Schürmann does not claim to present a canonical list: his concern lies primarily with the baptism in the Jordan and the table-action at the Last Supper which are widely acknowledged to be prophetic actions. Nevertheless, a more comprehensive study of the criteria for identifying an eschatological sign of fulfilment is required and, once established, a more rigorous application of these to a particular narrative is demanded.

Schürmann shows a commendable alertness to the dogmatic implications of his exegetical research. The soteriological import of his investigation of the attitude of Jesus to his violent death has been mentioned above. While the argument of those who follow the approach of Bultmann has been refuted, Schürmann has not settled all the questions concerning Jesus' understanding of his death. J.P. Galvin calls for further scrutiny into the words which accompany the table-actions in the accounts of the Last Supper and for a broader enquiry into other categories used to interpret the death of the Saviour in the passion theologies of the early Church.[93]

---

90 Indeed M.D. Hooker, *The Signs of a Prophet*, lists over thirty eight prophetic action in the gospel accounts.

91 M.D. Hooker, *The Signs of a Prophet*, 38-39.

92 Indeed, one may well ask how a prophetic action could be the 'embodiment of the divine purpose, which otherwise may well be at present hidden' without in some sense functioning as " a visual aid intended to assist in teaching."

93 J.P. Galvin, "Jesus' Approach to his Death: An examination of Some Recent Studies," 722-723, expresses his difficulty with Schürmann's method and conclusions as follows: "Schürmann seems excessively concerned with finding foundation in the life of Jesus for interpretation of his death in terms of atonement, while not considering in equal depth the possibility of a comparable basis for one or more of the other categories (death of the righteous man, death of a prophet-martyr) used in the Passion theologies of the early Church. Perhaps his particular

In his analysis of the prophetic washing by the Baptist in the Jordan and of the symbolic gestures of Jesus in the upper room, Schürmann contends that, in these eschatological signs of fulfilment, contrary to the situation pertaining in their Old Testament precursors, the fundamental relationship between sign and gift is reversed so that, pre-eminently, the sign follows the gift.[94] As Schürmann recognizes, the sacramental implications of such a conclusion are significant: "compared with the Greek conception of the sacraments, the direction of the symbolism is reversed."[95] However, beyond an initial delineation, the exegete does not elaborate further. This relationship between the sacramental sign and the grace conferred in the ritual celebration is discussed in Chapter 8.

2.3 *Karl Rahner: Channeling the Surge of Baptism*

The desire to overcome the scholastic extrinsicism with regard to the relationship between nature and grace, and between the sacred and the profane, is central to the theological project of Karl Rahner. The human person is forever "the infinite openness of the finite for God."[96] Every human search for truth or act of freedom ultimately affirm or deny God. The implications of such a starting point are manifold: it demands that every aspect of Christian life and doctrine be re-evaluated. Within the sacramental sphere, this approach has immediate repercussions on the traditional understanding of the relationships (i) between the ritual action and ordinary human life, (ii) between the rite and the Church

---

interest in the Last Supper tradition and in the early Christian Eucharist, while legitimate in itself, has contributed to a narrowing of the inquiry. As a result, the consequences of Wilhelm Thüsing's observation that a rudimentary theology of the Passion is already present when Jesus' acceptance of death is joined to the radical call to discipleship are not developed in Schürmann's work, though Thüsing's statement is quoted favourably. As valuable as Schürmann's treatment is, it remains incomplete."

[94] "Jesus' Words," 65: "John the Baptist by pouring water had already symbolically and effectively acted out the prophecy, 'I will sprinkle clean water upon you, and you shall be clean...' (Ez. 36:25f; cf. Zech. 13:1). Similarly, on this view, by his double action at the Last Supper, Jesus would have effectively proffered eschatological salvation as the fruit of his death, and by doing so also represented it symbolically. The Baptist's salvific action and that of Jesus presuppose the prophecy, take it up, make it a reality and apply it, and are therefore more than a prophetic *'ôt* ."

[95] "Jesus' Words," 65.

[96] K. Rahner, *Hearers of the Word*, 66: "The only thing which makes [man] a man is that he is forever on the road to God whether he is clearly aware of the fact or not, whether he wants to be or not, for he is always the infinite openness to the finite for God."

which performs it, (iii) between the action and the word which accompanies it, and (iv) between the liturgical activity and the praxis of the community which enacts it. In Chapter 5, the correspondence between Rahner's understanding of the sacraments and the Amsler-Schürmann analysis of Old and New Testament prophetic actions was underlined. This provided the justification for the application of the motif of baptism as symbolic event of eschatological salvation to the German Jesuit theologian's approach to the initiatory rite. In this section, the enhanced insights that have emerged from this study are evaluated in terms of the four relationships listed above in an effort to illumine further the prognostic dimension of this lustral rite.

Christian sacraments are not isolated events through which human beings leave the secular realm of time and space in order to enter into the sacred sphere where the sanctifying grace to be conferred is grasped as a reality beyond normal experience and consciousness. These ritual actions, Rahner rightly contends, are manifestations of that holiness which already penetrates every level of secular existence. They symbolically express the graced interaction with God in the lives of the participants so that they might arrive at a fuller actualization of this divine gift. Candidates who come forward to celebrate the sacrament of baptism have already experienced the offer of the divine self-communication and, insofar as they have responded to this grace in the joy and the struggle of "real" life, they are justified by the conscious or unconscious acceptance of this *res* prior to the celebration of the "religious" event in which it is joined to the *sacramentum.* In fact, Rahner continues, the subsequent celebration of the ecclesial rite of baptizing the candidates is possible precisely because they have encountered the self-communication of God within the depths of their ordinary lives. The primary *locus* for the renewal of the sacramental life of the Church, therefore is to be found not within the liturgical ambit *per se*, but within the "mystagogy" which opens the mystical depth of everyday experience to believers.[97] In this way, Rahner rescues the sacraments from the danger of magical abuse, and manifests them as privileged moments in the ongoing self-communication of God to humanity.

But what difference, then, does the water rite make? Immediately, Rahner offers two solutions: the pre-sacramental

---

[97] See "On the Theology of Worship," *TI* 19, 148; "Experience of the Holy Spirit," *TI* 18, 202.

indwelling of the Spirit finds a socio-historical embodiment in the ritual action, and thus attains a specific and definitive actualization; and, the ritual words and gestures visibly incorporate the recipient into the ecclesial community which realizes its own rite of initiation. While these responses to the dilemma are significant, they are not totally satisfactory. Both are formulated against the background of Rahner's ontology of symbol[98]: the former solution comprises a general application of his theory to the sacramental sphere, while the latter is a corollary derived from his ecclesiology. A more comprehensive answer emerges, however, if the particular sacramental sign and the divine grace associated with it were given due consideration. The lustral action not only averts to the divine plan to confer eternal beatitude in some heavenly time and place, but also assures the recipient that, in the midst of the ecclesial community, this fulfilment is already at hand. What the non-baptized justified person is to receive only in the *visio beatifica* is proleptically bestowed in the sacramental rite on the believer. In baptism, through water and the invocation of the Triune God, the form of eschatological life is imparted to the recipient.

Rahner situates his sacramental theory within an ecclesiological perspective: "the treatise *De sacramentis in genere* is not an abstract formulation of the nature of the individual sacraments, but a part of the treatise *De ecclesia*."[99] Jesus Christ is the primordial sacrament [*Ursakrament*]; the Church is the basic sacrament [*Grundsakrament*]. The individual rites are essential symbols in which the ecclesial community actualizes in the life of the recipients a particular dimension of its nature as the ongoing presence of the eschatological victory of Christ. The advantages of such an avenue of approach are evident. First of all, Rahner posits an essential relationship between the Church itself and the sacraments which it continually dispenses. The immediate effect, the *sacramentum et res*, of each rite is understood in an ecclesiological perspective. Secondly, he eschews the debate which

[98] This parallels the conclusion reached by M. Skelley, *The Liturgy of the World: Karl Rahner's Theology of Worship*. Skelley seeks to investigate the relationship between the Church's liturgy and of the "primordial liturgy" that takes place within the graced interaction with God in the ebb and flow of history. He concludes, 101, that "the liturgy of the Church is the explicit manifestation of the implicit liturgy of our lives. It is not simply identical with that liturgy of the world, but it is so derived from it and deeply united with it that it really expresses the cosmic liturgy and makes it present to us. In other words, explicit forms of worship are real symbols of the liturgy of the world."

[99] *CS*, 41.

seeks to locate the origin of the individual rites in specific statements of the pre- or post-paschal Jesus. The sacraments of the new law are implicitly instituted in the explicit institution of the Church by Christ. Yet, Rahner insists, this ecclesiological derivation of the individual rites does not obscure their fundamental christological source. There is a pneumatic link[100] between the sacramental rites of the Church and the words and actions of Jesus Christ, the eschatological prophet.

Rahner develops his sacramental theory also against the background of his theology of the word of God. Central to this is his conviction that the human person is "a hearer of the word." Since, according to Rahner, a transcendental reality necessarily finds a categorical expression, the inward self-communication of God must have an exhibitive character as an event of saving grace. The relationship between the word and the designated grace is reciprocal: the word is formed by the grace that seeks to communicate itself; the grace becomes efficacious from making itself heard in the word. History charters the ups and the downs in this divine-human dialogue which finds its fulfilment in the life, death and resurrection of Jesus Christ, the Word-made-flesh, and which is prolonged in the Spirit-endowed mission of the Church. Whenever this word is proclaimed through the Church in existentially decisive moments in the life of an individual, the irreversibly victorious promise of God is assured. As already noted in Chapter 5, this insight permits Rahner to bridge the post-reformation opposition between word and sacrament and to posit an understanding of the ecclesial rites as "one specific word-event within a theology of the word."[101] The sacrament of baptism, then, is celebrated most worthily when catechumens have first recognized that an infallible expression of the divine self-communication within them can be found in the external proclamation of the Good News in the Church, and when they wish to articulate their acceptance of this saving grace by undergoing the initiatory water ritual which assures them that they now stand on the threshold of eternal life.

Indeed, this is the understanding of baptism which is presented by the Sacred Congregation for Divine Worship in a general introduction to Christian Initiation which was promulgated together

---

[100] See "The Presence of Christ in the Sacrament of the Lord's Supper," *TI* 4, 287-311; "The Presence of the Lord in the Christian Community at Worship," *TI* 10, 71-83.

[101] "What is a Sacrament?" 138.

with the *Rite of Christian Initiation of Adults* (*RCIA*) on the Feast of the Epiphany in 1972.[102] It notes:

> Baptism, the door to life and to the kingdom of God, is the first sacrament of the New Law, which Christ offered to all, that they might have eternal life. He later entrusted this sacrament and the Gospel to his Church, when he had told his apostles: "Go, make disciples of all nations, and baptize them in the name of the Father, and of the Son and of the Holy Spirit." Baptism is therefore, and above all, the sacrament of that faith by which, enlightened by the grace of the Holy Spirit, we respond to the Gospel of Christ. That is why the Church believes that it is its most basic and necessary duty to inspire all, catechumens, parents of children still to be baptized, and all godparents, to that true and living faith by which they hold fast to Christ and enter into or confirm their commitment to the New Covenant. In order to enliven such faith, the Church prescribes the pastoral instruction of catechumens, the preparation of the children's parents, the celebration of God's word, and the profession of faith at the celebration of baptism.[103]

The text acknowledges that baptism is the sacrament whereby adults who are "enlightened by the gift of grace," "respond to the Gospel of Christ" and "confirm their commitment to the New Covenant." Clearly, the Congregation admits that one may be justified ("enlightened by the gift of grace") prior to the explicit proclamation of the Gospel and to the celebration of the sacrament. Since this grace "is offered to all, that they might have eternal life," the divine self-communication must be mediated in some transcendental manner before finding its categorical expression in the Word. If the "basic and necessary duty" of the Church is "to inspire all ... to that true and living faith by which they hold fast to Christ," then it can consist of a kerygmatic announcement of the *mirabilia* of salvation history, only if it is preceded or accompanied by a mystagogical awakening to the activity of divine grace in the everyday experience of the person. Then the celebration of the sacrament is a "confirmation" of that "commitment to the New Covenant" which has already been made by assenting to the self-communication of Absolute Mystery in the concrete history of the individual. Notice, too, how baptism is described as "the door to life and to the kingdom of God." Given the fact that the text allows for the justification of those who have not yet been baptized, it is

---

[102] *Rite of Christian Initiation for Adults. The Final Text with Commentaries.*
[103] *RCIA*, "General Introduction," no. 3.

unclear how this description is to be interpreted. However, the present exposition of baptism in terms of prophetic action offers a solution. While all the justified (baptized and non-baptized) are "enlightened" by grace and are admitted to life, those who undergo the sacramental washing proleptically participate in the form of eternal life which others only experience as a promise.

In proposing his theory of symbolic causality, Rahner seeks to overcome the fundamental flaw that he perceives in the traditional responses to the question of how sacraments confer grace. "How can one thing distinct from another produce the latter?," he queries.[104] His own response is to take seriously the much quoted axiom *sacramenta significando efficiunt gratiam*. The appropriate way to guarantee the intrinsic connection between sign and cause in the sacraments is to treat these rites as real symbols. This, in fact, is a particular application of the "ontology of symbol" which Rahner utilizes in anthropology, christology, ecclesiology and in other areas of his theological construct.[105] In this scheme, sacraments are causes of grace because they are its symbols; yet, they are symbols of grace because they are its causes. Rahner rejects the notion of transitive efficient causality on which the traditional approaches are based, and postulates instead the concept of quasi-formal causality.[106]

The benefits which accrue from this approach to sacraments are many. By situating the worship of the Church within the context of the "liturgy of the world" Rahner broadens the basis for Catholic sacramental practice, and transcends the magical interpretations which a narrower focus could so easily promote. This is particularly evident in Rahner's treatment of *ex opere operato* and *opus operantis*. In these, as in other areas, Rahner demonstrates a particular concern to demonstrate how his own insights are firmly rooted in the sacramental doctrine of the Church. His intention is not to dismiss the theories of the past, but

---

[104] *CS,* 37.

[105] See G. Vandervelde, "The Grammar of Grace: Karl Rahner as a Watershed in Contemporary Theology," *TS* 49 (1988) 445-459; J.J. Buckley, "On Being a Symbol: An Appraisal of Karl Rahner," *TS* 40 (1979) 453-473; B. Hurd, "Being is Being-Present-To-Self: Rahner's Key to Aquinas's Metaphysics," *Thom* 52 (1988) 63-78.

[106] See P. De Letter, "Divine Quasi-Formal Causality," *IThQ* 27 (1960) 221-228; D.A. Tappeiner, "Sacramental Causality in Aquinas and Rahner: Some Critical Thoughts," *SJTh* 28 (1975) 243-257; G. Mansini, "Quasi-Formal Causality and 'Change in the Other': A Note on Karl Rahner's Christology," *Thom* 52 (1988) 293-306.

to facilitate "concrete proclamation in the Church, to dialogue with people of today."[107] The similarities between Rahner's symbolic causality and the relationship between sign and reality in prophetic actions are emphasized in Chapter Five. Both advance a sacramental theory whereby the ritual celebration emerges at a particular moment in the ongoing dialogue between God and humanity; both foster an understanding of the sacrament as a word-event; both underpin the fact that the sacrament is primarily a sign or symbol of another reality which necessarily calls it into existence.

Rahner's recasting of the general principles of sacramental theory allows little time to consider the particular sign and the specific sacramental grace associated with each of the seven ecclesial rites. He readily admits that a saving gift necessarily creates its own symbol which expresses its deepest sense. In other words, the saving gift which finds expression in and is communicated by the ritual pouring of water with the accompanying trinitarian invocation cannot be totally identical with that saving gift which finds its self-expression and realizes its self-communication, for instance, in the ritual anointing of a sick person with oil which is accompanied by a prayer for healing and strength. According to Rahner, a sacrament is an ecclesial action: the establishment of the appropriate ritual gesture and formula takes place within the Spirit-filled community which prolongs the eschatological victory of Christ in history. This, however, cannot be an arbitrary prerogative of the Church. If the classical axiom quoted above is to be upheld, any alteration of the liturgical rite by the Church should ensure a more perspicacious relationship between the words and/or actions which constitute the symbol, and the underlying self-communication of God which it portrays. Certainly, the writings of Rahner do not deny this claim. Yet, it only becomes clear when Rahner's sacramental theory is complemented by the insights gleaned from the prior study of the analogical relationship between words and signs in prophetic actions.

Throughout his theological *corpus* Rahner insists that grace does not intervene in human life at particular religious moments only to recede from the secular reality as suddenly as it appeared. All of human history, all of earthly existence, is the stage on which the drama of divine self-communication unfolds. Positive as well as

---

[107] K. Rahner, *Karl Rahner in Dialogue: Conversations and Interviews, 1965-1982*, 334.

negative experiences, times of joy and suffering, are opportunities through which the presence of Mystery is glimpsed. "It has always been clear in my theology," Rahner claims, "that a 'transcendental experience' (of God and of grace) is always mediated through a categorical experience in history, in interpersonal relationships, and in society."[108] Salvation history, categorical revelation, church and sacraments are the privileged *loci* where this universal self-communication of God which is fulfilled in Jesus Christ is both irrefutably acknowledged and infallibly offered to humanity. It may seem strange, then, that the most serious critique of Rahner focuses on the relationship between Christian faith and praxis in the world. This, in fact, is the charge which J.B. Metz levels at his former professor.

Metz objects to the "transcendental-idealistic" approach of Rahner and charges that he secures the historical identity of Christian faith ahistorically, through a transcendental omnipresence.[109] Further, he asserts, the demands for a socio-practical mediation of Christian faith in the specific practice of solidarity with the suffering is attenuated in the transcendental thomist's theology. Metz faults Rahner on his understanding of the concept "anticipation" as the condition of the possibility of human subjectivity in freedom. In the rahnerian scheme it appears that grace is already vindicated in the world in the subjectivity of the subject, without having to "run the race" and seek its vindication in the world, in history and in society. J.A. Colombo,[110] in his analysis of the differences between master and student, points out that both affirm that religion is related to anticipation. Rahner is accused by Metz of foreclosing the openness and indeterminateness of history in a metaphysical trap. Metz insists that the anticipatory force of religion lies with its social, historical and practical mediation of the subversive memory of the passion and resurrection of Jesus. As the next section demonstrates, on this point, the position of Metz is similar to that of Schillebeeckx.

---

[108] K. Rahner, "Introduction" in J.J. Bacik, *Apologetics and the Eclipse of Mystery: Mystagogy According to Karl Rahner*, x. [Quoted from M. Skelley, *The Liturgy of the World: Karl Rahner's Theology of Worship*, 35, n. 9.]

[109] See, J.B. Metz, *Faith in History and Society: Towards a Practical Fundamental Theology*, 161-166.

[110] J.A. Colombo, "Rahner and his Critics: Lindbeck and Metz," *Thom* 56 (1992) 71-96.

2.4 *Edward Schillebeeckx: Following the Course of Baptism*

The writings of Edward Schillebeeckx reflect the development of theology in the twentieth century.[111] From the thomistic renewal of the earlier part of this century, through the existentialist and phenomenological schools of mid-century, to the social, critical and hermeneutical studies of the final decades of the second millennium, Schillebeeckx's work is a courageous attempt to articulate the perennial truth of Christianity for men and women against a changing socio-cultural and ecclesio-religious landscape. While certain questions have remained axial to his thought throughout his career, the answers have been formulated in different contexts.

His earlier work reflects the relatively secure intra-ecclesial theology of the pre-conciliar Church. Faith in God and the necessity of the Church are presumed. In formulating his theory of the Christian rites as an encounter with the risen Lord, Schillebeeckx displays an ample familiarity with the historical development of sacramental theory. Yet, he is not content merely to repeat the old dogmatic statements, but seeks to recast the mystery of ecclesial worship in categories which are more readily accessible and are more immediately intelligible to believers living in a secularized ambience. In order to attain this goal, the sacraments are presented not as things, but as symbolic acts of the Church by which the recipients encounter the Lord of Glory.

The eschatological implications were noted in Chapter 6. As an existence between passover and *parousia*, the present life of believers is a waiting in hope for the fulfilment in glory of that encounter which has been initiated in baptism. By virtue of the ritual enactment (present) of the historical mysteries of the life of Christ (past), believers encounter the *Eschaton* himself (future). Through the ecclesial rite, the recipients join with Christ in his eternal prayer of thanksgiving to the Father and in his intercession for the gift of the Spirit for all creation. In this way, the equilibrium between *epiclesis* and *anamnesis* in the liturgical action is maintained, and the prognostic dimension of the sacramental sign is given due emphasis together with its commemorative and demonstrative counterparts.

In his presentation of the institution of the seven sacraments, Schillebeeckx holds christological and ecclesiological

[111] In fact, P. Kennedy, *Schillebeeckx*, 4-5, suggests that Schillebeeckx's "works mirror twenty centuries of reflection on Christian belief."

considerations together. While Rahner is content to posit the implicit institution of the sacraments in the explicit institution of the Church, Schillebeeckx nuances this theory by insisting that the ecclesial determination of the sacramental words and actions must embody the meaning or signification determined by Jesus Christ. Like Rahner, Schillebeeckx understands the sacramental character as the permanent relationship with the visible community of the Church. However, he describes the baptismal character as the first investiture with the apostolic mission to give praise to God in life and in worship. Even at this early stage Schillebeeckx emphasizes the inherent link between membership in the Church and commitment to live for the service of others.

In Chapter 6, the two distinct phases in Schillebeeckx's thought were characterized by an epistemological conversion. In the earlier stage, the possibility of cognitive contact with, or theoretic participation in, a totality of meaning was postulated. In *Christ the Sacrament of the Encounter with God*, this human search for God finds its fullest expression in the sacraments of the Church. In the later phase, Schillebeeckx despairs of the possibility of any participation in a totality of theoretical meaning. Instead, he suggests that, by embracing the praxis of the kingdom, it is possible to anticipate that fulness which lies in the future. But, what is the fate of the Christian sacraments in this new perspective? Schillebeeckx makes little or no mention of these rites of the Church in his later writings. While this could be construed as a criticism of his more recent theological output, it is also symptomatic of the more global audience to which Schillebeeckx now addresses himself. Nevertheless, it is possible to construct a sacramental theory from the later christological and ecclesiological writings of the author. For this reason, the following cannot be construed either as an appraisal or as a critique of the later baptismal theology of Schillebeeckx. Rather, it seeks to sketch the outlines of the eschatological dimension of this initiatory rite which should naturally emerge from the cardinal points of Schillebeeckx's theology.

The memory of the saving mission of Jesus *(memoria passionis Christi)* is kept alive by the community which gathers in his name and which imitates his praxis of the values of the kingdom. Jesus is the eschatological prophet whose self-understanding derives from his extraordinary sense of the nearness of God whom he addresses as *Abba*-Father. The Church is the Spirit-filled community of men and women which continues to utter a prophetic "no" to the de-humanizing powers of the world. The pro-existent words and actions of Jesus reveal the cause of God as the cause of humanity, and unveil a new order in the life of his followers. As Schillebeeckx notes, this pro-existence, which is so plainly manifest at the Last Supper and at Calvary, is clearly discernible in the prophetic activity of the Nazarene from the moment of his baptism. By standing in the Jordan with sinners, Jesus performs his first prophetic act. This incipient gesture points to the fulfilment of the hope of Israel in the arrival of the eschatological prophet, and it anticipates a new reality within the human drama of suffering and death. This is the story which is enacted in the liturgy; this is the story which Christian praxis incarnates in the world. According to this scheme, Christian baptism is the sacrament by which believers express their commitment to live as members of the prophetic ecclesial community which seeks to anticipate a new world. By undergoing this lustral rite, they embark on a life-long mission of *being-for-others*. Sealed with the Spirit of justice, they utter a prophetic protest to the suffering and oppression which diminish humanity and establish signs which proleptically anticipate the world which lies in the future with God.

By reconciling message and action in his own person, Jesus overcame the disparity between orthodoxy and orthopraxis, and liberated people from religious and social oppression and injustice. Schillebeeckx is well aware that, in the history of human suffering, many have attempted to use religion to legitimize unjust structures or despotic regimes. How, then, can the Christian community be sure that its discipleship is truly a *sequela Christi*? In an article published in 1977, D. Hollenbach notes that the sacramental life can serve "as a touchstone for discerning the authenticity of prophetic statements which claim to be calls from God" and "as an important counterweight to the expressively futurist and critical approach of a purely eschatological theology or spirituality."[112] By activating the subversive memory of the life and death of the risen Lord, sacramental practice subjects all systems to the ultimate criterion, and unmasks idolatrous self-seeking and power. The liturgical rites of the Church confront the members of the Christian community with the challenge of verifying the "ritual memory" of Jesus' prophetic action with the "existential memory" of their own

[112] D. Hollenbach, "A Prophetic Church and the Catholic Sacramental Imagination" in J.C. Haughey, ed., *The Faith that Does Justice*, 251.

lives which take charge of history in his name.[113] In the celebration of baptism, for example, the ecclesial community comes face-to-face with the memory of the prophet from Nazareth who stands in solidarity with sinful men and women and who anticipates the definitive epiphany of the God of all peoples. Consequently, any bid to sabotage this rite for personal or exploitative motives is immediately shattered against the touchstone of the *memoria Jesu.*

In his later writings Schillebeeckx accepts the primacy of the future over the past. While human history continues, the fulness of truth cannot be articulated in any one metaphysical or linguistic framework, because the plenitude of meaning includes a tomorrow which has not yet been realized. But, belief in the *pleroma* which resides in the future is verified by the practical anticipation of those features which creation might eventually assume. Within this framework, then, there is a tension between present and future, between reality and promise, between *topia* and *utopia*. Baptism is the symbolic action that anticipates the fulness of divine life in the present experience of the community which seeks to live in the memory of Jesus. As such, it (and the other sacraments) functions as an important counterweight against an escape into the future which denies the moral imperative of the present. At the same time, baptism provides a vital swell against an imprisonment in the present which loses sight of the hidden indicative of the future. In other words, as a *signum rememorativum*, the ritual action recalls the radical pro-existence of the prophet from Nazareth; as a *signum demonstrativum*, it bestows new life in the Spirit on those who seek to participate in the ecclesial community's mission of justice; and, as a *signum prognosticum*, it proleptically imparts that fulness of life which has been promised to all.

Baptism is a *signum triplex*, a sign of the past, of the present, and of the future salvation which God imparts to all humanity. To focus on one aspect of this *sacrum lavacrum* to the exclusion or to the diminution of another is to sunder the mystery of salvation from its unique source, from its living font, or from its final destination. While this study has concentrated on the prognostic aspect of this symbolic action, it recognizes that the saving truth emphasized here can be appreciated only in the context of the other two.

---

[113] L.-M. Chauvet, *Symbol and Sacrament*, 260-261.

CHAPTER 8

Anticipating the Future

Baptism as a sacramental participation in the life and mission of Jesus Christ, the Alpha and the Omega

The aim of this final chapter is to present an overview of the understanding of baptism as a sacramental participation in the life and mission of Jesus Christ, the Alpha and the Omega, which emerges from this confluence of scriptural and systematic studies. The previous chapter was evaluative in scope and diachronic in approach: it evaluated in turn the contribution that each of the four authors have made to the theme under consideration. This final chapter is prognostic in extent and synchronic in style: it presents in overview the heightened understanding of the eschatological dimension of the lustral rite which derives from the attempt to juxtapose the biblical *'ôt* and the thomistic *signum prognosticum* which was conducted in the central part of this thesis.

In Chapter 1, the baptismal theology of St. Thomas Aquinas was presented under the heading *O Sacrum lavacrum*, paralleling the summary of the eucharistic doctrine of the Angelic Doctor which is to be found in the antiphon *O Sacrum convivium*. The enhanced understanding of baptism as symbolic act of eschatological salvation which emerges from this study is proposed in this concluding chapter under an analogous hymnic structure:

> O propheticum lavacrum,
> quo Christi ecclesiae quis incorporatur,
> vita venturi saeculi praefiguratur,
> passionis eius recolitur memoria,
> et peccati gratis nobis remissio datur.

The justification for each phrase emerges as the chapter unfolds.

1. "O propheticum lavacrum..."

Baptism is the symbolic action which derives from the Old Testament prophetic signs and, in turn, from the ritual washing which Jesus readily underwent in the Jordan. As such, it is more correctly described as a *propheticum lavacrum* than a *sacrum lavacrum*. The insights which derive from treating the sacramental sign as a prophetic action are treated in this section.

1.1 *Baptism as Divine Command*

In establishing signs of the future intervention of God among the chosen people, the Old Testament prophets never acted on their own initiative. Unlike the magicians of old, the prophets of Israel were the source neither of the power nor of the authority which their words and actions displayed. Rather, fundamental to their identity and mission was the conviction that prophets were called by Yahweh to speak and act on his behalf.[1] Normally, the whole of the prophetic *persona* was involved in communicating the divine word which was known from the depths of a personal relationship with God. According to Amsler, the decisive factor was not the precise modality of the communication event between God and individual prophets. That the latter understood their actions as a response to the divine spirit or word was of primary importance.

Even though the accounts of the activity of John the Baptist do not mention any explicit command to baptize, there is no doubt that he is acting in accordance with God's will in calling others to repentance. The Third Gospel insists that "the word of God came to John the son of Zechariah in the wilderness" (Luke 3:2). Like the prophets of old, John was a sign and a portent of the imminent intervention of God. His whole existence, his austere lifestyle and his intense preaching, were so associated with his message that he became synonymous with the dramatization of this rite of preparation for and anticipation of the Greater One. Everything that

---

[1]See *Les actes,* 51. Studies of the many call narratives in the Old Testament reveal that they do not follow any conventional pattern. According to G. von Rad, *The Message of the Prophets,* 36, the presence of the spirit of Yahweh was absolutely constitutive of the of the ninth-century prophets. For the prophets of the eighth and seventh centuries, however, the call was received through the direct and personal address of God to each one of them.

Jesus said and did pointed to the presence of the Kingdom. His whole person was linked to this eschatological proclamation: to accept Jesus was equivalent to embracing the reign of God; to reject Jesus was tantamount to refusing the divine offer of grace. Schillebeeckx underscores the novel and original experience of God as *Abba*-Father which was central to the self-understanding of Jesus. From the unfathomable depths of this relationship, he became aware of his identity as the Spirit-endowed eschatological prophet who was sent to bring the good news to the poor. This growing awareness impelled him to appropriate the Jordan rite, and propelled him on the journey to Calvary. The symbolic actions of Jesus, therefore, are pneumatic acts: they emerge from his maturing consciousness of being the Spirit-filled Son who is sent to unveil the eschatological nearness of the Father. They are also trinitarian actions: they find their origins in the inner mystery of God and find their fulfilment in the revelation of the divine life to all. Nowhere is this more evident than at the baptism of Jesus in the Jordan.

The Church, Rahner states repeatedly, is the historical continuation of the eschatological triumph of Christ in and through of those who believe in him.[2] A sacrament, then, is the realization of the very nature of the Church as the permanent presence of redemptive grace in the life of the individual.[3] While each sacrament is implicitly instituted in the explicit foundation of the Church,[4] there is a vital link between the ecclesial gesture and the prophetic actions of the Promised One.[5] When the Christian community celebrates the sacrament of baptism, it actualizes its very essence as the victorious mercy of Christ in the world. It expresses this reality in the rite of triple washing not just because this represents what Jesus did or may have commanded his disciples to do (the christological principle), but also because the Spirit-filled community recognizes this action as an authentic symbol of its self-accomplishment (pneumatological principle). In this approach to the institution of the sacrament (which is analogous to the command to perform a prophetic action), the christological, pneumatological, trinitarian and ecclesiological foundations of the lustral rite are held in dynamic tension.

---

[2] As already noted in Chapter 4, references to the Church as the historical continuation of the eschatological victory of Christ abound in Rahner's writings. See, for example, *CS,* 13; 18; 19; 21-24; 39; 63; 74; 76-77; 86; 94; 100.

[3] *CS*, 22.

[4] *CS*, 41.

[5] "Prophetism," *SM(E)* V, 113.

1.2 *Baptism as Word in Action*

The intrinsic relationship between the words which the prophets proclaimed and the actions which they performed was discussed in Chapter 3. According the Amsler, the prophetic act is a "visible word"[6] which overcomes audience resistance, which restores and prolongs the divine communication, even when in crisis, and which obliges the witnesses to reflect on their existential circumstances and to respond in a moral way. The act does not possess some ontological superiority over the oracle. Rather, as a word embodied through the person of the prophet, the symbolic action has an enhanced subjective impact in the community in which it is received.

Christian theology since the Reformation has been characterized by a false dichotomy between word and sacrament. The reformers' call for a renewed emphasis on the place of the word may well have been a sound reaction against the sacramental "inflation"[7] of the Middle Ages. In their joint study on the sacraments, K. Rahner and E. Jüngel have demonstrated how a contemporary approach to these sacred rites emphasises their continuity with the divine offer of grace in the proclamation of the Good News to God's people.[8] As L.-M. Chauvet remarks, the sacraments are a "precipitate of the Scriptures":

> From the table of the Scriptures to the table of the sacrament, the dynamic is traditional and irreversible. Traditional in that, from the time of Emmaus, one sees the distinctively sacramental moment preceded by a scriptural moment; irreversible in that this pattern is not at all arbitrary: we never pass from the table of the sacrament to that of the Scriptures.[9]

Clearly, then, the progression of the prophet from oracle to action provides a fortuitous matrix for an ecumenical understanding both of the common ground and of the qualitative difference between word and sacrament in the plan of the divine self-communication to humanity. Just as the prophetic action is a privileged moment within the on-going dialogue between Yahweh and Israel, so too, the sacramental rite is situated within the context of the proclamation of the Gospel in the Christian assembly. In fact, the post-conciliar revision of the rites of the Catholic Church places the

---

[6] *Les actes,* 55.
[7] L.-M. Chauvet, *Symbol and Sacrament,* 221.
[8] See Chapter 5, section 2.2.
[9] L.-M. Chauvet, *Symbol and Sacrament,* 220.

liturgy of the word as the indispensable, prior moment in the ritual celebration of each sacrament. In the first step of the Rite of Christian Initiation of Adults (RCIA), the candidates are invited to accept the Gospel as they are enrolled into the order of catechumens.

1.3 *Between Commemoration and Anticipation*

By word and deed, the Baptist had heralded the advent of the Greater One and had foretold a new future in which the eschatological gift of the Spirit would be bestowed. As a prophetic action, the ritual washing of John not only recalled the promises made in the Hebrew Scriptures, but also anticipated the end-time gift of the Paraclete which was associated with their fulfilment. When Jesus stepped into the Jordan the future which the baptism of John had proclaimed erupted into the present as the "one who is to come" paradoxically underwent the rite of his own anticipation. The analysis of Chapter 3 has established that a prophetic action proleptically anticipates a future intervention of God, grafting it into the present experience of the witnessing community. By stepping into the Jordan, the Son unleashes the eschatological gift of the Spirit which will be imparted to all by the post-paschal celebration of the sacrament of initiation.

To celebrate the sacrament of baptism, then, is to re-enact this dramatic anticipation both of the vicarious self-giving of the Son and of the universal out-pouring of the Spirit. While the former was fulfilled in the paschal events of the historical Jesus, the latter finds its definitive achievement in his second coming as the glorious Lord. In the Christian rite of initiation, recipients are mysteriously inserted into the saving death and resurrection of the Lord which it commemorates, and prophetically bestowed with the end-time gift of the Paraclete which it anticipates. The ritual action, then, is at once a *signum rememorativum* of the passion of Christ which is *effected in commemoration*, and a *signum prognosticum* of future glory which is *effected in anticipation*. It is also a *signum demonstrativum* of the present grace which is *realized in the interplay between commemoration and anticipation.*

1.4 *Baptism as Memorial in Anticipation*

On a first level, when the Christian community celebrates the sacrament of baptism, it imitates the symbolic action which Jesus performed in the Jordan. As the analysis of Amsler's understanding of Old Testament prophetic acts and of Schürmann's presentation of New Testament eschatological signs of fulfilment suggests, this ritual washing is oriented primarily towards the future. It effectively presages the impending intervention of God in the life, death and resurrection of the Son, and in the universal out-pouring of the Holy Spirit. When the Church repeats this action in its celebration of the sacrament of baptism it does so as an *anamnesis*, or as a recollection, of the eschatological sign of fulfilment which Jesus himself performed. Fundamental, however, to the religious consciousness of Israel is the belief that, in the liturgical representation of the events of history, the chosen people is inserted into the saving reality which is commemorated. Consequently, in the semitic order of things, to remember, is not just to recall, but also to reactivate in the present the effects of past events. The application of this Jewish category of *zikkārôn* to the Christian sacraments has already yielded considerable insights. The claim of this study is that, in the sacrament of baptism, the particular event which is recalled is essentially future-orientated. When the Church celebrates this lustral rite, it re-enacts Christ's action of "representative anticipation."[10]

In the *Summa Theologica*, St. Thomas noted that a sacrament is a sign of a triple reality, of the past, of the present, and of the future: it is commemorative of that which has been achieved, namely the passion of Christ (*signum rememorativum*); it is demonstrative of that which is effected in the present experience of the participants (*signum demonstrativum*); it is prognostic of the glory which awaits redeemed humanity (*signum prognosticum*).[11] Eclipsed in the sacramental theology of the commentators on St. Thomas at the beginning of the twentieth century, this threefold dimension of the sacramental sign has re-emerged with the help of the liturgical, patristic and biblical research which took place subsequently. Yet, as the historical survey in Chapter 2 suggests, while the sacramental words and actions clearly commemorate that saving gesture of Christ in the Jordan which finds fulfilment on the Cross, and strikingly point to the gift of forgiveness and of new life as the present effect of the liturgical rite, it is difficult to ground the prognostic dimension of the ritual act within the celebration.[12]

---

[10] This phrase is borrowed from A. Vonier, *KDE,* 156.

[11] *ST.* III, Q. 60, a. 3.

[12] Indeed, as the analysis of Chapter 2 suggests, this is the problem which beset both A. Vonier and O. Casel.

However, when the Church acknowledges that the saving event which it re-presents is fundamentally a symbol which anticipates the fulness of eschatological life, then the prognostic dimension of the sacrament is safeguarded.

The liturgical action is neither a straightforward memorial, nor a simple commemoration of an event which once had future implications. When the ecclesial community celebrates the memorial of the prophetic action of Jesus, it comes face to face with this historical event, but it also anticipates the end-time promise that it symbolizes. In recalling that past episode which is essentially an eschatological act, the proleptic power of the deed is unleashed. As the symbolic representation of one of the prophetic actions of Jesus, baptism is an *anticipation in memorial* of the plenitude of life which is offered to all humanity.

D.A. Lane concludes his recent work on eschatology with a chapter on the eucharist as the means *par excellence* of keeping hope alive.[13] Lane wisely notes the connection between the Last Supper and the other meals which Jesus shared both with his disciples and with "tax collectors and sinners." Given this background, together with "the emerging self-understanding of Jesus concerning the significance of his own death, the actions of cleansing the Temple, and the Passover setting," he concludes that "it is hardly surprising to discover that the Last Supper accounts are laden with eschatological symbolism and meaning."[14] Indeed, Lane argues that the double action of Jesus over the bread and wine will make sense only when is understood as a prophetic action.[15] This permits Lane to recognize the complementarity between memorial and anticipation in the ritual action. He notes that

> The distinctively Jewish theology of memory is an important part of the context and atmosphere surrounding the Last Supper. Jesus the Jew, in his farewell supper with his disciples around the time of the Passover, resurrects this rich background when he invites them to "do this in memory of me." The action of Jesus at the Last Supper is not only prophetic in terms of his own personal destiny that is about to take place but it is also eschatological insofar as it prefigures his own future and the future of humanity.[16]

---

[13] D.A. Lane, *Keeping Hope Alive,* 194-210.
[14] D.A. Lane, *Keeping Hope Alive,* 197.
[15] D.A. Lane, *Keeping Hope Alive,* 200.
[16] D.A. Lane, *Keeping Hope Alive,* 203-204.

According to Lane, then, the eucharist re-presents the saving mystery of the life, death and resurrection of Jesus in the liturgical assembly which gathers in his memory: "through the liberating power of memory the eucharist embodies the *Eschaton* in the world."[17] It also anticipates in memorial the future which is offered to all humanity.

While Lane acknowledges the complementarity of memorial and anticipation in the eucharistic event, the primary emphasis is placed on the former. "It is memory that makes the past operative in the present and in doing so holds out promise for the future,"[18] he notes. But, the question arises, how does the memory of the past experience generate a confident hope in the future? Is this confidence anything more than a psychological reassurance as the promises that God has made in the past are reactivated in the present? Lane asserts that the eucharist "gathers up all that Christ stood for, symbolized in his meals, prophetically formalized at the Last Supper and the washing of feet, and eschatologically realized in his death and resurrection."[19] Further, through the power of memory, it "stands out as a celebration of eschatology uniting the past and the future in the present."[20] But, is it sufficient to posit the eschatological force of the sacrament in the *anamnesis* as Lane so clearly does? The constant claim of this present study is that the reality which is re-presented in the baptismal action is one that is primarily oriented towards the future: eschatology is not surplus to ritual memory; it is constitutive of the liturgical action. When the ecclesial community celebrates the sacramental rite, it unveils in the present the power of the future. It is not just a matter of the liturgical assembly symbolizing "the dreams and hopes released by Jesus for the future of humanity and creation."[21] Rather, by re-enacting the prophetic action, the future which is signified in it is grafted into the present experience of the worshipping community.

Primarily, a prophetic act is a *signum prognosticum*: it heralds in the midst of history the future intervention of God. Implicitly, it is a *signum rememorativum*: it recalls the previous divine activity in the lives of the covenant people. If Christian baptism is a symbolic representation of the symbolic action of Jesus in the Jordan, then it is more appropriately termed a *memorial in anticipation* rather than

---

[17] D.A. Lane, *Keeping Hope Alive,* 194.
[18] D.A. Lane, *Keeping Hope Alive,* 203.
[19] D.A. Lane, *Keeping Hope Alive,* 205.
[20] D.A. Lane, *Keeping Hope Alive,* 205.
[21] D.A. Lane, *Keeping Hope Alive,* 209.

an *anticipation in memorial* as initially suggested above. This distinction captures the difference between the approach of Lane and that proposed in this study.

1.5 *Baptism as Worded Action*

The research into the prophetic acts found in the Hebrew Scriptures accentuates the inherent analogy between the action which is performed, the word of explanation which accompanies it, and the future reality which is unveiled in the present experience of the onlookers. The prophet Ahijah, it was noted, tore his cloak into twelve pieces, and used parallel words to describe an action which presaged the sundering of the twelve tribes of Israel.[22] Schürmann points out that this analogical structure is also apparent in the table-actions at the Last Supper: Jesus broke the bread and distributed the wine and, in offering the blessed elements to his disciples along with words indicating them as symbols of his own body and blood, he grafted the events of Good Friday onto the Holy Thursday experience of his commensals.

As a symbolic action which finds its roots in the dramatic acts of the Old Testament prophets and which emerges from the eschatological signs of fulfilment which Jesus performs in the Jordan and on Calvary, Christian baptism fittingly reflects this same analogical structure between the action, the words and the reality which is unveiled in the liturgical assembly. The rite of pouring water over the head of the candidate recalls the Johannine gesture, and points to the cleansing from sin which the sacramental waters bestow (*signum demonstrativum*). When baptism is administered as a triple immersion, however, all three aspects of the sacramental sign are more perfectly represented. In this latter scenario, the symbolic burial and resurrection not only renders visible the present effect of the ritual action, but also and more appropriately signifies both the passion of Christ (*signum rememorativum*) and the promise of future glory (*signum prognosticum*) which are eclipsed in the pouring of water. This point is acknowledged by the "General Introduction" to Christian Initiation which accompanies the texts of the *RCIA*. It notes that, while immersion or pouring may lawfully be used in the rite of baptizing, the former is "more suitable [than the latter] as a symbol of participation in the death and resurrection of Christ."[23]

---

22 1Kgs 11:29-31.
23 *RCIA*, "General Introduction," no. 22.

The formula of words which accompanies the lustral act makes no explicit reference to the threefold reality which is signified by the sacramental action. In the Latin Church, the baptismal formula is proclaimed in the present indicative tense ("I baptise you..."). According to St. Thomas, this pronouncement transforms the bodily washing into a spiritual cleansing of the soul.[24] As such, it appears to focus on the demonstrative signification of the rite to the exclusion of its commemorative and prognostic aspects. Faced with a similar dilemma as to why the passion of Christ, from which baptism receives its power, is not specifically mentioned in the sacramental form, the Angelic Doctor replied that, in mentioning the Trinity, the passion of Christ is included, because in this case the principal cause encompasses and implies the instrumental cause.[25] So, the argument unfolds, the fact that the passion of Christ is not explicitly mentioned in the form of baptism does not mean that Calvary is not signified by it. Similarly, it can be argued that, in the trinitarian invocation over the candidate for baptism, the gift of eschatological life is not omitted, because the principal cause (the Triune God) encompasses and implies the final cause (eternal beatitude). In principle, despite the scriptural provenance and the traditional use of the trinitarian formula, an expansion of these words which accompany the baptismal washing is possible so that they might allude more explicitly to the triple dimension of the sacramental sign.

In the rite of baptism, the formula for the blessing of water is steeped in biblical imagery. The waters of creation are "a rich symbol of the grace which is given in baptism." The waters of the great flood herald "an end to sin and a new beginning of goodness." The crossing of the Red Sea is recalled as "an image of God's holy people, set free from sin by baptism." Clearly, the emphasis is on the commemorative and demonstrative aspects of the sacramental sign; the prognostic dimension is noticeably absent. In Chapter 2, the preference for the typology of the Red Sea over that of the Jordan was linked to the predominance of the demonstrative (and, to a lesser extent, the commemorative) over the eschatological dimension of the sacramental sign. While the prayer of blessing is rich in Exodus imagery, no mention is made of

---

[24] *ST*. III, Q. 60, a. 6.

[25] See *ST*. III, Q. 66, a. 5, ad. 5. This objection is discusses in Chapter 1, section 1.2.3.

Israel's entrance into the promised land through the waters of the River Jordan.

From the New Testament, three episodes — the baptism of Jesus in the Jordan, the emergence of water and blood from his pierced side, and his post-resurrection command to baptize all nations — are recalled to justify the lustral activity of the Church. Following this *anamnesis*, the Holy Spirit is invoked:

> By the power of the Holy Spirit give to this water the grace of your Son, so that in the sacrament of baptism all those whom you have created in your likeness may be cleansed from sin and rise to a new birth of innocence by water and the Holy Spirit. We ask you, Father, with your Son to send the Holy Spirit upon the waters of this font. May all who are buried with Christ in the death of baptism rise also with him to newness of life.

According to this prayer, the primary effect of the sacramental rite is to "cleanse from sin" and to impart "a new birth." In other words, the rite is understood pre-eminently as a *signum demonstrativum*. The commemorative and prognostic aspects of the sacramental washing derive from this: "May all who are buried with Christ in the death of baptism rise also with him to newness of life." But, as this investigation has already shown, baptism is a *memorial in anticipation*. The order in the prayer of blessing, then, should be reversed. Precisely because the liturgical community first re-presents the saving events in the life of Jesus Christ as it dramatically pre-presents the gift of eschatological justice, it is possible that forgiveness and rebirth are bestowed on the candidates for baptism. This prayer is normally pronounced over the font during the Easter Vigil as the paschal candle is lowered three times into the water. The action acknowledges that the healing power of the font is unsealed as a *memorial in anticipation* of the *Eschaton*. This mystery should be articulated more deliberately in the words of blessing which are to be proclaimed over the baptismal waters.

The prayers which accompany the "explanatory rites" — the anointing with chrism, the clothing with the baptismal garment, and the presentation of a lighted candle — have a more explicit eschatological referent. The formula of anointing expresses the hope that the newly baptized "may remain forever members of Christ who is Priest, Prophet, and King." As they are clothed with the garment of the new creation, the neophytes are reminded that they must "bring it unstained to the judgement seat of our Lord Jesus Christ, so that [they] may have eternal life." The eschatological emphasis is reinforced when the garment is white: the end-time glory which is prefigured in the vision of *Revelation* (3:5, 18) is anticipated in the liturgical rite.[26] As the lighted candle is entrusted to the newly baptized, they are encouraged to "walk always as children of the light" and to "keep the flame of faith alive in [their] hearts." This is to ensure that "when the Lord comes, [they] may go out to meet him with all the saints in the heavenly kingdom."[27]

2. "... quo Christi ecclesiae quis incorporatur..."

According to St. Thomas Aquinas, character is the *sacramentum et res* of baptism. Traditionally, it is understood as an indelible mark which distinguishes believers from unbelievers, marks them for Christ, gives them a share in his priesthood, inserts them into the worshipping community, gives them access to the other rites of the Christian religion, and makes them capable of receiving further grace.[28] By approaching this intermediate effect from an ecclesiological perspective, Rahner and Schillebeeckx accentuate the correspondence between character and the immediate effect of a prophetic act. The ecclesial action claims the recipient as one of its own. The initiate is radically transformed by virtue of the irreversible word of grace which the Church addresses in God's name. Through the liturgical celebration the baptized acknowledge this saving gift and are granted title to a deeper participation in the divine life. To undergo the sacrament of baptism is to be commissioned to participate in the *doxa* offered in the liturgical assembly, and in the *diakonia* rendered in universal justice and love. The immediate effect of the symbolic action of baptism is an ecclesiological reality. As such, in this section, it is presented under the heading *quo Christi ecclesiae quis incorporatur.*

---

[26] See J. Daniélou, *BL*, 52-53.

[27] Patristic texts bear witness to other associated customs and rites which allude to the eschatological dimension of the baptismal washing. The octagonal shape of the baptistry, for example, refers to the eighth day of the new creation; the decoration of the baptistry with frescoes or mosaics of trees, flowers and fountains symbolizes the readmission to paradise which baptism initiates (See J. Daniélou, *The Bible and the Liturgy*, 35-37). Ambrose (*De sacramentis,* 5:15-15) describes how the neophytes are given a cup of mixed milk and honey as part of the eucharist that followed the baptismal rite. On the eschatological symbolism of the baptismal rites in the Orthodox Church, see A. Schmemann, *Of Water and the Spirit.*

[28] *ST*. III, Q. 63. See Chapter 1, section 2.2.

2.1 *Baptism as Community Action*

In Chapter 3 it was noted that, while magicians may divinise in secret and in favour of particular clients, prophets act publicly and on behalf of the community as a whole. The Old Testament prophets were not concerned with private communication or confidential revelation: their dramatic actions had implications beyond the immediate group of witnesses for all of God's people. Individuals hear the divine word of grace or of condemnation by virtue of their belonging to the covenant people which has been established as a sign to all nations. A similar scope is to be noted in the symbolic actions performed by Jesus. The significance of the establishment of the twelve, for example, is not confined to the vocation story of each disciple, momentous though that may be in itself on a personal level. Rather, it announces the in-breaking Kingdom and the "establishment of the eschatological people of God"[29] as a sign of salvation for all humanity.

As a rite which derives from the prophetic action of Jesus in the Jordan, baptism is not a private action between God and the recipient. Primarily, it is a word of grace that is addressed to the world, through the Church which celebrates it, and to the individuals who are committed to live in justice and love. Pastorally, this suggests that the notion of a "private baptism" is a contradiction it terms. The rite of initiation is not a magic moment performed for the benefit of an individual or of an exclusive *clique*. It is the public proclamation of the divine offer of grace which is freely bestowed on all.

To receive baptism is to declare publicly one's commitment to live as a member of the ecclesial community which is the sacrament, the instrument and the sign of the loving nearness of God in the world. The *RCIA* stresses that "the initiation of catechumens is a gradual process that takes place within the community of the faithful."[30] It calls all members of the community to a renewed conversion, to a more authentic living of that justice to which the Church is called to witness, and to a more profound appreciation of the paschal mystery which finds expression in worship and in service.

---

[29] J. Jeremias, *New Testament Theology*, I, 235: "The fact that Jesus' disciples number twelve does not mean that salvation is to be limited, in a particularistic way, to the empirical Jewish people; on the contrary, it announces the establishment of the *eschatological people of God,* to which, as we shall see, Jesus expected that even the Gentiles would attach themselves."

[30] *RCIA*, "Introduction," no. 4.

2.2 *Baptism as Prophetic Challenge*

The Old Testament prophetic acts were shocking, provocative actions. These unconventional, extravagant displays appalled and disturbed the social and religious sensibilities of the Hebrews. Theological presuppositions were undermined as the dramatic actions of the prophets prefigured a new future in the relationship between the God of Israel and the chosen people. Many of the things which Jesus said and did caused consternation among the religious people of his time: his attitude to the sabbath and the law; his association with tax-collectors and sinners; his claim to forgive sins; his reference to God as *Abba*. The inherently shocking aspect of Jesus' baptism in the Jordan should not be underestimated. The early Christian community recognized the potential embarrassment of this eschatological sign of fulfilment, and sought to modify its subversive impact in the scriptural accounts.

If the liturgical community so "tames" the rite that it is no longer provoked or challenged by it, then the Church does not celebrate in memory of Jesus of Nazareth. The sacraments constitute a "dangerous memory"[31]: when Christians repeat the ritual washing of Jesus, the disconcerting presence of the eschatological prophet must be palpable in the ecclesial gathering. Yet, in the passage from symbolic action to institutionalized rite, the prophetic challenge can be dulled as provisionality gives way to stability. What was once a provocative summons to justice and to integrity for all in the presence of the liberating Lord who comes, can easily become a defensive retreat into sectarianism and into self-preservation for a few in the memory of a vengeful god who came.

2.3 *Baptism as Effecting a New Relationship*

The correspondence between the initial impact of a prophetic action and the intermediate effect of the sacrament of baptism has already been noted in Chapter 5. The immediate effect of an Old Testament symbolic act was to place the spectators before the transcendent reality which was announced by the inspired messenger. Those who witnessed the dramatic action became a new people in the light of the anticipated divine intervention, taking on a new identity before God and each other. Such a transformation cannot be explained by either extrinsic or existential considerations:

---

[31] J. B. Metz, *Faith in History and Society*, 184.

it is necessary to speak of some ontological change in the individuals or in the community concerned. Even if a number of spectators reject the striking message of the prophet, they cannot deny that they have been radically altered by the divine word of salvation or of judgement which, once revealed, can never be revoked. Those who acknowledge the prophetic action as a proleptic manifestation of the divine will are constituted as a people who are committed to a specific ethical behaviour and who are open to the ulterior disclosure of saving grace in their concrete history.

In the later writings of Schillebeeckx, baptism emerges as the sacrament by which believers express their commitment to live as members of the ecclesial community which seeks to anticipate a new world. This rite of commitment entails a public declaration of belonging to the Church which can never be revoked. Furthermore, to undergo baptism is to pledge to live *for-others*: it is to embark on the Spirit-filled mission to anticipate proleptically in word, action and sacrament that new order which lies in the future with God. In this changed metaphysical context, Schillebeeckx makes no explicit reference to sacramental character. Yet, this later understanding of the immediate effect of the lustral rite which emerges from Schillebeeckx's writings is clearly rooted in his earlier presentation of the *sacramentum et res* of baptism. In both cases, the immediate effect is an ecclesiological reality, namely, membership in the church; in both cases, the liturgical rite is an initiation into, and a declaration in favour of, a life of cultic and diaconal service. By approaching the sacrament from the perspective of a prophetic action, the traditional teaching on baptismal character is retained, while a link is forged between the ritual action, the incorporation of the recipient into the Church, and the call to Christian orthopraxis as a practical anticipation of a new world.

2.4 *Baptism as Pro-existent Stance*

John had proclaimed a baptism for the forgiveness of sins and, under the threat and the promise of the presaged divine judgement, called the people to conversion and to righteousness. To undergo the rite of John was to declare publicly one's intention to live in obedience to the law and to conduct one's affairs in truth and honesty. By receiving baptism, Jesus affirmed John's dramatized message of the need for conversion and its concomitant moral appeal.

But, the scandal of the Sinless One who underwent this ritual of repentance was also a manifestation of his desire to stand in solidarity with sinful humanity. In this dramatic action, Jesus was neither object nor victim. Rather, he presented himself as subject and protagonist of a new reality. The pre-existent Son of God, who was born of Mary through the power of the Holy Spirit, was then revealed as the pro-existent Servant, who was anointed by the Paraclete to bring the "good news to the poor." The investigation of eschatological signs of fulfilment in Chapter 4 confirms that the symbolic action performed in the Jordan points towards Calvary. Already the *being-for* which was consummated on Holy Thursday and on Good Friday could be discerned (at least retrospectively) in the radical *being-with* which was disclosed in the initial eschatological sign of Jesus. Baptism, then, is not a rite for a moment but a life-long commitment to dedicate oneself to the loving service of others.

At its meeting in Lima in 1982, the World Council of Churches issued an agreed statement on three sacraments, baptism, eucharist and ministry.[32] The document represents the theological convergence that had been reached as the result of a fifty-year process of ecumenical study and reflection. The document states that:

> Baptism means participating in the life, death and resurrection of Jesus Christ. Jesus went down into the river Jordan and was baptized in solidarity with sinners in order to fulfil all righteousness (Matt 3:15). This baptism led Jesus along the way of the Suffering Servant, made manifest in his sufferings, death, and resurrection (Mark 10:38-40, 45). By baptism, Christians are immersed into the liberating death of Christ where their sins are buried, where the "old Adam" is crucified with Christ, and where the power of sin is broken. Thus, those baptized are no longer slaves to sin, but free. Fully identified with the death of Christ, they are buried with him and raised here and now to a new life in the power of the resurrection of Jesus Christ, confident that they will also be one with him in a resurrection like his (Rom 6:3-11; Col 2:13; 3:1; Eph 2:5-6).[33]

The text clearly states that, by going down into the Jordan, Jesus stands in solidarity with sinful humanity. The reason given for

---

[32] World Council of Churches, *Baptism Eucharist and Ministry* [Faith and Order Papers No. 111] (Geneva, 1882). [Hereafter *BEM*.]

[33] *BEM*, "Baptism," no. 3.

Jesus' self-alignment with the impure is his desire "to fulfil all righteousness."[34] In the face of moral indifference and legalistic isolation, Jesus stands in the Jordan waters with the marginalized of Israel and heralds the eschatological justice of his God and Father as a free offer which is already extended to all. This gracious proclamation, the text asserts, "led Jesus along the way of the Suffering Servant" to his death on the Cross. In other words, the saving mission which began in the Jordan, is brought to fulfilment on Calvary.

The statement also asserts that those who undergo the Christian rite of baptism are "immersed in the liberating death of Christ" and "raised here and now to a new life in the power of the resurrection of Jesus Christ." While the opening sentence of the quotation above states that "baptism means participation in the *life*, death and resurrection of Jesus Christ," the emphasis has shifted quickly from imitation of the Just One to union with the glorified Lord. All sacraments insert the Christian community more fully into the mystery of the death and resurrection of Jesus Christ which it celebrates. But, what is specific to baptism is that it "means a participation in the life" of Jesus, in the pro-existent solidarity with "tax-collectors and sinners" which leads to the Cross. Certainly, the document acknowledges later that baptism has "ethical implications."[35] However, this study of baptism as a prophetic action, which proleptically imparts the eschatological Sprit of justice, insists that the ethical behaviour that is demanded by celebrating this ritual is not some generic "striving for the realization of the will of God in all realms of life,"[36] but the specific participation of the ecclesial community in the mission of justice undertaken by the eschatological prophet.[37] The intrinsic

---

[34] P.J. Rosato, *Introduzione alla teologia dei sacramenti,* 62: "La purificazione volontaria ma inutile di un predicatore innocente per le mani di un altro che si dedica solo alla conversione di peccatori noti serve da critica palese all'indifferenza di sedicenti giusti per gli ingiusti. Gesù, unendo quest'ultimi nel suo gesto salvifico, li chiama a sentirsi solidali con lui, a praticare la giustizia ed a credere nell'inizio reale della loro inclusione futura nel Regno di Dio. In altre parole Gesù compie nel Giordano un atto più creatore che figurativo, nel senso che fa più che additare ad un evento salvifico da venire; il suo *ôt* constituirebbe per i peccatori astanti un'esperienza attuale della giustizia divina che è veramente definitiva o escatologica, poiché già nella storia 'il servo di Dio, il Diletto da Dio, si china sugli affranti'."

[35] *BEM*, "Baptism," no. 10.

[36] *BEM*, "Baptism," no. 10.

[37] In his encyclical letter, *Mediator Dei*, Pope Pius XII addressed the question of the presence of the historical mysteries of Christ in the sacraments and in the entire liturgical life of the Church. "These mysteries," he notes, "are still now

link between baptism and Christian praxis is treated later in this chapter.

3. "...vita venturi saeculi praefiguratur, passionis eius recolitur memoria, et peccati gratis nobis remissio datur."

A prophetic action proleptically anticipates a future intervention of God in the here and now of the covenant people. Primarily, then, it is a *signum prognosticum.* At the same time, it brings the previous interventions of God in history to mind. Implicitly, then, it is a *signum rememorativum.* Within this interplay between anticipation and memory the saving will of God is communicated. As such, it is a *signum demonstrativum.* Within this perspective, the ultimate effect of the sacrament of baptism as symbolic act of eschatological salvation is presented. In Chapter 1, the *res* of baptism was summarized as "*memoria passionis eius recolitur* (past), *mens impletur gratia* (present), *et futurae gloriae nobis porta reseratur* (future)." In this final chapter the emphasis is on the restored eschatological dimension of baptismal grace. Consequently, the movement is from the future ("*vita venturi saeculi praefiguratur*") to the past ("*passionis eius recolitur memoria*") to the present ("*peccati gratis nobis remissio datur*"). (See Diagram page 271)

3.1 *Baptism as Gift in Symbol*

The precise relationship between a symbolic action and the divine gift which is imparted has been a recurring theme throughout this work. In Chapter 3, this question was posed in terms of the connection between the Old Testament prophetic act and the future intervention of God which it grafts into the present experience of the community. This study has underscored that, while always a *prophetic* act, its ultimate power lies with the Lord who commands it: unlike a magician, the prophet does not exert pressure on the future from the present, but unveils the upcoming reality in the here and now of the people (*effect→sign*); unlike a messenger, a prophet does not merely announce a reality decided in the overall plan of

constantly present and active, not in the vague and nebulous way which recent authors describe, but as Catholic doctrine teaches us. The Doctors of the Church tell us that the mysteries of Christ's life are at the same time most excellent models of virtue for us to imitate and also sources of divine grace for us by reason of the merits and intercession of the Redeemer. They live on in their effect in us, since each of them is, according to its nature and its own way, the cause of our salvation" [ND 1333].

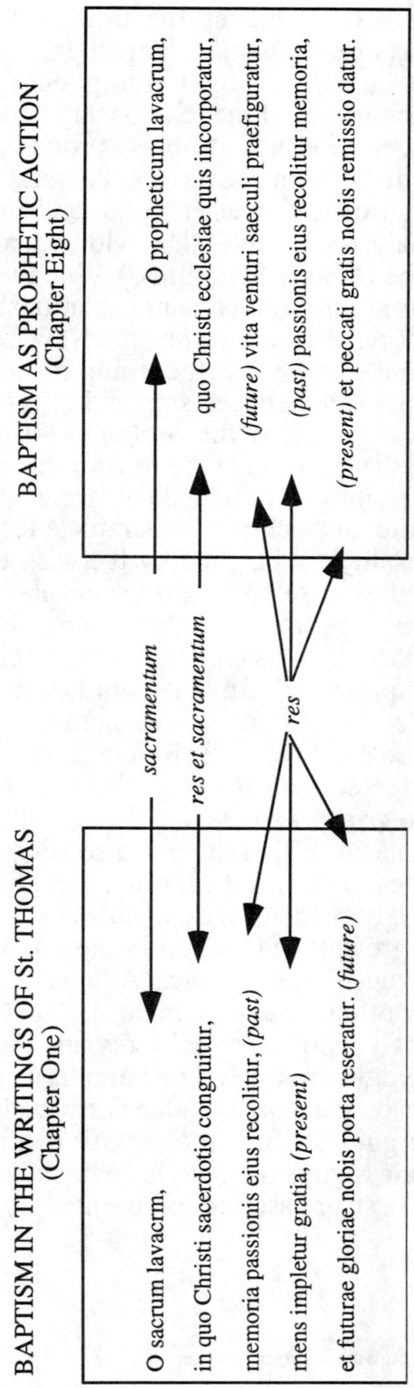
BAPTISM IN THE WRITINGS OF St. THOMAS
(Chapter One)
O sacrum lavacrm,
in quo Christi sacerdotio congruitur,
memoria passionis eius recolitur, (past)
mens impletur gratia, (present)
et futurae gloriae nobis porta reseratur. (future)
sacramentum
res et sacramentum
res
BAPTISM AS PROPHETIC ACTION
(Chapter Eight)
O propheticum lavacrum,
quo Christi ecclesiae quis incorporatur,
(future) vita venturi saeculi praefiguratur,
(past) passionis eius recolitur memoria,
(present) et peccati gratis nobis remissio datur.

God but, by the action, shapes the ulterior unfolding of the theological drama (*sign→effect*). A correct understanding is found with neither extreme: only by holding both truths together (*sign↔effect*) is the nature of the relationship between present and future, and between God and prophet, properly maintained. In Chapter 4, the discussion treats the correlation between an eschatological sign of fulfilment and the end-time gift which is conferred. The analysis concludes that, with regard to the prophetic acts recorded in the Hebrew Scriptures, within the interpenetrating *sign↔effect* scheme, the fundamental relationship followed the *sign→effect* strategy. However, since the New Testament actions are "marked from within by the time of fulfilment,"[38] the fundamental relationship between sign and gift is reversed so that, pre-eminently, the sign follows the gift (*effect→sign*).

In Chapter 5, the question of the relationship between sign and effect is transposed into sacramental categories. Rahner's attempt to recast the traditional teaching on sacramental causality in terms of "symbolic causality" is inspired by the wish to give due place to the nature of these rites as signs: *sacramenta significando efficiunt gratiam*. According to this approach, while the sign produces grace, it exists in its concrete form precisely because this grace wishes to express itself. In other words, the sign effects grace because the latter brings forth the sacrament as sign of the sanctification effected. Therefore, Rahner's symbolic causality is adequately represented neither by the linear *sign→grace* scheme nor by the inverse *grace→sign* strategy, but by the compenetrating *sign↔grace* scenario. This diagram also provides an adequate description of the relation between the sign and effect as it is explained in the early writings of Schillebeeckx.

Perhaps the greatest innovation in the sacramental theory of the *Summa Theologica* of St. Thomas Aquinas was the retrieval of the augustinian notion of a sacrament as "the sign of a sacred thing."[39] The analysis of Chapter 1 reveals, however, that this altered perspective was not given due emphasis in the writings of the commentators on the *Summa* in the early twentieth century. L.-M. Chauvet suggests that the relationship between this heterogeneous pair, sign and effect, is characterized by a "twofold impasse"[40]: the first impasse is represented by the approach of

---

[38] "DSJ," 35.
[39] *ST* III, Q. 60, a. 1.
[40] L.-M. Chauvet, *Symbol and Sacrament*, 410.

pre-conciliar Catholic theology; the second is exemplified by theories which emphasize the sacramental dimension of celebrating lived experience. While the former insists on the objective efficacy of the sacraments as instruments or means of grace, the latter understands the ecclesial rites as celebrations of the "already done" by God in the life of the community. But, sacraments are not just the summit of ecclesial life and worship; they also function as the source of Christian discipleship and prayer.[41] "In the wake of Vatican II," L.-M. Chauvet remarks, "it is in any case very clear that their [i.e., sacraments'] function as a 'means', without being ignored, is now subordinated to their quality as signs."[42] His own attempt to think of the sacraments simultaneously as both "revealers" and "operators" provides a framework for reformulating the relationship between sign and cause that readily accommodates the insights gleaned from this discussion of the Christian rites as prophetic actions.

Central to Chauvet's approach is the contention that the language proper to faith and liturgy is "illocutionary"[43]: the relationship between the communicating subjects is not the same after as it was before; it is found in performative verbs, such as "I promise you," "I bet you," "I commit myself to you."[44] Further, the language of faith is essentially self-implicative: the statement "God is Father" reveals the identity of God as Father and the believers' identity as sons and daughters, brothers and sisters; and, by revealing this identity, it makes effective the paternity of God, as well as the filiation of the believers and their condition as brothers and sisters.[45] This permits him to claim that,

> As the cornerstones of the architectonic structure of the Christian celebrations, sacramental formulas, with their eminently performative character joining gesture and word to show their operative goal, are the symbols which are repositories of the *illocutionary dimension of the whole of ritual language and, beyond that, of faith language*. Generally through the

---

[41] See *Sacrosanctum concilium*, 10.

[42] L.-M. Chauvet, *Symbol and Sacrament,* 414.

[43] Chauvet borrows this term from J.L. Austin, *Quand dire, c'est faire* (Paris, 1970). In formulating his theory of religious language he also draws from the works of J. Ladrière, *L'articulation du sens*, vol. 1 *Discours scientifique et parole et foi*, vol. 2 *Les langages de la foi* (Paris, 1984). See Y. Labbé, "Réceptions théologiques de la 'postmodernité'. A propos de deux livres récents de G. Lafont et L.-M. Chauvet," *RScPhTh* 72 (1988) 397-426.

[44] L.-M. Chauvet, *Symbol and Sacrament,* 132.

[45] L.-M. Chauvet, *Symbol and Sacrament,* 428.

> ordained minister, the official bearer of its symbolic capital, the Church is completely involved as the "sacrament" of Jesus Christ, that is, as at once institution and "mystery." It is its very identity it acts out here, proclaiming symbolically what it is and what it is yet to become. At the level of language, we have *the most expressive unfolding of its essence and truth.*[46]

Sacraments, then, are revealers which manifest symbolically the "already-there" of grace in the experience of faith. As such, they have an expressive function of response and gratitude to God for what he has done. They are also operators which bring about what the rite expresses. However, Chauvet insists, both truths must be held simultaneously. To deny that sacraments are revealers is to verge on magic; to repudiate that the New Testament rites are operators is to contradict the traditional teaching of the Church and to confute the specificity of the illocutionary-performative-ritual acts of language that constitute them.[47] Sacraments are revealers insofar as they are operators; they are operators insofar as they are revealers.[48]

When a minister of the Church pronounces the formula which accompanies the baptismal washing, the candidates are transformed by the language act. The perception that other believers have of the neophytes is also changed. So too, is their understanding of themselves, and of the behaviour they believe themselves bound to adopt in order to conform to this new state of affairs. The indicative mood of the sacramental action functions as a moral imperative: "become what you are."[49] The new relationship with God, brought about by baptism, is inseparable from a new relationship among the people: by immersing the candidates in the sacramental water, baptism creates "a relation of brotherly and sisterly union, itself founded on a relation of filiation in him, the Son, through the Spirit."[50] But, Chauvet adds, baptism is also a self-reception: "a receiving of oneself from God as son or daughter and from others as brother and sister."[51] The sacrament "ploughs the field that we ourselves are and thus renders it fruitful by converting it to the filiation and brotherly and sisterly love it proclaims to be

---

[46] L.-M. Chauvet, *Symbol and Sacrament,* 430.

[47] Notice the parallels between this statement and those on the relationship between prophetic sign and the presaged reality. See Chapter 3, section 3.1.2.

[48] L.-M. Chauvet, *Symbol and Sacrament,* 431; 437.

[49] Again, the parallels between this and the effect of a prophetic action are striking. See above, section 2.3.

[50] L.-M. Chauvet, *Symbol and Sacrament,* 440.

[51] L.-M. Chauvet, *Symbol and Sacrament,* 442.

eschatologically inaugurated in the person whom the Church acknowledges as the Son and our Brother."[52]

3.2 *Baptism as Form of Future Life*

In baptism, the pre-sacramental gift of grace makes itself visible. Rahner, however, insists that the lustral rite is not merely the subsequent notification of the antecedent indwelling of the Holy Spirit, or of the grace that has already been freely accepted. Rather, in the very act of positing itself (baptism as effect of grace), this grace attains its full historical and social nature in the water rite (baptism as cause of grace). It has already been noted that, while traditional Catholic theology focused on created grace in terms of efficient causality as an effect wrought by God on the human soul, Rahner accentuates the actuality of uncreated grace in terms of quasi-formal causality as the divine indwelling in the soul. The sacramental rite, then, specifies and imparts the form of future life: the baptized are incorporated into the eschatological community of the Son which draws life from the glorious future which God symbolically communicates to those who journey towards the fulness of salvation; they come face to face with the will of the Father to save, and are washed free from sin in the Spirit-giving waters. This conclusion was reached by combining the insights gleaned from the relationship between sign and effect in the prophetic actions of the New and Old Testaments with those garnered from the theory of symbolic causality developed by Rahner.

In his later theology Schillebeeckx does not address the issue of the specific difference that baptism makes. However, in the light of the resolution which he proposes to differentiate between the anticipatory praxis of the believer and that of the humanist, it is possible to postulate an answer. While both the humanist and the believer can perform prophetic actions in the hope of the ultimate triumph of justice, only the latter has a sure support for the transforming praxis which is undertaken. Christian faith, Schillebeeckx argues, is established on the "eschatological reminiscence of the death and resurrection of Jesus which is itself a promise that has not yet been fulfilled for humanity, though it nevertheless has a foundation."[53] The present activity of Christians on behalf of the betterment of humanity derives its inspiration from

---

[52] L.-M. Chauvet, *Symbol and Sacrament,* 442.
[53] *JWC,* 64.

the memory of the pro-existent prophet and receives its power from the eschatological victory of the glorified Lord. As the rite which initiates catechumens into the community of faith and justice, baptism assures them that the future which is sought by living in the memory of Jesus is a guaranteed promise. Baptism then is essentially an eschatological rite: it is a pledge that the form of new life has taken hold of the structures of the old world even as history continues to unfold.

3.3 *Baptism as a Commitment to Justice*

Working for human freedom and justice is an integral part of the proclamation of the Gospel.[54] The intrinsic link between orthodoxy and orthopraxis has been a recurring theme in post-conciliar theology.[55] The connection between life and liturgy has been underlined in contemporary approaches to the eucharist.[56] Baptism is the "basis of Christian living."[57] As such, it calls men and women to a life in service of their brothers and sisters, particularly the poor and the vulnerable. But, does this ethical imperative derive from the sacramental celebration, or is it a constitutive demand of the ritual action itself?

The sacramental rite functions in two directions: descending and ascending.[58] First of all, in descending motion, the ecclesial washing proclaims the gracious favour of the Father for all as the eschatological gift of the Spirit is imparted to the candidates who are anointed to share in the life and in the mission of the Son. In a second, ascending motion, the ecclesial community which enacts the washing as a rite of initiation performs a self-implicative act. In ritual word and gesture, the liturgical gathering acknowledges the free gift of God and, in response, asserts its own identity as the pneumatic community of fraternity and justice. The ethical dimension is not simply an extrinsic consequence of the baptismal rite: it belongs to it as an intrinsic element. Ethics is a "liturgical"

---

[54] Pope Paul VI, *Evangelii nuntiandi*, 29.

[55] See D.A. Lane, *Foundations for Social Theology: Praxis Process and Salvation*.

[56] Pope Paul VI, *Mysterium fidei*, 36. The International Eucharistic Congress held in Philadelphia in 1976 had the theme "The Eucharist and the Hunger of the Human Family." See P.J. Rosato, *Cena del Signore e amore sociale*.

[57] Pope John Paul II, *Tertio millennio adveniente*, 41.

[58] This traditional point is developed at length by Schillebeeckx. See *CSEG* 19; 37.

response to the free gift of God which is appropriated by the Christian community as that life which makes it what it is.

In his *De sacramentis*, St. Ambrose describes a controversial custom which was part of the ceremony of baptism in the Church of Milan. As soon as the candidates emerged from the font, their feet were washed by the "highest priest." He explains the meaning of this gesture as follows:

> What mystery is this? Surely, you have heard [John 13:4-11] that the Lord, after he had washed the feet of the other disciples, went to Peter, and Peter said to him: "Do you wash my feet?" That is: "Do you, Lord, wash the feet of a servant; do you without stain wash my feet; do you, the author of the heavens, wash my feet?" You have this also elsewhere [Matt 3:14]: He went to John and John said to him: "I ought to be baptized by you, and come you to me?" [1 Pet 2:22]. I am a sinner, and have you come to a sinner, that you who have not sinned may put aside your sins? Behold all justice [Matt 3:15], behold humility, behold grace, behold sanctification. He said: "If I do not wash your feet, you shall have no part with me" [John 13:8].[59]

In this text, Ambrose links the rite of baptism with that of the washing of feet.[60] Both gestures manifest the humility and justice of Jesus. In the former rite, the Sinless One takes part in a symbolic washing in the Jordan at the hands of a sinner so as to fulfil all justice. In the latter, the Lord of heaven and earth humbly stoops to wash the feet of his disciples to give an example which they should follow. When the neophytes emerge from the font of justice, they are cleansed from sin and sanctified by grace. According to the ambrosian rite, their feet are then washed so that, as the newly baptized, they can stand in solidarity with others in extending the justice of the Father to sinners, and can walk the path of humble service in bringing the good news to the poor. In other words, as they emerge reborn from the baptismal waters, Christians are charged to imitate the humility and justice which characterized the pro-existent mission of Jesus. Otherwise, the baptized are reminded, they shall have no part with him.[61]

---

[59] St. Ambrose, *De sacramentis,* 3, 4. ET: T.M. Finn, *Early Christian Baptism and the Catechumenate: Italy North Africa and Egypt*, 73-74.

[60] See E.J. Yarnold, "The Ceremonies of Initiation in the 'De Sacramentis' and 'De Mysteriis' of St. Ambrose," *Studia Patristica* 10 [TU 107] (1970) 453-463.

[61] The washing of the feet is also linked to baptism in the *Demonstrations* of Aphrahat, a Syrian-speaking Church leader who was born towards the end of the

3.4 *Baptism of Infants*

While the debate about infant baptism has largely subsided in the Christian Churches, the question is never far below the surface of theological discourse and of pastoral practice. Earlier this century protestant scholars were divided about the advisability of administering this sacrament to candidates who were unable to make a personal commitment to Jesus Christ.[62] Some like K. Barth,[63] his son M. Barth,[64] and K. Aland[65] insisted that the act of faith necessary for baptism required cognition and, as such, lay beyond the capacity of infants. Others, like O. Cullmann[66] and J. Jeremias,[67] defended the traditional practice of a *quamprimum* administration of the rite. However, because of the persuasive augustinian doctrine of original sin, this debate was never conducted with the same intensity within the Roman Catholic Church. The renewed interest in patristic and liturgical studies in the course of this century, and the restoration of the Easter Vigil by Pope Pius XII in 1951 gave rise to certain controversy about the baptismal polity of the Church in the years prior to the Second Vatican Council.[68] As A. Kavanagh ably demonstrates, the conciliar emphasis is clearly on adult baptism as the *norm*[69] for Christian initiation. Although there is not the slightest denigration of infant baptism in the conciliar documents, neither is there any suggestion that this practice represents the norm. Equally, Kavanagh remarks, the Council "nowhere suggests that the initiation of adults should be regarded either as exceptional or abnormal."[70]

---

third century. See T.M. Finn, *Early Christian Baptism and the Catechumenate: West and East Syria*, 148-149.

62 For an overview of the controversy, see A. Kavanagh, *The Shape of Baptism. The Rite of Christian Initiation.*

63 K. Barth, *The Teaching of the Church Regarding Baptism.* See H. Hartwell, "Karl Barth on Baptism," *SJTh* 22 (1969) 10-29; M. Romeo, "La posizione di Karl Barth sul battesimo," *RBR* 12/3 (1973) 89-94.

64 M. Barth, *Die Taufe: ein Sacrament?*

65 K. Aland, *Did the Early Church Baptize Infants?*

66 O. Cullmann, *Baptism in the New Testament.*

67 J. Jeremias, *Infant Baptism in the First Four Centuries.*

68 A. Kavanagh, *The Shape of Baptism*, 93-97, reports on the work of Ch.-V. Heris, A. M. Roguet and A.G. Martimort in France during the pre-conciliar period.

69 A. Kavanagh, *The Shape of Baptism*, 108: "A norm in this sense has nothing to do with the number of times a thing is done, but it has everything to do with the standard according to which a thing is done. ... Yet, to the extent possible, the norm must always be achieved to some extent lest it slip imperceptibly into the status of a mere 'ideal' all wish for but are under no obligation to realize."

70 A. Kavanagh, *The Shape of Baptism,* 109.

A full discussion of the issues concerned with infant baptism is beyond the scope of these pages. Nevertheless, it is reasonable to ask what, if anything, this study of baptism as symbolic act of eschatological salvation contributes to this controversy. Within the framework proposed by this thesis, baptism is primarily a word of grace addressed by God to humanity.[71] It is not a message of consolation for an individual, but a proclamation of salvation to all.[72] Baptism is an ecclesial word: it speaks of the victorious mercy of the Father which was made manifest in the obedient service of the Son, and is present as an on-going offer to all through the Spirit-filled mission of the Church which continues to symbolize and anticipate it. As such, baptism is an ecclesial proclamation of divine favour to saint and sinner, to Christian and pagan, to adult and infant alike.

Baptism, however, is never an abstract proclamation of grace. It is always celebrated with a water rite and with words spoken over some individuals who, *through the Church*, are committed to imitate the pro-existent life of Jesus. While adults may readily declare their willingness to live in such a fashion, this notification of personal commitment is impossible for infants. On this basis, many Christians Churches have decided that baptism should be administered only to believers. Those who continue to initiate infants claim that the response necessary for the celebration of the sacrament derives from the faith of parents, god-parents and the Christian community as a whole.[73]

When the Church celebrates the sacrament of baptism with a candidate, it welcomes that person, adult or infant, into a fellowship of faith and justice. This is the immediate effect of the initiatory rite; from this other rights and duties flow. Before it is a declaration

---

[71] See K. Rahner, "Baptism," 2-3.

[72] *Pastoralis actio*, the Instruction on Infant Baptism issued by the Sacred Congregation for the Doctrine of the Faith with the approval of Pope John Paul II (20 October 1980), notes (n. 9) that "Baptism is a manifestation of the Father's prevenient love, a sharing in the Son's Paschal Mystery, and a communication of new life in the Spirit" [ND 1443].

[73] *Pastoralis actio*, 14: "The fact that infants cannot yet profess faith does not prevent the Church from conferring this sacrament on them, since in reality it is in her own faith that she baptizes them. This point of doctrine was clearly defined by St. Augustine. ... This teaching is repeated by St. Thomas Aquinas and all the theologians after him: the child who is baptized believes not on its own account, by a personal act, but through others, "through the Church's faith communicated to it." (*ST* III, Q. 69, a. 6, ad. 3.) This same teaching is also expressed in the new Rite of Baptism, when the celebrant asks the parents and godparents to profess the faith of the Church, the faith in which the children are baptized" [ND 1444].

of personal commitment to Jesus Christ, baptism is the rite of initiation of a person into a community which seeks to live in the Spirit of the risen Lord. The quality of the discipleship of the neophytes will depend on the vitality of the faith into which they are baptized. Sometimes the impression is given that, while infants are baptized into the faith of the Church, adults are baptized into their own faith. But, all faith, adult or infant, is ecclesial faith. The primary question, therefore, is not "Is this person who is presented as a candidate for baptism able to make a commitment to live like Jesus?," but "Is this community, which initiates new members in baptism, committed to live according to the ritual of self-giving which it enacts?".

If baptism is celebrated by a group which is characterized by power and oppression and which is divided by hatred and self-seeking, then, whether the recipient is an adult or an infant, the reality which the sacrament rightfully expresses is obscured. But, when the symbolic act of Jesus is imitated by a community which is distinguished by service and liberation and which is united by love and self-giving, then, whether the candidate is an adult or an infant, the reality which the dramatic action expresses is likely to be brought to fulfilment in the existential history of the recipients. In other words, this study of baptism as symbolic action of eschatological salvation directs the question of who should be admitted to baptism not just at the candidates, but also at the ecclesial group which incorporates new members into the prophetic community and lives in anticipation of the new order that lies in the future with God.

Sacramental baptism is not absolutely necessary for salvation: baptism of desire is.[74] The pessimistic view which denied the fulness of beatitude to unbaptized infants no longer has such a fearful hold on the Catholic imagination. Theories of the *massa damnata* have been radically modified by confidence in the universal salvific will of God.[75] Parents no longer present their children for *quamprimum* baptism lest they die in a state of original sin and are consigned to limbo for all eternity. There is a growing awareness that the gift of justifying grace is confined neither to the Church nor to the administration of the sacraments.[76]

---

[74] DS 1524.

[75] DS 1922; 2005. See also *Gaudium et spes,* 22; *Ad gentes,* 3.

[76] This is not to deny that all salvation comes from Christ and that the Church is necessary for salvation. On this see, F.A. Sullivan, *Salvation Outside the Church: Tracing the History of the Catholic Response.*

To refuse baptism, then, is to foreclose neither the divine offer of grace nor the possibility of salvation. This is a point which needs to be stressed. Otherwise, this consideration over-rules all others in formulating a pastoral policy as to who should be admitted to the sacrament. This study insists that the lustral washing is more than a *signum demonstrativum* of the present gift of the remission of original sin. It is also a *signum prognosticum* of the fulness of life which lies in the future and a *signum rememorativum* of the saving mysteries which were completed in the past. The true meaning of baptism is fulfilled only when the recipient grows in Christian faith and praxis. In this way, the prognostic and the commemorative aspects of the sacramental sign are assured their rightful place together with the demonstrative dimension of the lustral action. In short, in establishing pastoral guidelines for infant baptism, this study resists any attempt to subordinate the future (*signum prognosticum*) or past (*signum rememorativum*) to the present dimension (*signum demonstrativum*) of the sacramental sign.

CONCLUSION

A PRAYER OVER BAPTISMAL WATERS

In both the revised *Rite of Baptism for Children* (1969) and the *Rite of Christian Initiation of Adults* (1972), the sacramental washing is preceded by the blessing of the baptismal waters. The text of this trinitarian prayer is rich in biblical imagery. It recalls the role that water has played in the history of salvation (*signum rememorativum*), and it underscores the symbolic cleansing and rebirth that are actually effected in the liturgical rite (*signum demonstrativum*). The eschatological symbolism of the water rite, however, receives little or no mention. This thesis concludes with a text for the prayer over baptismal waters which presents the commemorative, demonstrative and prognostic as three equal dimensions of the one sacramental sign. The original text is given on the left hand side; the eschatologically enhanced alternative is given in italics on the right.

Father,
you give us grace through sacramental signs,
which tell us of the wonders of your unseen power.

Father,
you give us grace through sacramental signs,
which foretell the wonders of your unseen power,
remind us of your loving care from one generation to the next,
and call your Church to holiness and service.

In baptism we use your gift of water,
which you have made a rich symbol of the grace
you give us in this sacrament.

In baptism we use your gift of water,
which you have made a rich symbol of the grace
you give us in this sacrament.

At the very dawn of creation
your Spirit breathed on the waters,
making them signs of all holiness.

At the very dawn of creation
your Spirit breathed on the waters,
making them the source of all goodness.

The waters of the great flood
you made a sign of the waters of baptism
that make an end to sin
and a new beginning of goodness.

The waters of the great flood
you made a sign of the waters of baptism:
a figure of the life to come,
an end to sin and a new beginning for all creation.

Through the waters of the Red Sea
you led Israel out of slavery
to be an image of God's holy people,
set free from sin by baptism.

Through the waters of the Red Sea
you led Israel out of slavery
to be an image of God's holy people,
journeying to the promised land.
Through the waters of the River Jordan
you bought your chosen ones to Canaan,
to live in integrity and peace.
The prophets announced a future washing
which would create a new heart and a new spirit.

In the waters of the Jordan
your Son was baptized by John
and anointed with the Spirit.

John the Baptist preached a baptism of repentance
for the forgiveness of sins
and dramatically prefigured the advent of redemption.
In the fulness of time,
Jesus went down into the waters
in solidarity with sinful men and women,

and was baptized by John.
As he emerged from the bath of justice,
he was anointed with the Spirit,
heralding the universal out pouring of the divine gift.

Your Son willed that water and blood should flow from his side as he hung upon the cross.

In fulfilment of his baptism,
your Son died upon the cross.
Water and blood flowed from his side,
and opened for us the way to salvation.

After his resurrection he told his disciples:
«Go out and teach all nations,
baptizing them in the name
of the Father, and of the Son, and of the Holy Spirit».

After his resurrection he told his disciples:
«Go out and teach all nations,
baptizing them in the name of the Father, and of the Son, and of the Holy Spirit».

Father,
look now upon your Church
and unseal for it the fountain of baptism.

Father,
look now upon your Church
and unseal for it the fountain of baptism.

By the power of the Holy Spirit
give to this water the grace of your Son,
so that in the sacrament of baptism
all those whom you have created in your likeness
may be cleansed from sin
and rise to a new birth of innocence
by water and the Holy Spirit.
We ask you Father, with your Son
to send the Holy Spirit upon the water of this font.
May all who are buried with Christ in the death of baptism
rise also with him to newness of life.

By the power of the Holy Spirit
give to this water the grace of your Son,
so that in the sacrament of baptism
all those whom you have created in your likeness
may become members of his Body
and heirs to future glory.
As they die to sin and rise to new birth,
may they emerge as sons and daughters of righteousness
forever witnessing to your victorious love.

We ask this through Christ our Lord.

BIBLIOGRAPHY

1. Magisterial Documents

COUNCIL OF TRENT, *Decretum de sacramentis*, DS 1600-1630.

LEO XIII, *Providentissimus Deus*, *AAS* 26 (1893/94) 269-292.

BENEDICT XV, *Spiritus Paraclitus*, *AAS* 12 (1920) 389-422.

PIUS XII, *Divino afflante Spiritu*, *AAS* 35 (1943) 297-325.

———, *Humani generis*, *AAS* 42 (1950) 561-578.

PONTIFICAL BIBLICAL COMMISSION, *Instructio de historica evangeliorum veritate*, *AAS* 56 (1964) 712-718; ET: "Instruction on the Historical Truth of the Gospels," in *A Christological Catechism. New Testament Answers*, ed. J.A. Fitzmyer, New York 1982, 131-140.

SECOND VATICAN COUNCIL, *Sacrosanctum concilium*, AAS 56 (1964) 97-138.

———, *Ad gentes*, AAS 57 (1965) 947-990.

———, *Dei verbum*, *AAS* 58 (1966) 817-835.

———, *Optatam totius*, *AAS* 58 (1966) 713-727.

———, *Gaudium et spes*, *AAS* 58 (1966) 1025-1120.

PAUL VI, *Divinae consortium naturae*, *AAS* 63 (1971) 657-664.

CONGREGATION FOR DIVINE WORSHIP, *Rite of Christian Initiation of Adults. The Final Texts with Commentaries.* [The Roman Ritual Revised by Decree of the Second Vatican Ecumenical Council and Published by Authority of Pope Paul VI on the Feast of the Epiphany 1972] Dublin 1986.

PAUL VI, *Evangelii nuntiandi*, *AAS* 68 (1975) 5-76.

INTERNATIONAL THEOLOGICAL COMMISSION, *Select Questions on Christology*, in *International Theological Commission. Texts and Documents 1969-1985*, ed. M.J. Sharkey, San Francisco 1986, 185-205.

CONGREGATION FOR THE DOCTRINE OF THE FAITH, *De quibus quaestionibus ad eschatologiam spectantibus*, *AAS* 91 (1979) 939-943; ET: "Some Current Questions in Eschatology," *IThQ* 58 (1992) 209-243.

CONGREGATION FOR THE DOCTRINE OF THE FAITH, *Pastoralis actio*, *AAS* 72 (1980) 1137-1156.

JOHN PAUL II, *Laborem exercens*, *AAS* 73 (1981) 577-647.

PONTIFICAL BIBLICAL COMMISSION, *De sacra scriptura et christologia*; ET: *Scripture and Christology. A Statement of the Pontifical Biblical Commission with a Commentary*, J.A. Fitzmyer, ed., New York 1986.

JOHN PAUL II, *Sollicitudo rei socialis*, *AAS* 80 (1988) 513-586.

———, *Centesimus annus*, *AAS* 83 (1991) 793-867.

PONTIFICAL BIBLICAL COMMISSION, *L'Interprétation de la Bible dans l'Eglise*, Città del Vaticano 1993; ET: *The Biblical Commission's Document "The Interpretation of the Bible in the Church". Text and Commentary*, J.A. Fitzmyer, ed., Roma 1995.

Cathechism of the Catholic Church, Dublin 1994.

2. Primary Texts

2.1 *Works by Samuel Amsler*

AMSLER, S., *Les actes des prophètes*, Genève 1985.

———, "Aggée - Zacharie 1-8," in S. Amsler, A. Lacoque, R. Vuilleumier (eds.), *Aggée - Zacharie, Malachie* [Commentaire de l'Ancien Testament XIc], Genève 1988[2].

———, "Amos," in E. Jacob, C. Keller, S. Amsler, ed., *Osée, Joël, Amos, Abdias, Jonas* [Commentaire de l'Ancien Testament XIa], Genève 1992[3].

———, "Amos, prophète de la onzième heure," *ThZ* 21 (1965) 318-328.

———, "L'Ancien Testament et la prédication de l'Evangile," in *Pratique et Théologie*, Fs. C. Bridel, Genève 1989, 131-139.

———, *L'Ancien Testament dans l'Eglise. Essai d'herméneutique chrétienne*, Neuchâtel-Paris 1960.

———, *Le dernier et l'avant-dernier. Etudes sur l'Ancien Testament*, Genève 1993.

———, "Le dernier et l'avant dernier. Le rapport entre le Nouveau et l'Ancien Testament," *RSR* 63 (1975) 385-396.

———, "La fonction prophétique de l'Eglise et dans l'Eglise. Remarques à partir de l'Ancien Testament," in J. Panagopoulos, ed., *Prophetic Vocation in the New Testament and Today* [N.T. Suppl. 45], Leiden 1977, 33-45.

———, "Lecture juive et lecture chrétienne de l'Ecriture sainte," *Jud* 17 (1961) 24-39.

AMSLER, S., "Les ministères de l'ancienne alliance: rois, prêtres et prophètes," *VC* 71/72 (1964) 29-41.

———, "Où en est la typologie de l'Ancien Testament?," *ETR* 27 (1952) 75-81.

———, "Paroles de Dieu et paroles des hommes," *CProt* (1981/3) 5-13.

———, "La parole visionnaire des prophètes," *VT* 31 (1981) 359-363.

———, "Problèmes d'herméneutique de l'Ancien Testament," *ÉeTh(O)* 24 (1961) 23-38.

———, "Les prophètes et la communication par les actes," in *Werden und Wirken des Alten Testaments*, Fs. C. Westermann, Göttingen 1980, 194-201.

———, "Les prophètes et la politique," *RThPh* 23 (1973) 14-31.

———, "Le thème du procès chez les prophètes d'Israël," *RThPh* 24 (1974) 116-131.

———, "La typologie de L'Ancien Testament chez saint Paul," *RThPh*, n.s. 37 (1949) 113-128.

———, "Typologie et prophétie," *RThPh* 3 (1953) 139-148.

2.2 *Works by Heinz Schürmann*

SCHÜRMANN, H., *Der Abendmahlsbericht Lukas 22,7-38 als Gottesdienstordnung, Gemeindeordnung, Lebensordnung*, Leipzig 1955.

———, *Der Einsetzungsbericht Lk 22:19-20. II. Teil einer quellenkritischen Untersuchung des lukanischen Abendmahlsberichtes Lk. 22:7-38* [Neutestamentliche Abhandlungen XX/4], Münster 1955.

———, "Das hermeneutische Hauptproblem der Verkündigung Jesu. Eschato-logie und Theologie im gegenseitigen Verhältnis," in *Gott in Welt*, Fs. Karl Rahner, Freiburg 1964, 579-607.

———, *Jesus. Gestalt und Geheimnis*, K. Scholtissek, ed., Paderborn 1994.

———, *Jesu Abschiedsrede Lk. 22:21-38. III. Teil einer quellenkritischen Untersuchung des lukanischen Abendmahlsberichtes Lk. 22:7-38* [Neutestamentliche Abhandlungen XX/5], Münster 1957.

———, *Jesu ureigener Tod. Exegetische Besinnungen und Ausblick*, Freiburg 1975.

———, "Jesus' Disciples: Prototype of Religious Life," *ThDig* 15 (1967) 138-143.

———, "Jesus' Words in the Light of His Actions at the Last Supper," *Conc* 4/10 (1968) 61-67.

SCHÜRMANN, H., *Das Lukasevangelium. Erster Teil. Kommentar zu Kap.1,1-9,50* [Herders theologischer Kommentar zum Neuen Testament III/1], Freiburg 1982[2].

———, *Das Lukasevangelium. Zweiter Teil. Erster Folge. Kommentar zu Kap.9,51-11,54* [Herders theologischer Kommentar zum Neuen Testament III/2], Freiburg 1994.

———, *Parola del Signore. Messaggio di Gesù sul Regno di Dio*, Torino 1966.

———, *Praying with Christ. The "Our Father" for Today*, New York 1964.

———, "Die Symbolhandlungen Jesu als eschatologische Erfüllungszeichen. Eine Rückfrage nach dem historischen Jesus," *BiLe* 11 (1970) 29-41; 73-78.

———, *Der Paschamahlbericht Lk 22:(7-14) 15-18. I. Teil einer quellenkritischen Untersuchung des lukanischen Abendmahlsberichtes Lk. 22:7-38* [Neutestamentliche Abhandlungen XIX/5], Münster 1953.

———, *La tradizione dei detti di Gesù*, Brescia 1980.

———, *Ursprung und Gestalt. Erörterungen und Besinnungen zum Neuen Testament*, Düsseldorf 1970.

2.3 *Works by Karl Rahner*

RAHNER, K., "The Abiding Influence of the Second Vatican Council," *TI* 20, 90-102.

———, "Anonymous Christians," *TI* 6, 390-398.

———, "Baptism and the Renewal of Baptism," *TI* 23, 195-204.

———, "The Christian among Unbelieving Relations," *TI* 3, 355-372.

———, "Christian Living Formerly and Today," *TI* 7, 3-24.

———, "Christmas, the Festival of Eternal Youth," *TI* 7, 121-126.

———, "Christology in the Setting of Modern Man's Understanding of Himself and His World," *TI* 11, 215-229.

———, "Christology within an Evolutionary View of the World," *TI* 5, 157-192.

———, *The Church and the Sacraments* [Quaestiones Disputatae 9], New York 1961.

———, "The Church's Redemptive Provenance from the Death and Resurrection of Jesus," *TI* 19, 24-38.

———, "The Concept of Mystery in Catholic Theology," *TI* 4, 36-73.

———, "Concerning the Relationship between Nature and Grace," *TI* 1, 297-318.

RAHNER, K., "Considerations on the Active Role of the Person in the Sacramental Event," *TI* 14, 161-184.

———, "A Copernican Revolution. Secular Life and the Sacraments 1," *Tablet* 225 (March 6, 1971) 236-238.

———, "Courage for an Ecclesial Christianity," *TI* 20, 3-12.

———, "Current Problems in Christology," *TI* 1, 149-200.

———, "The Death of Jesus and the Closure of Revelation," *TI* 18, 132-142.

———, "Dogmatic Notes on 'Ecclesiological Piety'," *TI* 5, 336-365.

———, "Dogmatic Questions on Easter," *TI* 4, 121-133.

———, "Encounters with the Risen Christ," *TI* 7,169-176.

———, "The Eternal Significance of the Humanity of Jesus for Our Relationship with God," *TI* 3, 35-46.

———, "The Eucharist and Our Daily Lives," *TI* 7, 211-226.

———, "The Eucharist and Suffering," *TI* 3,161-170.

———, "The Experience of God Today," *TI* 11, 149-165.

———, "Experience of the Holy Spirit," *TI* 18, 189-210.

———, "Experience of Self and Experience of God," *TI* 13, 122-132.

———, "Experience of the Spirit and Existential Commitment," *TI* 16, 24-34.

———, "Experiencing Easter," *TI* 7,159-168.

———, *Foundations of Christian Faith. An Introduction to the Idea of Christianity*, London 1978.

———, *Hearers of the Word*, New York 1969.

———, "The Hiddenness of God," *TI* 16, 227-243.

———, "History of the World and Salvation-History," *TI* 5, 97-114.

———, "Introductory Observations on Thomas Aquinas' Theology of the Sacraments in General," *TI* 14, 149-160.

———, *I Remember. An Autobiographical Interview with Meinhold Krauss*, New York 1985.

———, *Karl Rahner in Dialogue. Conversations and Interviews, 1965-1982*, P. Imhoff & H. Biallowons, ed., New York 1986.

———, "The Mass and the World: Secular Life and the Sacraments 2," *Tablet* 226 (March 13, 1971) 267-268.

———, *Meditations on the Sacraments*, New York 1977.

———, *Nature and Grace*, London 1963.

———, "The Old Testament and Christian Dogmatic Theology," *TI* 16, 177-190.

———, "Personal and Sacramental Piety," *TI* 2, 109-133.

RAHNER, K.,"The Position of Christology in the Church between Exegesis and Dogmatics," *TI* 11, 185-214.

———, *The Practice of the Faith. A Handbook of Contemporary Spirituality*, New York 1983.

———, "The Presence of Christ in the Sacrament of the Lord's Supper," *TI* 4, 287-311.

———, "The Presence of the Lord in the Christian Community at Worship," *TI* 10, 71-83.

———, "Prophet," in *Concise Theological Dictionary*, London 1965, 383-384.

———, "Prophetism," *SM(E)* V, 110-113.

———, "Reflections on the Experience of Grace," *TI* 3, 86-90.

———, "Remarks on the Importance of the History of Jesus for Catholic Dogmatics," *TI* 13, 201-212.

———, "Revelation," *SM(E)* V, 348-359.

———, "Some Implications of the Scholastic Notion of Uncreated Grace," *TI* 1, 319-346.

———, *Spirit in the World*, New York 1968.

———, "Theological Observations on the Concept of Time," *TI* 11, 288-308.

———, "The Theology of Symbol," *TI* 4, 221-252.

———, "On the Theology of Worship," *TI* 19, 141-149.

———, *The Trinity*, New York 1974.

———, "What is a Sacrament?," *TI* 14, 135-148.

———, "The Word and the Eucharist," *TI* 4, 253-286.

2.4 *Works By Edward Schillebeeckx*

SCHILLEBEECKX, E., "Can Christology be an Experiment?," *PCTSA* 36(1981) 1-14.

———, "The Christian and Political Engagement," *DoLi* 22 (1972) 118-127.

———, *Christ. The Experience of Jesus as Lord*, New York 1981.

———, *Christ the Sacrament of the Encounter with God*, London 1963.

———, *Church. The Human Story of God*, New York 1990.

———, *The Church with a Human Face. A New and Expanded Theology of Ministry*, London 1985.

———, "L'Eglise catholique aux Pays-Bas," *Septentrion* 1 (1972) 25-39.

———, *The Eucharist*, London 1968.

SCHILLEBEECKX, E., "Exegesis, Dogmatics and the Development of Dogma," in H. Vorgrimler, ed., *Dogmatics vs Biblical Theology*, London 1964, 115-145.

———, *For the Sake of the Gospel*, New York 1989.

———, *God Among Us. The Gospel Proclaimed*, New York 1983.

———, *God, the Future of Man*, London 1968.

———, *God and Man*, London 1969.

———, *God is New in Each Moment* [In Conversation with H. Oosterhuis & P. Hoogeveen], Edinburgh 1983.

———, *I am a Happy Theologian* [Conversations with F. Strazzari], London 1994.

———, *Interim Report on the Books "Jesus" and "Christ,"* New York 1980.

———, "The Interpretation of Eschatology," *Concilium* 5/1 (1969) 22-29.

———, *Jesus. An Experiment in Christology*, New York 1979.

———, *Jesus in Our Western Culture. Mysticism, Ethics and Politics*, London 1987.

———, "Liberation Theology between Medellin and Puebla," *ThDig* 28 (1980) 3-7.

———, *Marriage, Secular Reality and Saving Mystery*, London 1966.

———, *Ministry. A Case for Change*, London 1981.

———, *The Mission of the Church*, London 1973.

———, "Parole et sacrement dans l'Eglise," *LV(L)* 46 (1960) 25-45.

———, "Questions on Christian Salvation of and for Man," in D. Tracy, H. Küng, J.B. Metz, ed., *Towards Vatican III. The Work that Needs to be Done*, Dublin 1978, 27-44.

———, *Revelation and Theology. Revelation, Tradition and Theological Reflection* [Theological Soundings I/1], London 1967.

———, *Revelation and Theology. The Concept of Truth and Theological Renewal* [Theological Soundings I/2], London 1968.

———, *De Sacramentele Heilseconomie. Theologische bezinning op S. Thomas' sacramentenleer in het licht van de traditie en van de hedendaagse sacramentsproblematiek*, Bilthoven 1952.

———, *The Schillebeeckx Case. Official exchange of letters and documents in the investigation of Fr. Edward Schillebeeckx O.P. by the Sacred Congregation for the Doctrine of the Faith, 1976-1980*, T. Schoff, ed., New York 1984.

———, *The Schillebeeckx Reader*, ed. R.J. Schreiter, Edinburgh 1984.

———, "Les sacrements dans le plan de Dieu," *Présences* no. 102 (1968) 25-34.

———, "Transubstantiation, Transfinalization, Transignification," *Worship* 40 (1966) 324-338.

———, *The Understanding of Faith. Interpretation and Criticism*, London 1974.

———, *Vatican II. The Real Achievement*, London 1967.

———, *Vatican II. A Struggle of Minds and Other Essays*, Dublin 1963.

———, *World and Church*, London 1971.

3. Secondary Texts

ALBERIGO, G., "La riforma conciliare nel cammino del movimento liturgico e nella vita della Chiesa," in *Assisi 1956-1986. Il movimento liturgico fra riforma conciliare e attese del popolo di Dio*, Assisi 1987, 75-93.

ALAND, K., *Did the Early Church Baptize Infants?*, Philadelphia 1963.

D'ALÈS, A., *Baptême et confirmation*, Paris 1927.

ALTEN, D., "Baptism in Recent German Theology," *RestQ* 7 (1963) 124-131.

AUGÉ, M., "Movimento liturgico - Riforma liturgica - Rinnovamento liturgico," *EO* 6 (1989) 301-322.

AUNE, D.E., *Prophecy and Early Christianity*, Grand Rapids 1983.

DE BACIOCCHI, J., "Les sacrements, actes libres du Seigneur," *NRTh* 73 (1951) 681-706.

BAKER, K., "Rahner: The Transcendental Method," *Cont* 2 (1964) 51-59.

VON BALTHASAR, H. U., *Mysterium Pasquale*, Edinburgh 1990.

BARTH, K., *The Teaching of the Church Regarding Baptism*, London 1948.

BEASLEY-MURRAY, G.R., *Baptism in the New Testament*, Exeter 1979[3].

BECK, N.A., "The Last Supper as an Efficacious Symbolic Act," *JBL* 89 (1970) 192-198.

BECKER, K., "Der Gebrauch der Hl. Schrift in der dogmatischen Theologie," *Gr* 73 (1992) 667-687.

BECKER, J., *Johannes der Täufer*, Neukirchen 1972.

BECKER, W., *The Historical Jesus in the Face of His Death. His Comprehension of its Salvific Meaning in the Writings of Edward Schillebeeckx and Hans Urs von Balthasar*, Rome 1993-94.

BENOIT, P., "Les récits de l'institution et leur portée," *LV(L)* 31 (1957) 49-76.

BERGIN, H., "The Death of Jesus and its Impact on God," *IThQ* 52 (1986) 193-211.

BIFFI, I., "Misteri di Cristo, sacramenti, escatologia, nello *Scriptum super Sententiis* di San Tommaso d'Aquino," *ScC* 102 (1974) 569-623.

BILLOT, L., *De ecclesiae sacramentis. Commentarius in tertiam partem S. Thomae,* Tomus Prior, Romae 1900.

BLENKINSOPP, J., *Ezekiel*, Louisville 1990.

BONNETERRE, D., *Le mouvement liturgique de Dom Guéranger à Annibal Bugnini ou le Cheval de Troie dans la Cité de Dieu*, Escurolles 1980.

BORD, J.B., "De l'institution des sacraments par le Christ," *NRTh* 56 (1929) 667-670.

———, "Justification sacramentelle et extrasacramentelle," *NRTh* 52 (1925) 213-227; 292-297.

BORG, M.J., *Jesus. A New Vision*, San Francisco 1987.

———, *Jesus in Contemporary Scholarship*. Valley Forge 1994.

BORING, M.E., "How May We Identify Oracles of Christian Prophets in the Synoptic Tradition? Mark 3:28-29 as a Test Case," *JBL* 91 (1972) 501-521.

BOUËSSÉ, H., *Le Sauveur du monde*. IV. *L'Economie sacramentaire*, Chambery-Leysse 1951.

BOURGEOIS, H. – SESBOÜE, B. – TIHON, P., *Les signes du salut* [Histoire des Dogmes, Tome III], Paris 1995.

BOURKE, D., *The Sacraments* [St. Thomas Aquinas, *Summa Theologiae*, 3ª, 50-56. Vol. 56], Oxford 1975.

BOUYER, L., "Le symbolisme des rites baptismaux," *MD* 32 (1952) 5-17.

———, *Life and Liturgy*, London 1956.

BOWKER, J.W., "Prophetic Action and Sacramental Form," in *Studia Evangelica*, ed. F.L. Cross, III/II [TU 88], Berlin 1964, 129-137.

BRAND, E.L., "Reflections on the Ecumenical Aspects of the Liturgical Movement," *Worship* 51 (1977) 49-55.

BREDIN, E., *Disturbing the Peace: The Way of Discipleship*, Dublin 1993.

BRIDGEHOUSE, D., "Dom Odo Casel: A Short Appreciation and a Translation from his Works," *DR* 75 (1957) 140-148.

BRITO GUIMARÃES, P., *Os sacramentos como atos eclesiais e proféticos. Um contributo ao conceito dogmático de sacramento à luz da exegese contemporânea*, Roma 1995.

BROVELLI, F., "Per uno studio de *L'Année Liturgique* di P. Guéranger. Contributo alla storia del movimento liturgico," *EL* 95 (1981) 145-219.

———, "Radici, acquisizioni, istanze del movimento liturgico nel nostro secolo," in *Assisi 1956-1986: Il movimento liturgico fra riforma conciliare e attese del popolo di Dio*, Assisi 1987, 47-74.

BROVELLI, F., "Storia del movimento liturgico nel nostro secolo: dati, attese e linee di approfondimento," *EL* 99 (1985) 217-238.

BROWN, R.E., *Biblical Exegesis and Church Doctrine*, Mahwah 1985.

———, "Scripture and Dogma Today," *America* 157/12 (31 October 1987) 286-289.

BROWN, R.E. – COLLINS, T.A., "Church Pronouncements," *NJBC* II, 1166-1174.

BRUNO, C.G., *Il concetto di sacramento in Schillebeeckx*, Roma 1976.

BUCKLEY, J.J., "Karl Rahner as a Dogmatic Theologian," *Thom* 47 (1983) 364-394.

———, "On Being a Symbol: Appraisal of Rahner," *TS* 40 (1979) 454-473.

BULTMANN, R., *Jesus and the Word,* London, 1934.

BUZY, D, *Les symboles de l'Ancien Testament*, Paris 1923.

CADBURY, H.J, "Jesus and the Prophets," *JR* 5 (1925) 607-622.

CALLAHAN, C.A., "Karl Rahner's Theology of Symbol: Basis for his Theology of the Church and the Sacraments," *IThQ* 49 (1982) 195-205.

CAMELOT, P.T., "Il Battesimo e la cresima nella teologia contemporanea," in *Problemi e orientamenti di teologia dogmatica,* II, Milano 1957, 795-829.

CAMELOT, P.T., "Bulletin de théologie dogmatique: sacrements," *RScPhTh* 50 (1966) 279-289.

———, *Spiritualité du baptême* [Lex Orandi 30], Paris 1960.

CAROBENE, A., *La teologia sacramentale in genere di Karl Rahner*, Roma 1978.

CARROLL, R.P., *From Chaos to Covenant. Uses of Prophecy in the Book of Jeremiah*, New York 1981.

———, *Jeremiah* [Old Testament Guides] , Sheffield 1989.

———, *Jeremiah. A Commentary*, London 1986.

CASEL, O., "Das Mysteriengedächtnis der Meßliturgie im Lichte der Tradition," *JL* 6 (1926) 113-204.

———, *The Mystery of Christian Worship*, London 1962.

———, "Das Wort 'sacramentum'," *ThRv* 24 (1925) 41-47.

CENTI, T.S., "Introduzione e note," in *La Somma teologica. I sacramenti in genere. Battesimo e Cresima*, XXVII, Bologna 1984.

CHAUVET, L.-M., *Symbol and Sacrament. A Sacramental Reinterpretation of Christian Experience*, Collegeville 1995.

CHENU, M.-D., "Le plan de la Somme théologique de Saint Thomas," *RThom* 47 (1939) 93-107.

CHILDS, B.S., *Memory and Tradition in Israel*, London 1962.

CIAPPI, A.M., *De sacramentis in communi. Commentarius in tertiam partem S. Thomae*, Torino 1957.

———, "De praesentia Domini in communitate cultus ratione characteris baptismalis," in *Acta Conventus Internationalis de Theologia Concilii Vaticani II*, Roma 1968, 272-282.

CINCINNATI, A., *Pneumatological Ecclesiology in the Writings of Abbot Anscar Vonier, O.S.B.*, Roma 1994.

COCCOPALMERIO, F., "La dottrina dell'appartenenza alla Chiesa nell'insegnamento del Vaticano II," *ScC* 98 (1970) 215-238.

CODY, A., *Ezekiel* [Old Testament Message], Dublin 1984.

COFFEY, R.M., "St. Thomas Aquinas" in *The Summa of St. Thomas Aquinas,* Vol. III, 3063-3071.

COLLINS, J.J. – CROSSAN, J.D., *The Biblical Heritage in Modern Catholic Scholarship*, Fs. Bruce Vawter, Wilmington 1986.

COLOMBO, G., "Dove va la teologia sacramentaria?," *ScC* 102 (1974) 673-717.

COLOMBO, J.A., "Rahner and His Critics. Lindbeck and Metz," *Thom* 56 (1992) 71-96.

COMBÓN, E., *L'ortoprassi nel pensiero di E. Schillebeeckx*, Roma 1974.

CONGAR, Y., *A History of Theology*, Garden City 1968.

———, "Bulletin de Théologie: Sacrements," *RScPhTh* 24 (1935) 717-723.

CONNELL, F., *De sacramentis Ecclesiae tractatus dogmatici.* I. *De sacramentis in communi, de baptismo, de confirmatione, de SS. Eucharistia*, Brugis 1933.

CONROY, C., "Prophets," in *DFT,* 798-801.

COOKE, B.J., "*De Sacramentis* and the Seminary Course," in ed., *Apostolic Renewal in the Seminary in the Light of Vatican Council II,* [The Papers of the Second Christopher Study Weeks], ed. J. Keller & R. Armstrong, New York 1965, 185-193.

———, "Review of Books on Sacraments, 1955-65," *Worship* 40 (1966) 73-79.

COX, D., *The Psalms in the Life of God's People*, Middlegreen 1984.

CRANFIELD, C., "The Baptism of Our Lord," *SJTh* 8 (1955) 55-63.

CREHAN, J.H., "Ten Years Work on Baptism and Confirmation: 1945-1955," *TS* 17 (1956) 494-515.

CRICHTON, J.D., *Christian Celebration. The Sacraments*, London 1973.

CROSSAN, J.D., *The Historical Jesus. The Life of a Mediterranean Jewish Peasant*, Edinburgh 1991.

CULLMANN, O., *Baptism in the New Testament*, London 1950.

CULLMANN, O., *The Christology of the New Testament*, London 1959.

———, *Les sacrements dans l'évangile johannique,* Paris 1951.

CUNNINGHAM, J.J., *Baptism and Confirmation* [St. Thomas Aquinas, *Summa Theologiae*, 3a, 66-72. Vol. 57], Oxford 1975.

DANIÉLOU, J., *The Bible and the Liturgy*, Ann Arbor 1956.

———, "Bulletin d'histoire de la théologie sacramentaire," *RSR* 34 (1947) 369-384.

———, "Le Christ Prophète," *VS* 78 (1945) 154-170.

———, "Le dimanche comme huitième jour," in *Le Dimanche*, ed. B. Botte, Paris 1965.

———, *L'entrée dans l'histoire du salut. Baptême et confirmation*, Paris 1967.

———, "Sacraments and Parousia," *OF* 25 (1951) 400-404.

———, *Sacramentum Futuri. Études sur les origines de la typologie biblique*, Paris 1950.

———, "Le Symbolisme baptismal du véhicule," *ScEc* 10 (1958) 127-138.

———, "Le symbolisme de l'eau vive," *RSR* 32 (1958) 335-346.

———, "Le symbolisme des rites baptismaux," *DViv* 1 (1945) 17-43.

———, "Traversée de la Mer Rouge et baptême aux premiers siècles," *RSR* 33 (1946) 402-430.

DAVIS, C., "Notes on Recent Works. Dogmatic Theology," *CleR* 42 (1957) 152-167.

DAVIES, P.E., "Did Jesus Die as a Martyr-Prophet?" *BR* 2 (1957) 19-30. [Reprinted 19 (1974) 37-47.]

———, "Jesus and the Role of Prophet", *JBL* 64 (1945) 241-254.

DELHAYE, P., "Presentation," in Commision Théologique Internationale, "Quelques questions touchant la Christologie," *EeV* 90 (1980) 609-610.

DELORME, J., "The Practice of Baptism in Judaism at the Beginning of the Christian Era," in *Baptism in the New Testament*, ed. A. George, London 1964, 25-60.

DENKEN, M., "Pour une christologie de la pro-existence," *RSR* 82 (1988) 255-290.

DESCAMPS, A.-L., "Cénacle et Calvaire: Les vues de H. Schürmann," *RTL* 10 (1979) 335-347.

DIDIER, J.-C., "Bulletin de théologie sacramentaire," *AmiCl* 73 (1963) 577-586.

———, "À propos du caractère sacramentel," *AmiCl* 72 (1962) 167-171.

DILLENBERGER, J., *Martin Luther. Selections from His Writings*, Garden City 1961.

DIX, G., *The Shape of the Liturgy*, London 1945.

DONDAINE, H.-F., "La définition des sacrements dans la 'Somme Théologique'," *RScPhTh* 31 (1947) 213-228.

DODD, C.H., "Jesus as Teacher and Prophet," in *Mysterium Christi*, ed. G.K.A. Bell & D.A. Deissmann, London 1930, 53-66.

———, *The Parables of the Kingdom*, London 1935.

DORONZO, E., *De baptismo et confirmatione*, Milwaukee 1947.

———, *De sacramentis in genere*, Milwaukee 1945.

DUDLEY, M., "On Reading Rahner," *SJTh* 37 (1984) 81-96.

DUFFY, R.A., ed., *Alternative Futures for Worship. I. General Introduction*, Collegeville 1987.

———, "Justification and Sacrament," *JES* 16 (1979) 672-690.

———, "The Post-Rahnerian Formulation," *TS* 55 (1994) 665-675.

DULLES, A., "The Succession of Prophets in the Church," *Conc* 4/4 (1968) 28-32.

———, "The Use of Scripture in Theology," in *The Craft of Theology: From Symbol to System*, New York 1992, 69-85.

DUNN, J.D.G., *Baptism in the Holy Spirit*, London 1970.

DUPONT, J., "'Ceci est mon corps', 'Ceci est mon sang'," *NRTh* 80 (1968) 1025-1041.

DUPUIS, J., *Who Do You Say I Am?* Maryknoll 1994.

DUPUY, B.D., "Bulletin de théologie dogmatique: sacrements," *RScPhTh* 47 (1963) 290-309.

DURWELL, F.-X., "La transfiguration de Jésus," *VS* 85 (1951) 115-126.

DYCH, W.V., "The Achievement of Karl Rahner," *ThDig* 31 (1984) 325-333.

———, *Karl Rahner* [Outstanding Christian Thinkers Series], London 1992.

EMERTON, J.A., ed., *Prophecy*, Fs. G. Fohrer, Berlin-New York 1980.

EMERY, P.Y., "Le baptême: appartenance fondamentale à l'Eglise," *VC* 76 (1965) 57-68.

ESPINEL, J.L., "Biblia y moral cristiana," *CTom* 113 (1986) 583-595.

———, *La cena del Señor, acción profética*, Madrid 1976.

———, "Teología profética," *CTom* 114 (1987) 503-520.

EVANS, C., "Jesus' Action in the Temple: Cleansing or Portent of Destruction?," *CBQ* 51 (1989) 237-270.

FAHEY, M.A., "1904-1994, Karl Rahner, Theologian," *PCTSA* 39 (1984) 84-98.

FARRELL, D., *The Dogmatic Foundations of Bernard Häring's Thought on Christian Morality as a Sacramental Way of Life*, Roma 1988.

FEUILLET, A., "La coupe et le baptême de la passion," *RB* 74 (1967) 356-391.

FEUILLET, A., "La personnalité de Jésus entrevue à partir de sa soumission au rite de repentance du précurseur," *RB* 77 (1970) 30-49.

FILTHAUT, T., *La théologie des mystères. Exposé de la controverse. Dossier complet de la controverse*, Tournai 1954.

FINN, T.M., *Early Christian Baptism and the Catechumenate. Italy, North Africa, and Egypt* [Message of the Fathers of the Church 6], Collegeville 1992.

———, *Early Christian Baptism and the Catechumenate. West and East Syria* [Message of the Fathers of the Church 5], Collegeville 1992.

FISCHEL, H.A., "Martyr and Prophet," *JQR* 37 (1946/47) 265-280; 363-386.

FISICHELLA, R., "Prophecy," in *DFT*, 788-798.

FITZMYER, J.A., *A Christological Catechism. New Testament Answers*, New York 1991².

———, *Essays on the Semitic Background of the New Testament*, London 1971.

———, *Scripture, the Soul of Theology*, Mahwah 1994.

FLEMINGTON, W.F., *The New Testament Doctrine of Baptism*, London 1948.

FOGARTY, G.P., *American Catholic Biblical Scholarship. A History from the Early Republic to Vatican II*, San Francisco 1989.

FOHRER, G., "Die Gattung der Berichte über symbolische Handlungen der Propheten," *ZAW* 64 (1952) 101-120.

———, *History of Israelite Religion*, Nashville – New York 1972.

———, *Introduction to the Old Testament*, London 1968.

———, "Prophetie und Geschichte," *ThLZ* 89 (1964) 481-500.

———, "Prophetie und Magie," *ZAW* 78 (1966) 25-47.

———, "Remarks on Modern Interpretation of the Prophets," *JBL* 80 (1961) 309-319.

———, *Die symbolischen Handlungen der Propheten*, Zürich 1968².

FOWLER, J.W., "The RCIA and Christian Religious Education," *Worship* 56 (1982) 336-342.

FRANKLIN, R.W., "The Nineteenth-Century Liturgical Movement," *Worship* 53 (1979) 12-39.

———, "Response: Humanism and Transcendence in the Nineteenth Century Liturgical Movement," *Worship* 59 (1985) 342-353.

FRASER, E.R., "Symbolic Acts of the Prophets," *SBT* 4 (1974) 45-53.

FREYNE, S., *Galilee, Jesus and the Gospels. Literary Approaches and Historical Investigations*, Philadelphia 1988.

FRIEDRICH, G., "*προφήτης κτλ*," in *TDNT* VI (1968) 781-861.

FROHLE, C., *The Idea of the Sacred According to Abbot Anscar Vonier*, Rome 1971.

FRUTSAERT, E., "La définition du sacrement dans S. Thomas," *NRTh* 60 (1928) 401-409.

FULLER, R.H., *The Foundations of New Testament Christology*, London 1965.

———, *The Mission and Achievement of Jesus*, London 1954.

FUNK, R.W. - HOOVER, R.W., ed., *The Five Gospels: The Search for the Authentic Words of Jesus*, New York 1993.

GAILLARD, J., "Chronique de liturgie," *RThom* 57 (1957) 510-551.

GALVIN, J.P., "The Death of Jesus in Contemporary Theology: Systematic Perspectives and Historical Issues," *Horizons* 13 (1986) 239-252.

———, "Jesus' Approach to Death: An Examination of Some Recent Studies," *TS* 41 (1980) 713-744.

GARLAND, P.B., *The Definition of Sacrament according to Saint Thomas*, Ottawa 1959.

GAVIN, F., *The Jewish Antecedents of the Christian Sacraments*, New York 1969.

GEFFRÉ, C., "Du symbolisme au symbole: les sacrements," *MD* 142 (1980) 59-55.

GELINEAU, J., "Eredità del movimento liturgico e nuove attese," in *Assisi 1956-1986. Il movimento liturgico fra riforma conciliare e attese del popolo di Dio*, Assisi 1987, 111-123.

GENEVOIS, M.A., "Théologie sacramentaire (Bulletin)," *RThom* 77 (1977) 679-683.

GEORGE, A., ed., *Baptism in the New Testament*, London 1964.

———, "Comment Jésus a-t-il perçu sa mort?," *LV(L)* 20 (1971) 34-59.

GHERARDINI, B., "Sul concetto di sacramento, ieri e oggi," *Div* 19 (1975) 292-334.

GILBERT, M., "New Horizons and Present Needs: Exegesis Since Vatican II," in *Vatican II: Assessment and Perspectives*, ed. R. Latourelle, I, New York 1988, 321-343.

GILBY, T., *Christian Theology* [St. Thomas Aquinas, *Summa Theologiae,* 1ª, 1. Vol. 1], Oxford, 1963.

GILMORE, A., ed., *Christian Baptism. A Fresh Attempt to Understand the Rite in Terms of Scripture, History and Theology*, London 1959.

GILS, F., *Jésus prophète d'après les évangiles synoptiques*, Louvain 1957.

GNILKA, J., "Wie urteilte Jesus über seinen Tod?," in *Der Tod Jesu: Deutungen im Neuen Testament,* ed. K. Kertelge [Quaestiones Disputatae 74], Freiburg 1976, 13-50.

GOGUEL, M., "Pneumatisme et eschatologie," *RHR* 132 (1946) 124-169.

GRABMANN, M., *Einführung in die "Summa Theologiae" des heiligen Thomas von Aquin*, Freiburg 1928.

GRAF, E., *Abbot of Buckfast. A Study of Anscar Vonier*, London 1963.

GRANT, R.M. – TRACY, D., *A Short History of the Interpretation of the Bible*, Philadelphia 1975[2].

GREENBERG, M., *Ezekiel 1-20* [AncB 22], Garden City 1983.

GROOT, J., "The Church as Sacrament of the World," *Conc* 4/1 (1968) 27-34.

GUGLIELMETTI, P., *L' estensione e l'approfondimento della nozione di sacramento in K. Rahner, E. Schillebeeckx, O. Semmelroth*, Roma 1971.

GUILLAUME, A., *Prophecy and Divination among the Hebrews and Other Semites*, London 1938.

GUILLET, J., *Jésus devant sa vie et devant sa mort,* Paris 1971.

GUZIE, T., *The Book of Sacramental Basics*, New York 1981.

———, *Jesus and the Eucharist*, New York 1974.

GY, P.-M., "Bulletin de théologie dogmatique. Sacrements," *RScPhTh* 41 (1957) 550-552.

———, "L'office du *Corpus Christi* et S. Thomas D'Aquin. Etat d'une recherche," *RScPhTh* 64 (1980) 491-507.

———, "Problèmes de théologie sacramentaire," *MD* 110 (1972) 129-143.

DE HAES, R., *Pour une théologie prophétique. Lecture thématique de la théologie de Karl Rahner*, Louvain 1972.

HAIGHT, R., *The Experience and Language of Grace*, Dublin 1979.

HAMEL, E., "L'Ecriture, âme de la théologie," *Gr* 52 (1971) 511-535.

HAPPEL, S., "The 'Bent World': Sacraments as Orthopraxis," *PCTSA* 35 (1980) 88-101.

HARRINGTON, J.P., "The Jewishness of Jesus. Facing Some Problems," *CBQ* 49 (1987) 1-13.

HART, J.G., "The Cult-Mystery Revisited," *DR* 91 (1973) 141-153.

HARTWELL, H., "Karl Barth on Baptism," *SJTh* 22 (1969) 10-29.

HASTINGS, A., "The Sacramentality of the Church," *ECQ* 16 (1964) 219-225.

HAQUIN, A., "Les moines bénédictins dans le mouvement liturgique des XIXe et XXe siècles," *ComLi* 61 (1979) 380-390.

HAÜSLING, A.A., "Bibliografie Odo Casel O.S.B. 1967-1985. Mit einzelnen Nachträgen aus den früheren Jahren," *ALW* 28 (1986) 26-42.

HELFMEYER, F.J., "twOa *'ôth*," in *TDOT* I (1974) 167-188.

HENNESSY, R.J., *The Incarnate Word* [St. Thomas Aquinas, *Summa Theologiae*, 3ª, 1-6. Vol. 48], London 1976.

HENRY, P., *Leçons sur le baptême*, Paris 1965.

HIGGINS, A.B.J., "Jesus as Prophet," *ExT* 57 (1945/46) 292-294.

HILD, J., "L'Encyclique *Mediator* et la sacramentalité des actes liturgiques," *QLP* 29 (1948) 186-203.

———, "L'Encyclique *Mediator Dei* et le mouvement liturgique de Maria-Laach," *MD* 14 (1948) 15-29.

HILL, D., *New Testament Prophecy*, London 1979.

HOLLENBACH, D.A., "A Prophetic Church and the Catholic Sacramental Imagination," in J.C. Haughey, ed., *The Faith That Does Justice* [Woodstock Studies 2], New York 1977, 234-263.

HOOKER, M.D., *The Signs of a Prophet. The Prophetic Actions of Jesus*, London 1997.

HORSLEY, R., "'Like One of the Prophets of Old': Two Types of Popular Prophets at the Time of Jesus," *CBQ* 47 (1985) 435-463.

HOUSSIAU, A., "The Rediscovery of the Liturgy by Sacramental Theology (1950-1980)," *StLi* 15 (1982/83) 158-177.

HOUSSIAU, D., "The Church and Her Ministry from the Viewpoint of Eschatology," in *The Christian Priesthood,* ed. N. Lash – J. Rhymer; [9th Downside Symposium], London 1970.

HOVARTH, T., "After Rahner What? A Tribute to His Memory and Achievement," *Thom* 49 (1985) 157-167.

HOWARD, V., "Did Jesus Speak about His Own Death?," *CBQ* 39 (1977) 515-527.

HURD, B., "Being is Being-Present-To-Self: Rahner's Key to Aquinas's Metaphysics," *Thom* 52 (1988) 63-78.

VAN IERSEL, B., "Some Biblical Roots of the Christian Sacraments," *Conc* 4/1 (1968) 4-11.

IRWIN, K.W., *Context and Text. Method in Liturgical Theology*, Collegeville 1994.

———, "Recent Sacramental Theology: A Review Discussion," *Thom* 47 (1983) 592-608; 52 (1988) 124-147; 53 (1989) 281-313.

JANZ, D.R., *Luther on Thomas Aquinas. The Angelic Doctor in the Thought of the Reformer*, Stuttgart 1989.

JASPER, R.C.D., "Liturgical Movement," *NDCTh* (1983) 335-336.

JEREMIAS, J., *The Eucharistic Words of Jesus*, London 1966³.

———, *Infant Baptism in the First Four Centuries*, London 1960.

———, *The Parables of Jesus,* London 1972.

JUNGMANN, J.A., "Liturgical Movement," *SM(E)* III, 319-320.

KALAYIL, C.G., *The Co-Relation of the Common and Ministerial Modes of Christian Priesthood According to Karl Rahner*, Rome 1994.

KARIMATTAM, M., *Jesus the Prophet*, Rome 1979.

KÄSEMANN, E., "The Quest for the Historical Jesus," in *Essays on New Testament Themes*, London 1964, 15-47.

KASPER, W., *The God of Jesus Christ*, London 1983.

———, *Jesus the Christ*, London 1976.

KAVANAGH, A., "Sacraments as an Act of Service," *Worship* 39 (1965) 89-95.

———, *The Shape of Baptism. The Rite of Christian Initiation*, New York 1978.

———, "Symbolic Implications of Christian Initiation in Roman Catholicism since the Second Vatican Council" in *I simboli dell'iniziazione cristiana* [Analecta Liturgica 7], Roma 1993, 223-241.

KEIFER, R.A., "Response: The RCIA and Sacramental Efficacy," *Worship* 56 (1982) 327-332.

KELSEY, D.H., *The Uses of Scripture in Recent Theology*, Philadelphia 1975.

KEMP, R., "The Rite of Christian Initiation of Adults at Ten Years," *Worship* 56 (1982) 309-326.

KENNEDY, P., *Deus Humanissimus: The Knowability of God in the Theology of Edward Schillebeeckx* [Ökumenische Beihefte 22], Freiburg 1993.

———, *Schillebeeckx* [Outstanding Christian Thinkers Series], London 1993.

KERKETTA, J., *Jesus Christ, the Universal Saviour. Christology in the Perspective of God's Universal Saving Will*, Roma 1988.

KODELL, J., *The Eucharist in the New Testament* [Zacchaeus Studies: New Testament], Wilmington 1988.

KUJUR, S.K., *The Eucharistic Theology of Dom Anscar Vonier, O.S.B.*, Roma 1992.

LAMPE, G.W.H., *The Seal of the Spirit. A Study of the Doctrine of Baptism and Confirmation in the New Testament and the Fathers*, London 1951.

LANE, D.A., *Christ at the Centre*, Dublin 1990.

———, *Foundations for Social Theology. Praxis, Process and Salvation*, Dublin 1984.

———, *Keeping Hope Alive. Stirrings in Christian Theology*, Dublin 1996.

———, *The Reality of Jesus*, Dublin 1975.

LANG, B., "Street Theater, Raising the Dead and the Zoroastrian Connection in Ezekiel's Prophecy," in *Ezekiel and His Book. Textual and Literary Criticism and Their Interrelation,* ed. J. Lust, [BETL LXXIV], Leuven 1986, 297-316.

LATTEY, C., *Six Sacraments*, London 1929.

LEBEAU, P., *Jean Daniélou*, Paris 1967.

LEEMING, B., *Principles of Sacramental Theology*, London1960.

———, "Recent Trends in Sacramental Theology," *IThQ* 23 (1956) 195-217.

LÉGASSE, S., *Naissance du baptême* [Lectio Divina 153], Paris 1993.

LEGENDRE, A., *Introduction à l'étude de la Somme Théologique de Saint Thomas d'Aquin*, Paris 1923.

LEIJSSEN, L., "La contribution de Karl Rahner (1904-1984) au renouvellement de la sacramentaire," *QuLi* 75 (1994) 84-102.

LELOIR, L., "La sainte Ecriture, âme de toute la théologie," *Seminarium* 16 (1966) 880-891.

LENNERZ, H., *De sacramento baptismi*, Roma 1955[3].

———, *De sacramentis novae legis in genere*, Roma 1950[3].

LÉON-DUFOUR, X., "L'exégèse, trente ans après," *Etudes* 340 (1974) 299-283.

———, "Jésus face à la mort menaçante," *NRTh* 100 (1978) 802-821.

———, "Teologia e sacra scrittura," in *Problemi e prospettive di teologia dogmatica*, ed. K.H. Neufeld, Brescia 1983, 44-69.

LÉPICIER, A.-M., *Tractatus de baptismo et de confirmatione* [3, Quaest. LXVI-LXXII], Roma 1923.

———, *Tractatus de sacramentis in communi*, Paris 1921.

DE LETTER, P., "Divine Quasi-Formal Causality," *IThQ* 27 (1960) 221-228.

LINDBLOM, J., *Prophecy in Ancient Israel*, Oxford 1962.

LONERGAN, B., "The Transition from a Classicist World-View to Historical Mindedness," in *A Second Collection*, ed. W.J.F. Ryan – B.J. Tyrrell, London 1974, 1-9.

MCCOOL, G.A., "Philosophical Pluralism and an Evolving Thomism," *Cont* 2 (1964) 3-16.

MCCORMACK, S., "The Configuration of the Sacramental Character," *Thom* 7 (1944) 458-491.

MCCOWN, C.C., "The Scene of John's Ministry and its Relation to the Purpose and Outcome of His Mission," *JBL* 49 (1940) 113-131.

MCDONNELL, K. – MONTAGUE, G.T., *Christian Initiation and Baptism in the Holy Spirit. Evidence from the First Eight Centuries*, Collegeville 1991.

MCKEATING, H., "The Prophet Jesus," *ExT* 73 (1961/62) 4-7; 50-53.

MACQUARRIE, J., *Jesus Christ in Modern Thought*, London 1990.

Made, Not Born. New Perspectives on Christian Initiation and the Catechumenate [The Murphy Center for Liturgical Research], London 1976.

MAGGIONI, B., "I sacramenti e la 'historia salutis'," *RivLi* 54 (1967) 7-20.

MANN, P., "Masters in Israel IV: The Later Theology of Karl Rahner," *CleR* 54 (1969) 939-948

MANSINI, G., "Quasi Formal Causality and 'Change in the Other': A Note on Karl Rahner's Christology," *Thom* 52 (1988) 293-306.

MANSON, T.W., "John the Baptist," *BJRL* 36 (1953/54) 395-412.

MARSH, H.G., *The Origin and Significance of New Testament Baptism*, Manchester 1941.

MARSH, T., "The History and Significance of the Post-Baptismal Rites," *IThQ* 39 (1972) 175-206.

———, "The Sacramental Character," in D. O'Callaghan, ed., *Sacraments*, Dublin 1964, 109-138.

MARTIN-ACHARD, R., "Souvenir et mémorial selon l'Ancien Testament," *RThPh* 15 (1965) 302-310.

MASON, S., *Josephus and the New Testament,* Peabody, Mass., 1992.

MAYEUR, J.-M., "Magistère et théologiens sous Pie XII," *QF* 12 (1980) 113-119.

MEIER, J.P., "The Bible as a Source for Theology," *PCTSA* 43 (1988) 1-14.

———, *A Marginal Jew: Rethinking the Historical Jesus* [AncBRL]. I. *The Roots and the Problem of the Person*, New York 1991. II. *Mentor, Message and Miracles*, New York 1994.

MERCURIO, R., "A Baptismal Motif in the Gospel Narratives of the Burial," *CBQ* 21 (1959) 39-54.

METZ, J.B., *Faith in History and Society*, New York 1980.

———, "Theology Today: New Crises and New Visions," *PCTSA* 40 (1985) 1-14.

MEYER, B.F., *The Aims of Jesus*, London 1979.

MICHEL, M., "Le retour de l'eschatologie dans la théologie contemporaine," *RSR* 58 (1984) 180-195.

MIKHAEL, R., *Jésus comme prophète dans la christologie contemporaine de la langue française*, Roma 1992.

MILLER, M., "The Sacramental Theology of Hans Urs von Balthasar," *Worship* 64 (1990) 48-66.

MIRALLES GARCÍA, A., "La noción de sacramento en Santo Tomás," in *Tommaso d'Aquino nel suo settimo centenario*, Napoli 1975-1978, 373-392.

MOLTMANN, J., *The Crucified God*, London 1974.

———, *Theology of Hope*, London 1967.

———, *The Trinity and the Kingdom of God*, London 1981.

MUMMADI, J., *Eschatological Aspects of Baptism*, Roma 1974.

MÚNERA DUQUE, A. – BOARDA, A., "La sacramentalidad de la Iglesia según los teólogos actuales (Rahner, Semmelroth, Schillebeeckx)," *EX* 15 (1965) 69-90.

MURPHY, R.E. – PETER, C.J., "The Role of the Bible in Roman Catholic Theology," *Interp* 25 (1971) 78-92.

NEUNHEUSER, B., "Baptism. Sacrament of Baptism," *SM(E)* I (1968) 136-144.

———, *Baptism and Confirmation*, New York 1964.

———, "Les conceptions fondamentales des premiers maîtres du mouvement liturgique: leur caractère traditionel et leur nouveauté," in A.M. Triacca – A. Pistoia, ed., *Liturgie, Spiritualité, Cultures* [Conferences Saint-Serge. XXIXe Semaine d'études liturgiques. Paris, 29 juin - 2 juillet 1982], Roma 1983, 221-230.

———, "In memoria di Dom Odo Casel. Il centenario della nascita: 27 settembre 1886-1986," *Not* 22 (1986) 368-372.

———, "Masters in Israel. Odo Casel," *CleR* 55 (1970) 194-212.

———, "Movimento liturgico," in *NDL*, 904-918.

———, "Il movimento liturgico nella storia recente della Chiesa. Intervista a cura di L. Vaccaro," *Hum(B)* 37 (1982) 959-965.

———, "Mystery Presence," *Worship* 34 (1960) 120-127.

———, "The Mystery Presence. Dom Odo Casel and the Latest Research," *DR* 76 (1958) 266-273.

———, "Odo Casel and the Meaning of the Liturgical Year," *StLi* 15 (1982/1983) 210-213.

———, "Odo Casel," *NCE* III, 176-177.

———, "Odo Casel in Retrospect and Prospect," *Worship* 50 (1976) 489-504.

———, "La théologie de la vie monastique chez Dom Casel (1886-1948)," *RMab* 50 (1961) 257-263.

———, "La théologie des mystères de Odo Casel dans la tradition catholique," *EL* 94 (1980) 297-310.

NICHOLAS, J.-H., "Les sacrements et l'attente du Christ," *VS* 107 (1962) 391-402.

NOLAN, A., *Jesus before Christianity*, London 1992.

O'CALLAGHAN, D., ed., *Sacraments*, Dublin 1964.

O'COLLINS, G., *Christology: A Biblical, Historical, and Systematic Study of Jesus*, Oxford 1995.

———, *The Easter Jesus*, London 1980[2].

———, *Interpreting Jesus*, London 1983.

———, *Jesus Risen*, Mahwah 1987.

———, *Retrieving Fundamental Theology*, Mahwah 1993.

O'CONNELL, M.J., "New Perspectives in Sacramental Theology," *Worship* 39 (1965) 195-206.

———, "The Sacraments in Theology Today," *Thought* 30 (1961) 40-58.

O'DONOVAN, L.J., ed., "A Changing Ecclesiology in a Changing Church: A Symposium on Development in the Ecclesiology of Karl Rahner," *TS* 38 (1977) 736-762.

———, "The Ethical Imperative of Schillebeeckx's Christology," *PCTSA* 38 (1983) 119-122.

———, "Orthopraxis and Theological Method: Rahner," *PCTSA* 35 (1980) 47-65.

———, *A World of Grace. An Introduction to the Themes and Foundations of Karl Rahner's Theology*, New York 1981.

Ó FEARGHAIL, F., *The Introduction to Luke-Acts. A Study of Lk. 1:1 - 4:44 in the Composition of Luke's Two-Volume Work* [AnBib 126], Roma 1991.

O'MEARA, T.F., "The Origins of the Liturgical Movement and German Romanticism," *Worship* 59 (1985) 326-342.

O'NEILL, C.E., "I sacramenti," in *Bilancio della teologia del XX secolo*, ed. H. Vorgrimler – R. Van Der Gucht, III, Roma 1972, 263-313.

OSBORNE, K.B., *Sacramental Theology*, New York 1988.

OTTO, R., *The Kingdom of God and the Son of Man*, London 1938.

OURY, G., "Aux origines du mouvement liturgique. Les *Institutions liturgiques* de Dom Guéranger," *EeV* 86 (1976) 120-126; 139-143; 157-160.

OVERHOLT, T.W., "Prophecy: The Problem of Cross-Cultural Comparison," in B. Lang, ed., *Anthropological Approaches to the Old Testament* [Issues in Religion and Theology 9] , London 1985, 60-82.

———, "Seeing is Believing. The Social Setting of Prophetic Acts of Power," *JSOT* 23 (1982) 3-31.

PALMER, P.F., *Sacraments and Worship. Liturgy and Doctrinal Development of Baptism, Confirmation and the Eucharist* [Sources of Christian Theology 1], Westminster 1955.

PAYNE, E.A., "Baptism in Recent Discussion," in A. Gilmore, ed., *Christian Baptism. A Fresh Attempt to Understand the Rite in terms of Scripture, History and Theology*, London 1959, 15-24.

PEDLEY, C.J., "An English Bibliographical Aid to Karl Rahner," *HeyJ* 25 (1984) 319-365; 26 (1985) 310.

PEPPERDENE, M., "Baptism in the Early British and Irish Churches," *IThQ* 22 (1955) 110-123.

PESCH, C., *De sacramentis*. Pars I [Praelectiones Dogmaticae, Tomus IV], Friburgi 1900.

PESCH, R., "The Last Supper and Jesus' Understanding of His Death," *BiBh* 3 (1977) 58-75.

PLUS, R., *Baptême et confirmation*, Paris 1929.

POHLE, J., *The Sacraments in General. Baptism. Confirmation. A Dogmatic Treatise* I [Adapted by A. Preuss], St. Louis 1931^6.

DE LA POTTERIE, I., "L'onction du Christ," *NRTh* 80 (1958) 225-252.

POU Y RIUS, R., "Perspectivas actuales en la teología de los sacramentos," *Phase* 12 (1972) 433-448.

POWER, D.N., "Sacraments: Symbolizing God's Power in the Church," *PCTSA* 37 (1982) 50-66.

———, *Unsearchable Riches. The Symbolic Nature of the Liturgy*, New York 1984.

POWERS, J.M., *Symbolic Instrumentality in the Sacramental Theology of E.H. Schillebeeckx*, Roma 1972.

PRYKE, J., "The Sacraments of Holy Baptism and Holy Communion in the Light of the Ritual Washings and Sacred Meals at Qumran," *RdQ* 5 (1966) 543-552.

PRZEWOZNY, B., *Church as Sacrament of the Unity of all Mankind in "Lumen Gentium," "Gaudium et Spes" and in Semmelroth, Schillebeeckx and Rahner*, Roma 1979.

QUICK, O.C., *The Christian Sacraments*, London 1928.

VON RAD, G., *The Message of the Prophets*, London 1968.

———, *Old Testament Theology*, II, London 1965.

RASCO, E., "Biblical Theology. Its Revival and Influence on Theological Formation," in R. Latourelle, ed., *Vatican II: Assessment and Perspectives. Twenty-five Years After (1962-1987)*, III, Mahwah 1989, 337-360.

RATZINGER, J., "Biblical Interpretation in Crisis: On the Question of the Foundations and Approaches of Exegesis Today" in R.J. Neuhaus, ed., *Biblical Interpretation in Crisis. The Ratzinger Conference on Bible and Church*, Grand Rapids 1989, 1-23.

RATZINGER, J., "Sacred Scripture in the Life of the Church" [Commentary on *Dei Verbum*, ch. 6], in H. Vorgrimler, ed., *Commentary on the Documents of Vatican II*, III, London 1969, 262-272.

ROBERTS, L., "The Collision of Rahner and Balthasar," *Cont* 5 (1968) 753-757.

ROBINSON, H.W., "Prophetic Symbolism," in *Old Testament Essays*, London 1927, 1-17.

———, "Hebrew Sacrifice and Prophetic Symbolism," *JTS* 43 (1942) 129-139.

ROBINSON, W., "The Sacraments and Eschatology," *Theol* 55 (1952) 52-59.

ROCCHETTA, C., "*Mistica* e sacramenti nel pensiero del Card. J. Daniélou," *RVS* 30 (1976) 182-193.

———, *I sacramenti della fede. Saggio di teologia biblica sui sacramenti quali meraviglie della salvezza nel tempo della chiesa,* Bologna 1987[3].

———, *I sacramenti e la storia della salvezza. Dai "Magnalia Dei" ai "Sacramenta fidei" nel pensiero teologico del card. J. Daniélou*, Roma 1976.

———, "Sacramenti e vita spirituale nel pensiero teologico del Card. J. Daniélou," *RVS* 30 (1976) 32-51.

ROGUET, A.-M., *Christ Acts through the Sacraments*, Collegeville 1954.

———, "La consommation des sacrements," *VS* 108 (1963) 660-667.

———, "I sacramenti nel loro valore di segni," *SacDo* 45 (1967) 79-92.

———, *Les sacrements* [*Somme théologique* (3ª. 60-65)], Paris 1945.

———, "Les sacrements nous jugent," *VS* 108 (1963) 516-523.

ROMEO, M., "La posizione di Karl Barth sul battesimo," *RBR* 12/3 (1973) 89-94.

VAN ROO, W., *The Christian Sacraments*, Roma 1992.

———, *De sacramentis in genere*, Roma 1966.

———, "Reflections on Karl Rahner's 'Kirche und Sakramente'," *Gr* 44 (1963) 465-500.

ROSATO, P.J., "Celebrazione e missione. Il carattere provocario ed anticipativo dei sacramenti come atti profetici," *RPLi* 24 (1987) 9-17.

———, *Cena del Signore e amore sociale*, Ponteranica 1994.

———, *Introduzione alla teologia dei sacramenti* [Introduzione alle discipline teologiche 9], Casale Monferrato 1992.

———, "Perché studiare la teologia a Roma?," in K.H. Neufeld, ed., *Problemi e prospettive di teologia dogmatica*, Brescia 1983, 495-520.

ROSATO, P.J., "The Prophetic Acts of Jesus, the Sacraments and the Kingdom," in *Gottes Zukunft - Zukunft der Welt*, Fs. J. Moltmann, München 1986, 59-67.

ROUSSEAU, O., *Storia del movimento liturgico*, Roma 1961.

RUFFINI, E., "Character as a Concrete Manifestation of a Sacrament in Relation to the Church," *Conc* 4/1 (1968) 52-58.

———, "I grandi temi della teologia contemporanea dei sacramenti," *RivLi* 54 (1967) 39-52.

———, "Il battesimo nell'economia sacramentale," *RivLi* 57 (1970) 383-404.

———, "Teologia del battesimo. Dal Vaticano II al nuovo *Ordo baptismi parvulorum*," *RPLi* 8 (1970) 32-42.

RYAN, W.F., "The Teaching of St. Thomas in the *Summa* Concerning the Baptismal Character," *AmEcclRev* 149 (1963) 361-385.

RYSKA, J.M., "Lépicier, Alexis," *NCE* VIII, 666.

SALERNO, L., "Tomismo, pluralismo culturale e Concilio Vaticano II," *SapDom* 18 (1965) 45-86.

SANCHEZ DE MURILLO, J., *Dimensíon escatológica de la vida cristiana según Karl Rahner. Aportacíon a la teología de la esperanza*, Roma 1971.

SANDERS, E.P., *The Historical Figure of Jesus*, London 1993.

———, *Jesus and Judaism*, Philadelphia 1985.

SANTAGADA, O.D., "Dom Odo Casel: Contributo monografico per una bibliografia generale delle sue opere, degli studi sulla sua dottrina, e della sua influenza nella teologia contemporanea," *ALW* 10 (1967) 7-77.

SARTORE, D., "Alcuni recenti trattati di sacramentaria fondamentale. Considerazioni di un liturgista," *RivLi* 3 (1988) 321-339.

SARTORI, L., "Il battesimo nella teologia attuale," *StPat* 7 (1960) 7-42.

SCHLECK, C.A., "The Sacramental Character of Baptism and Worship," in S.C. Sullivan, ed., *Readings in Sacramental Theology*, Englewood Cliffs 1964, 165-186.

———, "St. Thomas on the Nature of Sacramental Grace," *Thom* 18 (1955) 1-30; 242-278.

SCHMEMANN, A., *Of Water and the Spirit*, St. Vladimir's Seminary 1974.

SCHMIDT, K.W., "Prophetic Delegation: A Form-Critical Inquiry," *Bib* 63 (1982) 206-218.

SCHNACKENBURG, R., *Baptism in the Thought of St. Paul*, Oxford 1964.

———, ed., *Die Kirche des Anfangs*, Fs. Heinz Schürmann, Leipzig 1977.

SCHNEIDER, F., *Jesus der Prophet* [OBO 2], Freiburg 1973.

SCHREITER, R. J. – HILKERT, M.C., *The Praxis of Christian Experience. An Introduction to the Theology of E. Schillebeeckx*, San Francisco 1989.

SCHULTES, R.M., "Circa doctrinam S. Thomae de iustificatione," *Ang* 3 (1926) 166-175; 345-354.

SCHÜSSLER FIORENZA, E., *In Memory of Her. A Feminist Theological Reconstruction of Christian Origins*, London 1983.

SCIPIONI, L., "Il battesimo: incorporazione al Cristo ed alla Chiesa," *SacDo* 12 (1967) 457-474.

SCOBIE, C.H.H., *John the Baptist*, London 1964.

SEARLE, M., ed., *Alternative Futures for Worship,* II. *Baptism and Confirmation*, Collegeville 1987.

———, *Christening. The Making of Christians*, Collegeville 1980.

SEEDLEY, D., "Jesus' Temple Act," *CBQ* 55 (1993) 263-283.

SENIOR, D., *Jesus. A Gospel Portrait*, New York 1992.

SEQUEIRA, A.M., *The Doctrine of Vatican II on Baptism in the Dogmatic Constitution "Lumen gentium,"* Roma 1983.

SHEEHAN, K., *Karl Rahner. The Philosophical Foundations*, Athens, Ohio 1987.

SIKORSKI, T., "Le rôle des sacrements dans la présentation et l'accomplissement des obligations morales. Pour une dimension eschatologique et mystérique de la morale sacramentelle," *CollTh* 47 (1977) 57-68.

SKELLEY, M., *The Liturgy of the World. Karl Rahner's Theology of Worship*, Collegeville 1991.

SLOYAN, G.S., *Jesus in Focus. A Life in Its Setting*, Mystic 1983.

DE SMET, A., *Tractatus dogmatico-moralis de sacramentis in genere, de baptismo et confirmatione*, Brugis 1925.

SMITH, B., "The More Original Form of the Words of Institution," *ZNW* 83 (1992) 166-186.

SOGGIN, J.A., "Memoria, ricordo ed anamnesi in Oriente e nell'Antico Testamento," *Protest* 21 (1966) 83-86.

STACEY, W.D., "The Lord's Supper as Prophetic Drama," in M.D. Hooker, *The Signs of a Prophet. The Prophetic Actions of Jesus*, London 1997, 80-95.

———, *Prophetic Drama in the Old Testament*, London 1990.

STÄHLIN, G., *Die Gleichnishandlungen Jesu*, Kassel 1953.

STANLEY, D.M., "The New Testament Doctrine on Baptism," *TS* 18 (1957) 169-215.

STÉPHAN, J., "Anscar Vonier," *NCE* XIV, 751.

STRACHAN, R.H., *The Fourth Gospel*, London 1946.

SWINDLER, A., "Prophets and Prophetic Acts Today," *BiTod* 19 (1981) 182-187.

TABORDA, F., "A dimensão eclesial dos sacramentos segundo Karl Rahner," *PerTeol* 8/14 (1976) 3-30; 8/15 (1976) 35-68.

TAPPEINER, D.A. "Sacramental Causality in Aquinas and Rahner: Some Critical Thoughts," *SJTh* 28 (1975) 243-257.

TATUM, W.B., *John the Baptist and Jesus. A Report on the Jesus Seminar*, Sonoma 1994.

THIERRY D'ARGENLIEU, B., "La doctrine de S. Thomas d'Aquin sur le caractère sacramentel dans les 'Sentences'," *RThom* 34 (1929) 219-233.

———, "La doctrine de S. Thomas d'Aquin sur le caractère sacramentel dans la 'Somme'," *RThom* 34 (1929) 289-303.

THISELTON, A.C., "The Supposed Power of Words," *JTS* 25 (1974).

THOMPSON, W.M., *The Jesus Debate*, New York 1985.

THONDIPARAMBIL, J., *Prophecy as Theatre. An Exegetico-Theological Study of Symbolic Acts in the Book of Jeremiah*, Rome 1989.

TILLARD, J.M.R., "La triple dimension du signe sacramentel (A propos de 'Summa Theologica' III, 60,3.)," *NRTh* 83 (1961) 225-254.

TORRANCE, T.F., "The Origins of Baptism," *SJTh* 11 (1958) 158-171.

TRIACCA, A.M., "Odo Casel e il movimento liturgico," *EL* 101 (1987) 153-181.

———, "Dom Burkhard Neunheuser interprete di Dom Odo Casel (Rassegna bibliografica)," *Sales* 40 (1978) 625-632.

TURRADO, A., "La teología sacramental del P.E.H. Schillebeeckx, O.P.. Causalidad simbólica instrumental," *Aug* 2 (1962) 40-72.

UEHLINGER, C., "'Zeichne eine Stadt ... und belagere sie!' Bild und Wort in einer Zeichenhandlung Ezechiels gegen Jerusalem (Ez 4f)," in M. Kücher – C. Uehlinger, ed., *Jerusalem. Texte - Bilder - Steine...* [Novum Testamentum et Orbis Antiquus 6], Freiburg, Schweiz–Göttingen 1987, 111-200.

UPSON. W., "Anscar Vonier," *DublR* 206 (April, 1939) 236-246.

VACEK, E., "Development within Rahner's Theology," *IThQ* 42 (1975) 36-49.

VANDERVELDE, G., "The Grammar of Grace: Karl Rahner as a Watershed in Contemporary Theology," *TS* 49 (1988) 445-459.

VANHOYE, A., "Esegesi biblica e teologia: la questione dei metodi," *Seminarium* 31 (1991) 267-278.

VAWTER, B. – HOPPE, L.J., *A New Heart. A Commentary on the Book of Ezekiel*, Edinburgh 1991.

VELIATH, D., *Theological Approaches and Evaluation of Religions. A Study of Contrast of the Positions of Jean Daniélou and Raimundo Pannikar*, Roma 1985.

VERMES, G., *Jesus and the World of Judaism*, London 1983.

———, *Jesus the Jew*, London 1994[2].

———, *The Religion of Jesus the Jew*, London 1993.

VÖGTLE, A., "Todesankündigunden und Todesverständnis Jesu" in K. Kertelge ed., *Der Tod Jesu. Deutungen im Neuen Testament* [Quaestiones Disputatae 74], Freiburg 1976, 51-113.

VOLLERT, C., "The Eucharist: Quests for Insights from Scripture," *TS* 21 (1960) 404-443.

VONIER, A., *A Key to the Doctrine of the Eucharist*, London 1925.

VORGRIMLER, H., *Karl Rahner. His Life, Thought and Works*, London 1965.

———, "Karl Rahner: The Theologian's Contribution," in A. Stackpoole, ed., *Vatican II by Those Who Were There*, London 1986, 32-46.

———, *Sacramental Theology*, Collegeville 1992.

———, *Understanding Karl Rahner. An Introduction to His Life and Thought*, London 1986.

WAINWRIGHT, G., "Christian Initiation in the Ecumenical Movement," *StLi* 12 (1977) 67-86.

———, "Développements baptismaux depuis 1967," *ETR* 49 (1974) 67-93.

———, *Eucharist and Eschatology*, New York 1981.

———, "Sacramental Theology and the World Church," *PCTSA* 39(1984) 69-83.

———, "Sacramental Time," *StLi* 14 (1982, 2-4) 135-146.

WANSBROUGH, H., "The Mission of Jesus II: The Prophet," *CleR* 57 (1972) 513-522.

WARE, R., "The Use of Scripture in Current Theology," in R. Murphy, ed., *Theology, Exegesis, and Proclamation* [*Concilium* 70], New York 1971, 115-128.

WICKS, J., "Biblical Criticism Criticised," *Gr* 72 (1991) 117-128.

———, *Introduction to Theological Method* [Introduction to the Theological Disciplines 1], Casale Monferrato 1994.

———, *Luther and His Spiritual Legacy*, Wilmington 1983.

WILDE, J.A., ed., *Commentaries. Rite of Christian Initiation of Adults*, Chicago 1988.

WINLING, R., "La théologie catholique en France au XXe siècle," *NRTh* 111 (1989) 537-555.

———, *La théologie contemporaine (1945-1980)*, Paris 1983.

WINZEN, D., "La dottrina sacramentale di S. Tommaso e la religiosità moderna," *Studium* 32 (1936) 200-209.

WITHERUP, R.D., "Modern New Testament Criticism," *NJBC* II, 1130-1145.

WOLFF, H.W., *Anthropology of the Old Testament*, Philadelphia 1974.

WORLD COUNCIL OF CHURCHES, *Baptism, Eucharist and Ministry* [Faith and Order Papers No. 111], Geneva 1982.

WRIGHT, J., "The Bible and the Hermeneutical Horizon: The Use of Scripture in Theology," *TS* 43 (1982) 651-672.

YARNOLD, E.J., "The Ceremonies of Initiation in the 'De Sacramentis' and 'De Mysteriis' of St. Ambrose," *Studia Patristica* 10 [TU 107] (1970) 453-463.

YOUNG, F.W., "Jesus the Prophet: A Re-examination," *JBL* 68 (1949) 285-299.

ZADRA, D., "I sacramenti e il tempo" in K.H. Neufeld, ed., *Problemi e prospettive di teologia dogmatica*, Brescia 1983, 253-273.

ZIMMERLI, W., *Ezekiel*, I, 1979; II, Philadelphia 1983.

ZITNIK, M., *Sacramenta. Bibliografia Internationalis* [4 Vol.], Roma 1992.

Finito di stampare
nel mese di dicembre 1999

presso la tipografia
"Giovanni Olivieri" di E. Montefoschi
00187 Roma - Via dell'Archetto, 10,11,12